TECHNICAL ANALYSIS
ANALYSIS
OF THE FINANCIAL
MARKETS

A COMPREHENSIVE GUIDE TO TRADING
METHODS AND APPLICATIONS

TECHNICAL ANALYSIS OF THE FINANCIAL MARKETS

A COMPREHENSIVE GUIDE TO TRADING METHODS AND APPLICATIONS

JOHN J. MURPHY

NEW YORK INSTITUTE OF FINANCE

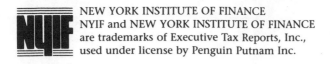

NEW YORK INSTITUTE OF FINANCE
NYIF and NEW YORK INSTITUTE OF FINANCE
are trademarks of Executive Tax Reports, Inc.,
used under license by Penguin Putnam Inc.

Portions of this book were previously published as
Technical Analysis of the Futures Markets (New York INstitute of Finance, 1985).

Library of Congress Cataloging-in-Publication Data

Murphy, John J., [date]
    Technical analysis of the financial markets / John J. Murphy.
        p.   cm.
        Rev. ed. of: Technical analysis of the futures markets. c1986.
        Includes bibliographical references and index.
        ISBN 0-7352-0066-1
        1. Futures market.   2. Commodity exchanges.   I. Murphy, John J.
    Technical analysis of the futures markets.   II. Title.
    HG6046.M87   1999
    332.64'4—dc21   98-38531
                                                                                CIP

Printed in the United States of America

15 14 13 12 11 10

This publication is designed to provide accurate and authoritative information in regard
to the subject matter covered. It is sold with the understanding that the publisher is not
engaged in rendering legal, accounting, or other professional service. If legal advice or
other expert assistance is required, the services of a competent professional person
should be sought.

—From the Declaration of Principles jointly adopted by a Committee of the American Bar
Association and a Committee of Publishers and Associations.

Most NYIF and New York Institute of Finance books are available at special
quantity discounts for bulk purchases for sales promotions, premiums, fund-
raising, or educational use. Special books, or book excerpts, can also be created
to fit specific needs.

For details, write: Special Markets, Penguin Putnam Inc., 375 Hudson Street,
New York, New York 10014.

ISBN 0-7352-0066-1

To my parents,
Timothy and Margaret
and
To Patty, Clare, and Brian

Contents

2
Dow Theory   *23*

3 Chart Construction   35

4 Basic Concepts of Trend   49

6 Continuation Patterns 129

7 Volume and Open Interest 157

8
Long Term Charts   *181*

12
Japanese Candlesticks *297*

13
Elliott Wave Theory *319*

14
Time Cycles   *343*

15 Computers and Trading Systems   *377*

16 Money Management and Trading Tactics   *393*

The Link Between Stocks and Futures: Intermarket Analysis

18
Stock Market Indicators   *433*

D
Continuous Futures Contracts   *505*

About the Author

John J. Murphy has been applying technical analysis for three decades. He was formerly Director of Futures Technical Research and the senior managed account trading advisor with Merrill Lynch. Mr. Murphy was the technical analyst for CNBC-TV for seven years. He is the author of three books, including *Technical Analysis of the Futures Markets,* the predecessor to this book. His second book, *Intermarket Technical Analysis,* opened up a new branch of analysis. His third book, *The Visual Investor,* applies technical work to mutual funds.

In 1996, Mr. Murphy founded MURPHYMORRIS, Inc., along with software developer Greg Morris, to produce interactive educational products and online analysis for investors. Their Web site address is:

www.murphymorris.com.

He is also head of his own consulting firm, JJM Technical Advisors, located in Oradell, New Jersey.

About the Contributors

Thomas E. Aspray (Appendix A) is a Capital Market Analyst with Princeton Economic Institute Ltd., located in Princeton, New Jersey. Mr. Aspray has been trading markets since the 1970s. Many of the techniques he pioneered in the early 1980s are now used by other professional traders.

Dennis C. Hynes (Appendix B) is Managing Director and cofounder of R.W. Pressprich & Co., Inc., a fixed income broker/dealer located in New York City. He also serves as the firm's Chief Market Strategist. Mr. Hynes is a futures and options trader and a CTA (Commodity Trading Advisor). He has an MBA in Finance from the University of Houston.

Greg Morris (Chapter 12 and Appendix D) has been developing trading systems and indicators for 20 years for investors and traders to be used with major technical analysis software programs. He is the author of two books on candlestick charting (see Chapter 12). In August 1996, Mr. Morris teamed with John Murphy to found MURPHYMORRIS Inc., a Dallas-based firm dedicated to educating investors.

Fred G. Schutzman, CMT (Appendix C) is the President and Chief Executive Officer of Briarwood Capital Management, Inc., a New York-based Commodity Trading Advisor. He is also responsible for technical research and trading system development at Emcor Eurocurrency Management Corporation, a risk management consulting firm. Mr. Schutzman is a member of the Market Technicians Association and is currently serving on their Board of Directors.

Introduction

I had no idea when *Technical Analysis of the Futures Markets* was published in 1986 that it would create such an impact on the industry. It has been referred to by many in the field as the "Bible" of technical analysis. The Market Technicians Association uses it as a primary source in their testing process for the Chartered Market Technician program. The Federal Reserve has cited it in research studies that examine the value of the technical approach. In addition, it has been translated into eight foreign languages. I was also unprepared for the long shelf life of the book. It continues to sell as many copies ten years after it was published as it did in the first couple of years.

It became clear, however, that a lot of new material had been added to the field of technical analysis in the past decade. I added some of it myself. My second book, *Intermarket Technical Analysis* (Wiley, 1991), helped create that new branch of technical analysis, which is widely used today. Old techniques like Japanese candlestick charting and newer ones like Market Profile have become part of the technical landscape. Clearly, this new work needed to be included in any book that attempted to present a comprehensive picture of technical analysis. The focus of my work changed as well.

While my main interest ten years ago was in the futures markets, my recent work has dealt more with the stock market. That also brought me full circle, since I began my career as a stock analyst thirty years ago. That was also one of the side effects of my being the technical analyst for CNBC-TV for seven years. That focus on what the general public was doing also led to my third book, *The Visual Investor* (Wiley, 1996). That book focused on the use of technical tools for market sectors, primarily through mutual funds, which have become extremely popular in the 1990s.

Many of the technical indicators that I wrote about ten years ago, which had been used primarily in the futures markets, have been incorporated into stock market work. It was time to show how that was being done. Finally, like any field or discipline, writers also evolve. Some things that seemed very important to me ten years ago aren't as important today. As my work has evolved into a broader application of technical principles to all financial markets, it seemed only right that any revision of that earlier work should reflect that evolution.

I've tried to retain the structure of the original book. Therefore, many of the original chapters remain. However, they have been revised with new material and updated with new graphics. Since the principles of technical analysis are universal, it wasn't that difficult to broaden the focus to include all financial markets. Since the original focus was on futures, however, a lot of stock market material has been added.

Three new chapters have been added. The two previous chapters on point and figure charting (Chapters 11 and 12) have been merged into one. A new Chapter 12 on candlestick charting has been inserted. Two additional chapters have also been added at the end of the book. Chapter 17 is an introduction to my work on intermarket analysis. Chapter 18 deals with stock market indicators. We've replaced the previous appendices with new ones. Market Profile is introduced in Appendix B. The other appendices show some of the more advanced technical indicators and explain how to build a technical trading system. There's also a glossary.

I approached this revision with some trepidation. I wasn't sure redoing a book considered a "classic" was such a good idea. I hope I've succeeded in making it even better. I approached this work from the perspective of a more seasoned and mature writer and analyst. And, throughout the book, I tried to show the respect I have always had for the discipline of technical analysis and for the many talented analysts who practice it. The success of their work, as well as their dedication to this field, has always been a source of comfort and inspiration to me. I only hope I did justice to it and to them.

John Murphy

Acknowledgments

The person who deserves the most credit for the second edition of this book is Ellen Schneid Coleman, Executive Editor at Simon & Schuster. She convinced me that it was time to revise *Technical Analysis of the Futures Markets* and broaden its scope. I'm glad she was so persistent. Special thanks go to the folks at Omega Research who provided me with the charting software I needed and, in particular, Gaston Sanchez who spent a lot of time on the phone with me. The contributing authors—Tom Aspray, Dennis Hynes, and Fred Schutzman—added their particular expertise where it was needed. In addition, several analysts contributed charts including Michael Burke, Stan Ehrlich, Jerry Toepke, Ken Tower, and Nick Van Nice. The revision of Chapter 2 on Dow Theory was a collaborative effort with Elyce Picciotti, an independent technical writer and market consultant in New Orleans, Louisiana. Greg Morris deserves special mention. He wrote the chapter on candlestick charting, contributed the article in Appendix D, and did most of the graphic work. Fred Dahl of Inkwell Publishing Services (Fishkill, NY), who handled production of the first edition of this book, did this one as well. It was great working with him again.

TECHNICAL ANALYSIS
OF THE FINANCIAL
MARKETS

A COMPREHENSIVE GUIDE TO TRADING
METHODS AND APPLICATIONS

Philosophy of Technical Analysis

INTRODUCTION

Before beginning a study of the actual techniques and tools used in technical analysis, it is necessary first to define what technical analysis is, to discuss the philosophical premises on which it is based, to draw some clear distinctions between technical and fundamental analysis and, finally, to address a couple of criticisms frequently raised against the technical approach.

The author's strong belief is that a full appreciation of the technical approach must begin with a clear understanding of what technical analysis claims to be able to do and, maybe even more importantly, the philosophy or rationale on which it bases those claims.

First, let's define the subject. *Technical analysis is the study of market action, primarily through the use of charts, for the purpose of forecasting future price trends.* The term "market action" includes the three principal sources of information available to the technician—price, volume, and open interest. (Open interest is used only in futures and options.) The term "price action," which is often used, seems too narrow because most technicians include volume and open interest as an integral part of their market analysis. With this distinction made, the terms "price action" and "market action" are used interchangeably throughout the remainder of this discussion.

PHILOSOPHY OR RATIONALE

There are three premises on which the technical approach is based:

1. Market action discounts everything.
2. Prices move in trends.
3. History repeats itself.

Market Action Discounts Everything

The statement "market action discounts everything" forms what is probably the cornerstone of technical analysis. Unless the full significance of this first premise is fully understood and accepted, nothing else that follows makes much sense. The technician believes that anything that can possibly affect the price—fundamentally, politically, psychologically, or otherwise—is actually reflected in the price of that market. It follows, therefore, that a study of price action is all that is required. While this claim may seem presumptuous, it is hard to disagree with if one takes the time to consider its true meaning.

All the technician is really claiming is that price action should reflect shifts in supply and demand. If demand exceeds supply, prices should rise. If supply exceeds demand, prices should fall. This action is the basis of all economic and fundamental forecasting. The technician then turns this statement around to arrive at the conclusion that if prices are rising, for whatever the specific reasons, demand must exceed supply and the fundamentals must be bullish. If prices fall, the fundamentals must be bearish. If this last comment about fundamentals seems surprising in the context of a discussion of technical analysis, it shouldn't. After all, the technician is indirectly studying fundamentals. Most technicians would probably agree that it is the underlying forces of supply and demand, the economic fundamentals of a market, that cause bull and bear markets. The charts do not in themselves cause markets to move up or down. They simply reflect the bullish or bearish psychology of the marketplace.

As a rule, chartists do not concern themselves with the reasons why prices rise or fall. Very often, in the early stages of a price trend or at critical turning points, no one seems to know exactly why a market is performing a certain way. While the technical approach may sometimes seem overly simplistic in its claims, the logic behind this first premise—that markets discount everything—becomes more compelling the more market experience one gains. It follows then that if everything that affects market price is ultimately reflected in market price, then the study of that market price is all that is necessary. By studying price charts and a host of supporting technical indicators, the chartist in effect lets the market tell him or her which way it is most likely to go. The chartist does not necessarily try to outsmart or outguess the market. All of the technical tools discussed later on are simply techniques used to aid the chartist in the process of studying market action. The chartist knows there are reasons why markets go up or down. He or she just doesn't believe that knowing what those reasons are is necessary in the forecasting process.

Prices Move in Trends

The concept of trend is absolutely essential to the technical approach. Here again, unless one accepts the premise that markets do in fact trend, there's no point in reading any further. The whole purpose of charting the price action of a market is to identify trends in early stages of their development for the purpose of trading in the direction of those trends. In fact, most of the techniques used in this approach are trend-following in nature, meaning that their intent is to identify and follow existing trends. (See Figure 1.1.)

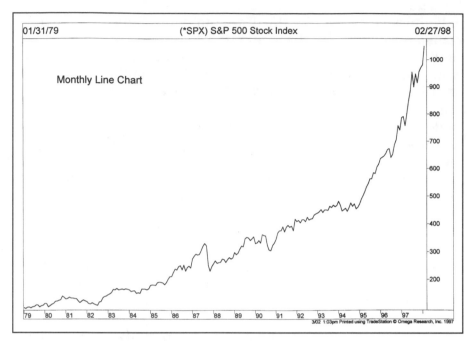

| 01/31/79 | (*SPX) S&P 500 Stock Index | 02/27/98 |

Monthly Line Chart

3/02 1:03pm Printed using TradeStation © Omega Research, Inc. 1997

Figure 1.1   *Example of an uptrend. Technical analysis is based on the premise that markets trend and that those trends tend to persist.*

There is a corollary to the premise that prices move in trends—*a trend in motion is more likely to continue than to reverse.* This corollary is, of course, an adaptation of Newton's first law of motion. Another way to state this corollary is that a trend in motion will continue in the same direction until it reverses. This is another one of those technical claims that seems almost circular. But the entire trend-following approach is predicated on riding an existing trend until it shows signs of reversing.

History Repeats Itself

Much of the body of technical analysis and the study of market action has to do with the study of human psychology. Chart patterns, for example, which have been identified and categorized over the past one hundred years, reflect certain pictures that appear on price charts. These pictures reveal the bullish or bearish psychology of the market. Since these patterns have worked well in the past, it is assumed that they will continue to work well in the future. They are based on the study of human psychology, which tends not to change. Another way of saying this last premise—that history repeats itself—is that the key to understanding the future lies in a study of the past, or that the future is just a repetition of the past.

TECHNICAL VERSUS FUNDAMENTAL FORECASTING

While technical analysis concentrates on the study of market action, fundamental analysis focuses on the economic forces of supply and demand that cause prices to move higher, lower, or stay the same. The fundamental approach examines all of the relevant factors affecting the price of a market in order to determine the intrinsic value of that market. The intrinsic value is what the fundamentals indicate something is actually worth based on the law of supply and demand. If this intrinsic value is under the current market price, then the market is overpriced and should be sold. If market price is below the intrinsic value, then the market is undervalued and should be bought.

Both of these approaches to market forecasting attempt to solve the same problem, that is, to determine the direction prices are likely to move. They just approach the problem from different directions. *The fundamentalist studies the cause of market movement, while the technician studies the effect.* The technician, of course, believes that the effect is all that he or she wants or needs to know and that the reasons, or the causes, are unnecessary. The fundamentalist always has to know why.

Most traders classify themselves as either technicians or fundamentalists. In reality, there is a lot of overlap. Many fundamentalists have a working knowledge of the basic tenets of chart analysis. At the same time, many technicians have at least a passing awareness of the fundamentals. The problem is that the charts and fundamentals are often in conflict with each other. Usually at the beginning of important market moves, the fundamentals do not explain or support what the market seems to be doing. It is at these critical times in the trend that these two approaches seem to differ the most. Usually they come back into sync at some point, but often too late for the trader to act.

One explanation for these seeming discrepancies is that *market price tends to lead the known fundamentals*. Stated another way, *market price acts as a leading indicator of the fundamentals* or the conventional wisdom of the moment. While the known fundamentals have already been discounted and are already "in the market," prices are now reacting to the unknown fundamentals. Some of the most dramatic bull and bear markets in history have begun with little or no perceived change in the fundamentals. By the time those changes became known, the new trend was well underway.

After a while, the technician develops increased confidence in his or her ability to read the charts. The technician learns to be comfortable in a situation where market movement disagrees with the so-called conventional wisdom. A technician begins to enjoy being in the minority. He or she knows that eventually the reasons for market action will become common knowledge. It is just that the technician isn't willing to wait for that added confirmation.

In accepting the premises of technical analysis, one can see why technicians believe their approach is superior to the fundamentalists. If a trader had to choose only one of the two approaches to use, the choice would logically have to be the technical. Because, by definition, the technical approach includes the fundamental. If the fundamentals are reflected in market price, then the study of those fundamentals becomes unnecessary. Chart reading becomes a shortcut form of fundamental analysis. The reverse, however, is not true. Fundamental analysis does not include a study of price action. It is possible to trade financial markets using just the technical approach. It is doubtful that anyone could trade off the fundamentals alone with no consideration of the technical side of the market.

ANALYSIS VERSUS TIMING

This last point is made clearer if the decision making process is broken down into two separate stages—analysis and timing.

Because of the high leverage factor in the futures markets, timing is especially crucial in that arena. It is quite possible to be correct on the general trend of the market and still lose money. Because margin requirements are so low in futures trading (usually less than 10%), a relatively small price move in the wrong direction can force the trader out of the market with the resulting loss of all or most of that margin. In stock market trading, by contrast, a trader who finds him or herself on the wrong side of the market can simply decide to hold onto the stock, hoping that it will stage a comeback at some point.

Futures traders don't have that luxury. A "buy and hold" strategy doesn't apply to the futures arena. Both the technical and the fundamental approach can be used in the first phase—the forecasting process. However, the question of timing, of determining specific entry and exit points, is almost purely technical. Therefore, considering the steps the trader must go through before making a market commitment, it can be seen that the correct application of technical principles becomes indispensable at some point in the process, even if fundamental analysis was applied in the earlier stages of the decision. Timing is also important in individual stock selection and in the buying and selling of stock market sector and industry groups.

FLEXIBILITY AND ADAPTABILITY OF TECHNICAL ANALYSIS

One of the great strengths of technical analysis is its adaptability to virtually any trading medium and time dimension. There is no area of trading in either stocks or futures where these principles do not apply.

The chartist can easily follow as many markets as desired, which is generally not true of his or her fundamental counterpart. Because of the tremendous amount of data the latter must deal with, most fundamentalists tend to specialize. The advantages here should not be overlooked.

For one thing, markets go through active and dormant periods, trending and nontrending stages. The technician can concentrate his or her attention and resources in those markets that display strong trending tendencies and choose to ignore the rest. As a result, the chartist can rotate his or her attention and capital to take advantage of the rotational nature of the markets. At different times, certain markets become "hot" and experience important trends. Usually, those trending periods are followed by quiet and relatively trendless market conditions, while another market or group takes over. The technical trader is free to pick and choose. The fundamentalist, however, who tends to specialize in only one group, doesn't have that kind of flexibility. Even if he or she were free to switch groups, the fundamentalist would have a much more difficult time doing so than would the chartist.

Another advantage the technician has is the "big picture." By following all of the markets, he or she gets an excellent feel for what markets are doing in general, and avoids the "tunnel vision" that can result from following only one group of markets. Also, because so many of the markets have built-in economic relationships and react to similar economic factors, price action in one market or group may give valuable clues to the future direction of another market or group of markets.

TECHNICAL ANALYSIS APPLIED TO DIFFERENT TRADING MEDIUMS

The principles of chart analysis apply to both *stocks* and *futures*. Actually, technical analysis was first applied to the stock market and later adapted to futures. With the introduction of *stock index futures,* the dividing line between these two areas is rapidly disappearing. *International stock markets* are also charted and analyzed according to technical principles. (See Figure 1.2.)

Financial futures, including *interest rate markets* and *foreign currencies,* have become enormously popular over the past decade and have proven to be excellent subjects for chart analysis.

Technical principles play a role in *options trading.* Technical forecasting can also be used to great advantage in the *hedging process.*

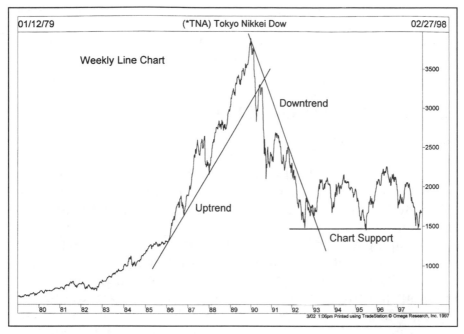

Figure 1.2 *The Japanese stock market charts very well as do most stock markets around the world.*

TECHNICAL ANALYSIS APPLIED TO DIFFERENT TIME DIMENSIONS

Another strength of the charting approach is its ability to handle different time dimensions. Whether the user is trading the intra-day tic-by-tic changes for *day trading purposes* or *trend trading* the intermediate trend, the same principles apply. A time dimension often overlooked is *longer range technical forecasting*. The opinion expressed in some quarters that charting is useful only in the short term is simply not true. It has been suggested by some that fundamental analysis should be used for long term forecasting with technical factors limited to short term timing. The fact is that longer range forecasting, using weekly and monthly charts going back several years, has proven to be an extremely useful application of these techniques.

Once the technical principles discussed in this book are thoroughly understood, they will provide the user with tremendous flexibility as to how they can be applied, both from the standpoint of the medium to be analyzed and the time dimension to be studied.

ECONOMIC FORECASTING

Technical analysis can play a role in economic forecasting. For example, the direction of commodity prices tells us something about the direction of inflation. They also give us clues about the strength or weakness of the economy. Rising commodity prices generally hint at a stronger economy and rising inflationary pressure. Falling commodity prices usually warn that the economy is slowing along with inflation. The direction of interest rates is affected by the trend of commodities. As a result, charts of commodity markets like gold and oil, along with Treasury Bonds, can tell us a lot about the strength or weakness of the economy and inflationary expectations. The direction of the U.S. dollar and foreign currency futures also provide early guidance about the strength or weakness of the respective global economies. Even more impressive is the fact that trends in these futures markets usually show up long before they are reflected in traditional economic indicators that are released on a monthly or quarterly basis, and usually tell us what has already happened. As their name implies, futures markets usually give us insights into the future. The S&P 500 stock market index has long been counted as an official leading economic indicator. A book by one of the country's top experts on the business cycle, *Leading Indicators for the 1990s* (Moore), makes a compelling case for the importance of commodity, bond, and stock trends as economic indicators. All three markets can be studied employing technical analysis. We'll have more to say on this subject in Chapter 17, "The Link Between Stocks and Futures."

TECHNICIAN OR CHARTIST?

There are several different titles applied to practitioners of the technical approach: technical analyst, chartist, market analyst, and visual analyst. Up until recently, they all meant pretty much the same thing. However, with increased specialization in the field, it has become necessary to make some further distinctions and define the terms a bit more carefully. Because virtually all technical analysis was based on the use of charts up until the last decade, the terms "technician" and "chartist" meant the same thing. This is no longer necessarily true.

The broader area of technical analysis is being increasingly divided into two types of practitioners, the traditional chartist and, for want of a better term, statistical technicians. Admittedly, there is a lot of overlap here and most technicians combine both areas to some extent. As in the case of the technician versus the fundamentalist, most seem to fall into one category or the other.

Whether or not the traditional chartist uses quantitative work to supplement his or her analysis, charts remain the primary working tool. Everything else is secondary. Charting, of necessity, remains somewhat subjective. The success of the approach depends, for the most part, on the skill of the individual chartist. The term "art charting" has been applied to this approach because chart reading is largely an art.

By contrast, the statistical, or quantitative, analyst takes these subjective principles, quantifies, tests, and optimizes them for the purpose of developing mechanical trading systems. These systems, or trading models, are then programmed into a computer that generates mechanical "buy" and "sell" signals. These systems range from the simple to the very complex. However, the intent is to reduce or completely eliminate the subjective human element in trading, to make it more scientific. These statisticians may or may not use price charts in their work, but they are considered technicians as long as their work is limited to the study of market action.

Even computer technicians can be subdivided further into those who favor mechanical systems, or the "black box" approach, and those who use computer technology to develop better technical indicators. The latter group maintains control over the interpretation of those indicators and also the decision making process.

One way of distinguishing between the chartist and the statistician is to say that all chartists are technicians, but not all technicians are chartists. Although these terms are used interchangeably throughout this book, it should be remembered that charting represents only one area in the broader subject of technical analysis.

A BRIEF COMPARISON OF TECHNICAL ANALYSIS IN STOCKS AND FUTURES

A question often asked is whether technical analysis as applied to futures is the same as the stock market. The answer is both yes and no. The basic principles are the same, but there are some significant differences. The principles of technical analysis were first applied to stock market forecasting and only later adapted to futures. Most of the basic tools—bar charts, point and figure charts, price patterns, volume, trendlines, moving averages, and oscillators, for example—are used in both areas. Anyone who has learned these concepts in either stocks or futures wouldn't have too much trouble making the adjustment to the other side. However, there are some general areas of difference having more to do with the different nature of stocks and futures than with the actual tools themselves.

Pricing Structure

The pricing structure in futures is much more complicated than in stocks. Each commodity is quoted in different units and increments. Grain markets, for example, are quoted in cents per bushel, livestock markets in cents per pound, gold and silver in dollars per ounce, and interest rates in basis points. The trader must learn the contract details of each market: which exchange it is traded on, how each contract is quoted, what the minimum and maximum price increments are, and what these price increments are worth.

Limited Life Span

Unlike stocks, futures contracts have expiration dates. A March 1999 Treasury Bond contract, for example, expires in March of

1999. The typical futures contract trades for about a year and a half before expiration. Therefore, at any one time, at least a half dozen different contract months are trading in the same commodity at the same time. The trader must know which contracts to trade and which ones to avoid. (This is explained later in this book.) This limited life feature causes some problems for longer range price forecasting. It necessitates the continuing need for obtaining new charts once old contracts stop trading. The chart of an expired contract isn't of much use. New charts must be obtained for the newer contracts along with their own technical indicators. This constant rotation makes the maintenance of an ongoing chart library a good deal more difficult. For computer users, it also entails greater time and expense by making it necessary to be constantly obtaining new historical data as old contracts expire.

Lower Margin Requirements

This is probably the most important difference between stocks and futures. All futures are traded on margin, which is usually less than 10% of the value of the contract. The result of these low margin requirements is tremendous leverage. Relatively small price moves in either direction tend to become magnified in their impact on overall trading results. For this reason, it is possible to make or lose large sums of money very quickly in futures. Because a trader puts up only 10% of the value of the contract as margin, then a 10% move in either direction will either double the trader's money or wipe it out. By magnifying the impact of even minor market moves, the high leverage factor sometimes makes the futures markets seem more volatile than they actually are. When someone says, for example, that he or she was "wiped out" in the futures market, remember that he or she only committed 10% in the first place.

From the standpoint of technical analysis, the high leverage factor makes timing in the futures markets much more critical than it is in stocks. The correct timing of entry and exit points is crucial in futures trading and much more difficult and frustrating than market analysis. Largely for this reason, technical trading skills become indispensable to a successful futures trading program.

Time Frame Is Much Shorter

Because of the high leverage factor and the need for close monitoring of market positions, the time horizon of the commodity trader is much shorter of necessity. Stock market technicians tend to look more at the longer range picture and talk in time frames that are beyond the concern of the average commodity trader. Stock technicians may talk about where the market will be in three or six months. Futures traders want to know where prices will be next week, tomorrow, or maybe even later this afternoon. This has necessitated the refinement of very short term timing tools. One example is the moving average. The most commonly watched averages in stocks are 50 and 200 days. In commodities, most moving averages are under 40 days. A popular moving average combination in futures, for example, is 4, 9, and 18 days.

Greater Reliance on Timing

Timing is everything in futures trading. Determining the correct direction of the market only solves a portion of the trading problem. If the timing of the entry point is off by a day, or sometimes even minutes, it can mean the difference between a winner or a loser. It's bad enough to be on the wrong side of the market and lose money. Being on the right side of the market and still losing money is one of the most frustrating and unnerving aspects of futures trading. It goes without saying that timing is almost purely technical in nature, because the fundamentals rarely change on a day-to-day basis.

LESS RELIANCE ON MARKET AVERAGES AND INDICATORS

Stock market analysis is based heavily on the movement of broad market averages—such as the Dow Jones Industrial Average or the S&P 500. In addition, technical indicators that measure the strength or weakness of the broader market—like the NYSE advance-decline line or the new highs-new lows list—are heavily employed. While commodity markets can be tracked using measures like the Commodity Research Bureau Futures Price Index, less emphasis is placed on the broader market approach. Commodity market analysis concentrates more on individual market action. That being the case, technical indicators that measure broader commodity trends aren't used much. With only about 20 or so active commodity markets, there isn't much need.

Specific Technical Tools

While most of the technical tools originally developed in the stock market have some application in commodity markets, they are not used in the exact same way. For example, chart patterns in futures often tend not to form as fully as they do in stocks.

Futures traders rely more heavily on shorter term indicators that emphasize more precise trading signals. These points of difference and many others are discussed later in this book.

Finally, there is another area of major difference between stocks and futures. Technical analysis in stocks relies much more heavily on the use of *sentiment indicators* and *flow of funds* analysis. *Sentiment indicators* monitor the performance of different groups such as odd lotters, mutual funds, and floor specialists. Enormous importance is placed on sentiment indicators that measure the overall market bullishness and bearishness on the theory that the majority opinion is usually wrong. *Flow of funds* analysis refers to the cash position of different groups, such as mutual funds or large institutional accounts. The thinking here is that the larger the cash position, the more funds that are available for stock purchases.

Technical analysis in the futures markets is a much purer form of price analysis. While contrary opinion theory is also used to some extent, much more emphasis is placed on basic trend analysis and the application of traditional technical indicators.

SOME CRITICISMS OF THE TECHNICAL APPROACH

A few questions generally crop up in any discussion of the technical approach. One of these concerns is the *self-fulfilling prophe-*

cy. Another is the question of whether or not past price data can really be used to forecast future price direction. The critic usually says something like: "Charts tell us where the market has been, but can't tell us where it is going." For the moment, we'll put aside the obvious answer that a chart won't tell you anything if you don't know how to read it. The Random Walk Theory questions whether prices trend at all and doubts that any forecasting technique can beat a simple *buy and hold* strategy. These questions deserve a response.

The Self-Fulfilling Prophecy

The question of whether there is a self-fulfilling prophecy at work seems to bother most people because it is raised so often. It is certainly a valid concern, but of much less importance than most people realize. Perhaps the best way to address this question is to quote from a text that discusses some of the disadvantages of using chart patterns:

> a. The use of most chart patterns has been widely publicized in the last several years. Many traders are quite familiar with these patterns and often act on them in concert. This creates a "self-fulfilling prophecy," as waves of buying or selling are created in response to "bullish" or "bearish" patterns. . .
>
> b. Chart patterns are almost completely subjective. No study has yet succeeded in mathematically quantifying any of them. They are literally in the mind of the beholder.... (Teweles et al.)

These two criticisms contradict one another and the second point actually cancels out the first. If chart patterns are "completely subjective" and "in the mind of the beholder," then it is hard to imagine how everyone could see the same thing at the same time, which is the basis of the self-fulfilling prophecy. Critics of charting can't have it both ways. They can't, on the one hand, criticize charting for being so objective and obvious that everyone will act in the same way at the same time (thereby causing the price pattern to be fulfilled), and then also criticize charting for being too subjective.

The truth of the matter is that charting is very subjective. Chart reading is an art. (Possibly the word "skill" would be more to the point.) Chart patterns are seldom so clear that even experienced chartists always agree on their interpretation. There is always an element of doubt and disagreement. As this book demonstrates, there are many different approaches to technical analysis that often disagree with one another.

Even if most technicians did agree on a market forecast, they would not all necessarily enter the market at the same time and in the same way. Some would try to anticipate the chart signal and enter the market early. Others would buy the "breakout" from a given pattern or indicator. Still others would wait for the pullback after the breakout before taking action. Some traders are aggressive; others are conservative. Some use stops to enter the market, while others like to use market orders or resting limit orders. Some are trading for the long pull, while others are day trading. Therefore, the possibility of all technicians acting at the same time and in the same way is actually quite remote.

Even if the self-fulfilling prophecy were of major concern, it would probably be "self-correcting" in nature. In other words, traders would rely heavily on charts until their concerted actions started to affect or distort the markets. Once traders realized this was happening, they would either stop using the charts or adjust their trading tactics. For example, they would either try to act before the crowd or wait longer for greater confirmation. So, even if the self-fulfilling prophecy did become a problem over the near term, it would tend to correct itself.

It must be kept in mind that bull and bear markets only occur and are maintained when they are justified by the law of supply and demand. Technicians could not possibly cause a major market move just by the sheer power of their buying and selling. If this were the case, technicians would all become wealthy very quickly.

Of much more concern than the chartists is the tremendous growth in the use of computerized technical trading systems in the futures market. These systems are mainly trend-following in nature, which means that they are all programmed to identify and trade major trends. With the growth in professionally managed money in the futures industry, and the proliferation of mul-timillion-dollar public and private funds, most of which are using these technical systems, tremendous concentrations of money are chasing only a handful of existing trends. Because the universe of futures markets is still quite small, the potential for these systems distorting short term price action is growing. However, even in cases where distortions do occur, they are generally short term in nature and do not cause major moves.

Here again, even the problem of concentrated sums of money using technical systems is probably self-correcting. If all of the systems started doing the same thing at the same time, traders would make adjustments by making their systems either more or less sensitive.

The self-fulfilling prophecy is generally listed as a criticism of charting. It might be more appropriate to label it as a compliment. After all, for any forecasting technique to become so popular that it begins to influence events, it would have to be pretty good. We can only speculate as to why this concern is seldom raised regarding the use of fundamental analysis.

Can the Past Be Used to Predict the Future?

Another question often raised concerns the validity of using past price data to predict the future. It is surprising how often critics of the technical approach bring up this point because every known method of forecasting, from weather predicting to fundamental analysis, is based completely on the study of past data. What other kind of data is there to work with?

The field of statistics makes a distinction between *descriptive statistics* and *inductive statistics*. *Descriptive statistics* refers to the graphical presentation of data, such as the price data on a standard bar chart. *Inductive statistics* refers to generalizations, predictions, or extrapolations that are inferred from that data. Therefore, the price chart itself comes under the heading of the descriptive, while the analysis technicians perform on that price data falls into the realm of the inductive.

As one statistical text puts it, "The first step in forecasting the business or economic future consists, thus, of gathering observations from the past." (Freund and Williams) Chart analysis is just another form of *time series analysis,* based on a study of the past, which is exactly what is done in all forms of time series analysis. The only type of data anyone has to go on is past data. We can only estimate the future by projecting past experiences into that future.

So it seems that the use of past price data to predict the future in technical analysis is grounded in sound statistical concepts. If anyone were to seriously question this aspect of technical forecasting, he or she would have to also question the validity of every other form of forecasting based on historical data, which includes all economic and fundamental analysis.

RANDOM WALK THEORY

The *Random Walk Theory,* developed and nurtured in the academic community, claims that price changes are "serially independent" and that price history is not a reliable indicator of future price direction. In a nutshell, price movement is random and unpredictable. The theory is based on the *efficient market hypothesis,* which holds that prices fluctuate randomly about their intrinsic value. It also holds that the best market strategy to follow would be a simple "buy and hold" strategy as opposed to any attempt to "beat the market."

While there seems little doubt that a certain amount of randomness or "noise" does exist in all markets, it's just unrealistic to believe that *all* price movement is random. This may be one of those areas where empirical observation and practical experience prove more useful than sophisticated statistical techniques, which seem capable of proving anything the user has in mind or incapable of disproving anything. It might be useful to keep in mind that randomness can only be defined in the negative sense of an inability to uncover systematic patterns in price action. The fact that many academics have not been able to discover the presence of these patterns does not prove that they do not exist.

The academic debate as to whether markets trend is of little interest to the average market analyst or trader who is forced to deal in the real world where market trends are clearly visible. If the reader has any doubts on this point, a casual glance through any chart book (randomly selected) will demonstrate the presence of trends in a very graphic way. How do the "random walkers" explain the persistence of these trends if prices are serially independent, meaning that what happened yesterday, or last week, has no bearing on what may happen today or tomorrow? How do they explain the profitable "real life" track records of many trend-following systems?

How, for example, would a buy and hold strategy fare in the commodity futures markets where timing is so crucial? Would those long positions be held during bear markets? How would traders even know the difference between bull and bear markets if prices are unpredictable and don't trend? In fact, how could a bear market even exist in the first place because that would imply a trend? (See Figure 1.3.)

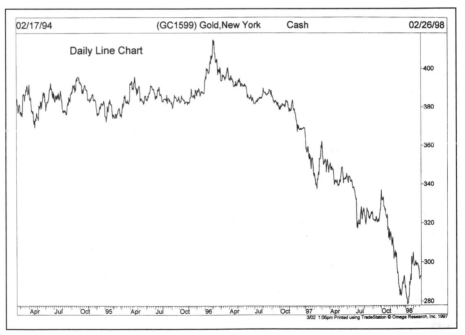

Figure 1.3 *A "random walker" would have a tough time convincing a holder of gold bullion that there's no real trend on this chart.*

It seems doubtful that statistical evidence will ever totally prove or disprove the Random Walk Theory. However, the idea that markets are random is totally rejected by the technical community. If the markets were truly random, no forecasting technique would work. Far from disproving the validity of the technical approach, the *efficient market hypothesis* is very close to the technical premise that *markets discount everything*. The academics, however, feel that because markets quickly discount all information, there's no way to take advantage of that information. The basis of technical forecasting, already touched upon, is that important market information is discounted in the market price long before it becomes known. Without meaning to, the academics have very eloquently stated the need for closely monitoring price action and the futility of trying to profit from fundamental information, at least over the short term.

Finally, it seems only fair to observe that any process appears random and unpredictable to those who do not understand the rules under which that process operates. An electrocardiogram printout, for example, might appear like a lot of random noise to a layperson. But to a trained medical person, all those little blips make a lot of sense and are certainly not random. The working of the markets may appear random to those who have not taken the time to study the rules of market behavior. *The illusion of randomness gradually disappears as the skill in chart reading improves.* Hopefully, that is exactly what will happen as the reader progresses through the various sections of this book.

There may even be hope for the academic world. A number of leading American universities have begun to explore Behavioral Finance which maintains that human psychology and securities pricing are intertwined. That, of course, is the primary basis of technical analysis.

UNIVERSAL PRINCIPLES

When an earlier version of this book was published twelve years ago, many of the technical timing tools that were explained were used mainly in the futures markets. Over the past decade, however, these tools have been widely employed in analyzing stock market trends. The technical principles that are discussed in this book can be applied universally to all markets—even mutual funds. One additional feature of stock market trading that has gained wide popularity in the past decade has been sector investing, primarily through index options and mutual funds. Later in the book we'll show how to determine which sectors are hot and which are not by applying technical timing tools.

2
Dow Theory

INTRODUCTION

Charles Dow and his partner Edward Jones founded Dow Jones & Company in 1882. Most technicians and students of the markets concur that much of what we call *technical analysis* today has its origins in theories first proposed by Dow around the turn of the century. Dow published his ideas in a series of editorials he wrote for the *Wall Street Journal*. Most technicians today recognize and assimilate Dow's basic ideas, whether or not they recognize the source. *Dow Theory* still forms the cornerstone of the study of technical analysis, even in the face of today's sophisticated computer technology, and the proliferation of newer and supposedly better technical indicators.

On July 3, 1884, Dow published the first stock market average composed of the closing prices of eleven stocks: nine railroad companies and two manufacturing firms. Dow felt that these eleven stocks provided a good indication of the economic health of the country. In 1897, Dow determined that two separate indices would better represent that health, and created a 12 stock industrial index and a 20 stock rail index. By 1928 the industrial index had grown to include 30 stocks, the number at which it stands today. The editors of *The Wall Street Journal* have updated the list numerous times in the ensuing years, adding a utility index in 1929. In 1984, the year that marked the one hundredth anniversary of Dow's first publication, the Market Technicians Association presented a Gorham-silver bowl to Dow Jones & Co. According to the MTA, the award recognized "the lasting contribution that Charles Dow made to the field of investment analysis. His index, the forerunner of what today is regarded as the leading barometer of stock market activity, remains a vital tool for market technicians 80 years after his death."

Unfortunately for us, Dow never wrote a book on his theory. Instead, he set down his ideas of stock market behavior in a series of editorials that *The Wall Street Journal* published around the turn of the century. In 1903, the year after Dow's death, S.A. Nelson compiled these essays into a book entitled *The ABC of Stock Speculation.* In that work, Nelson first coined the term "Dow's Theory." Richard Russell, who wrote the introduction to a 1978 reprint, compared Dow's contribution to stock market theory with Freud's contribution to psychiatry. In 1922, William Peter Hamilton (Dow's associate and successor at the Journal) categorized and published Dow's tenets in a book entitled *The Stock Market Barometer.* Robert Rhea developed the theory even further in the *Dow Theory* (New York: Barron's), published in 1932.

Dow applied his theoretical work to the stock market averages that he created; namely the Industrials and the Rails. However, most of his analytical ideas apply equally well to all market averages. This chapter will describe the six basic tenets of Dow Theory and will discuss how these ideas fit into a modern study of technical analysis. We will discuss the ramifications of these ideas in the chapters that follow.

BASIC TENETS

1. The Averages Discount Everything.

> The sum and tendency of the transactions of the Stock Exchange represent the sum of all Wall Street's knowl-

edge of the past, immediate and remote, applied to the discounting of the future. There is no need to add to the averages, as some statisticians do, elaborate compilations of commodity price index numbers, bank clearings, fluctuations in exchange, volume of domestic and foreign trades or anything else. Wall Street considers all these things (Hamilton, pp. 40–41).

Sound familiar? The idea that the markets reflect every possible knowable factor that affects overall supply and demand is one of the basic premises of technical theory, as was mentioned in Chapter 1. The theory applies to market averages, as well as it does to individual markets, and even makes allowances for "acts of God." While the markets cannot anticipate events such as earthquakes and various other natural calamities, they quickly discount such occurrences, and almost instantaneously assimilate their affects into the price action.

2. The Market Has Three Trends.

Before discussing how trends behave, we must clarify what Dow considered a trend. Dow defined an uptrend as a situation in which each successive rally closes higher than the previous rally high, and each successive rally low also closes higher than the previous rally low. In other words, an uptrend has a pattern of rising peaks and troughs. The opposite situation, with successively lower peaks and troughs, defines a downtrend. Dow's definition has withstood the test of time and still forms the cornerstone of trend analysis.

Dow believed that the laws of action and reaction apply to the markets just as they do to the physical universe. He wrote, "Records of trading show that in many cases when a stock reaches top it will have a moderate decline and then go back again to near the highest figures. If after such a move, the price again recedes, it is liable to decline some distance" (Nelson, page 43).

Dow considered a trend to have three parts, *primary, secondary,* and *minor,* which he compared to the tide, waves, and ripples of the sea. The primary trend represents the tide, the secondary or intermediate trend represents the waves that make up the tide, and the minor trends behave like ripples on the waves.

An observer can determine the direction of the tide by noting the highest point on the beach reached by successive waves.
If each successive wave reaches further inland than the preceding
one, the tide is flowing in. When the high point of each successive wave recedes, the tide has turned out and is ebbing. Unlike
actual ocean tides, which last a matter of hours, Dow conceived
of market tides as lasting for more than a year, and possibly for
several years.

The secondary, or intermediate, trend represents corrections in the primary trend and usually lasts three weeks to three
months. These intermediate corrections generally retrace between
one-third and two-thirds of the previous trend movement and
most frequently about half, or 50%, of the previous move.

According to Dow, the minor (or near term) trend usually
lasts less than three weeks. This near term trend represents fluctuations in the intermediate trend. We will discuss trend concepts
in greater detail in Chapter 4, "Basic Concepts of Trends," where
you will see that we continue to use the same basic concepts and
terminology today.

3. Major Trends Have Three Phases.

Dow focused his attention on primary or major trends, which he
felt usually take place in three distinct phases: an accumulation
phase, a public participation phase, and a distribution phase. The
accumulation phase represents informed buying by the most
astute investors. If the previous trend was down, then at this
point these astute investors recognize that the market has assimi-
lated all the so-called "bad" news. The public participation phase,
where most technical trend-followers begin to participate, occurs
when prices begin to advance rapidly and business news
improves. The distribution phase takes place when newspapers
begin to print increasingly bullish stories; when economic news is
better than ever; and when speculative volume and public participation increase. During this last phase the same informed
investors who began to "accumulate" near the bear market bottom (when no one else wanted to buy) begin to "distribute"
before anyone else starts selling.

Students of Elliott Wave Theory will recognize this division of a major bull market into three distinct phases. R. N. Elliott elaborated upon Rhea's work in *Dow Theory,* to recognize that a bull market has three major, upward movements. In Chapter 13, "Elliott Wave Theory," we'll show the close similarity between Dow's three phases of a bull market and the five wave Elliott sequence.

4. The Averages Must Confirm Each Other.

Dow, in referring to the Industrial and Rail Averages, meant that no important bull or bear market signal could take place unless both averages gave the same signal, thus confirming each other. He felt that both averages must exceed a previous secondary peak to confirm the inception or continuation of a bull market. He did not believe that the signals had to occur simultaneously, but recognized that a shorter length of time between the two signals provided stronger confirmation. When the two averages diverged from one another, Dow assumed that the prior trend was still maintained. (Elliott Wave Theory only requires that signals be generated in a single average.) Chapter 6, "Continuation Patterns," will cover the key concepts of confirmation and divergence. (See Figures 2.1 and 2.2.)

5. Volume Must Confirm the Trend.

Dow recognized volume as a secondary but important factor in confirming price signals. Simply stated, *volume should expand or increase in the direction of the major trend.* In a major uptrend, volume would then increase as prices move higher, and diminish as prices fall. In a downtrend, volume should increase as prices drop and diminish as they rally. Dow considered volume a secondary indicator. He based his actual buy and sell signals entirely on closing prices. In Chapter 7, "Volume and Open Interest," we'll cover the subject of volume and build on Dow's ideas. Today's sophisticated volume indicators help determine whether volume is increasing or falling off. Savvy traders then compare this information to price action to see if the two are confirming each other.

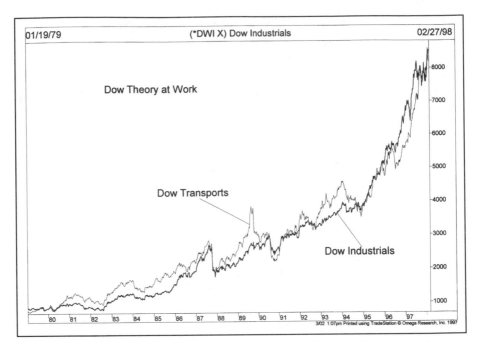

Figure 2.1   *A long term view of the Dow Theory at work. For a major bull trend to continue, both the Dow Industrials and the Dow Transports must advance together.*

6. A Trend Is Assumed to Be in Effect Until It Gives Definite Signals That It Has Reversed.

This tenet, which we touched upon in Chapter 1, forms much of the foundation of modern trend-following approaches. It relates a physical law to market movement, which states that an object in motion (in this case a trend) tends to continue in motion until some external force causes it to change direction. A number of technical tools are available to traders to assist in the difficult task of spotting reversal signals, including the study of support and resistance levels, price patterns, trendlines, and moving averages. Some indicators can provide even earlier warning signals of loss of momentum. All of that not withstanding, the odds usually favor that the existing trend will continue.

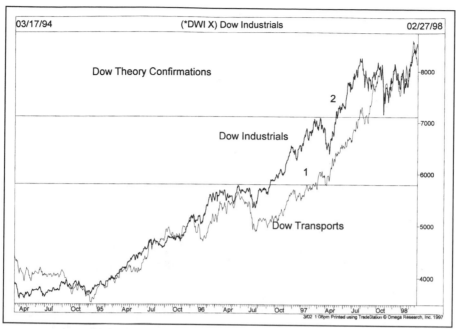

Figure 2.2 *Examples of two Dow Theory confirmations. At the start of 1997 (point 1), the Dow Transports confirmed the earlier breakout in the Industrials. The following May (point 2), the Dow Industrials confirmed the earlier new high in the Transports.*

The most difficult task for a Dow theorist, or any trend-follower for that matter, is being able to distinguish between a normal secondary correction in an existing trend and the first leg of a new trend in the opposite direction. Dow theorists often disagree as to when the market gives an actual reversal signal. Figures 2.3a and 2.3b show how this disagreement manifests itself.

Figures 2.3a and 2.3b illustrate two different market scenarios. In Figure 2.3a, notice that the rally at point C is lower than the previous peak at A. Price then declines below point B. The presence of these two lower peaks and two lower troughs gives a clear-cut sell signal at the point where the low at B is broken (point S). This reversal pattern is sometimes referred to as a "failure swing."

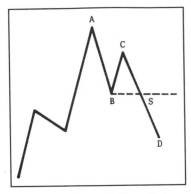

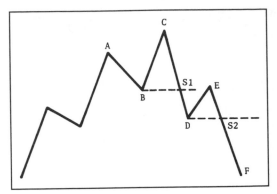

Figure 2.3a   *Failure Swing.*
The failure of the peak at C to
overcome A, followed by the
violation of the low at B, con-
stitutes a "sell" signal at S.

Figure 2.3b   *Nonfailure Swing. Notice*
that C exceeds A before falling below B.
Some Dow theorists would see a "sell" sig-
nal at S1, while others would need to see a
lower high at E before turning bearish at S2.

In Figure 2.3b, the rally top at C is higher than the previous
peak at A. Then price declines below point B. Some Dow theorists
would not consider the clear violation of support, at S1, to be a
bona fide sell signal. They would point out that only lower lows
exist in this case, but not lower highs. They would prefer to see a
rally to point E which is lower than point C. Then they would look
for another new low under point D. To them, S2 would represent
the actual sell signal with two lower highs and two lower lows.

The reversal pattern shown in Figure 2.3b is referred to as a
"nonfailure swing." A failure swing (shown in Figure 2.3a) is a
much weaker pattern than the nonfailure swing in Figure 2.3b.
Figures 2.4a and 2.4b show the same scenarios at a market bottom.

THE USE OF CLOSING PRICES AND THE PRESENCE OF LINES

Dow relied exclusively on *closing prices*. He believed that averages
had to *close* higher than a previous peak or lower than a previous
trough to have significance. Dow did not consider intraday penetrations valid.

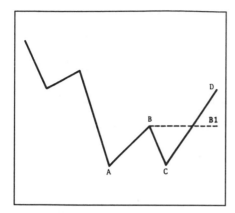

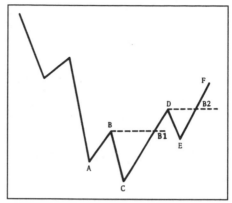

Figure 2.4a *Failure Swing Bottom. The "buy" signal takes place when point B is exceeded (at B1).*

Figure 2.4b *Nonfailure Swing Bottom. "Buy" signals occur at points B1 or B2.*

When traders speak of *lines* in the averages, they are referring to horizontal patterns that sometimes occur on the charts. These sideways trading ranges usually play the role of corrective phases and are usually referred to as consolidations. In more modern terms, we might refer to such lateral patterns as "rectangles."

SOME CRITICISMS OF DOW THEORY

Dow Theory has done well over the years in identifying major bull and bear markets, but has not escaped criticism. On average, Dow Theory misses 20 to 25% of a move before generating a signal. Many traders consider this to be too late. A Dow Theory buy signal usually occurs in the second phase of an uptrend as price penetrates a previous intermediate peak. This is also, incidentally, about where most trend-following technical systems begin to identify and participate in existing trends.

In response to this criticism, traders must remember that Dow never intended to anticipate trends; rather he sought to recognize the emergence of major bull and bear markets and to capture the large middle portion of important market moves.

Available records suggest that Dow's Theory has performed that function reasonably well. From 1920 to 1975, Dow Theory signals captured 68% of the moves in the Industrial and Transportation Averages and 67% of those in the S&P 500 Composite Index (Source: Barron's). Those who criticize Dow Theory for failing to catch actual market tops and bottoms lack a basic understanding of the trend-following philosophy.

STOCKS AS ECONOMIC INDICATORS

Dow apparently never intended to use his theory to forecast the direction of the stock market. He felt its real value was to use stock market direction as a barometric reading of general business conditions. We can only marvel at Dow's vision and genius. In addition to formulating a great deal of today's price forecasting methodology, he was among the first to recognize the usefulness of stock market averages as a leading economic indicator.

DOW THEORY APPLIED TO FUTURES TRADING

Dow's work considered the behavior of stock averages. While most of that original work has significant application to commodity futures, there are some important distinctions between stock and futures trading. For one thing, Dow assumed that most investors follow only the major trends and would use intermediate corrections for timing purposes only. Dow considered the minor or near term trends to be unimportant. Obviously, this is not the case in futures trading in which most traders who follow trends trade the intermediate instead of the major trend. These traders must pay a great deal of attention to minor swings for timing purposes. If a futures trader expected an intermediate uptrend to last for a couple of months, he or she would look for short term dips to signal purchases. In an intermediate downtrend, the trader would use minor bounces to signal short sales. The minor trend, therefore, becomes extremely important in futures trading.

NEW WAYS TO TRADE THE DOW AVERAGES

For the first 100 years of its existence, the Dow Jones Industrial Average could only be used as a market indicator. That all changed on October 6, 1997 when futures and options began trading on Dow's venerable average for the first time. The Chicago Board of Trade launched a futures contract on the Dow Jones Industrial Average, while options on the Dow (symbol: DJX) started trading at the Chicago Board Options Exchange. In addition, options were also launched on the Dow Jones Transportation Average (symbol: DJTA) and the Dow Jones Utility Index (symbol: DJUA). In January 1998, the American Stock Exchange started trading the Diamonds Trust, a unit investment trust that mimics the 30 Dow industrials. In addition, two mutual funds were offered based on the 30 Dow benchmark. Mr. Dow would probably be happy to know that, a century after their creation, it would now be possible to trade his Dow averages, and actually put his Dow Theory into practice.

CONCLUSION

This chapter presented a relatively quick review of the more important aspects of the Dow Theory. It will become clear, as you continue through this book, that an understanding and appreciation of Dow Theory provides a solid foundation for any study of technical analysis. Much of what is discussed in the following chapters represents some adaptation of Dow's original theory. The standard definition of a trend, the classification of a trend into three categories and phases, the principles of confirmation and divergence, the interpretation of volume, and the use of percentage retracements (to name a few), all derive, in one way or another, from Dow Theory.

In addition to the sources already cited in this chapter, an excellent review of the principles of Dow Theory can be found in *Technical Analysis of Stock Trends* (Edwards & Magee).

3

Chart Construction

INTRODUCTION

This chapter is primarily intended for those readers who are unfamiliar with bar chart construction. We'll begin by discussing the different types of charts available and then turn our focus to the most commonly used chart—*the daily bar chart*. We'll look at how the price data is read and plotted on the chart. *Volume and open interest* are also included in addition to price. We'll then look at other variations of the bar chart, including *longer range weekly and monthly charts*. Once that has been completed, we'll be ready to start looking at some of the analytical tools applied to that chart in the following chapter. Those readers already familiar with the charts themselves might find this chapter too basic. Feel free to move on to the next chapter.

TYPES OF CHARTS AVAILABLE

The daily bar chart has already been acknowledged as the most widely used type of chart in technical analysis. There are, however, other types of charts also used by technicians, such as line charts, point and figure charts, and more recently, candlesticks. Figure 3.1 shows a standard daily bar chart. It's called a bar chart because each day's range is represented by a vertical bar. The bar chart shows the open, high, low, and closing prices. The tic to the right of the vertical bar is the closing price. The opening price is the tic to the left of the bar.

Figure 3.2 shows what the same market looks like on a line chart. In the line chart, only the closing price is plotted for each successive day. Many chartists believe that because the closing price is the most critical price of the trading day, a line (or close-only) chart is a more valid measure of price activity.

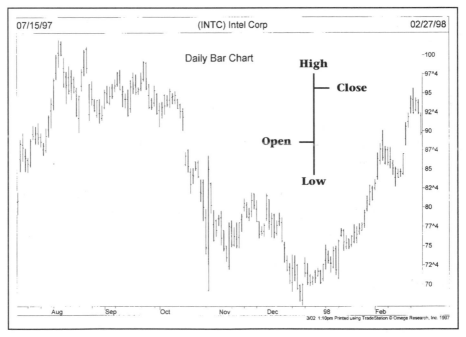

Figure 3.1 *A daily bar chart of Intel. Each vertical bar represents one day's action.*

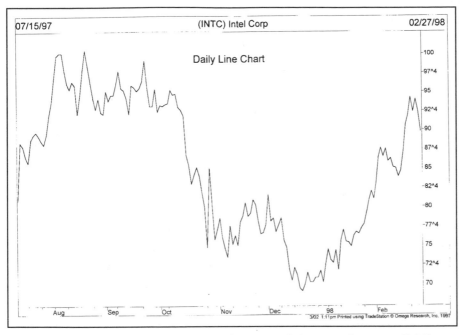

Figure 3.2 *A line chart of Intel. This type of chart produces a solid line by connecting the successive closing prices.*

A third type of chart, the point and figure chart, is shown in Figure 3.3. Notice here that the point and figure chart shows the same price action but in a more compressed format. Notice the alternating column of x's and o's. The x columns show rising prices and the o columns, declining prices. Buy and sell signals are more precise and easier to spot on the point and figure chart than on the bar chart. This type of chart also has a lot more flexibility. Chapter 11 covers point and figure charts.

CANDLESTICKS

Candlestick charts are the Japanese version of bar charting and have become very popular in recent years among western chartists. The Japanese candlestick records the same four prices as the traditional bar chart—the open, the close, the high, and the

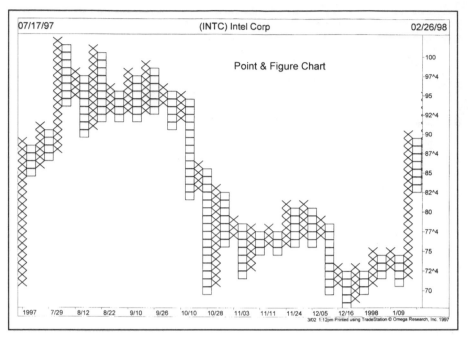

Figure 3.3 *A point and figure chart of Intel. Notice the alternating columns of x's and o's. The x column shows rising prices. The o column shows falling prices. Buy and sell signals are more precise on this type of chart.*

low. The visual presentation differs however. On the candlestick chart, a thin line (called the *shadow*) shows the day's price range from the high to the low. A wider portion of the bar (called the *real body*) measures the distance between the open and the close. If the close is higher than the open, the real body is white (positive). If the close is lower than the open, the real body is black (negative). (See Figure 3.4.)

The key to candlestick charts is the relationship between the open and the close. Possibly because of the growing popularity of candlesticks, western chartists now pay a lot more attention to the opening tic on their bar charts. You can do everything with a candlestick chart that you can do with a bar chart. In other words, all the technical tools and indicators we'll be showing you for the bar chart can also be used on candlesticks. We'll show you a bit later in the chapter how to construct bar charts for weekly

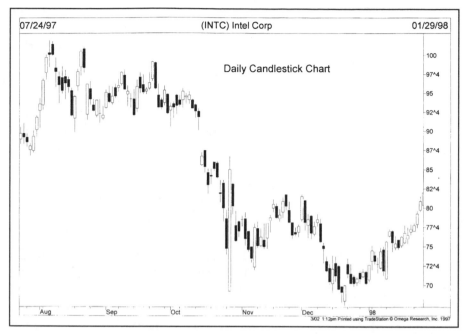

Daily Candlestick Chart

Figure 3.4   *A candlestick chart of Intel. The color of the candlestick is determined by the relationship between the open and the close. White candlesticks are positive, while black candlesticks are negative.*

and monthly periods. You can do the same with candlesticks. Chapter 12, "Japanese Candlesticks," provides a more thorough explanation of candlestick charting.

ARITHMETIC VERSUS LOGARITHMIC SCALE

Charts can be plotted using arithmetic or logarithmic price scales. For some types of analysis, particularly for very long range trend analysis, there may be some advantage to using logarithmic charts. (See Figures 3.5 and 3.6.) Figure 3.5 shows what the different scales would look like. On the arithmetic scale, the vertical price scale shows an equal distance for each price unit of change. Notice in this example that each point on the arithmetic scale is equidistant. On the log scale, however, note that the percentage

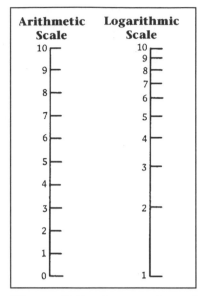

Figure 3.5   *A comparison of an arithmetic and logarithmic scale. Notice the equal spacing on the scale to the left. The log scale shows percentage changes (right scale).*

increases get smaller as the price scale increases. The distance from points 1 to 2 is the same as the distance from points 5 to 10 because they both represent the same doubling in price. For example, a move from 5 to 10 on an arithmetic scale would be the same distance as a move from 50 to 55, even though the former represents a doubling in price, while the latter is a price increase of only 10%. Prices plotted on ratio or log scales show equal distances for similar percentage moves. For example, a move from 10 to 20 (a 100% increase) would be the same distance on a log chart as a move from 20 to 40 or 40 to 80. Many stock market chart services use log charts, whereas futures chart services use arithmetic. Charting software packages allow both types of scaling, as shown in Figure 3.6.

CONSTRUCTION OF THE DAILY BAR CHART

The construction of the daily bar chart is extremely simple. The bar chart is both a price and a time chart. The vertical axis (the y axis) shows a scale representing the price of the contract. The horizontal axis (the x axis) records the passage of time. Dates are marked along the bottom of the the chart. All the user has to do is plot a vertical bar in the appropriate day from the day's high to the day's low (called the range). Place a horizontal tic to the right of the vertical bar identifying the daily closing price. (See Figure 3.7.)

The reason for placing the tic to the right of the bar is to distinguish it from the opening price, which chartists record to

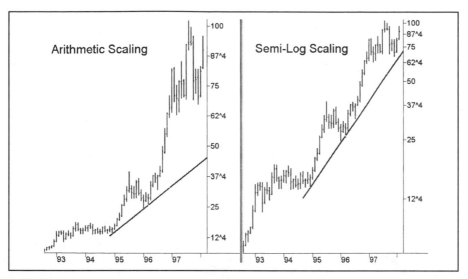

Figure 3.6 *Longer view of Intel using two different price scales. The chart to the left shows the traditional arithmetic scale. The chart on the right shows a logarithmic scale. Notice that the three year up trendline worked better on the log chart.*

the left of the bar. Once that day's activity has been plotted, the user moves one day to the right to plot the next day's action. Most chart services use five day weeks. Weekends are not shown on the chart. Whenever an exchange is closed during the trading week, that day's space is left blank. The bars along the bottom of the chart measure volume. (See Figure 3.7.)

VOLUME

Another piece of important information should be included on the bar chart—volume. *Volume* represents the total amount of trading activity in that market for that day. It is the total number of futures contracts traded during the day or the number of common stock shares that change hands on a given day in the stock market. The volume is recorded by a vertical bar at the bottom of the chart under that day's price bar. A higher volume bar means

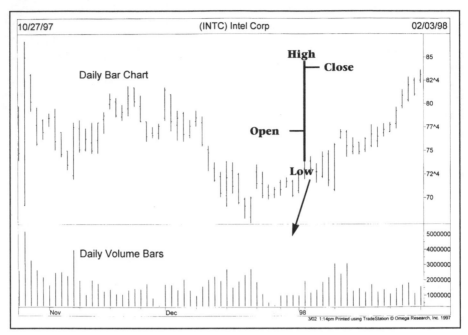

Figure 3.7 *A closer look at the Intel daily bar chart. Each bar measures the day's price range. The opening price is marked by the small tic to the left of each bar. The closing tic is to the right. The bars along the bottom measure each day's volume.*

the volume was heavier for that day. A smaller bar represents lighter volume. A vertical scale along the bottom of the chart is provided to help plot the data, as shown in Figure 3.7.

FUTURES OPEN INTEREST

Open interest is the total number of outstanding futures contracts that are held by market participants at the end of the day. Open interest is the number of outstanding contracts held by the longs or the shorts, not the total of both. Remember, because we're dealing with futures contracts, for every long there must also be a short. Therefore, we only have to know the totals on one side. Open interest is marked on the chart with a solid line along the bottom, usually just above the volume but below the price. (See Figure 3.8.)

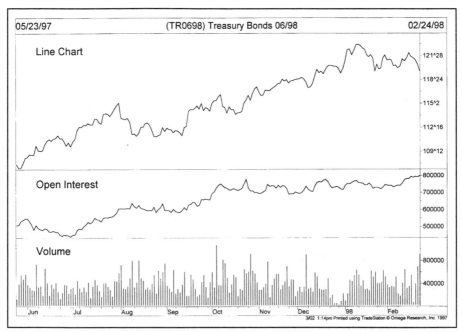

| 05/23/97 | (TR0698) Treasury Bonds 06/98 | 02/24/98 |

Line Chart

121^28
118^24
115^2
112^16
109^12

Open Interest

800000
700000
600000
500000

Volume

800000
400000

Jun Jul Aug Sep Oct Nov Dec '98 Feb

3/02 1:14pm Printed using TradeStation © Omega Research, Inc. 1997

Figure 3.8   *A daily line chart of a Treasury Bond futures contract. The vertical bars along the bottom measure the total daily volume. The solid line along the middle represents the total outstanding open interest for the Treasury Bond futures market.*

Total Versus Individual Volume and Open Interest Numbers in Futures

Futures chart services, along with most futures technicians, use only the *total* volume and open interest figures. Although figures are available for each individual delivery month, the total figures for each commodity market are the ones that are used for forecasting purposes. There is a good reason for this.

In the early stages of a futures contract's life, volume and open interest are usually quite small. The figures build up as the contract reaches maturity. In the last couple of months before expiration, however, the numbers begin to drop again. Obviously, traders have to liquidate open positions as the contract approaches expiration. Therefore, the increase in the numbers in the first few months of life and the decline near the end of trading have nothing to do with market direction and are just a function of the limited life feature of a commodity futures contract. To provide the necessary continuity in volume and open interest numbers, and to give them forecasting value, the total numbers are generally used. (Stock charts plot total volume figures, but do not include open interest.)

Volume and Open Interest Reported a Day Late in Futures

Futures volume and open interest numbers are reported a day late. Therefore, the chartist must be content with a day's lag in obtaining and interpreting the figures. The numbers are usually reported during the following day's trading hours, but too late for publication in the day's financial newspapers. Estimated volume figures are available, however, after the markets close and are included in the following morning's paper. Estimated volume numbers are just that, but they do at least give the futures technician some idea of whether trading activity was heavier or lighter the previous day. In the morning paper, therefore, what the reader gets is the last day's futures prices along with an estimated volume figure. Official volume and open interest numbers, however, are given for the day before. Stock chartists don't have that problem. Volume totals for stocks are immediately available.

The Value of Individual Volume and Open Interest Numbers in Futures

The individual open interest numbers in futures do provide valuable information. They tell us which contracts are the most liquid for trading purposes. *As a general rule, trading activity should be limited to those delivery months with the highest open interest. Months with low open interest numbers should be avoided.* As the term implies, higher open interest means that there is more interest in certain delivery months.

WEEKLY AND MONTHLY BAR CHARTS

We've focused so far on the daily bar chart. However, be aware that a bar chart can be constructed for any time period. The intraday bar chart measures the high, low, and last prices for periods as short as five minutes. The average daily bar chart covers from six to nine months of price action. For longer range trend analysis, however, weekly and monthly bar charts must be used. The value of using these longer range charts is covered in Chapter 8. But the method of constructing and updating the charts is essentially the same. (See Figures 3.9 and 3.10.)

On the weekly chart, one bar represents the price activity for the entire week. On the monthly chart, each bar shows the

Figure 3.9 *A weekly bar chart of the U.S. Dollar Index. Each bar represents one week's price data. By compressing the price data, the weekly chart allows for chart analysis of longer range price trends, usually in the vicinity of five years.*

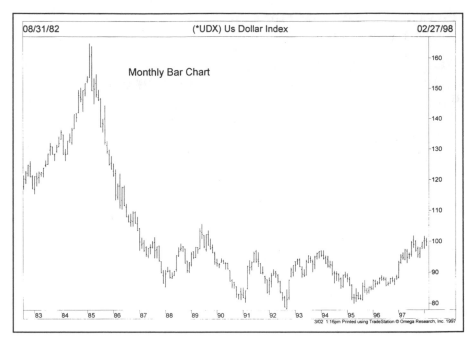

Figure 3.10 *A monthly bar chart of the U.S. Dollar Index. Each bar represents one month's price data. By compressing the data even further, the monthly chart allows chart analysis for periods as long as twenty years.*

entire month's price action. Obviously, weekly and monthly charts compress the price action to allow for much longer range trend analysis. A weekly chart can go back as much as five years and a monthly chart up to 20 years. It's a simple technique that helps the chartist study the markets from a longer range perspective—a valuable perspective that is often lost by relying solely on daily charts.

CONCLUSION

Now that we know how to plot a bar chart, and having introduced the three basic sources of information—price, volume, and open interest—we're ready to look at how that data is interpreted. Remember that the chart only records the data. In itself, it has little value. It's much like a paint brush and canvas. By themselves, they have no value. In the hands of a talented artist, however, they can help create beautiful images. Perhaps an even better comparison is a scalpel. In the hands of a gifted surgeon, it can help save lives. In the hands of most of us, however, a scalpel is not only useless, but might even be dangerous. A chart can become an extremely useful tool in the art or skill of market forecasting once the rules are understood. Let's begin the process. In the next chapter, we'll look at some of the basic concepts of trend and what I consider to be the building blocks of chart analysis.

4

Basic Concepts of Trend

DEFINITION OF TREND

The concept of *trend* is absolutely essential to the technical approach to market analysis. All of the tools used by the chartist—support and resistance levels, price patterns, moving averages, trendlines, etc.—have the sole purpose of helping to measure the trend of the market for the purpose of participating in that trend. We often hear such familiar expressions as "always trade in the direction of the trend," "never buck the trend," or "the trend is your friend." So let's spend a little time to define what a trend is and classify it into a few categories.

In a general sense, the trend is simply the direction of the market, which way it's moving. But we need a more precise definition with which to work. First of all, markets don't generally move in a straight line in any direction. Market moves are characterized by a series of *zigzags*. These zigzags resemble a series of successive waves with fairly obvious peaks and troughs. *It is the direction of those peaks and troughs that constitutes market trend.* Whether those peaks and troughs are moving up, down, or sideways tells us the trend of the market. An *uptrend* would be defined as a series of successively higher peaks and troughs; a *downtrend* is just the opposite, a series of declining peaks and troughs; horizontal peaks and troughs would identify a sideways price trend. (See Figures 4.1a-d.)

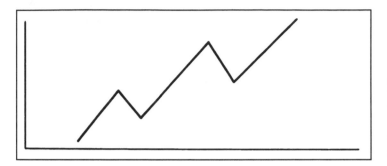

Figure 4.1a
Example of an uptrend with ascending peaks and troughs.

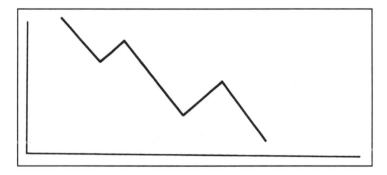

Figure 4.1b
Example of a downtrend with descending peaks and troughs.

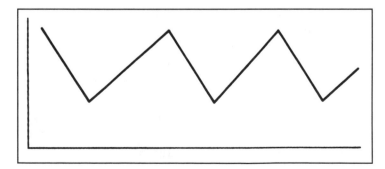

Figure 4.1c
Example of a sideways trend with horizontal peaks and troughs. This type of market is often referred to as "trendless."

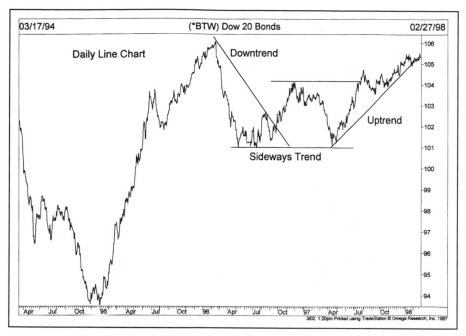

| 03/17/94 | (*BTW) Dow 20 Bonds | 02/27/98 |

Figure 4.1d *Example of a downtrend turning into an uptrend. The first portion to the left shows a downtrend. From April 1996 to April 1997, the market traded sideways. During the summer 1997, the trend turned up.*

TREND HAS THREE DIRECTIONS

We've mentioned an uptrend, downtrend, and sideways trend for a very good reason. Most people tend to think of markets as being always in either an uptrend or a downtrend. The fact of the matter is that markets actually move in three directions—up, down, and sideways. It is important to be aware of this distinction because for at least a third of the time, by a conservative estimate, prices move in a flat, horizontal pattern that is referred to as a *trading range.* This type of sideways action reflects a period of equilibrium in the price level where the forces of supply and demand are in a state of relative balance. (If you'll recall, Dow Theory refers to this type of pattern as a *line.*) Although we've defined a flat market as having a sideways trend, it is more commonly referred to as being *trendless.*

Most technical tools and systems are trend-following in nature, which means that they are primarily designed for markets that are moving up or down. They usually work very poorly, or not at all, when markets enter these lateral or "trendless" phases. It is during these periods of sideways market movement that technical traders experience their greatest frustration, and systems traders their greatest equity losses. A trend-following system, by its very definition, needs a trend in order to do its stuff. The failure here lies not with the system. Rather, the failure lies with the trader who is attempting to apply a system designed for trending markets into a nontrending market environment.

There are three decisions confronting the trader—whether to buy a market (go long), sell a market (go short), or do nothing (stand aside). When a market is rising, the buying strategy is preferable. When it is falling, the second approach would be correct. *However, when the market is moving sideways, the third choice— to stay out of the market—is usually the wisest.*

TREND HAS THREE CLASSIFICATIONS

In addition to having three directions, trend is usually broken down into the three categories mentioned in the previous chapter. Those three categories are the *major, intermediate*, and *near term trends*. In reality, there are almost an infinite number of trends interacting with one another, from the very short term trends covering minutes and hours to superlong trends lasting 50 or 100 years. Most technicians, however, limit trend classifications to three. There is a certain amount of ambiguity, however, as to how different analysts define each trend.

Dow Theory, for example, classifies the *major trend* as being in effect for longer than a year. Because futures traders operate in a shorter time dimension than do stock investors, I would be inclined to shorten the major trend to anything over six months in the commodity markets. Dow defined the intermediate, or secondary, trend as three weeks to as many months, which also appears about right for the futures markets. The near term trend is usually defined as anything less than two or three weeks.

Each trend becomes a portion of its next larger trend. For example, the intermediate trend would be a *correction* in the major trend. In a long term uptrend, the market pauses to correct itself for a couple of months before resuming its upward path. That secondary correction would itself consist of shorter waves that would be identified as near term dips and rallies. This theme recurs many times—that each trend is part of the next larger trend and is itself comprised of smaller trends. (See Figures 4.2a and b.)

In Figure 4.2a, the major trend is up as reflected by the rising peaks and troughs (points 1, 2, 3, 4). The corrective phase (2-3) represents an intermediate correction within the major uptrend. But notice that the wave 2-3 also breaks down into three smaller waves (A, B, C). At point C, the analyst would say that the major trend was still up, but the intermediate and near term trends were down. At point 4, all three trends would be up. It is important to understand the distinction between the various degrees of trend. When someone asks what the trend is in a given market, it is difficult, if not impossible, to respond until you know

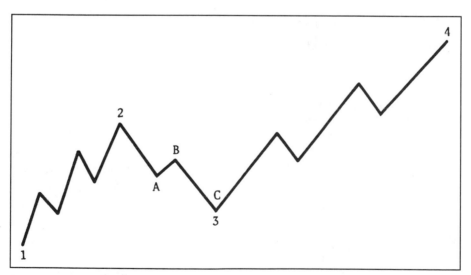

Figure 4.2a *Example of the three degrees of trend: major, secondary, and near term. Points 1, 2, 3, and 4 show the major uptrend. Wave 2-3 represents a secondary correction within the major uptrend. Each secondary wave in turn divides into near term trends. For example, secondary wave 2-3 divides into minor waves A-B-C.*

| 12/08/95 | (*DWI X) Dow Industrials | 11/28/97 |

Three Degrees of Trend

2

1
Intermediate
Trend Is Down

Short Trend Is Down

3

Major Trend Is Up

8000

7500

7000

6500

6000

5500

'96   Apr   Jul   Oct   '97   Apr   Jul   Oct

3/02 1:30pm Printed using TradeStation © Omega Research, Inc. 1997

Figure 4.2b   *The major trend (over a year) is up during 1997. A short term correction occurred during March. An intermediate correction lasted from August to November (three months). The intermediate correction broke down into three short term trends.*

which trend the person is inquiring about. You may have to respond in the manner previously discussed by defining the three different trend classifications.

Quite a bit of misunderstanding arises because of different traders' perceptions as to what is meant by a trend. To long term position traders, a few days' to a few weeks' price action might be insignificant. To a day trader, a two or three day advance might constitute a major uptrend. It's especially important, then, to understand the different degrees of trend and to make sure that all involved in a transaction are talking about the same ones.

As a general statement, most trend-following approaches focus on the intermediate trend, which may last for several months. The near term trend is used primarily for timing purposes. In an intermediate uptrend, short term setbacks would be used to initiate long positions.

SUPPORT AND RESISTANCE

In the previous discussion of trend, it was stated that prices move in a series of peaks and troughs, and that the direction of those peaks and troughs determined the trend of the market. Let's now give those peaks and troughs their appropriate names and, at the same time, introduce the concepts of *support* and *resistance*.

The troughs, or reaction lows, are called *support*. The term is self-explanatory and indicates that support is a level or area on the chart *under the market* where buying interest is sufficiently strong to overcome selling pressure. As a result, a decline is halted and prices turn back up again. Usually a support level is identified beforehand by a previous reaction low. In Figure 4.3a, points 2 and 4 represent support levels in an uptrend. (See Figures 4.3a and b.)

Resistance is the opposite of support and represents a price level or area *over the market* where selling pressure overcomes buying pressure and a price advance is turned back. Usually a resis-

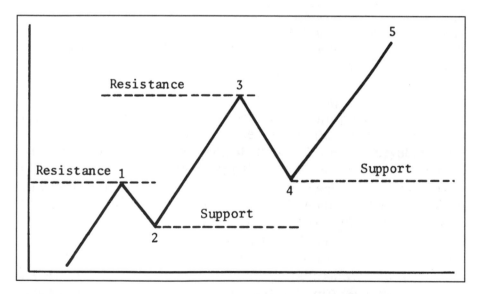

Figure 4.3a *Shows rising support and resistance levels in uptrend. Points 2 and 4 are support levels which are usually previous reaction lows. Points 1 and 3 are resistance levels, usually marked by previous peaks.*

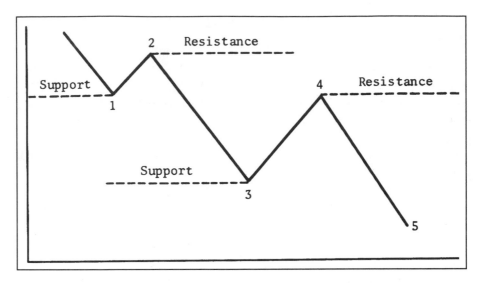

Figure 4.3b   *Shows support and resistance in a downtrend.*

tance level is identified by a previous peak. In Figure 4.3a, points 1 and 3 are resistance levels. Figure 4.3a shows an uptrend. In an uptrend, the support and resistance levels show an ascending pattern. Figure 4.3b shows a downtrend with descending peaks and troughs. In the downtrend, points 1 and 3 are support levels under the market and points 2 and 4 are resistance levels over the market.

A solid grasp of the concepts of support and resistance is necessary for a full understanding of the concept of trend. For an uptrend to continue, each successive low (support level) must be higher than the one preceding it. Each rally high (resistance level) must be higher than the one before it. If the corrective dip in an uptrend comes all the way down to the previous low, it may be an early warning that the uptrend is ending or at least moving from an uptrend to a sideways trend. If the support level is violated, then a trend *reversal* from up to down is likely.

In an uptrend, the resistance levels represent pauses in that uptrend and are usually exceeded at some point. In a downtrend, support levels are not sufficient to stop the decline permanently, but are able to check it at least temporarily.

Each time a previous resistance peak is being tested, the uptrend is in an especially critical phase. Failure to exceed a previous peak in an uptrend, or the ability of prices to bounce off the previous support low in a downtrend, is usually the first warning that the existing trend is changing. Chapters 5 and 6 on *price patterns* show how the testing of these support and resistance levels form pictures on the charts that suggest either a trend reversal in progress or merely a pause in the existing trend. But the basic building blocks on which those price patterns are based are support and resistance levels.

Figures 4.4a-c are examples of a classic trend reversal. Notice, in Figure 4.4a, that at point 5 prices failed to exceed the previous peak (point 3) before turning down to violate the previous low at point 4. This trend reversal could have been identified simply by watching the support and resistance levels. In our coverage of price patterns, this type of reversal pattern will be identified as a *double top*.

How Support and Resistance Levels Reverse Their Roles

So far we've defined "support" as a previous low and "resistance" as a previous high. However, this is not always the case. This leads us to one of the more interesting and lesser known aspects of support and resistance—their reversal of roles. *Whenever a support or*

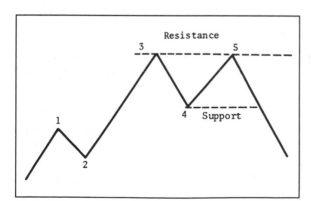

Figure 4.4a *Example of a trend reversal. The failure of prices at point 5 to exceed the previous peak at point 3 followed by a downside violation of the previous low at point 4 constitutes a downside trend reversal. This type of pattern is called a double top.*

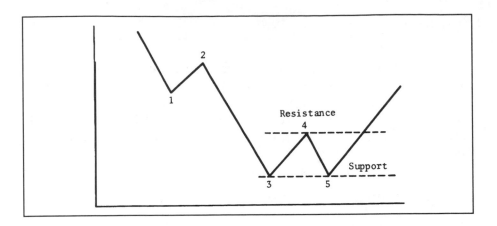

Figure 4.4b   *Example of a bottom reversal pattern. Usually the first sign of a bottom is the ability of prices at point 5 to hold above the previous low at point 3. The bottom is confirmed when the peak at 4 is overcome.*

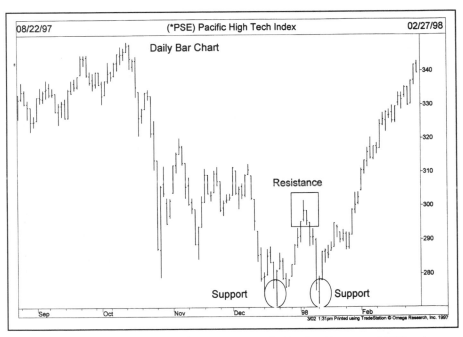

Figure 4.4c   *Example of a bottom reversal. During January 1998 prices retested the December support low and bounced off it, forming a second support level. The upside penetration of the middle resistance peak signaled a new uptrend.*

resistance level is penetrated by a significant amount, they reverse their roles and become the opposite. In other words, a resistance level becomes a support level and support becomes resistance. To understand why this occurs, perhaps it would be helpful to discuss some of the psychology behind the creation of support and resistance levels.

The Psychology of Support and Resistance

To illustrate, let's divide the market participants into three categories—the longs, the shorts, and the uncommitted. The longs are those traders who have already purchased contracts; the shorts are those who have already committed themselves to the sell side; the uncommitted are those who have either gotten out of the market or remain undecided as to which side to enter.

Let's assume that a market starts to move higher from a support area where prices have been fluctuating for some time. The longs (those who bought near the support area) are delighted, but regret not having bought more. If the market would dip back near that support area again, they could add to their long positions. The shorts now realize (or strongly suspect) that they are on the wrong side of the market. (How far the market has moved away from that support area will greatly influence these decisions, but we'll come back to that point a bit later.) The shorts are hoping (and praying) for a dip back to that area where they went short so they can get out of the market where they got in (their break even point).

Those sitting on the sidelines can be divided into two groups—those who never had a position and those who, for one reason or another, liquidated previously held long positions in the support area. The latter group are, of course, mad at themselves for liquidating their longs prematurely and are hoping for another chance to reinstate those longs near where they sold them.

The final group, the undecided, now realize that prices are going higher and resolve to enter the market on the long side on the next good buying opportunity. All four groups are resolved to "buy the next dip." They all have a "vested interest" in that support area under the market. Naturally, if prices do decline near that support, renewed buying by all four groups will materialize to push prices up.

The more trading that takes place in that support area, the more significant it becomes because more participants have a vested interest in that area. The amount of trading in a given support or resistance area can be determined in three ways: the amount of time spent there, volume, and how recently the trading took place.

The longer the period of time that prices trade in a support or resistance area, the more significant that area becomes. For example, if prices trade sideways for three weeks in a congestion area before moving higher, that support area would be more important than if only three days of trading had occurred.

Volume is another way to measure the significance of support and resistance. If a support level is formed on heavy volume, this would indicate that a large number of units changed hands, and would mark that support level as more important than if very little trading had taken place. Point and figure charts that measure the intraday trading activity are especially useful in identifying these price levels where most of the trading took place and, consequently, where support and resistance will be most likely to function.

A third way to determine the significance of a support or resistance area is how recently the trading took place. Because we are dealing with the reaction of traders to market movement and to positions that they have already taken or failed to take, it stands to reason that the more recent the activity, the more potent it becomes.

Now let's turn the tables and imagine that, instead of moving higher, prices move lower. In the previous example, because prices advanced, the combined reaction of the market participants caused each downside reaction to be met with additional buying (thereby creating new support). However, if prices start to drop and move below the previous support area, the reaction becomes just the opposite. All those who bought in the support area now realize that they made a mistake. For futures traders, their brokers are now calling frantically for more margin money.

Because of the highly leveraged nature of futures trading, traders cannot sit with losses very long. They must put up additional margin money or liquidate their losing positions.

What created the previous support in the first place was the predominance of buy orders under the market. Now, however, all of the previous buy orders under the market have become sell orders over the market. *Support has become resistance.* And the more significant that previous support area was—that is, the more recent and the more trading that took place there—the more potent it now becomes as a resistance area. All of the factors that created support by the three categories of participants—the longs, the shorts, and the uncommitted—will now function to put a ceiling over prices on subsequent rallies or bounces.

It is useful once in a while to pause and reflect on why the price patterns used by chartists, and concepts like support and resistance, actually do work. It's not because of some magic produced by the charts or some lines drawn on those charts. These patterns work because they provide pictures of what the market participants are actually doing and enable us to determine their reactions to market events. Chart analysis is actually a study of human psychology and the reactions of traders to changing market conditions. Unfortunately, because we live in the fast-paced world of financial markets, we tend to rely heavily on chart terminology and shortcut expressions that overlook the underlying forces that created the pictures on the charts in the first place. There are sound psychological reasons why support and resistance levels can be identified on price charts and why they can be used to help predict market movements.

Support Becoming Resistance and Vice Versa: Degree of Penetration

A support level, penetrated by a significant margin, becomes a resistance level and vice versa. Figures 4.5a-c are similar to Figures 4.3a and b but with one added refinement. Notice that as prices are rising in Figure 4.5a the reaction at point 4 stops at or above the top of the peak at point 1. That previous peak at point 1 had been a resistance level. But once it was decisively penetrated by

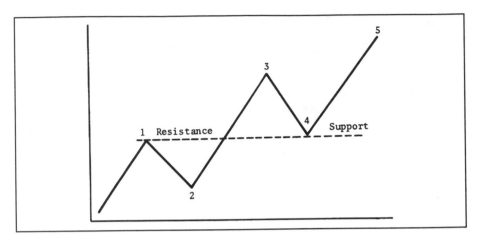

Figure 4.5a   *In an uptrend, resistance levels that have been broken by a significant margin become support levels. Notice that once resistance at point 1 is exceeded, it provides support at point 4. Previous peaks function as support on subsequent corrections.*

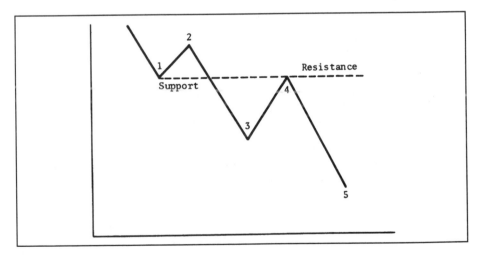

Figure 4.5b   *In a downtrend, violated support levels become resistance levels on subsequent bounces. Notice how previous support at point 1 became resistance at point 4.*

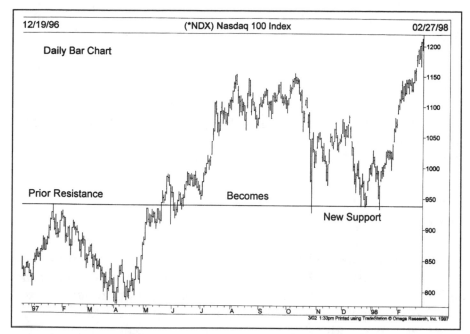

Figure 4.5c   *Role reversal at play. Once the early 1997 resistance peak was broken, it reversed roles to become a support level. A year later, the intermediate price decline found support right at that prior resistance peak which had become new support.*

wave 3, that previous resistance peak became a support level. All of the previous selling near the top of wave 1 (creating the resistance level) has now become buying under the market. In Figure 4.5b, showing declining prices, point 1 (which had been a previous support level under the market) has now become a resistance level over the market acting as a ceiling at point 4.

It was mentioned earlier that the distance prices traveled away from support or resistance increased the significance of that support or resistance. This is particularly true when support and resistance levels are penetrated and reverse roles. For example, it was stated that support and resistance levels reverse roles only after a significant penetration. But what constitutes significant? There is quite a bit of subjectivity involved here in determining whether a penetration is significant or not. As a benchmark, some chartists use a 3% penetration as a criteria, particularly for major support and resistance levels. Shorter term support and resistance areas would probably require a much smaller number, like 1%. In reality, each analyst must decide for himself or herself what constitutes a significant penetration. It's important to remember, however, that support and resistance areas only reverse roles when the market moves far enough away to convince the market participants that they have made a mistake. The farther away the market moves, the more convinced they become.

The Importance of Round Numbers as Support and Resistance

There is a tendency for round numbers to stop advances or declines. Traders tend to think in terms of important round numbers, such as 10, 20, 25, 50, 75, 100 (and multiples of 1000), as price objectives and act accordingly. These round numbers, therefore, will often act as "psychological" support or resistance levels. A trader can use this information to begin taking profits as an important round number is approached.

The gold market is an excellent example of this phenomenon. The 1982 bear market low was right at $300. The market then rallied to just above $500 in the first quarter of 1983 before falling to $400. A gold rally in 1987 stopped at $500 again. From 1990 to 1997, gold failed each attempt to break through $400. The Dow Jones Industrial Average has shown a tendency to stall at multiples of 1000.

One trading application of this principle is to *avoid placing trading orders right at these obvious round numbers.* For example, if the trader is trying to buy into a short term market dip in an uptrend, it would make sense to place limit orders just above an important round number. Because others are trying to buy the market at the round number, the market may never get there. Traders looking to sell on a bounce should place resting sell orders just below round numbers. The opposite would be true when placing protective stops on existing positions. As a general rule, *avoid placing protective stops at obvious round numbers.*

In other words, protective stops on long positions should be placed below round numbers and on short positions, above such numbers. The tendency for markets to respect round numbers, and especially the more important round numbers previously referred to, is one of those peculiar market characteristics that can prove most helpful in trading and should be kept in mind by the technically oriented trader.

TRENDLINES

Now that we understand support and resistance, let's add another building block to our arsenal of technical tools—*the trendline.* (See Figures 4.6a-c.) The basic trendline is one of the simplest of the technical tools employed by the chartist, but is also one of the most valuable. An *up trendline* is a straight line drawn upward to the right along successive reaction lows as shown by the solid line in Figure 4.6a. A *down trendline* is drawn downward to the right along successive rally peaks as shown in Figure 4.6b.

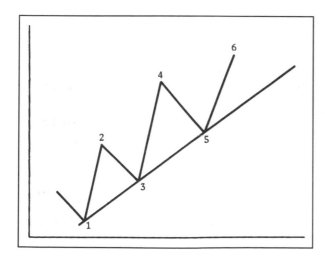

Figure 4.6a
Example of an up trendline. The up trendline is drawn under the rising reaction lows. A tentative trendline is first drawn under two successively higher lows (points 1 and 3), but needs a third test to confirm the validity of the trendline (point 5).

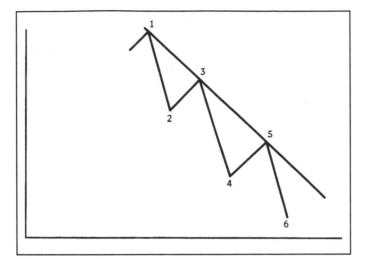

Figure 4.6b
*A down trend-
line is drawn
over the succes-
sively lower rally
highs. The ten-
tative down
trendline needs
two points (1
and 3) to be
drawn and a
third test (5) to
confirm its
validity.*

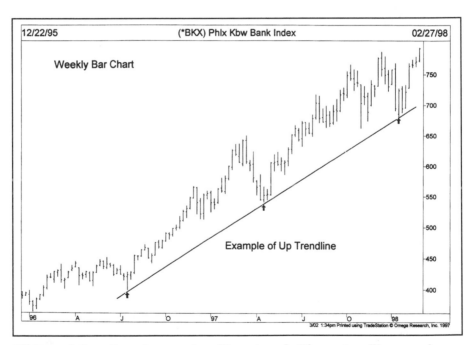

Figure 4.6c   *Long term up trendline at work. The up trendline was drawn
upward and to the right along the first two reaction lows (see arrows). The
third low at the start of 1998 bounced right off the rising trendline, thereby
keeping the uptrend intact.*

Drawing a Trendline

The correct drawing of trendlines is a lot like every other aspect of charting and some experimenting with different lines is usually necessary to find the correct one. Sometimes a trendline that looks correct may have to be redrawn. But there are some useful guidelines in the search for that correct line.

First of all, there must be evidence of a trend. This means that, for an up trendline to be drawn, there must be at least two reaction lows with the second low higher than the first. Of course, it always takes two points to draw any straight line. In Figure 4.6a, for example, only after prices have begun to move higher from point 3 is the chartist reasonably confident that a reaction low has been formed, and only then can a tentative up trendline be drawn under points 1 and 3.

Some chartists require that the peak at point 2 be penetrated to confirm the uptrend before drawing the trendline. Others only require a 50% retracement of wave 2-3, or that prices approach the top of wave 2. While the criteria may differ, the main point to remember is that the chartist wants to be reasonably sure that a reaction low has been formed before identifying a valid reaction low. Once two ascending lows have been identified, a straight line is drawn connecting the lows and projected up and to the right.

Tentative Versus the Valid Trendline

So far, all we have is a *tentative trendline*. In order to confirm the validity of a trendline, however, that line should be touched a third time with prices bouncing off of it. Therefore, in Figure 4.6a, the successful test of the up trendline at point 5 confirmed the validity of that line. Figure 4.6b shows a downtrend, but the rules are the same. The successful test of the trendline occurs at point 5. To summarize, two points are needed to draw the trendline, and a third point to make it a *valid trendline*.

How to Use the Trendline

Once the third point has been confirmed and the trend proceeds in its original direction, that trendline becomes very useful in a variety of ways. One of the basic concepts of trend is that a trend in motion will tend to remain in motion. As a corollary to that, once a trend assumes a certain slope or rate of speed, as identified by the trendline, it will usually maintain the same slope. The trendline then helps not only to determine the extremities of the corrective phases, but maybe even more importantly, tells us when that trend is changing.

In an uptrend, for example, the inevitable corrective dip will often touch or come very close to the up trendline. Because the intent of the trader is to buy dips in an uptrend, that trendline provides a support boundary under the market that can be used as a buying area. A down trendline can be used as a resistance area for selling purposes. (See Figures 4.7a and b.)

As long as the trendline is not violated, it can be used to determine buying and selling areas. However, at point 9 in Figures 4.7a-b, the violation of the trendline signals a trend change, calling for liquidation of all positions in the direction of the previous trend. Very often, *the breaking of the trendline is one of the best early warnings of a change in trend.*

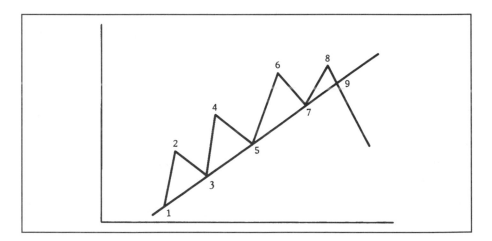

Figure 4.7a *Once the up trendline has been established, subsequent dips near the line can be used as buying areas. Points 5 and 7 in this example could have been used for new or additional longs. The breaking of the trendline at point 9 called for liquidation of all longs by signaling a downside trend reversal.*

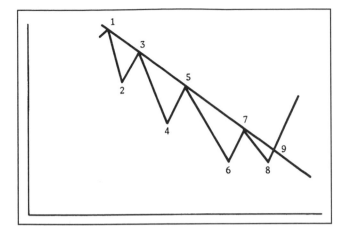

Figure 4.7b
Points 5 and 7 could have been used as selling areas. The breaking of the trendline at point 9 signaled an upside trend reversal.

How to Determine the Significance of a Trendline

Let's discuss some of the refinements of the trendline. First, what determines the significance of a trendline? The answer to that question is twofold—*the longer it has been intact and the number of times it has been tested.* A trendline that has been successfully tested eight times, for example, that has continually demonstrated its validity, is obviously a more significant trendline than one that has only been touched three times. Also, a trendline that has been in effect for nine months is of more importance than one that has been in effect for nine weeks or nine days. The more significant the trendline, the more confidence it inspires and the more important is its penetration.

Trendlines Should Include All Price Action

Trendlines on bar charts should be drawn over or under the entire day's price range. Some chartists prefer to draw the trendline by connecting only the closing prices, but that is not the more standard procedure. The closing price may very well be the most important price of the day, but it still represents only a small sample of that day's activity. The technique of including the day's price range takes into account all of the activity and is the more common usage. (See Figure 4.8.)

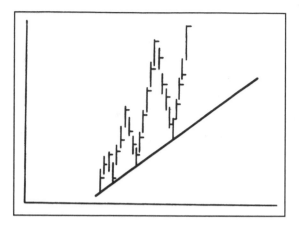

Figure 4.8 *The correct drawing of a trendline should include the entire day's trading range.*

How to Handle Small Trendline Penetrations

Sometimes prices will violate a trendline on an intraday basis, but then close in the direction of the original trend, leaving the analyst in some doubt as to whether or not the trendline has actually been broken. (See Figure 4.9.) Figure 4.9 shows how such a situation might look. Prices did dip under the trendline during the day, but closed back above the up trendline. Should the trendline be redrawn?

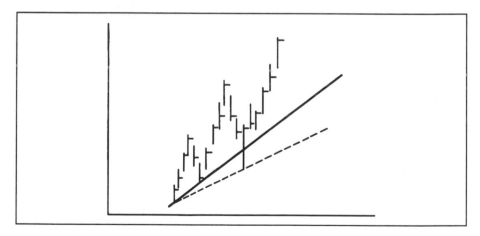

Figure 4.9 *Sometimes an intraday violation of a trendline will leave the chartist in doubt as to whether the original trendline is still valid or if a new line should be drawn. A compromise is to keep the original trendline, but draw a new dotted line until it can be better determined which is the truer line.*

Unfortunately, there's no hard and fast rule to follow in such a situation. Sometimes it is best to ignore the minor breach, especially if subsequent market action proves that the original line is still valid.

What Constitutes a Valid Breaking of a Trendline?

As a general rule, *a close beyond the trendline is more significant than just an intraday penetration.* To go a step further, sometimes even a closing penetration is not enough. Most technicians employ a variety of time and price filters in an attempt to isolate valid trendline penetrations and eliminate bad signals or "whipsaws." One example of a price filter is the 3% *penetration criteria.* This price filter is used mainly for the breaking of longer term trendlines, but requires that the trendline be broken, on a closing basis, by at least 3%. (The 3% rule doesn't apply to some financial futures, such as the interest rate markets.)

If, for example, gold prices broke a major up trendline at $400, prices would have to close below that line by 3% of the price level where the line was broken (in this case, prices would have to close $12 below the trendline, or at $388). Obviously, a $12 penetration criteria would not be appropriate for shorter term trading. Perhaps a 1% criterion would serve better in such cases. The % rule represents just one type of price filter. Stock chartists, for example, might require a full point penetration and ignore fractional moves. There is tradeoff involved in the use of any type of filter. If the filter is too small, it won't be very useful in reducing the impact of whipsaws. If it's too big, then much of the initial move will be missed before a valid signal is given. Here again, the trader must determine what type of filter is best suited to the degree of trend being followed, always making allowances for the differences in the individuals markets.

An alternative to a price filter (requiring that a trendline be broken by some predetermined price increment or percentage amount) is a *time filter.* A common time filter is the *two day rule.* In other words, to have a valid breaking of a trendline, prices must close beyond the trendline for two successive days. To break an up trendline, therefore, prices must close under the trendline two days in a row. A one day violation would not count. The 1-3% rule and the two day rule are also applied to the breaking of important support and resistance levels, not just to major trendlines. Another filter would require a Friday close beyond a major breakout point to ensure a weekly signal.

How Trendlines Reverse Roles

It was mentioned earlier that support and resistance levels became the opposite once violated. The same principle holds true of trendlines. (See Figures 4.10a-c.) In other words, an up trendline (a support line) will usually become a resistance line once it's decisively broken. A down trendline (a resistance line) will often become a support line once it's decisively broken. This is why it's usually a good idea to project all trendlines as far out to the right on the chart as possible even after they've been broken. It's surprising how often old trendlines act as support and resistance lines again in the future, but in the opposite role.

Measuring Implications of Trendlines

Trendlines can be used to help determine price objectives. We'll have a lot more to say about price objectives in the next two chap-

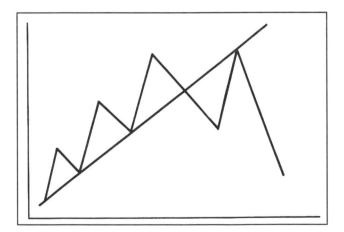

Figure 4.10a
Example of a rising support line becoming resistance. Usually a support line will function as a resistance barrier on subsequent rallies, after it has been broken on the downside.

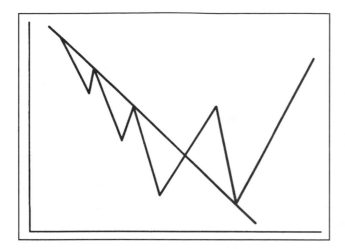

Figure 4.10b
Very often a down trendline will become a support line once it's been broken on the upside.

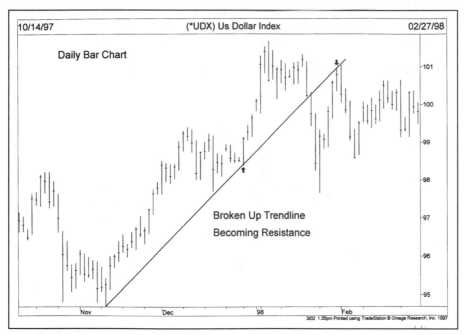

Figure 4.10c *Trendlines also reverse roles. On this chart, the broken up trendline became a resistance barrier on the following rally attempt.*

ters on price patterns. In fact, some of the price objectives addressed that are derived from various price patterns are similar to the one we'll cover here with trendlines. Stated briefly, once a trendline is broken, prices will usually move a distance beyond the trendline equal to the vertical distance that prices achieved on the other side of the line, prior to the trend reversal.

In other words, if in the prior uptrend, prices moved $50 above the up trendline (measured vertically), then prices would be expected to drop that same $50 below the trendline after it's broken. In the next chapter, for example, we'll see that this measuring rule using the trendline is similar to that used for the well-known *head and shoulders* reversal pattern, where the distance from the "head" to the "neckline" is projected beyond that line once it's broken.

THE FAN PRINCIPLE

This brings us to another interesting use of the trendline—the *fan principle*. (See Figures 4.11a-c.) Sometimes after the violation of an up trendline, prices will decline a bit before rallying back to the bottom of the old up trendline (now a resistance line). In Figure 4.11a, notice how prices rallied to but failed to penetrate line 1. A

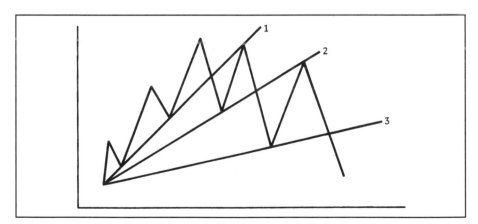

Figure 4.11a   *Example of the fan principle. The breaking of the third trendline signals the reversal of a trend. Notice also that the broken trendlines 1 and 2 often become resistance lines.*

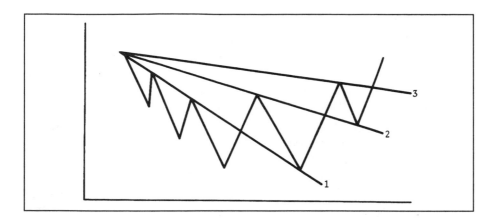

Figure 4.11b *The fan principle at a bottom. The breaking of the third trendline signals the upside trend reversal. The previously broken trendlines (1 and 2) often become support levels.*

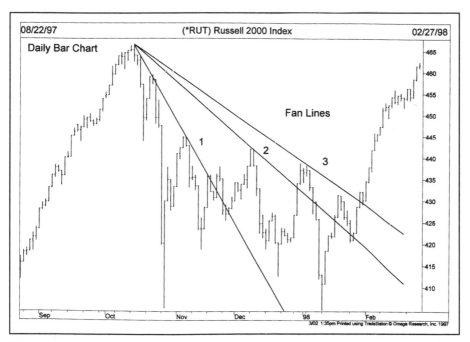

Figure 4.11c *Fan lines are drawn along successive peaks as shown in this chart. The breaking of the third fan line usually signals the start of the uptrend.*

second trendline (line 2) can now be drawn, which is also broken. After another failed rally attempt, a third line is drawn (line 3). *The breaking of that third trendline is usually an indication that prices are headed lower.* In Figure 4.11b, the breaking of the third down trendline (line 3) constitutes a new uptrend signal. Notice in these examples how previously broken support lines became resistance and resistance lines became support. The term "fan principle" derives from the appearance of the lines that gradually flatten out, resembling a fan. *The important point to remember here is that the breaking of the third line is the valid trend reversal signal.*

THE IMPORTANCE OF THE NUMBER THREE

In examining the three lines in the fan principle, it's interesting to note how often the number three shows up in the study of technical analysis and the important role it plays in so many technical approaches. For example, the fan principle uses three lines; major bull and bear markets usually have three major phases (Dow Theory and Elliott Wave Theory); there are three kinds of *gaps* (to be covered shortly); some of the more commonly known reversal patterns, such as the *triple top* and the *head and shoulders,* have three prominent peaks; there are three different classifications of trend (major, secondary, and minor) and three trend directions (up, down, and sideways); among the generally accepted continuation patterns, there are three types of *triangles*—the symmetrical, ascending, and descending; there are three principle sources of information—price, volume, and open interest. For whatever the reason, the number three plays a very prominent role throughout the entire field of technical analysis.

THE RELATIVE STEEPNESS OF THE TRENDLINE

The relative steepness of the trendline is also important. In general, most important up trendlines tend to approximate an average slope of 45 degrees. Some chartists simply draw a 45 degree

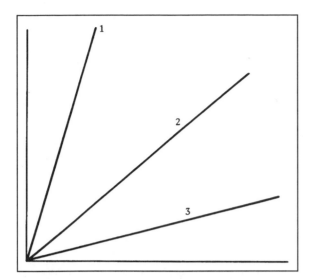

Figure 4.12 *Most valid trendlines rise at an angle approximating 45 degrees (see line 2). If the trendline is too steep (line 1), it usually indicates that the rate of ascent is not sustainable. A trendline that is too flat (line 3) suggests that the uptrend is too weak and probably suspect. Many technicians use 45 degree lines from previous tops or bottoms as major trendlines.*

line on the chart from a prominent high or low and use this as a major trendline. The 45 degree line was one of the techniques favored by W. D. Gann. Such a line reflects a situation where prices are advancing or declining at such a rate that price and time are in perfect balance.

If a trendline is too steep (see line 1 in Figure 4.12), it usually indicates that prices are advancing too rapidly and that the current steep ascent will not be sustained. The breaking of that steep trendline may be just a reaction back to a more sustainable slope closer to the 45 degree line (line 2). If a trendline is too flat (see line 3), it may indicate that the uptrend is too weak and not to be trusted.

How to Adjust Trendlines

Sometimes trendlines have to be adjusted to fit a slowing or an accelerating trend. (See Figure 4.13 and Figures 4.14a and b.) For example, as shown in the previous case, if a steep trendline is broken, a slower trendline might have to be drawn. If the original trendline is too flat, it may have to be redrawn at a steeper angle. Figure 4.13 shows a situation where the breaking of the steeper trendline (line 1) necessitated the drawing of a slower line (line 2).

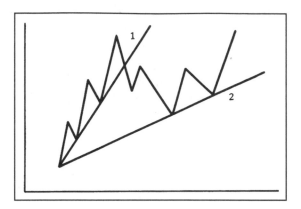

Figure 4.13 *Example of a trendline that is too steep (line 1). The original up trendline proved too steep. Often the breaking of a steep trendline is only an adjustment to a slower and more sustainable up trendline (line 2).*

In Figure 4.14a, the original trendline (line 1) is too flat and has to be redrawn at a steeper angle (line 2). The uptrend accelerated, requiring a steeper line. A trendline that is too far away from the price action is obviously of little use in tracking the trend.

In the case of an accelerating trend, sometimes several trendlines may have to be drawn at increasingly steeper angles. In my experience, however, where steeper trendlines become necessary, it is best to resort to another tool—the moving average—which is the same as a curvilinear trendline. One of the advantages

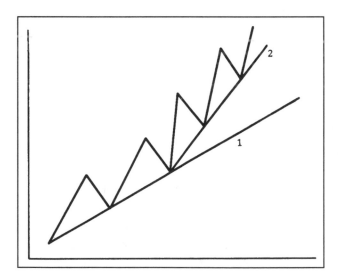

Figure 4.14a *Example of an up trendline that is too flat (line 1). Line 1 proved too slow as the uptrend accelerated. In this case, a second and steeper trendline (line 2) should be drawn to more closely track the rising trend.*

Figure 4.14b *An accelerating uptrend requires the drawing of steeper trendlines as shown in this chart. The steepest trendline becomes the most important one.*

of having access to several different types of technical indicators is being able to choose the one most appropriate for a given situation. All of the techniques covered in this book work well in certain situations, but not so well in others. By having an arsenal of tools to fall back on, the technician can quickly switch from one tool to another that might work better in a given situation. An accelerated trend is one of those cases where a moving average would be more useful than a series of steeper and steeper trendlines.

Just as there are several different degrees of trend in effect at any one time, so is there a need for different trendlines to measure those various trends. A major up trendline, for example, would connect the low points of the major uptrend, while a shorter and more sensitive line might be used for secondary swings. An even shorter line can measure the short term movements. (See Figure 4.15.)

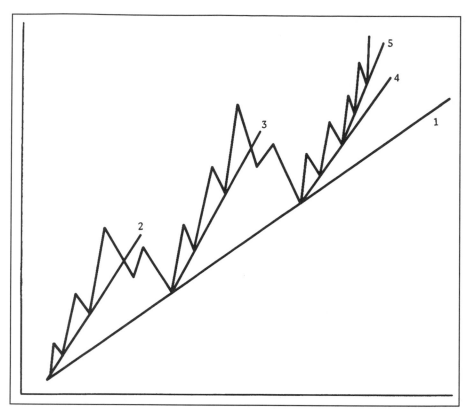

Figure 4.15 *Different trendlines are used to define the different degrees of trend. Line 1 in the above example is the major up trendline, defining the major uptrend. Lines 2, 3, and 4 define the intermediate uptrends. Finally, line 5 defines a shorter term advance within the last intermediate uptrend. Technicians use many different trendlines on the same chart.*

THE CHANNEL LINE

The *channel line,* or the *return line* as it is sometimes called, is another useful variation of the trendline technique. Sometimes prices trend between two parallel lines—the basic trendline and the channel line. Obviously, when this is the case and when the analyst recognizes that a channel exists, this knowledge can be used to profitable advantage.

The drawing of the channel line is relatively simple. In an uptrend (see Figure 4.16a), first draw the basic up trendline along

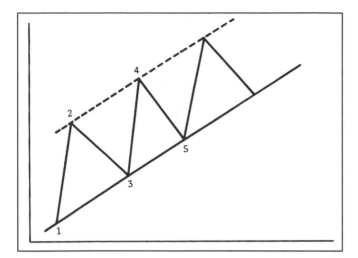

Figure 4.16a
Example of a trend channel. Once the basic up trendline is drawn (below points 1 and 3) a channel, or return, line (dotted line) can be projected over the first peak at 2, which is parallel to the basic up trendline.

the lows. Then draw a dotted line from the first prominent peak (point 2), which is parallel to the basic up trendline. Both lines move up to the right, forming a channel. If the next rally reaches and backs off from the channel line (at point 4), then a channel may exist. If prices then drop back to the original trendline (at point 5), then a channel probably does exist. The same holds true for a downtrend (Figure 4.16b), but of course in the opposite direction.

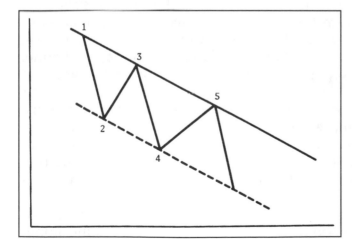

Figure 4.16b
A trend channel in a downtrend. The channel is projected downward from the first low at point 2, parallel to the down trendline along the 1 and 3 peaks. Prices will often remain within such a trend channel.

| 03/31/70 | (*DWU) Dow Utilities | 02/28/95 |

Monthly Line Chart

Long Term Channel Lines

3/02 1:37pm Printed using TradeStation © Omega Research, Inc. 1997

Figure 4.16c   *Notice how prices fluctuated between the upper and lower parallel channels over a period of 25 years. The 1987, 1989, and 1993 tops occurred right at the upper channel line. The 1994 bottom bounced off the lower trendline.*

The reader should immediately see the value of such a situation. The basic up trendline can be used for the initiation of new long positions. The channel line can be used for short term profit taking. More aggressive traders might even use the channel line to initiate a countertrend short position, although trading in the opposite direction of the prevailing trend can be a dangerous and usually costly tactic. As in the case of the basic trendline, the longer the channel remains intact and the more often it is successfully tested, the more important and reliable it becomes.

The breaking of the major trendline indicates an important change in trend. But the breaking of a rising channel line has exactly the opposite meaning, and signals an acceleration of the existing trend. Some traders view the clearing of the upper line in an uptrend as a reason to add to long positions.

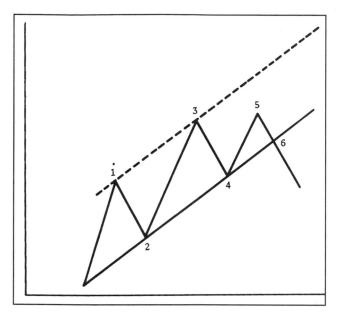

Figure 4.17
The failure to reach the upper end of the channel is often an early warning that the lower line will be broken. Notice the failure to reach the upper line at point 5 is followed by the breaking of the basic up trendline at point 6.

Another way to use the channel technique is to spot failures to reach the channel line, usually a sign of a weakening trend. In Figure 4.17, the failure of prices to reach the top of the channel (at point 5) may be an early warning that the trend is turning, and increases the odds that the other line (the basic up trendline) will be broken. As a general rule of thumb, the failure of any move within an established price channel to reach one side of the channel usually indicates that the trend is shifting, and increases the likelihood that the other side of the channel will be broken.

The channel can also be used to adjust the basic trendline. (See Figures 4.18 and 4.19.) If prices move above a projected rising channel line by a significant amount, it usually indicates a strengthening trend. Some chartists then draw a steeper basic up trendline from the last reaction low parallel to the new channel line (as demonstrated in Figure 4.18). Often, the new steeper support line functions better than the old flatter line. Similarly, the failure of an uptrend to reach the upper end of a channel justifies the drawing of a new support line under the last reaction low parallel to the new resistance line over the past two peaks (as shown in Figure 4.19).

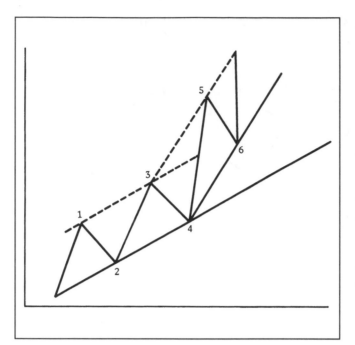

Figure 4.18
When the upper channel line is broken (as in wave 5), many chartists will redraw the basic up trendline parallel to the new upper channel line. In other words, line 4-6 is drawn parallel to line 3-5. Because the uptrend is accelerating, it stands to reason that the basic up trendline will do likewise.

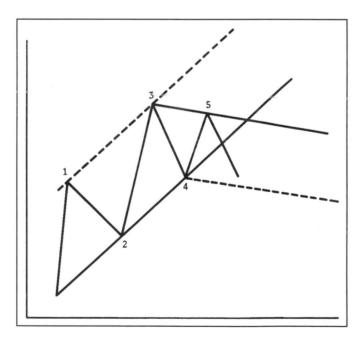

Figure 4.19
When prices fail to reach the upper channel line, and a down trendline is drawn over the two declining peaks (line 3-5), a tentative channel line can be drawn from the low at point 4 parallel to line 3-5. The lower channel line sometimes indicates where initial support will be evident.

Channel lines have measuring implications. *Once a break-out occurs from an existing price channel, prices usually travel a distance equal to the width of the channel.* Therefore, the user has to simply measure the width of the channel and then project that amount from the point at which either trendline is broken.

It should always be kept in mind, however, that of the two lines, the basic trendline is by far the more important and the more reliable. The channel line is a secondary use of the trendline technique. But the use of the channel line works often enough to justify its inclusion in the chartist's toolkit.

PERCENTAGE RETRACEMENTS

In all of the previous examples of uptrends and downtrends, the reader has no doubt noticed that after a particular market move, prices retrace a portion of the previous trend before resuming the move in the original direction. These countertrend moves tend to fall into certain predictable percentage parameters. The best known application of the phenomenon is the 50% *retracement.* Let's say, for example, that a market is trending higher and travels from the 100 level to the 200 level. Very often, the subsequent reaction retraces about half of the prior move, to about the 150 level, before upward momentum is regained. This is a very well-known market tendency and happens quite frequently. Also, these percentage retracements apply to any degree of trend—major, secondary, and near term.

Besides the 50% retracement, there are minimum and maximum percentage parameters that are also widely recognized—*the one-third and the two-thirds retracements.* In other words, the price trend can be divided into thirds. Usually, a minimum retracement is about 33% and a maximum about 66%. What this means is that, in a correction of a strong trend, the market usually retraces at least a third of the previous move. This is very useful information for a number of reasons. If a trader is looking for a buying area under the market, he or she can just compute a 33-50% zone on the chart and use that price zone as a general frame of reference for buying opportunities. (See Figures 4.20a and b.)

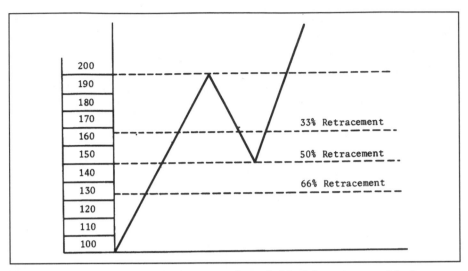

Figure 4.20a   *Prices often retrace about half of the prior trend before resuming in the original direction. This example shows a 50% retracement. The minimum retracement is one-third and the maximum, two-thirds of the prior trend.*

The maximum retracement parameter is 66%, which becomes an especially critical area. If the prior trend is to be maintained, the correction must stop at the two-thirds point. This then becomes a relatively low risk buying area in an uptrend or selling area in a downtrend. If prices move beyond the two-thirds point, the odds then favor a trend reversal rather than just a retracement. The move usually then retraces the entire 100% of the prior trend.

You may have noticed that the three percentage retracement parameters we've mentioned so far—50%, 33%, and 66%—are taken right from the original Dow Theory. When we get to the Elliott Wave Theory and Fibonacci ratios, we will see that followers of that approach use percentage retracements of 38% and 62%. I prefer to combine both approaches for a minimum retracement zone of 33-38% and a maximum zone of 62-66%. Some technicians round off these numbers even further to arrive at a 40-60% retracement zone.

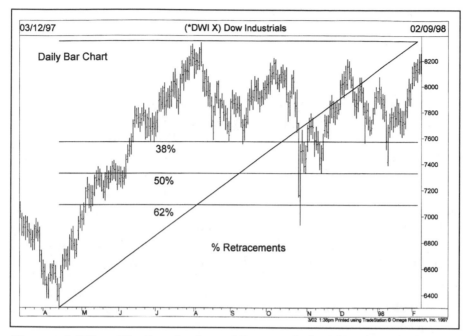

Figure 4.20b *The three horizontal lines mark the 38%, 50%, and 62% retracement levels measured from the April 1997 low to the August high. The first decline fell to the 38% line, the second decline to the 62% line, and the third near the 50% line. Most corrections will find support in the 38% to 50% retracement zones. The 38% and 62% lines are Fibonacci retracements and are popular with chartists.*

Students of W. D. Gann are aware that he broke down the trend structure into eighths—$^1/_8$, $^2/_8$, $^3/_8$, $^4/_8$, $^5/_8$, $^6/_8$, $^7/_8$, $^8/_8$. However, even Gann attached special importance to the $^3/_8$ (38%), $^4/_8$ (50%), and $^5/_8$ (62%) retracement numbers and also felt it was important to divide the trend into thirds—$^1/_3$ (33%) and $^2/_3$ (66%).

SPEED RESISTANCE LINES

Speaking of thirds, let's touch on another technique that combines the trendline with percentage retracements—*speedlines*. This technique, developed by Edson Gould, is actually an adaptation of the idea of dividing the trend into thirds. The main difference from the percentage retracement concept is that the speed resistance lines (or speedlines) measure the rate of ascent or descent of a trend (in other words, its speed).

To construct a bullish *speedline,* find the highest point in the current uptrend. (See Figure 4.21a.) From that high point on the chart, a vertical line is drawn toward the bottom of the chart to where the trend began. That vertical line is then divided into thirds. A trendline is then drawn from the beginning of the trend through the two points marked off on the vertical line, representing the one-third and two-thirds points. In a downtrend, just reverse the process. Measure the vertical distance from the low point in the downtrend to the beginning of the trend, and draw two lines from the beginning of the trend through the one-third and two-thirds points on the vertical line. (See Figures 4.21a and b.)

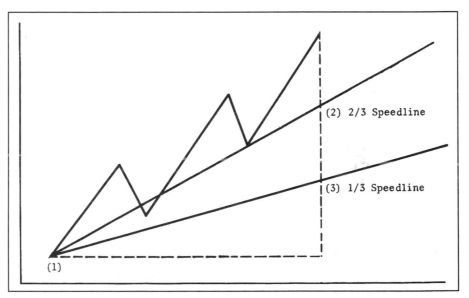

Figure 4.21a *Examples of speed resistance lines in an uptrend. The vertical distance from the peak to the beginning of the trend is divided into thirds. Two trendlines are then drawn from point 1 through points 2 and 3. The upper line is the $^2/_3$ speedline and the lower, the $^1/_3$. The lines should act as support during market corrections. When they're broken, they revert to resistance lines on bounces. Sometimes these speedlines intersect price action.*

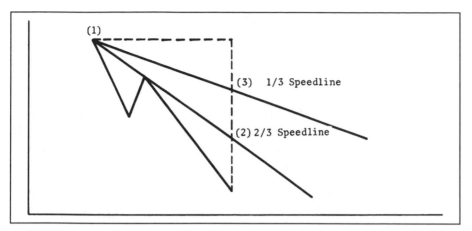

Figure 4.21b   *Speedlines in a downtrend.*

Each time a new high is set in an uptrend or a new low in a downtrend, a new set of lines must be drawn (because there is now a new high or low point). Because the *speedlines* are drawn from the beginning of the trend to the one-third and two-thirds points, those trendlines may sometimes move through some of the price action. This is one case where trendlines are not drawn under lows or over highs, but actually through the price action.

If an uptrend is in the process of correcting itself, the downside correction will usually stop at the higher speedline (the $2/_3$ speedline). If not, prices will drop to the lower speedline (the $1/_3$ speedline). If the lower line is also broken, prices will probably continue all the way to the beginning of the prior trend. In a downtrend, the breaking of the lower line indicates a probable rally to the higher line. If that is broken, a rally to the top of the prior trend would be indicated.

As with all trendlines, speedlines reverse roles once they are broken. Therefore, during the correction of an uptrend, if the upper line ($2/_3$ line) is broken and prices fall to the $1/_3$ line and rally from there, that upper line becomes a resistance barrier. Only when that upper line is broken would a signal be given that the old highs will probably be challenged. The same principle holds true in downtrends.

GANN AND FIBONACCI FAN LINES

Charting software also allows the drawing of *Gann* and *Fibonacci* fan lines. *Fibonacci* fan lines are drawn in the same fashion as the speedline. Except that Fibonacci lines are drawn at 38% and 62% angles. (We'll explain where those 38% and 62% numbers come from in Chapter 13, "Elliott Wave Theory.") *Gann* lines (named after the legendary commodity trader, W.D. Gann) are trendlines drawn from prominent tops or bottoms at specific geometric angles. The most important Gann line is drawn at a 45 degree angle from a peak or trough. Steeper Gann lines can be drawn during an uptrend at $63^3/_4$ degree and 75 degree angles. Flatter Gann lines can be drawn at $26^1/_4$ and 15 degree lines. It's possible to draw as many as nine different Gann lines.

Gann and Fibonacci lines are used in the same way as speedlines. They are supposed to provide support during downward corrections. When one line is broken, prices will usually fall to the next lower line. Gann lines are somewhat controversial. Even if one of them works, you can't be sure in advance which one it will be. Some chartists question the validity of drawing geometric trendlines at all.

INTERNAL TRENDLINES

These are variations of the trendline that don't rely on extreme highs or lows. Instead, *internal* trendlines are drawn through the price action and connect as many internal peaks or troughs as possible. Some chartists develop a good eye for this type of trendline and find them useful. The problem with internal trendlines is that their drawing is very subjective; whereas the rules for drawing of more traditional trendlines along the extreme highs and lows are more exact. (See Figure 4.21c.)

REVERSAL DAYS

Another important building block is the *reversal day*. This particular chart formation goes by many names—the top reversal day,

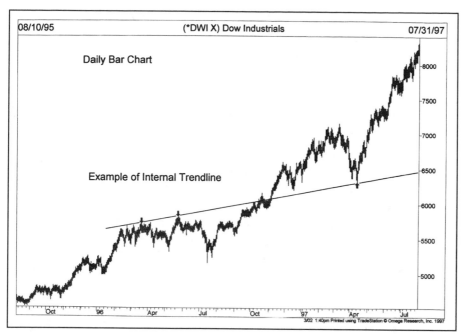

Figure 4.21c *Internal trendlines are drawn through the price action connecting as many highs and lows as possible. This internal trendline drawn along the early 1996 highs provided support a year later during the spring of 1997.*

the bottom reversal day, the *buying* or *selling climax,* and the key reversal day. By itself, this formation is not of major importance. But, taken in the context of other technical information, it can sometimes be significant. Let's first define what a reversal day is.

A *reversal day* takes place either at a top or a bottom. The generally accepted definition of a *top reversal day* is the setting of a new high in an uptrend, followed by a lower close on the same day. In other words, prices set a new high for a given upmove at some point during the day (usually at or near the opening) then weaken and actually close lower than the previous day's closing. A *bottom reversal day* would be a new low during the day followed by a higher close.

The wider the range for the day and the heavier the volume, the more significant is the signal for a possible near term trend reversal. Figures 4.22a-b show what both would look like on a bar chart. Note the heavier volume on the reversal day. Also notice that both the high and low on the reversal day exceed the range of the previous day, forming an *outside day*. While an outside day is not a requirement for a reversal day, it does carry more significance. (See Figure 4.22c.)

The bottom reversal day is sometimes referred to as a *selling climax*. This is usually a dramatic turnaround at the bottom of a down move where all the discouraged longs have finally been forced out of the market on heavy volume. The subsequent absence of selling pressure creates a vacuum over the market, which prices quickly rally to fill. The selling climax is one of the more dramatic examples of the reversal day and, while it may not mark the final bottom of a falling market, it usually signals that a significant low has been seen.

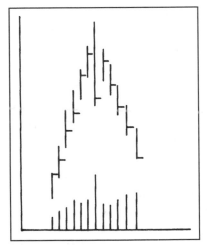

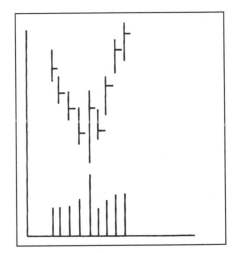

Figure 4.22a   *Example of a top reversal day. The heavier the volume on the reversal day and the wider the range, the more important it becomes.*

Figure 4.22b   *Example of a bottom reversal day. If volume is especially heavy, bottom reversals are often referred to as "selling climaxes."*

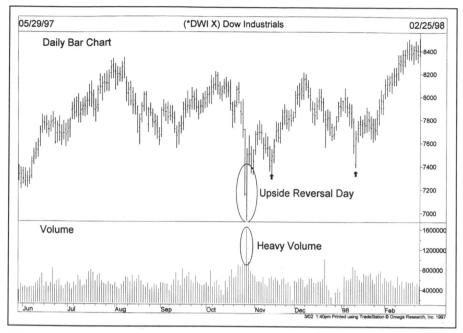

Figure 4.22c *The chart action of October 28, 1997 was a classic example of an upside reversal day or a "selling climax." Prices opened sharply lower and closed sharply higher. The unusually heavy volume bar for that day added to its importance. Two less dramatic upside reversal days (see arrows) also marked price bottoms.*

Weekly and Monthly Reversals

This type of reversal pattern shows up on weekly and monthly bar charts, and with much greater significance. On a weekly chart, each bar represents the entire week's range with the close registered on Friday. An *upside weekly reversal,* therefore, would occur when the market trades lower during the week, makes a new low for the move, but on Friday closes above the previous Friday's close.

Weekly reversals are much more significant than daily reversals for obvious reasons and are watched closely by chartists as signaling important turning points. By the same token, monthly reversals are even more important.

PRICE GAPS

Price *gaps* are simply areas on the bar chart where no trading has taken place. In an uptrend, for example, prices open above the highest price of the previous day, leaving a gap or open space on the chart that is not filled during the day. In a downtrend, the day's highest price is below the previous day's low. Upside gaps are signs of market strength, while downside gaps are usually signs of weakness. Gaps can appear on long term weekly and monthly charts and, when they do, are usually very significant. But they are more commonly seen on daily bar charts.

Several myths exist concerning the interpretation of gaps. One of the maxims often heard is that "gaps are always filled." This is simply not true. Some should be filled and others shouldn't. We'll also see that gaps have different forecasting implications depending on which types they are and where they occur.

Three Types of Gaps

There are three general types of gaps—the *breakaway, runaway (or measuring)*, and *exhaustion gaps*.

The Breakaway Gap. The *breakaway gap* usually occurs at the completion of an important price pattern, and usually signals the beginning of a significant market move. After a market has completed a major basing pattern, the breaking of resistance often occurs on a breakaway gap. Major breakouts from topping or basing areas are breeding grounds for this type of gap. The breaking of a major trendline, signaling a reversal of trend, might also see a breakaway gap.

Breakaway gaps usually occur on heavy volume. More often than not, breakaway gaps are not filled. Prices may return to the upper end of the gap (in the case of a bullish breakout), and may even close a portion of the gap, but some portion of the gap is often left unfilled. As a rule, the heavier the volume after such a gap appears, the less likely it is to be filled. Upside gaps usually act as support areas on subsequent market corrections. It's important that prices not fall below gaps during an uptrend. In all cases a close below an upward gap is a sign of weakness. (See Figures 4.23a and b.)

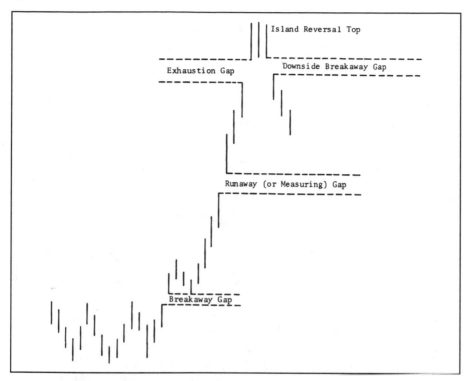

Figure 4.23a *The three types of gaps. The breakaway gap signaled the completion of the basing pattern. The runaway gap occurred at about the midway point (which is why it is also called the measuring gap). An exhaustion gap to the upside, followed within a week by a breakaway gap to the downside, left an island reversal top. Notice that the breakaway and runaway gaps were not filled on the way up, which is often the case.*

The Runaway or Measuring Gap. After the move has been underway for awhile, somewhere around the middle of the move, prices will leap forward to form a second type of gap (or a series of gaps) called the *runaway gap*. This type of gap reveals a situation where the market is moving effortlessly on moderate volume. In an uptrend, it's a sign of market strength; in a downtrend, a sign of weakness. Here again, runaway gaps act as support under the market on subsequent corrections and are often not filled. As in the case of the breakaway, a close below the runaway gap is a negative sign in an uptrend.

Figure 4.23b *The first box shows an "exhaustion" gap near the end of the rally. Prices falling below that gap signaled a top. The second box is a "measuring" gap about halfway through the downtrend. The third box is another "exhaustion" gap at the bottom. The move back above that gap signaled higher prices.*

This variety of gap is also called a *measuring gap* because it usually occurs at about the halfway point in a trend. By measuring the distance the trend has already traveled, from the original trend signal or breakout, an estimate of the probable extent of the remaining move can be determined by doubling the amount already achieved.

The Exhaustion Gap.   The final type of gap appears near the end of a market move. After all objectives have been achieved and the other two types of gaps (breakaway and runaway) have been identified, the analyst should begin to expect the *exhaustion gap.* Near the end of an uptrend, prices leap forward in a last gasp, so to speak. However, that upward leap quickly fades and prices turn lower within a couple of days or within a week. When prices close under that last gap, it is usually a dead giveaway that the exhaustion gap has made its appearance. This is a classic example where falling below a gap in an uptrend has very bearish implications.

The Island Reversal

This takes us to *the island reversal pattern.* Sometimes after the upward exhaustion gap has formed, prices will trade in a narrow range for a couple of days or a couple of weeks before gapping to the downside. Such a situation leaves the few days of price action looking like an "island" surrounded by space or water. The exhaustion gap to the upside followed by a breakaway gap to the downside completes the island reversal pattern and usually indicates a trend reversal of some magnitude. Of course, the major significance of the reversal depends on where prices are in the general trend structure. (See Figure 4.23c.)

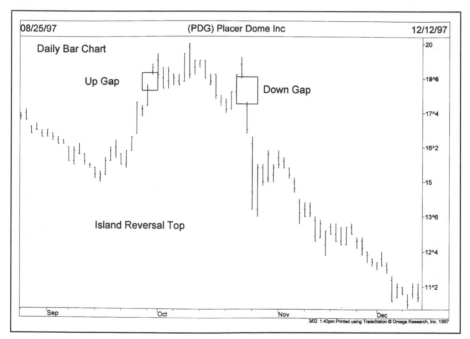

Figure 4.23c *The two gaps on this daily chart form an "island reversal" top. The first box shows an up gap after a rally. The second box shows a down gap three weeks later. That combination of gaps usually signals an important top.*

CONCLUSION

This chapter introduced introductory technical tools that I consider to be the building blocks of chart analysis—support and resistance, trendlines and channels, percentage retracements, speed resistance lines, reversal days, and gaps. Every technical approach covered in later chapters uses these concepts and tools in one form or another. Armed with a better understanding of these concepts, we're now ready to begin a study of price patterns.

Major Reversal Patterns

INTRODUCTION

So far we've touched on Dow Theory, which is the basis of most trend following work being used today. We've examined the basic concepts of trend, such as support, resistance, and trendlines. And we've introduced volume and open interest. We're now ready to take the next step, which is a study of chart patterns. You'll quickly see that these patterns build on the previous concepts.

In Chapter 4, the definition of a trend was given as a series of ascending or descending peaks and troughs. As long as they were ascending, the trend was up; if they were descending, the trend was down. It was stressed, however, that markets also move sideways for a certain portion of the time. It is these periods of sideways market movement that will concern us most in these next two chapters.

It would be a mistake to assume that most changes in trend are very abrupt affairs. The fact is that important changes in trend usually require a period of transition. The problem is that these periods of transition do not always signal a trend reversal. Sometimes these sideways periods just indicate a pause or consolidation in the existing trend after which the original trend is resumed.

PRICE PATTERNS

The study of these transition periods and their forecasting implications leads us to the question of price patterns. First of all, what are price patterns? Price patterns are pictures or formations, which appear on price charts of stocks or commodities, that can be classified into different categories, and that have predictive value.

TWO TYPES OF PATTERNS: REVERSAL AND CONTINUATION

There are two major categories of price patterns—reversal and continuation. As these names imply, reversal patterns indicate that an important reversal in trend is taking place. The continuation patterns, on the other hand, suggest that the market is only pausing for awhile, possibly to correct a near term overbought or oversold condition, after which the existing trend will be resumed. The trick is to distinguish between the two types of patterns as early as possible during the formation of the pattern.

In this chapter, we'll be examining the five most commonly used major reversal patterns: the head and shoulders, triple tops and bottoms, double tops and bottoms, spike (or V) tops and bottoms, and the rounding (or saucer) pattern. We will examine the price formation itself, how it is formed on the chart, and how it can be identified. We will then look at the other important considerations—the accompanying *volume pattern* and *measuring implications*.

Volume plays an important confirming role in all of these price patterns. In times of doubt (and there are lots of those), a study of the volume pattern accompanying the price data can be the deciding factor as to whether or not the pattern can be trusted.

Most price patterns also have certain *measuring techniques* that help the analyst to determine minimum price objectives. While these objectives are only an approximation of the size of the subsequent move, they are helpful in assisting the trader to determine his or her reward to risk ratio.

In Chapter 5, we'll look at a second category of patterns—the continuation variety. There we will examine triangles, flags, pennants, wedges, and rectangles. These patterns usually reflect pauses in the existing trend rather than trend reversals, and are usually classified as intermediate and minor as opposed to major.

Preliminary Points Common to All Reversal Patterns

Before beginning our discussion of the individual major reversal patterns, there are a few preliminary points to be considered that are common to all of these reversal patterns.

1. A prerequisite for any reversal pattern is the existence of a prior trend.
2. The first signal of an impending trend reversal is often the breaking of an important trendline.
3. The larger the pattern, the greater the subsequent move.
4. Topping patterns are usually shorter in duration and more volatile than bottoms.
5. Bottoms usually have smaller price ranges and take longer to build.
6. Volume is usually more important on the upside.

The Need for a Prior Trend.　　The existence of a prior major trend is an important prerequisite for any reversal pattern. A market must obviously have something to reverse. A formation occasionally appears on the charts, resembling one of the reversal patterns. If that pattern, however, has not been preceded by a trend, there is nothing to reverse and the pattern is suspect. Knowing where certain patterns are most apt to occur in the trend structure is one of the key elements in pattern recognition.

A corollary to this point of having a prior trend to reverse is the matter of measuring implications. It was stated earlier that most of the measuring techniques give only *minimum* price objectives. The *maximum* objective would be the total extent of the prior move. If a major bull market has occurred and a major topping pattern is being formed, the maximum implication for the potential move to the downside would be a 100% retracement of the bull market, or the point at which it all began.

The Breaking of Important Trendlines. The first sign of an impending trend reversal is often the breaking of an important trendline. Remember, however, that the violation of a major trendline does not necessarily signal a trend reversal. What is being signaled is a change in trend. The breaking of a major up trendline might signal the beginning of a sideways price pattern, which later would be identified as either the reversal or consolidation type. Sometimes the breaking of the major trendline coincides with the completion of the price pattern.

The Larger the Pattern, the Greater the Potential. When we use the term "larger," we are referring to the height and the width of the price pattern. The height measures the volatility of the pattern. The width is the amount of time required to build and complete the pattern. The greater the size of the pattern—that is, the wider the price swings within the pattern (the volatility) and the longer it takes to build—the more important the pattern becomes and the greater the potential for the ensuing price move.

Virtually all of the measuring techniques in these two chapters are based on the *height* of the pattern. This is the method applied primarily to bar charts, which use a *vertical* measuring criteria. The practice of measuring the *horizontal* width of a price pattern usually is reserved for point and figure charting. That method of charting uses a device known as the *count,* which assumes a close relationship between the width of a top or bottom and the subsequent price target.

Differences Between Tops and Bottoms. Topping patterns are usually shorter in duration and are more volatile than bottoms. Price swings within the tops are wider and more violent. Tops usually take less time to form. Bottoms usually have smaller price ranges, but take longer to build. For this reason it is usually easier and less costly to identify and trade bottoms than to catch market tops. One consoling factor, which makes the more treacherous topping patterns worthwhile, is that *prices tend to decline faster than they go up.* Therefore, the trader can usually make more money a lot faster by catching the short side of a bear market than by trading the long side of a bull market. Everything in life is a tradeoff between reward and risk. The greater risks are compensated for by greater rewards and vice versa. Topping patterns are harder to catch, but are worth the effort.

Volume is More Important on the Upside. Volume should generally increase in the direction of the market trend and is an important confirming factor in the completion of all price patterns. The completion of each pattern should be accompanied by a noticeable increase in volume. However, in the early stages of a trend reversal, *volume is not as important at market tops.* Markets have a way of "falling of their own weight" once a bear move gets underway. Chartists like to see an increase in trading activity as prices drop, but it is not critical. At bottoms, however, the volume pickup is absolutely essential. If the volume pattern does not show a significant increase during the upside price *breakout,* the entire price pattern should be questioned. We will be taking a more indepth look at volume in Chapter 7.

THE HEAD AND SHOULDERS REVERSAL PATTERN

Let's take a close look now at what is probably the best known and most reliable of all major reversal patterns—*the head and shoulders reversal.* We'll spend more time on this pattern because it is important and also to explain all the nuances involved. Most of the other reversal patterns are just variations of the head and shoulders and will not require as extensive a treatment.

This major reversal pattern, like all of the others, is just a further refinement of the concepts of trend covered in Chapter 4. Picture a situation in a major uptrend, where a series of ascending peaks and troughs gradually begin to lose momentum. The uptrend then levels off for awhile. During this time the forces of supply and demand are in relative balance. Once this distribution phase has been completed, support levels along the bottom of the horizontal trading range are broken and a new downtrend has been established. That new downtrend now has descending peaks and troughs.

Let's see how this scenario would look on a *head and shoulders* top. (See Figures 5.1a and b.) At point A, the uptrend is proceeding as expected with no signs of a top. Volume expands on the price move into new highs, which is normal. The corrective

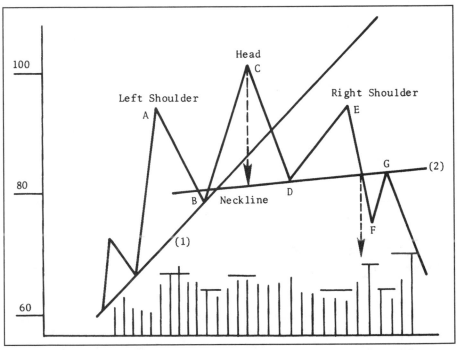

Figure 5.1a *Example of a head and shoulders top. The left and right shoulders (A and E) are at about the same height. The head (C) is higher than either shoulder. Notice the lighter volume on each peak. The pattern is completed on a close under the neckline (line 2). The minimum objective is the vertical distance from the head to the neckline projected downward from the breaking of the neckline. A return move will often occur back to the neckline, which should not recross the neckline once it has been broken.*

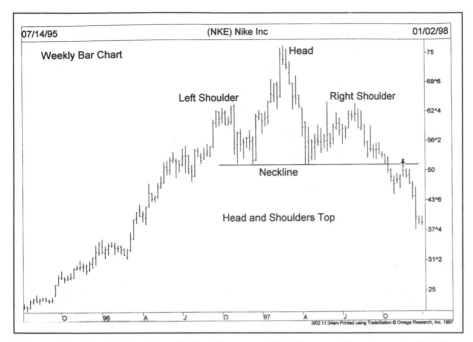

Figure 5.1b *A head and shoulders top. The three peaks show the head higher than either shoulder. The return move (see arrow) back to the neckline occurred on schedule.*

dip to point B is on lighter volume, which is also to be expected. At point C, however, the alert chartist might notice that the volume on the upside breakout through point A is a bit lighter than on the previous rally. This change is not in itself of major importance, but a little yellow caution light goes on in the back of the analyst's head.

Prices then begin to decline to point D and something even more disturbing happens. The decline carries below the top of the previous peak at point A. Remember that, in an uptrend, a penetrated peak should function as support on subsequent corrections. The decline well under point A, almost to the previous reaction low at point B, is another warning that something may be going wrong with the uptrend.

The market rallies again to point E, this time on even lighter volume, and isn't able to reach the top of the previous peak at point C. (That last rally at point E will often retrace one-half to two-thirds of the decline from points C to D.) To continue an uptrend, each high point must exceed the high point of the rally preceding it. The failure of the rally at point E to reach the previous peak at point C fulfills half of the requirement for a new downtrend—namely, descending peaks.

By this time, the major up trendline (line 1) has already been broken, usually at point D, constituting another danger signal. But, despite all of these warnings, all that we know at this point is that the trend has shifted from up to sideways. This might be sufficient cause to liquidate long positions, but not necessarily enough to justify new short sales.

The Breaking of the Neckline Completes the Pattern

By this time, a flatter trendline can be drawn under the last two reaction lows (points B and D), which is called a *neckline* (see line 2). This line generally has a slight upward slope at tops (although it's sometimes horizontal and, less often, tilts downward). *The deciding factor in the resolution of the head and shoulders top is a decisive closing violation of that neckline.* The market has now violated the trendline along the bottom of points B and D, has broken under support at point D, and has completed the requirement for a new downtrend—descending peaks and troughs. The new downtrend is now identified by the declining highs and lows at points C, D, E, and F. Volume should increase on the breaking of the neckline. A sharp increase in downside volume, however, is not critically important in the initial stages of a market top.

The Return Move

Usually a *return move* develops which is a bounce back to the bottom of the neckline or to the previous reaction low at point D (see point G), both of which have now become overhead resistance. The return move does not always occur or is sometimes only a very minor bounce. Volume may help determine the size of the bounce. If the initial breaking of the neckline is on very heavy trading, the odds for a return move are diminished because the increased activity reflects greater downside pressure. Lighter volume on the initial break of the neckline increases the likelihood of a return move. That bounce, however, should be on light volume and the subsequent resumption of the new downtrend should be accompanied by noticeably heavier trading activity.

Summary

Let's review the basic ingredients for a head and shoulders top.

1. A prior uptrend.
2. A left shoulder on heavier volume (point A) followed by a corrective dip to point B.
3. A rally into new highs but on lighter volume (point C).
4. A decline that moves below the previous peak (at A) and approaches the previous reaction low (point D).
5. A third rally (point E) on noticeably light volume that fails to reach the top of the head (at point C).
6. A close below the neckline.
7. A return move back to the neckline (point G) followed by new lows.

What has become evident is three well defined peaks. The middle peak (the head) is slightly higher than either of the two shoulders (points A and E). The pattern, however, is not complete until the neckline is decisively broken on a closing basis. Here again, the 1-3% penetration criterion (or some variation thereof) or the requirement of two successive closes below the neckline (the two day rule) can be used for added confirmation. Until that downside violation takes place, however, there is always the possibility that the pattern is not really a head and shoulders top and that the uptrend may resume at some point.

THE IMPORTANCE OF VOLUME

The accompanying volume pattern plays an important role in the development of the head and shoulders top as it does in all price patterns. As a general rule, the second peak (the head) should take place on lighter volume than the left shoulder. This is not a requirement, but a strong tendency and an early warning of diminishing buying pressure. The most important volume signal takes place during the third peak (the right shoulder). Volume should be noticeably lighter than on the previous two peaks. Volume should then expand on the breaking of the neckline, decline during the return move, and then expand again once the return move is over.

As mentioned earlier, volume is less critical during the completion of market tops. But, at some point, volume should begin to increase if the new downtrend is to be continued. Volume plays a much more decisive role at market bottoms, a subject to be discussed shortly. Before doing so, however, let's discuss the measuring implications of the head and shoulders pattern.

FINDING A PRICE OBJECTIVE

The method of arriving at a price objective is based on the *height* of the pattern. Take the vertical distance from the head (point C) to the neckline. Then project that distance from the point where the neckline is broken. Assume, for example, that the top of the head is at 100 and the neckline is at 80. The vertical distance, therefore, would be the difference, which is 20. That 20 points would be measured downward from the level at which the neckline is broken. If the neckline in Figure 5.1a is at 82 when broken, a downside objective would be projected to the 62 level (82 – 20 = 62).

Another technique that accomplishes about the same task, but is a bit easier, is to simply measure the length of the first wave of the decline (points C to D) and then double it. In either case, the greater the height or volatility of the pattern, the greater the objective. Chapter 4 stated that the measurement taken from a trendline penetration was similar to that used in the head and shoulders pattern. You should be able to see that now. Prices travel roughly the same distance below the broken neckline as they do above it. You'll see throughout our entire study of price patterns that *most price targets on bar charts are based on the height or volatility of the various patterns.* The theme of measuring the height of the pattern and then projecting that distance from a breakout point will be constantly repeated.

It's important to remember that the objective arrived at is only a minimum target. Prices will often move well beyond the objective. Having a minimum target to work with, however, is very helpful in determining beforehand whether there is enough potential in a market move to warrant taking a position. If the market exceeds the price objective, that's just icing on the cake. The *maximum* objective is the size of the prior move. If the previous bull market went from 30 to 100, then the maximum downside objective from a topping pattern would be a complete retracement of the entire upmove all the way down to 30. Reversal patterns can only be expected to reverse or retrace what has gone before them.

Adjusting Price Objectives

A number of other factors should be considered while trying to arrive at a price objective. The measuring techniques from price patterns, such as the one just mentioned for the head and shoulders top, are only the first step. There are other technical factors to take into consideration. For example, where are the prominent support levels left by the reaction lows during the previous bull move? Bear markets often pause at these levels. What about percentage retracements? The *maximum objective* would be a 100% retracement of the previous bull market. But where are the 50% and 66% retracement levels? Those levels often provide significant support under the market. What about any prominent gaps underneath? They often function as support areas. Are there any long term trendlines visible below the market?

The technician must consider other technical data in trying to pinpoint price targets taken from price patterns. If a downside price measurement, for example, projects a target to 30, and there is a prominent support level at 32, then the chartist would be wise to adjust the downside measurement to 32 instead of 30. As a general rule, when a slight discrepancy exists between a projected price target and a clearcut support or resistance level, it's usually safe to adjust the price target to that support or resistance level. It is often necessary to adjust the measured targets from price patterns to take into account additional technical information. The analyst has many different tools at his or her disposal. The most skillful technical analysts are those who learn to blend all of those tools together properly.

THE INVERSE HEAD AND SHOULDERS

The head and shoulders bottom, or the *inverse head and shoulders* as it is sometimes called, is pretty much a mirror image of the topping pattern. As Figure 5.2a shows, there are three distinct bot-

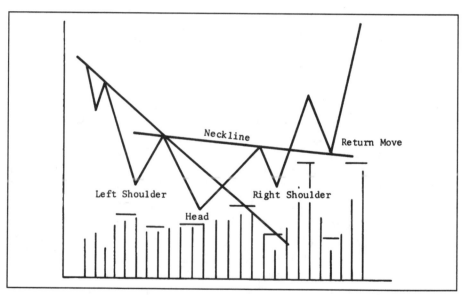

Figure 5.2a *Example of an inverse head and shoulders. The bottom version of this pattern is a mirror image of the top. The only significant difference is the volume pattern in the second half of the pattern. The rally from the head should see heavier volume, and the breaking of the neckline should see a burst of trading activity. The return move back to the neckline is more common at bottoms.*

toms with the head (middle trough) a bit lower than either of the two shoulders. A decisive close through the neckline is also necessary to complete the pattern, and the measuring technique is the same. One slight difference at the bottom is the greater tendency for the return move back to the neckline to occur after the bullish breakout. (See Figure 5.2b.)

The most important difference between the top and bottom patterns is the volume sequence. Volume plays a much more critical role in the identification and completion of a head and shoulders bottom. This point is generally true of all bottom patterns. It was stated earlier that markets have a tendency to "fall of their own weight." At bottoms, however, markets require a significant increase in buying pressure, reflected in greater volume, to launch a new bull market.

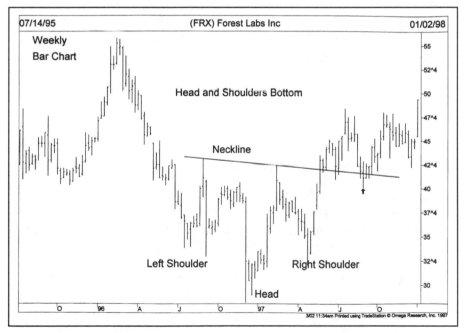

Figure 5.2b *A head and shoulders bottom. The neckline has a slight downward slant, which is normally the case. The pullback after the breakout (see arrow) nicked the neckline a bit, but then resumed the uptrend.*

A more technical way of looking at this difference is that a market can fall just from inertia. Lack of demand or buying interest on the part of traders is often enough to push a market lower; but a market does not go up on inertia. Prices only rise when demand exceeds supply and buyers are more aggressive than sellers.

The volume pattern at the bottom is very similar to that at the top for the first half of the pattern. That is, the volume at the head is a bit lighter than that at the left shoulder. The rally from the head, however, should begin to show not only an increase in trading activity, but the level of volume often exceeds that registered on the rally from the left shoulder. The dip to the right shoulder should be on very light volume. The critical point occurs at the rally through the neckline. This signal must be accompanied by a sharp burst of trading volume if the breakout is for real.

This point is where the bottom differs the most from the top. At the bottom, heavy volume is an absolutely essential ingredient in the completion of the basing pattern. The return move is more common at bottoms than at tops and should occur on light volume. Following that, the new uptrend should resume on heavier volume. The measuring technique is the same as at the top.

The Slope of the Neckline

The neckline at the top usually slopes slightly upward. Sometimes, however, it is horizontal. In either case, it doesn't make too much of a difference. Once in a while, however, a top neckline slopes downward. This slope is a sign of market weakness and is usually accompanied by a weak right shoulder. However, this is a mixed blessing. The analyst waiting for the breaking of the neckline to initiate a short position has to wait a bit longer, because the signal from the down sloping neckline occurs much later and only after much of the move has already taken place. For basing patterns, most necklines have a slight downward tilt. A rising neckline is a sign of greater market strength, but with the same drawback of giving a later signal.

COMPLEX HEAD AND SHOULDERS PATTERNS

A variation of the head and shoulders pattern sometimes occurs which is called the *complex head and shoulders pattern*. These are patterns where two heads may appear or a double left and right shoulder. These patterns are not that common, but have the same forecasting implications. A helpful hint in this regard is the strong tendency toward symmetry in the head and shoulders pattern. This means that a single left shoulder usually indicates a single right shoulder. A double left shoulder increases the odds of a double right shoulder.

Tactics

Market tactics play an important role in all trading. Not all technical traders like to wait for the breaking of the neckline before initiating a new position. As Figure 5.3 shows, more aggressive traders, believing that they have correctly identified a head and shoulders bottom, will begin to probe the long side during the formation of the right shoulder. Or they will buy the first technical signal that the decline into the right shoulder has ended.

Some will measure the distance of the rally from the bottom of the head (points C to D) and then buy a 50% or 66% retracement of that rally. Still others would draw a tight down trendline along the decline from points D to E and buy the first upside break of that trendline. Because these patterns are reasonably symmetrical, some will buy into the right shoulder as it approaches the same level as the bottom of the left shoulder. A lot of anticipatory buying takes place during the formation of the right shoulder. If the initial long probe proves to be profitable, additional positions can be added on the actual penetration of the neckline or on the return move back to the neckline after the breakout.

The Failed Head And Shoulders Pattern

Once prices have moved through the neckline and completed a head and shoulders pattern, *prices should not recross the neckline*

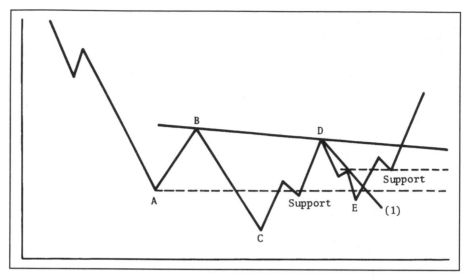

Figure 5.3 *Tactics for a head and shoulders bottom. Many technical traders will begin to initiate long positions while the right shoulder (E) is still being formed. One-half to two-thirds pullback of the rally from points C to D, a decline to the same level as the left shoulder at point A, or the breaking of a short term down trendline (line 1) all provide early opportunities for market entry. More positions can be added on the breaking of the neckline or the return move back to the neckline.*

again. At a top, once the neckline has been broken on the downside, any decisive close back above the neckline is a serious warning that the initial breakdown was probably a bad signal, and creates what is often called, for obvious reasons, *a failed head and shoulders.* This type of pattern starts out looking like a classic head and shoulders reversal, but at some point in its development (either prior to the breaking of the neckline or just after it), prices resume their original trend.

There are two important lessons here. The first is that none of these chart patterns are infallible. They work most of the time, but not always. The second lesson is that technical traders must always be on the alert for chart signs that their analysis is incorrect. One of the keys to survival in the financial markets is to keep trading losses small and to exit a losing trade as quickly as possible. One of the greatest advantages of chart analysis is its ability to quickly alert the trader to the fact that he or she is on the wrong side of the market. The ability and willingness to quickly recognize trading errors and to take defensive action immediately are qualities not to be taken lightly in the financial markets.

The Head And Shoulders as a Consolidation Pattern

Before moving on to the next price pattern, there's one final point to be made on the head and shoulders. We started this discussion by listing it as the best known and most reliable of the major reversal patterns. You should be warned, however, that this formation can, on occasion, act as a consolidation rather than a reversal pattern. When this does happen, it's the exception rather than the rule. We'll talk more about this in Chapter 6, "Continuation Patterns."

TRIPLE TOPS AND BOTTOMS

Most of the points covered in the treatment of the head and shoulders pattern are also applicable to other types of reversal patterns. (See Figures 5.4a-c.) The *triple top* or *bottom,* which is much rarer in occurrence, is just a slight variation of that pattern. The main difference is that the three peaks or troughs in the *triple top* or *bottom* are at about the same level. (See Figure 5.4a.) Chartists often disagree as to whether a reversal pattern is a head and shoulders or a triple top. The argument is academic, because both patterns imply the exact same thing.

The volume tends to decline with each successive peak at the top and should increase at the breakdown point. The triple top is not complete until support levels along both of the intervening lows have been broken. Conversely, prices must close through the two intervening peaks at the bottom to complete a triple bottom. (As an alternate strategy, the breaking of the nearest peak or trough can also be used as a reversal signal.) Heavy upside volume on the completion of the bottom is also essential.

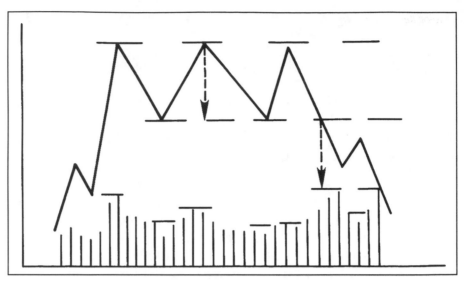

Figure 5.4a *A triple top. Similar to the head and shoulders except that all peaks are at the same level. Each rally peak should be on lighter volume. The pattern is complete when both troughs have been broken on heavier volume. The measuring technique is the height of the pattern projected downward from the breakdown point. Return moves back to the lower line are not unusual.*

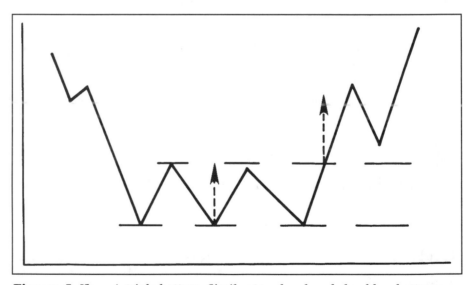

Figure 5.4b *A triple bottom. Similar to a head and shoulders bottom except that each low is at the same level. A mirror image of the triple top except that volume is more important on the upside breakout.*

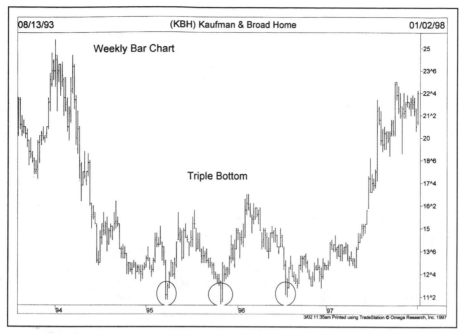

Figure 5.4c   *A triple bottom reversal pattern. Prices found support just below 12 three times on this chart before launching a major advance. The bottom formation on this weekly chart lasted two full years, thereby giving it major significance.*

The measuring implication is also similar to the head and shoulders, and is based on the height of the pattern. Prices will usually move a minimum distance from the breakout point at least equal to the height of the pattern. Once the breakout occurs, a return move to the breakout point is not unusual. Because the triple top or bottom represents only a minor variation of the head and shoulders pattern, we won't say much more about it here.

DOUBLE TOPS AND BOTTOMS

A much more common reversal pattern is the *double top or bottom.* Next to the *head and shoulders,* it is the most frequently seen and the most easily recognized. (See Figures 5.5a-e.) Figures 5.5a and

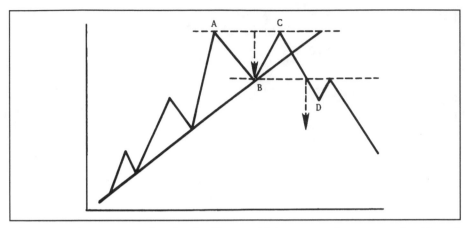

Figure 5.5a *Example of a double top. This pattern has two peaks (A and C) at about the same level. The pattern is complete when the middle trough at point B is broken on a closing basis. Volume is usually lighter on the second peak (C) and picks up on the breakdown (D). A return move back to the lower line is not unusual. The minimum measuring target is the height of the top projected downward from the breakdown point.*

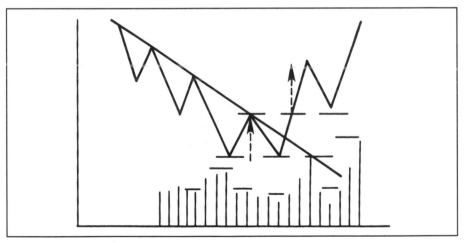

Figure 5.5b *Example of a double bottom. A mirror image of the double top. Volume is more important on the upside breakout. Return moves back to the breakout point are more common at bottoms.*

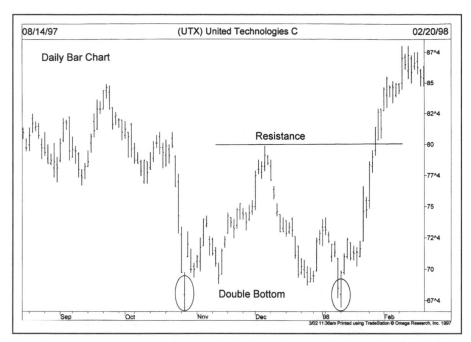

Figure 5.5c   *Example of a double bottom. This stock bounced sharply off the 68 level twice over a span of three months. Note that the second bottom was also an upside reversal day. The breaking of resistance at 80 completed the bottom.*

5.5b show both the top and bottom variety. For obvious reasons, the top is often referred to as an "M" and the bottom as a "W." The general characteristics of a *double top* are similar to that of the head and shoulders and triple top except that only two peaks appear instead of three. The volume pattern is similar as is the measuring rule.

In an uptrend (as shown in Figure 5.5a), the market sets a new high at point A, usually on increased volume, and then declines to point B on declining volume. So far, everything is proceeding as expected in a normal uptrend. The next rally to point C, however, is unable to penetrate the previous peak at A on a closing basis and begins to fall back again. A potential *double top* has been set up. I use the word "potential" because, as is the case with all reversal patterns, the reversal is not complete until the

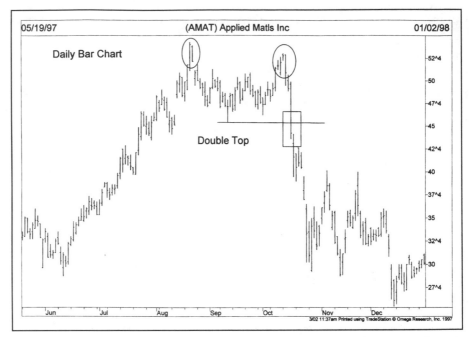

Figure 5.5d   *Example of a double top. Sometimes the second peak doesn't quite reach the first peak as in this example. This two month double top signaled a major decline. The actual signal was the breaking of support near 46 (see box).*

previous support point at B is violated on a closing basis. Until that happens, prices could be in just a sideways consolidation phase, preparing for a resumption of the original uptrend.

The ideal top has two prominent peaks at about the same price level. Volume tends to be heavier during the first peak and lighter on the second. A decisive close under the middle trough at point B on heavier volume completes the pattern and signals a reversal of trend to the downside. A return move to the breakout point is not unusual prior to resumption of the downtrend.

Measuring Technique for the Double Top

The measuring technique for the double top is the height of the pattern projected from the breakdown point (the point where the

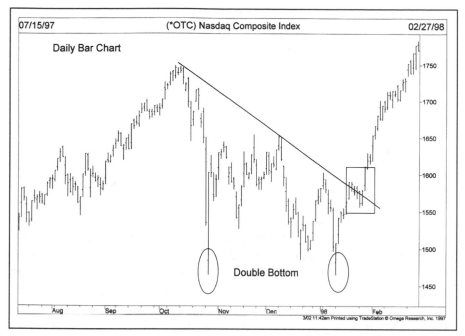

07/15/97   (*OTC) Nasdaq Composite Index   02/27/98

Daily Bar Chart

Double Bottom

Figure 5.5e   *Price patterns show up regularly on the charts of major stock averages. On this chart, the Nasdaq Composite Index formed a double bottom near the 1470 level before turning higher. The break of the down trendline (see box) confirmed the upturn.*

middle trough at point B is broken). As an alternative, measure the height of the first downleg (points A to B) and project that length downward from the middle trough at point B. Measurements at the bottom are the same, but in the other direction.

VARIATIONS FROM THE IDEAL PATTERN

As in most other areas of market analysis, real-life examples are usually some variation of the ideal. For one thing, sometimes the two peaks are not at exactly the same price level. On occasion, the second peak will not quite reach the level of the first peak, which is not too problematical. What does cause some problems is when the second peak actually exceeds the first peak by a slight margin. What at first may appear to be a valid upside breakout and resumption of the uptrend may turn out to be part of the topping process. To help resolve this dilemma, some of the filtering criteria already mentioned may come in handy.

Filters

Most chartists require a close beyond a previous resistance peak instead of just an intraday penetration. Second, a price filter of some type might be used. One such example is a percentage penetration criterion (such as 1% or 3%). Third, the two day penetration rule could be used as an example of a time filter. In other words, prices would have to close beyond the top of the first peak for two consecutive days to signal a valid penetration. Another time filter could be a Friday close beyond the previous peak. The volume on the upside breakout might also provide a clue to its reliability.

These filters are certainly not infallible, but do serve to reduce the number of false signals (or whipsaws) that often occur. Sometimes these filters are helpful, and sometimes they're not. The analyst must face the realization that he or she is dealing with percentages and probabilities, and that there will be times when bad signals occur. That's simply a fact of trading life.

It's not that unusual for the final leg or wave of a bull market to set a new high before reversing direction. In such a case, the final upside breakout would become a "bull trap." (See Figures 5.6a and b.) We'll show you some indicators later on that may help you spot these false breakouts.

The Term "Double Top" Greatly Overused

The terms "double top and bottom" are greatly overused in the financial markets. Most potential double tops or bottoms wind up being something else. The reason for this is that prices have a strong tendency to back off from a previous peak or bounce off a previous low. These price changes are a natural reaction and do not in themselves constitute a reversal pattern. Remember that, at a top, prices must actually violate the previous reaction low before the double top exists.

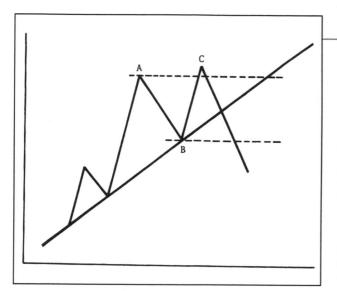

Figure 5.6a
Example of a false breakout, usually called a bull trap. Sometimes near the end of a major uptrend, prices will exceed a previous peak before failing. Chartists use various time and price filters to reduce such whipsaws. This topping pattern would probably qualify as a double top.

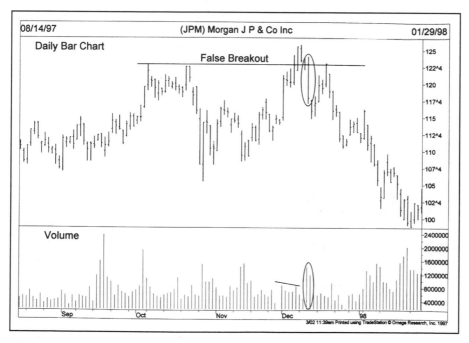

Figure 5.6b *Example of a false breakout. Notice that the upside breakout was on light volume and the subsequent decline on heavy volume—a negative chart combination. Watching the volume helps avoid some false breakouts, but not all.*

Notice in Figure 5.7a that the price at point C backs off from the previous peak at point A. This is perfectly normal action in an uptrend. Many traders, however, will immediately label this pattern as a double top as soon as prices fail to clear the first peak on the first attempt. Figure 5.7b shows the same situation in a downtrend. It is very difficult for the chartist to determine whether the pullback from the previous peak or the bounce from the previous low is just a temporary setback in the existing trend or the start of a double top or bottom reversal pattern. Because the technical odds usually favor continuation of the present trend, it is usually wise to await completion of the pattern before taking action.

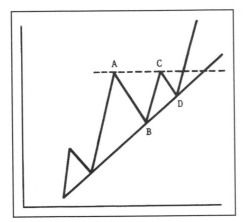 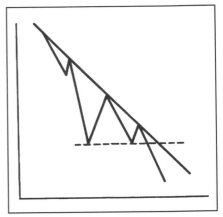

Figure 5.7a *Example of a normal pullback from a previous peak before resumption of the uptrend. This is normal market action and not to be confused with a double top. The double top only occurs when support at point B is broken.*

Figure 5.7b *Example of a normal bounce off a previous low. This is normal market action and not to be confused with a double bottom. Prices will normally bounce off a previous low at least once, causing premature calls for a double bottom.*

Time Between Peaks or Troughs
Is Important

Finally, the size of the pattern is always important. The longer the time period between the two peaks and the greater the height of the pattern, the greater the potential impending reversal. This is true of all chart patterns. In general, most valid double tops or bottoms should have at least a month between the two peaks or troughs. Some will even be two or three months apart. (On longer range monthly and weekly charts, these patterns can span several years.) Most of the examples used in this discussion have described market tops. The reader should be aware by now that bottoming patterns are mirror images of tops except for some of the general differences already touched upon at the beginning of the chapter.

SAUCERS AND SPIKES

Although not seen as frequently, reversal patterns sometimes take the shape of saucers or rounding bottoms. The *saucer bottom* shows a very slow and very gradual turn from down to sideways to up. It is difficult to tell exactly when the saucer has been completed or to measure how far prices will travel in the opposite direction. Saucer bottoms are usually spotted on weekly or monthly charts that span several years. The longer they last, the more significant they become. (See Figure 5.8.)

Spikes are the hardest market turns to deal with because the spike (or V pattern) happens very quickly with little or no transition period. They usually take place in a market that has gotten so overextended in one direction, that a sudden piece of adverse news causes the market to reverse direction very abruptly. A daily or weekly reversal, on very heavy volume, is sometimes the only warning they give us. That being the case, there's not much more we can say about them except that we hope you don't run into too many of them. Some technical indicators we discuss in later chapters will help you determine when markets have gotten dangerously over-extended. (See Figure 5.9.)

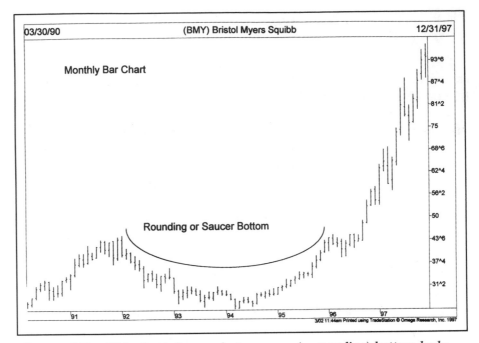

Figure 5.8 *This chart shows what a saucer (or rounding) bottom looks like. They're very slow and gradual, but usually mark major turns. This bottom lasted four years.*

Figure 5.9 *Example of a v reversal pattern. These sudden reversals take place with little or no warning. A sudden price drop on heavy volume is usually the only telltale sign. Unfortunately, these sudden turns are hard to spot in advance.*

CONCLUSION

We've discussed the five most commonly used major reversal patterns—the head and shoulders, double and triple tops and bottoms, the saucer, and the V, or spike. Of those, the most common are the head and shoulders, and double tops and bottoms. These patterns usually signal important trend reversals in progress and are classified as major reversal patterns. There is another class of patterns, however, which are shorter term in nature and usually suggest trend consolidations rather than reversals. They are aptly called *continuation* patterns. Let's look at this other type of pattern in Chapter 6.

6

Continuation Patterns

INTRODUCTION

The chart patterns covered in this chapter are called *continuation* patterns. These patterns usually indicate that the sideways price action on the chart is nothing more than a pause in the prevailing trend, and that the next move will be in the same direction as the trend that preceded the formation. This distinguishes this group of patterns from those in the previous chapter, which usually indicate that a major trend reversal is in progress.

Another difference between reversal and continuation patterns is their time duration. Reversal patterns usually take much longer to build and represent major trend changes. Continuation patterns, on the other hand, are usually shorter term in duration and are more accurately classified as near term or intermediate patterns.

Notice the constant use of the term "usually." The treatment of all chart patterns deals of necessity with general tendencies as opposed to rigid rules. There are always exceptions. Even the grouping of price patterns into different categories sometimes becomes tenuous. Triangles are usually continuation patterns, but sometimes act as reversal patterns. Although triangles are usually considered intermediate patterns, they may occasionally appear on long term charts and take on major trend significance. A variation of the triangle—the inverted variety—usually signals a major market top. Even the head and shoulders pattern, the best known of the major reversal patterns, will on occasion be seen as a consolidation pattern.

Even with allowances for a certain amount of ambiguity and the occasional exception, chart patterns do generally fall into the above two categories and, if properly interpreted, can help the chartist determine what the market will probably do most of the time

TRIANGLES

Let's begin our treatment of continuation patterns with the *triangle*. There are three types of triangles—*symmetrical, ascending,* and *descending.* (Some chartists include a fourth type of triangle known as an *expanding triangle,* or *broadening formation.* This is treated as a separate pattern later.) Each type of triangle has a slightly different shape and has different forecasting implications.

Figures 6.1a-c show examples of what each triangle looks like. The symmetrical triangle (see Figure 6.1a) shows two converging trendlines, the upper line descending and the lower line ascending. The vertical line at the left, measuring the height of the pattern, is called the *base.* The point of intersection at the right, where the two lines meet, is called the *apex.* For obvious reasons, the symmetrical triangle is also called a *coil.*

The ascending triangle has a rising lower line with a flat or horizontal upper line (see Figure 6.1b). The descending triangle (Figure 6.1c), by contrast, has the upper line declining with a flat or horizontal bottom line. Let's see how each one is interpreted.

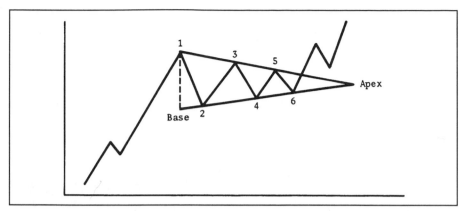

Figure 6.1a *Example of a bullish symmetrical triangle. Notice the two converging trendlines. A close outside either trendline completes the pattern. The vertical line at the left is the base. The point at the right where the two lines meet is the apex.*

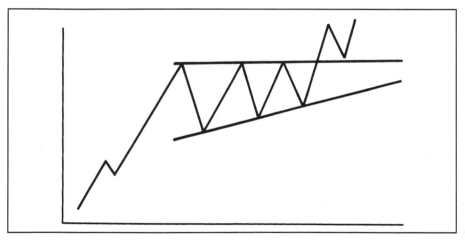

Figure 6.1b *Example of an ascending triangle. Notice the flat upper line and the rising lower line. This is generally a bullish pattern.*

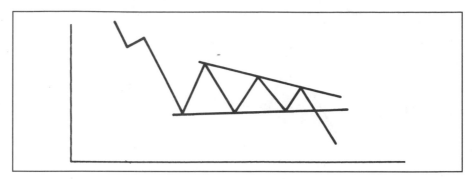

Figure 6.1c *Example of a descending triangle. Notice the flat bottom line and the declining upper line. This is usually a bearish pattern.*

THE SYMMETRICAL TRIANGLE

The *symmetrical triangle* (or the *coil*) is usually a continuation pattern. It represents a pause in the existing trend after which the original trend is resumed. In the example in Figure 6.1a, the prior trend was up, so that the percentages favor resolution of the triangular consolidation on the upside. If the trend had been down, then the symmetrical triangle would have bearish implications.

The minimum requirement for a triangle is four reversal points. Remember that it always takes two points to draw a trendline. Therefore, in order to draw two converging trendlines, each line must be touched at least twice. In Figure 6.1a, the triangle actually begins at point 1, which is where the consolidation in the uptrend begins. Prices pull back to point 2 and then rally to point 3. Point 3, however, is lower than point 1. The upper trendline can only be drawn once prices have declined from point 3.

Notice that point 4 is higher than point 2. Only when prices have rallied from point 4 can the lower upslanting line be drawn. It is at this point that the analyst begins to suspect the he or she is dealing with the symmetrical triangle. Now there are four reversal points (1, 2, 3, and 4) and two converging trendlines.

While the minimum requirement is four reversal points, many triangles have six reversal points as shown in Figure 6.1a.

This means that there are actually three peaks and three troughs that combine to form five waves within the triangle before the uptrend resumes. (When we get to the Elliott Wave Theory, we'll have more to say about the five wave tendency within triangles.)

Time Limit for Triangle Resolution

There is a time limit for the resolution of the pattern, and that is the point where the two lines meet—at the apex. As a general rule, prices should break out in the direction of the prior trend somewhere between two-thirds to three-quarters of the horizontal width of the triangle. That is, the distance from the vertical base on the left of the pattern to the apex at the far right. Because the two lines must meet at some point, that time distance can be measured once the two converging lines are drawn. An upside breakout is signaled by a penetration of the upper trendline. If prices remain within the triangle beyond the three-quarters point, the triangle begins to lose its potency, and usually means that prices will continue to drift out to the apex and beyond

The triangle, therefore, provides an interesting combination of price and time. The converging trendlines give the price boundaries of the pattern, and indicate at what point the pattern has been completed and the trend resumed by the penetration of the upper trendline (in the case of an uptrend). But these trendlines also provide a time target by measuring the width of the pattern. If the width, for example, were 20 weeks long, then the breakout should take place sometime between the 13th and the 15th week. (See Figure 6.1d.)

The actual trend signal is given by a closing penetration of one of the trendlines. Sometimes a return move will occur back to the penetrated trendline after the breakout. In an uptrend, that line has become a support line. In a downtrend, the lower line becomes a resistance line once it's broken. The apex also acts as an important support or resistance level after the breakout occurs. Various penetration criteria can be applied to the breakout, similar to those covered in the previous two chapters. A minimum penetration criterion would be a closing price outside the trendline and not just an intraday penetration.

Figure 6.1d   *Dell formed a bullish symmetrical triangle during the fourth quarter of 1997. Measured from left to right, the triangle width is 18 weeks. Prices broke out on the 13th week (see circle), just beyond the two-thirds point.*

Importance of Volume

Volume should diminish as the price swings narrow within the triangle. This tendency for volume to contract is true of all consolidation patterns. But the volume should pick up noticeably at the penetration of the trendline that completes the pattern. The return move should be on light volume with heavier activity again as the trend resumes.

Two other points should be mentioned about volume. As is the case with reversal patterns, volume is more important on the upside than on the downside. An increase in volume is essential to the resumption of an uptrend in all consolidation patterns.

The second point about volume is that, even though trading activity diminishes during formation of the pattern, a close inspection of the volume usually gives a clue as to whether the heavier volume is occurring during the upmoves or down-moves. In an uptrend, for example, there should be a slight tendency for volume to be heavier during the bounces and lighter on the price dips.

Measuring Technique

Triangles have measuring techniques. In the case of the symmetrical triangle, there are a couple of techniques generally used. The simplest technique is to measure the height of the vertical line at the widest part of the triangle (the base) and measure that distance from the breakout point. Figure 6.2 shows the distance projected from the breakout point, which is the technique I prefer.

The second method is to draw a trendline from the top of the base (at point A) parallel to the lower trendline. This upper channel line then becomes the upside target in an uptrend. It is possible to arrive at a rough time target for prices to meet the upper channel line. Prices will sometimes hit the channel line at the same time the two converging lines meet at the apex.

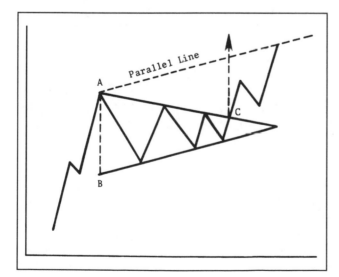

Figure 6.2 *There are two ways to take a measurement from a symmetrical triangle. One is to measure the height of the base (AB); project that vertical distance from the breakout point at C. Another method is to draw a parallel line upward from the top of the baseline (A) parallel to the lower line in the triangle.*

THE ASCENDING TRIANGLE

The ascending and descending triangles are variations of the symmetrical, but have different forecasting implications. Figures 6.3a and b show examples of an *ascending triangle.* Notice that the upper trendline is flat, while the lower line is rising. This pattern indicates that buyers are more aggressive than sellers. It is considered a bullish pattern and is usually resolved with a breakout to the upside.

Both the ascending and descending triangles differ from the symmetrical in a very important sense. No matter where in the trend structure the ascending or descending triangles appear, they have very definite forecasting implications. The ascending triangle is bullish and the descending triangle is bearish. The symmetrical triangle, by contrast, is inherently a neutral pattern. This does not mean, however, that the symmetrical triangle does not have forecasting value. On the contrary, because the symmetrical

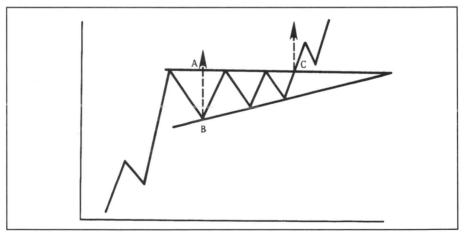

Figure 6.3a   *An ascending triangle. The pattern is completed on a decisive close above the upper line. This breakout should see a sharp increase in volume. That upper resistance line should act as support on subsequent dips after the breakout. The minimum price objective is obtained by measuring the height of the triangle (AB) and projecting that distance upward from the breakout point at C.*

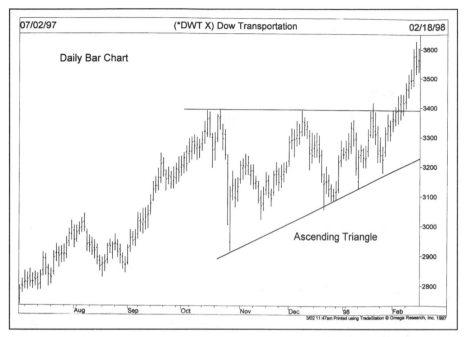

| 07/02/97 | (*DWT X) Dow Transportation | 02/18/98 |

Daily Bar Chart

Ascending Triangle

3/02 11:47am Printed using TradeStation © Omega Research, Inc. 1997

Figure 6.3b *The Dow Transports formed a bullish ascending triangle near the end of 1997. Notice the flat upper line at 3400 and the rising lower line. This is normally a bullish pattern no matter where it appears on the chart.*

triangle is a continuation pattern, the analyst must simply look to see the direction of the previous trend and then make the assumption that the previous trend will continue.

Let's get back to the ascending triangle. As already stated, more often than not, the ascending triangle is bullish. The bullish breakout is signaled by a decisive closing above the flat upper trendline. As in the case of all valid upside breakouts, volume should see a noticeable increase on the breakout. A return move back to the support line (the flat upper line) is not unusual and should take place on light volume.

Measuring Technique

The measuring technique for the ascending triangle is relatively simple. Simply measure the height of the pattern at its widest point and project that vertical distance from the breakout point. This is just another example of using the volatility of a price pattern to determine a minimum price objective.

The Ascending Triangle as a Bottom

While the ascending triangle most often appears in an uptrend and is considered a continuation pattern, it sometimes appears as a bottoming pattern. It is not unusual toward the end of a downtrend to see an ascending triangle develop. However, even in this situation, the interpretation of the pattern is bullish. The breaking of the upper line signals completion of the base and is considered a bullish signal. Both the ascending and descending triangles are sometimes also referred to as *right angle* triangles.

THE DESCENDING TRIANGLE

The *descending triangle* is just a mirror image of the ascending, and is generally considered a bearish pattern. Notice in Figures 6.4a and b the descending upper line and the flat lower line. This pattern indicates that sellers are more aggressive than buyers, and is usually resolved on the downside. The downside signal is registered by a decisive close under the lower trendline, usually on increased volume. A return move sometimes occurs which should encounter resistance at the lower trendline.

The measuring technique is exactly the same as the ascending triangle in the sense that the analyst must measure the height of the pattern at the base to the left and then project that distance down from the breakdown point.

The Descending Triangle as a Top

While the descending triangle is a continuation pattern and usually is found within downtrends, it is not unusual on occasion for the descending triangle to be found at market tops. This type of pattern is not that difficult to recognize when it does appear in the top setting. In that case, a close below the flat lower line would signal a major trend reversal to the downside.

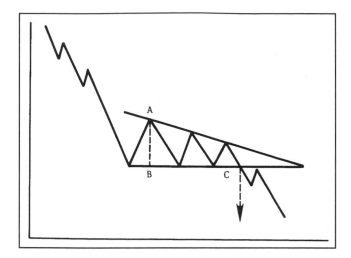

Figure 6.4a *A descending triangle. The bearish pattern is completed with a decisive close under the lower flat line. The measuring technique is the height of the triangle (AB) projected down from the breakout at point C.*

Figure 6.4b *A bearish descending triangle formed in Du Pont during the autumn of 1997. The upper line is descending while the lower line is flat. The break of the lower line in early October resolved the pattern to the downside.*

The Volume Pattern

The volume pattern in both the ascending and descending triangles is very similar in that the volume diminishes as the pattern works itself out and then increases on the breakout. As in the case of the symmetrical triangle, during the formation the chartist can detect subtle shifts in the volume pattern coinciding with the swings in the price action. This means that in the ascending pattern, the volume tends to be slightly heavier on bounces and lighter on dips. In the descending formation, volume should be heavier on the downside and lighter during the bounces.

The Time Factor in Triangles

One final factor to be considered on the subject of triangles is that of the time dimension. The triangle is considered an intermediate pattern, meaning that it usually takes longer than a month to form, but generally less than three months. A triangle that lasts less than a month is probably a different pattern, such as a pennant, which will be covered shortly. As mentioned earlier, triangles sometimes appear on long term price charts, but their basic meaning is always the same.

THE BROADENING FORMATION

This next price pattern is an unusual variation of the triangle and is relatively rare. It is actually an inverted triangle or a triangle turned backwards. All of the triangular patterns examined so far show converging trendlines. The *broadening formation,* as the name implies, is just the opposite. As the pattern in Figure 6.5 shows, the trendlines actually diverge in the broadening formation, creating a picture that looks like an expanding triangle. It is also called a megaphone top.

The volume pattern also differs in this formation. In the other triangular patterns, volume tends to diminish as the price swings grow narrower. Just the opposite happens in the broadening formation. *The volume tends to expand along with the wider price swings.* This situation represents a market that is out of control

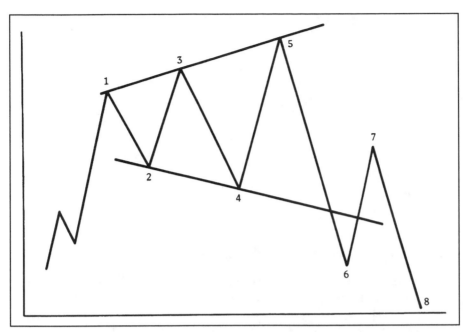

Figure 6.5   *A broadening top. This type of expanding triangle usually occurs at major tops. It shows three successively higher peaks and two declining troughs. The violation of the second trough completes the pattern. This is an unusually difficult pattern to trade and fortunately is relatively rare.*

and unusually emotional. Because this pattern also represents an unusual amount of public participation, it most often occurs at major market tops. *The expanding pattern, therefore, is usually a bearish formation.* It generally appears near the end of a major bull market.

FLAGS AND PENNANTS

The *flag* and *pennant* formations are quite common. They are usually treated together because they are very similar in appearance, tend to show up at about the same place in an existing trend, and have the same volume and measuring criteria.

The *flag* and *pennant* represent brief pauses in a dynamic market move. In fact, one of the requirements for both the flag and the pennant is that they be preceded by a sharp and almost straight line move. They represent situations where a steep advance or decline has gotten ahead of itself, and where the market pauses briefly to "catch its breath" before running off again in the same direction.

Flags and pennants are among the most reliable of continuation patterns and only rarely produce a trend reversal. Figures 6.6a-b show what these two patterns look like. To begin with, notice the steep price advance preceding the formations on heavy volume. Notice also the dramatic drop off in activity as the consolidation patterns form and then the sudden burst of activity on the upside breakout.

Construction of Flags and Pennants

The construction of the two patterns differs slightly. The flag resembles a parallelogram or rectangle marked by two parallel trendlines that tend to slope against the prevailing trend. In a downtrend, the flag would have a slight upward slope.

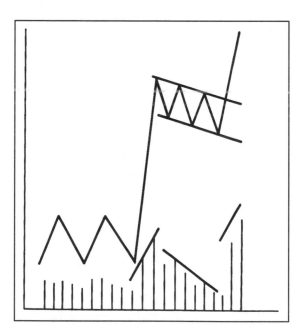

Figure 6.6a *Example of a bullish flag. The flag usually occurs after a sharp move and represents a brief pause in the trend. The flag should slope against the trend. Volume should dry up during the formation and build again on the breakout. The flag usually occurs near the midpoint of the move.*

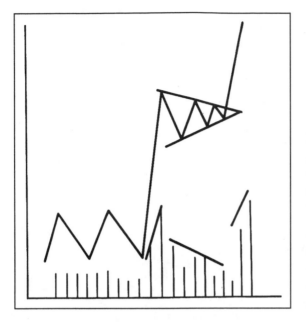

Figure 6.6b *A bullish pennant. Resembles a small symmetrical triangle, but usually lasts no longer than three weeks. Volume should be light during its formation. The move after the pennant is completed should duplicate the size of the move preceding it.*

The pennant is identified by two converging trendlines and is more horizontal. It very closely resembles a small symmetrical triangle. An important requirement is that volume should dry up noticeably while each of the patterns is forming.

Both patterns are relatively short term and should be completed within one to three weeks. Pennants and flags in downtrends tend to take even less time to develop, and often last no longer than one or two weeks. Both patterns are completed on the penetration of the upper trendline in an uptrend. The breaking of the lower trendline would signal resumption of downtrends. The breaking of those trendlines should take place on heavier volume. As usual, upside volume is more critically important than downside volume. (See Figures 6.7a-b.)

Measuring Implications

The measuring implications are similar for both patterns. Flags and pennants are said to "fly at half-mast" from a *flagpole*. The flagpole is the prior sharp advance or decline. The term "half-mast" suggests that these minor continuation patterns tend to

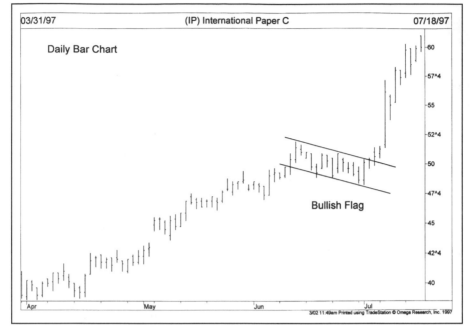

Figure 6.7a   *A bullish flag in International Paper. The flag looks like a down-sloping parallelogram. Notice that the flag occurred right at the halfway point of the uptrend.*

appear at about the halfway point of the move. In general, the move after the trend has resumed will duplicate the flagpole or the move just prior to the formation of the pattern.

To be more precise, measure the distance of the preceding move from the original breakout point. That is to say, the point at which the original trend signal was given, either by the penetration of a support or resistance level or an important trendline. That vertical distance of the preceding move is then measured from the breakout point of the flag or pennant—that is, the point at which the upper line is broken in an uptrend or the lower line in a downtrend.

Summary

Let's summarize the more important points of both patterns.

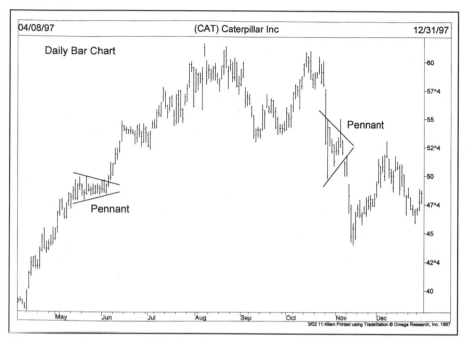

Figure 6.7b *A couple of pennants are flying on this Caterpillar chart. Pennants are short term continuation patterns that look like small symmetrical triangles. The pennant to the left continued the uptrend, while the one to the right continued the downtrend.*

1. They are both preceded by an almost straight line move (called a flagpole) on heavy volume.
2. Prices then pause for about one to three weeks on very light volume.
3. The trend resumes on a burst of trading activity.
4. Both patterns occur at about the midpoint of the market move.
5. The pennant resembles a small horizontal symmetrical triangle.
6. The flag resembles a small parallelogram that slopes against the prevailing trend.
7. Both patterns take less time to develop in downtrends.
8. Both patterns are very common in the financial markets.

THE WEDGE FORMATION

The *wedge* formation is similar to a symmetrical triangle both in terms of its shape and the amount of time it takes to form. Like the symmetrical triangle, it is identified by two converging trendlines that come together at an *apex*. In terms of the amount of time it takes to form, the wedge usually lasts more than one month but not more than three months, putting it into the intermediate category.

What distinguishes the *wedge* is its noticeable slant. The wedge pattern has a noticeable slant either to the upside or the downside. As a rule, like the flag pattern, the wedge slants against the prevailing trend. Therefore, a *falling wedge is considered bullish and a rising wedge is bearish.* Notice in Figure 6.8a that the bullish wedge slants downward between two converging trendlines. In the downtrend in Figure 6.8b, the converging trendlines have an unmistakable upward slant.

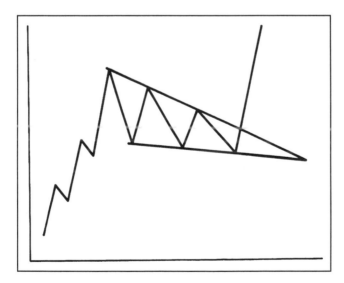

Figure 6.8a
Example of a bullish falling wedge. The wedge pattern has two converging trendlines, but slopes against the prevailing trend. A falling wedge is usually bullish.

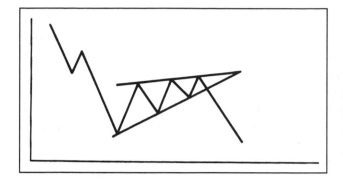

Figure 6.8b
Example of a bearish wedge. A bearish wedge should slope upward against the prevailing down-trend.

Wedges as Tops and Bottom Reversal Patterns

Wedges show up most often within the existing trend and usually constitute continuation patterns. The wedge can appear at tops or bottoms and signal a trend reversal. But that type of situation is much less common. Near the end of an uptrend, the chartist may observe a clearcut rising wedge. Because a continuation wedge in an uptrend should slope downward against the prevailing trend, the rising wedge is a clue to the chartist that this is a bearish and not a bullish pattern. At bottoms, a falling wedge would be a tip-off of a possible end of a bear trend.

Whether the wedge appears in the middle or the end of a market move, the market analyst should always be guided by the general maxim that *a rising wedge is bearish and a falling wedge is bullish*. (See Figure 6.8c.)

THE RECTANGLE FORMATION

The *rectangle formation* often goes by other names, but is usually easy to spot on a price chart. It represents a pause in the trend during which prices move sideways between two parallel horizontal lines. (See Figures 6.9a-c.)

The rectangle is sometimes referred to as a *trading range* or a *congestion area*. In Dow Theory parlance, it is referred to as a *line*. Whatever it is called, it usually represents just a consolidation period in the existing trend, and is usually resolved in the direc-

Figure 6.8c   *Example of a bearish rising wedge. The two converging trend-lines have a definite upward slant. The wedge slants against the prevailing trend. Therefore, a rising wedge is bearish, and a falling wedge is bullish.*

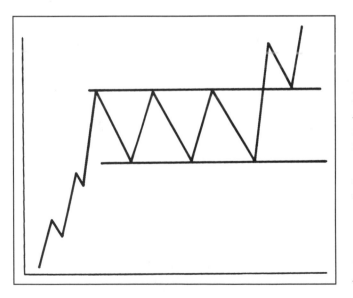

Figure 6.9a
Example of a bull-ish rectangle in an uptrend. This pat-tern is also called a trading range, and shows prices trading between two horizontal trendlines. It is also called a con-gestion area.

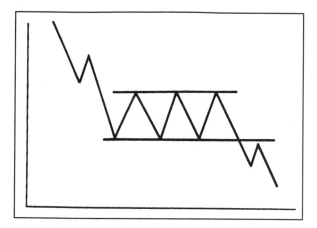

Figure 6.9b *Example of a bearish rectangle. While rectangles are usually considered continuation patterns, the trader must always be alert for signs that it may turn into a reversal pattern. such as a triple bottom.*

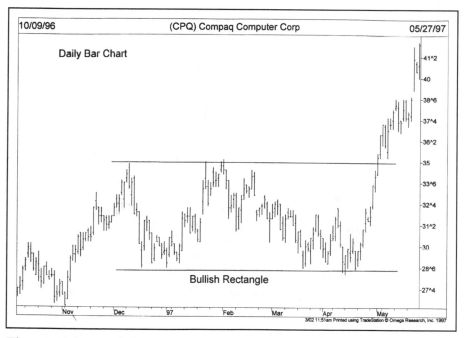

Figure 6.9c *A bullish rectangle. Compaq's uptrend was interrupted for four months while it traded sideways. The break above the upper line in early May completed the pattern and resumed the uptrend. Rectangles are usually continuation patterns.*

tion of the market trend that preceded its occurrence. In terms of forecasting value, it can be viewed as being similar to the symmetrical triangle but with flat instead of converging trendlines.

A decisive close outside either the upper or lower boundary signals completion of the rectangle and points the direction of the trend. The market analyst must always be on the alert, however, that the rectangular consolidation does not turn into a reversal pattern. In the uptrend shown in Figure 6.9a, for example, notice that the three peaks might initially be viewed as a possible triple top reversal pattern.

The Importance of the Volume Pattern

One important clue to watch for is the volume pattern. Because the price swings in both directions are fairly broad, the analyst should keep a close eye on which moves have the heavier volume. If the rallies are on heavier and the setbacks on lighter volume, then the formation is probably a continuation in the uptrend. If the heavier volume is on the downside, then it can be considered a warning of a possible trend reversal in the works.

Swings Within the Range Can Be Traded

Some chartists trade the swings within such a pattern by buying dips near the bottom and selling rallies near the top of the range. This technique enables the short term trader to take advantage of the well defined price boundaries, and profit from an otherwise trendless market. Because the positions are being taken at the extremes of the range, the risks are relatively small and well defined. If the trading range remains intact, this countertrend trading approach works quite well. When a breakout does occur, the trader not only exits the last losing trade immediately, but can reverse the previous position by initiating a new trade in the direction of the new trend. Oscillators are especially useful in sideways trading markets, but less useful once the breakout has occurred for reasons discussed in Chapter 10.

Other traders assume the rectangle is a continuation pattern and take long positions near the lower end of the price band in an uptrend, or initiate short positions near the top of the range in downtrends. Others avoid such trendless markets altogether and await a clearcut breakout before committing their funds. Most trend-following systems perform very poorly during these periods of sideways and trendless market action.

Other Similarities and Differences

In terms of duration, the rectangle usually falls into the one to three month category, similar to triangles and wedges. The volume pattern differs from other continuation patterns in the sense that the broad price swings prevent the usual dropoff in activity seen in other such patterns.

The most common measuring technique applied to the rectangle is based on the height of the price range. Measure the height of the trading range, from top to bottom, and then project that vertical distance from the breakout point. This method is similar to the other vertical measuring techniques already mentioned, and is based on the volatility of the market. When we cover the count in point and figure charting, we'll say more on the question of horizontal price measurements.

Everything mentioned so far concerning volume on breakouts and the probability of return moves applies here as well. Because the upper and lower boundaries are horizontal and so well defined in the rectangle, support and resistance levels are more clearly evident. This means that, on upside breakouts, the top of the former price band should now provide solid support on any selloffs. After a downside breakout in downtrends, the bottom of the trading range (the previous support area) should now provide a solid ceiling over the market on any rally attempts.

THE MEASURED MOVE

The *measured move,* or the *swing* measurement as it is sometimes called, describes the phenomenon where a major market advance or decline is divided into two equal and parallel moves, as shown in Figure 6.10a. For this approach to work, the market moves

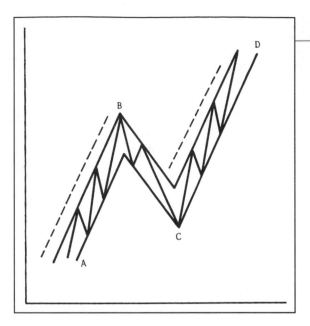

Figure 6.10a
Example of a measured move (or the swing measurement) in an uptrend. This theory holds that the second leg in the advance (CD) duplicates the size and slope of the first upleg (AB). The corrective wave (BC) often retraces a third to a half of AB before the uptrend is resumed.

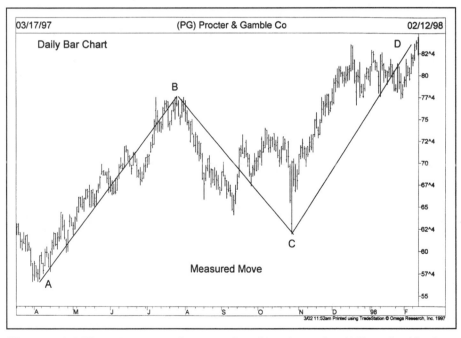

Figure 6.10b *A measured move takes the prior upleg (AB) and adds that value to the bottom of the correction at C. On this chart, the prior uptrend (AB) was 20 points. Adding that to the lowpoint at C (62) yielded a price target to 82 (D).*

should be fairly orderly and well defined. The measured move is really just a variation of some of the techniques we've already touched on. We've seen that some of the consolidation patterns, such as flags and pennants, usually occur at about the halfway point of a market move. We've also mentioned the tendency of markets to retrace about a third to a half of a prior trend before resuming that trend.

In the measured move, when the chartist sees a well-defined situation, such as in Figure 6.10a, with a rally from point A to point B followed by a countertrend swing from point B to point C (which retraces a third to a half of wave AB), it is assumed that the next leg in the uptrend (CD) will come close to duplicating the first leg (AB). The height of wave (AB), therefore, is simply measured upward from the bottom of the correction at point C.

THE CONTINUATION HEAD AND SHOULDERS PATTERN

In the previous chapter, we treated the head and shoulders pattern at some length and described it as the best known and most trustworthy of all reversal patterns. The head and shoulders pattern can sometimes appear as a continuation instead of a reversal pattern.

In the continuation head and shoulders variety, prices trace out a pattern that looks very similar to a sideways rectangular pattern except that the middle trough in an uptrend (see Figure 6.11a) tends to be lower than either of the two shoulders. In a downtrend (see Figure 6.11b), the middle peak in the consolidation exceeds the other two peaks. The result in both cases is a head and shoulders pattern turned upside down. Because it is turned upside down, there is no chance of confusing it with the reversal pattern.

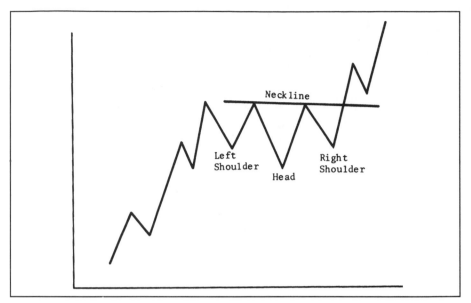

Figure 6.11a *Example of a bullish continuation head and shoulders pattern.*

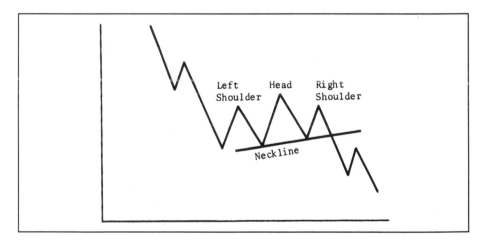

Figure 6.11b *Example of a bearish continuation head and shoulders pattern.*

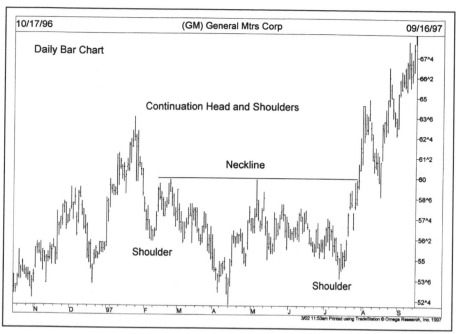

Figure 6.11c *General Motors formed a continuation head and shoulders pattern during the first half of 1997. The pattern is very clear but shows up in an unusual place. The pattern was completed and the uptrend resumed with the close above the neckline at 60.*

CONFIRMATION AND DIVERGENCE

The principle of *confirmation* is one of the common themes running throughout the entire subject of market analysis, and is used in conjunction with its counterpart—*divergence*. We'll introduce both concepts here and explain their meaning, but we'll return to them again and again throughout the book because their impact is so important. We're discussing confirmation here in the context of chart patterns, but it applies to virtually every aspect of technical analysis. *Confirmation* refers to the comparison of all technical signals and indicators to ensure that most of those indicators are pointing in the same direction and are confirming one another.

Divergence is the opposite of confirmation and refers to a situation where different technical indicators fail to confirm one another. While it is being used here in a negative sense, divergence is a valuable concept in market analysis, and one of the best early warning signals of impending trend reversals. We'll discuss the principle of divergence at greater length in Chapter 10, "Oscillators and Contrary Opinion."

CONCLUSION

This concludes our treatment of price patterns. We stated earlier that the three pieces of raw data used by the technical analyst were *price, volume,* and *open interest.* Most of what we've said so far has focused on price. Let's take a closer look now at volume and open interest and how they are incorporated into the analytical process.

Volume and Open Interest

INTRODUCTION

Most technicians in the financial markets use a multidimensional approach to market analysis by tracking the movement of three sets of figures—*price, volume,* and *open interest.* Volume analysis applies to all markets. Open interest applies primarily to futures markets. Chapter 3 discussed the construction of the daily bar chart and showed how the three figures were plotted on that type of chart. It was stated then that even though volume and open interest figures are available for each delivery month in futures markets, the *total* figures are the ones generally used for forecasting purposes. Stock chartists simply plot total volume along with the accompanying price.

Most of the discussion of charting theory to this point has concentrated mainly on price action with some mention of volume. In this chapter, we'll round out the three dimensional approach by taking a closer look at the role played by volume and open interest in the forecasting process.

VOLUME AND OPEN INTEREST AS SECONDARY INDICATORS

Let's begin by placing volume and open interest in their proper perspective. *Price* is by far the most important. *Volume* and *open interest* are secondary in importance and are used primarily as confirming indicators. Of those two, volume is the more important.

Volume

Volume is the number of entities traded during the time period under study. Because we'll be dealing primarily with daily bar charts, our main concern is with daily volume. That daily volume is plotted by a vertical bar at the bottom of the chart under the day's price action. (See Figure 7.1.)

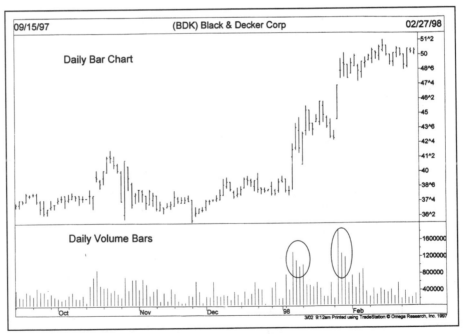

Figure 7.1   *Notice that the volume bars are noticeably larger as prices are rallying (see circles). That means that volume is confirming the price rise and is bullish.*

Volume can be plotted for *weekly* bar charts as well. In that case, total volume for the week would simply be plotted under the bar representing that week's price action. Volume is usually not used, however, on *monthly* bar charts.

Open Interest in Futures

The total number of outstanding or unliquidated contracts at the end of the day is *open interest*. In Figure 7.2, open interest is the solid line plotted on the chart under its corresponding price data for the day, but above the volume bars. Remember that official volume and open interest figures are reported a day late in the futures markets and are, therefore, plotted with a one day lag. (Only estimated volume figures are available for the last trading day.) That means that each day the chartist plots the high, low, and closing price bar for the last day of trading, but plots the official volume and open interest figures for the previous day.

Open interest represents the total number of outstanding longs or shorts in the market, *not the sum of both*. Open interest is the number of contracts. A contract must have both a *buyer* and a *seller*. Therefore, two market participants—a *buyer* and a *seller*—combine to create only one contract. The open interest figure reported each day is followed by either a positive or negative number showing the increase or decrease in the number of contracts for that day. It is those changes in the open interest levels, either up or down, that give the chartist clues as to the changing character of market participation and give open interest its forecasting value.

How Changes in Open Interest Occur. In order to grasp the significance of how changes in the open interest numbers are interpreted, the reader must first understand how each trade produces a change in those numbers.

Every time a trade is completed on the floor of the exchange, the open interest is affected in one of three ways—it increases, decreases, or stays unchanged. Let's see how those changes occur.

Buyer	Seller	Change in Open Interest
1. Buys new long	Sells new short	Increases
2. Buys new long	Sells old long	No change
3. Buys old short	Sells new short	No change
4. Buys old short	Sells old long	Decreases

In the first case, both the buyer and seller are initiating a new position and a new contract is established. In case 2, the buyer is initiating a new long position, but the seller is merely liquidating an old long. One is entering and the other exiting a trade. The result is a standoff and no change takes place in the number of contracts. In case 3, the same thing happens except this time it is the seller who is initiating a new short and the buyer who is only covering an old short. Because one of the traders is entering and the other exiting a trade, again no change is produced. In case 4, both traders are liquidating an old position and the open interest decreases accordingly.

To sum up, if both participants in a trade are initiating a new position, the open interest will increase. If both are liquidating an old position, the open interest will decline. If, however, one is initiating a new trade while the other is liquidating an old trade, open interest will remain unchanged. By looking at the net change in the total open interest at the end of the day, the chartist is able to determine whether money is flowing into or out of the market. This information enables the analyst to draw some conclusions about the strength or weakness of the current price trend.

General Rules for Interpreting Volume and Open Interest

The futures technician incorporates volume and open interest information into market analysis. The rules for the interpretation of volume and open interest are generally combined because they are so similar. There are, however, some distinctions between the two that should be addressed. We'll begin here with a statement of the general rules for both. Having done that, we'll then treat each one separately before combining them again at the end.

Price	Volume	Open Interest	Market
Rising	Up	Up	Strong
Rising	Down	Down	Weak
Declining	Up	Up	Weak
Declining	Down	Down	Strong

If volume and open interest are both increasing, then the current price trend will probably continue in its present direction (either up or down). If, however, volume and open interest are declining, the action can be viewed as a warning that the current price trend may be nearing an end. Having said that, let's now take a look at volume and open interest separately. (See Figure 7.2.)

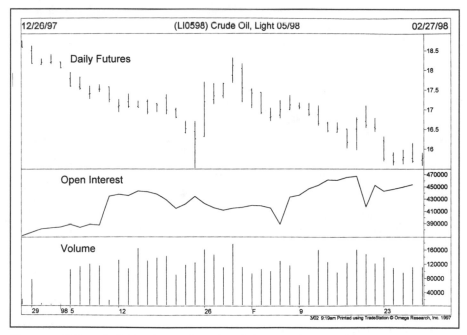

Figure 7.2 *A daily chart of crude oil futures shows volume and open interest (solid line). The open interest line is rising as prices are falling, which is bearish.*

INTERPRETATION OF VOLUME
FOR ALL MARKETS

The level of volume measures the intensity or urgency behind the price move. Heavier volume reflects a higher degree of intensity or pressure. By monitoring the level of volume along with price action, the technician is better able to gauge the buying or selling pressure behind market moves. This information can then be used to confirm price movement or warn that a price move is not to be trusted. (See Figures 7.3 and 7.4.)

   To state the rule more concisely, *volume should increase or expand in the direction of the existing price trend.* In an uptrend, volume should be heavier as the price moves higher, and should decrease or contract on price dips. As long as this pattern continues, volume is said to be confirming the price trend.

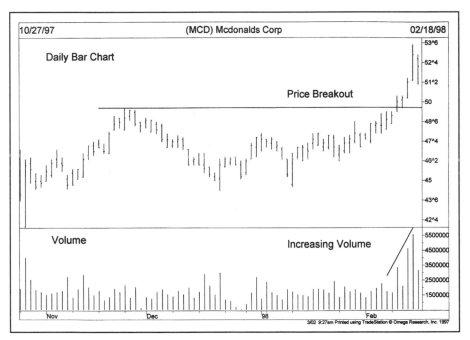

Figure 7.3   *The upside price breakout by McDonalds through the November 1997 peak was accompanied by a noticeable burst of trading activity. That's bullish.*

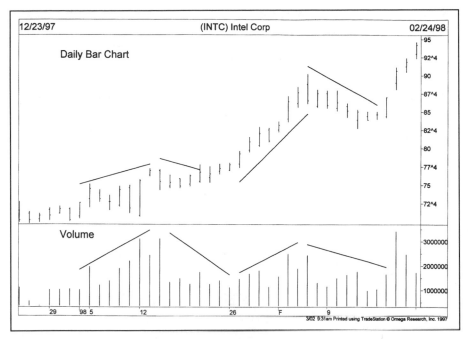

Figure 7.4 *The volume bars are following Intel's price uptrend. Volume is heavier as prices are rising, and drops off as prices weaken. Notice the burst of trading activity during the last three days' price jump.*

The chartist is also watching for signs of *divergence* (there's that word again). Divergence occurs if the penetration of a previous high by the price trend takes place on declining volume. This action alerts the chartist to diminishing buying pressure. If the volume also shows a tendency to pick up on price dips, the analyst begins to worry that the uptrend is in trouble.

Volume as Confirmation in Price Patterns

During our treatment of price patterns in Chapters 5 and 6, volume was mentioned several times as an important confirming indicator. One of the first signs of a *head and shoulders* top occurred when prices moved into new highs during the formation of the *head* on light volume with heavier activity on the subsequent decline to the *neckline*. The *double* and *triple tops* saw lighter volume on each successive peak followed by heavier downside activity. Continuation patterns, like the *triangle,* should be accompanied by a gradual drop off in volume. As a rule, the resolution of all price patterns (the breakout point) should be accompanied by heavier trading activity if the signal given by that breakout is real. (See Figure 7.5.)

In a downtrend, the volume should be heavier during down moves and lighter on bounces. As long as that pattern continues, the selling pressure is greater than buying pressure and the downtrend should continue. It's only when that pattern begins to change that the chartist starts looking for signs of a bottom.

Volume Precedes Price

By monitoring the price and volume together, we're actually using two different tools to measure the same thing—pressure. By

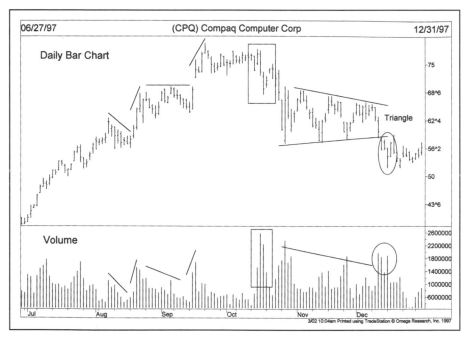

Figure 7.5   *The first half of this chart shows a positive trend with heavier volume on up days. The box at the top shows a sudden downturn on heavy volume—a negative sign. Notice the increase in trading as the continuation triangle is broken on the downside.*

the mere fact that prices are trending higher, we can see that there is more buying than selling pressure. It stands to reason then that the greater volume should take place in the same direction as the prevailing trend. Technicians believe that *volume precedes price,* meaning that the loss of upside pressure in an uptrend or downside pressure in a downtrend actually shows up in the volume figures before it is manifested in a reversal of the price trend.

On Balance Volume

Technicians have experimented with many volume indicators to help quantify buying or selling pressure. Trying to "eyeball" the vertical volume bars along the bottom of the chart is not always precise enough to detect significant shifts in the volume flow. The simplest and best known of these volume indicators is *on balance volume* or *OBV.* Developed and popularized by Joseph Granville in his 1963 book, *Granville's New Key to Stock Market Profits,* OBV actually produces a curving line on the price chart. This line can be used either to confirm the quality of the current price trend or warn of an impending reversal by diverging from the price action.

Figure 7.6 shows the price chart with the OBV line along the bottom of the chart instead of the volume bars. Notice how much easier it is to follow the volume trend with the OBV line.

The construction of the OBV line is simplicity itself. The total volume for each day is assigned a plus or minus value depending on whether prices close higher or lower for that day. A higher close causes the volume for that day to be given a plus value, while a lower close counts for negative volume. A running cumulative total is then maintained by adding or subtracting each day's volume based on the direction of the market close.

It is the direction of the OBV line (its trend) that is important and not the actual numbers themselves. The actual OBV values will differ depending on how far back you are charting. Let the computer handle the calculations. Concentrate on the direction of the OBV line.

The *on balance volume* line should follow in the same direction as the price trend. If prices show a series of higher peaks and

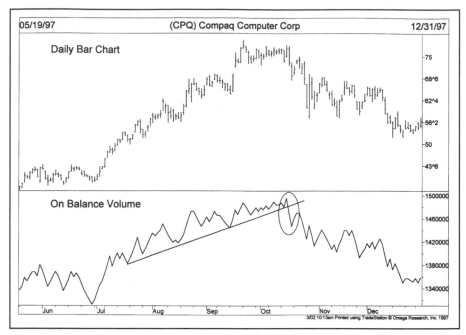

Figure 7.6   *The line along the bottom shows on balance volume (OBV) for the same Compaq chart. Notice how much easier it was to spot the downturn in October 1997.*

troughs (an uptrend), the OBV line should do the same. If prices are trending lower, so should the OBV line. It's when the volume line fails to move in the same direction as prices that a divergence exists and warns of a possible trend reversal.

Alternatives to OBV

The *on balance volume* line does its job reasonably well, but it has some shortcomings. For one thing, it assigns an entire day's volume a plus or minus value. Suppose a market closes up on the day by some minimal amount such as one or two tics. Is it reasonable to assign all of that day's activity a positive value? Or consider a situation where the market spends most of the day on the upside, but then closes slightly lower. Should all of that day's volume be given a negative value? To resolve these questions, technicians have experimented with many variations of OBV in an attempt to discover the true upside and downside volume.

One variation is to give greater weight to those days where the trend is the strongest. On an up day, for example, the volume is multiplied by the amount of the price gain. This technique still assigns positive and negative values, but gives greater weight to those days with greater price movement and reduces the impact of those days where the actual price change is minimal.

There are more sophisticated formulas that blend volume (and open interest) with price action. James Sibbet's Demand Index, for example, combines price and volume into a leading market indicator. The Herrick Payoff Index uses open interest to measure money flow. (See Appendix A for an explanation of both indicators.)

It should be noted that volume reporting in the stock market is much more useful than in the futures markets. Stock trading volume is reported immediately, while it is reported a day late for futures. Levels of upside and downside volume are also available for stocks, but not in futures. The availability of volume data for stocks on each price change during the day has facilitated an even more advanced indicator called Money Flow, developed by Laszlo Birinyi, Jr. This real-time version of OBV tracks the level of volume on each price change in order to determine if money is flowing into or out of a stock. This sophisticated calculation, however, requires a lot of computer power and isn't readily available to most traders.

These more sophisticated variations of OBV have basically the same intent—to determine whether the heavier volume is taking place on the upside (bullish) or the downside (bearish). Even with its simplicity, the OBV line still does a pretty good job of tracking the volume flow in a market—either in futures or stocks. And OBV is readily available on most charting software. Most charting packages even allow you to plot the OBV line right over the price data for even easier comparison. (See Figures 7.7 and 7.8.)

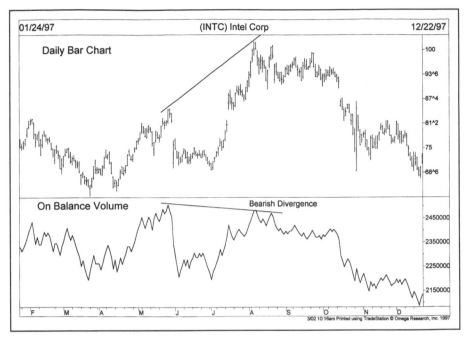

Figure 7.7   *An excellent example of how a bearish divergence between the on balance volume line (bottom) and the price of Intel correctly warned of a major downturn.*

Other Volume Limitations in Futures

We've already mentioned the problem of the one day lag in reporting futures volume. There is also the relatively awkward practice of using total volume numbers to analyze individual contracts instead of each contract's actual volume. There are good reasons for using total volume. But how does one deal with situations when some contracts close higher and others lower in the same futures market on the same day? *Limit* days produce other problems. Days when markets are locked *limit up* usually produce very light volume. This is a sign of strength as the numbers of buyers so overwhelm the sellers that prices reach the maximum trading limit and cease trading. According to the traditional rules of interpretation, light volume on a rally is bearish. The light volume on *limit* days is a violation of that principle and can distort OBV numbers.

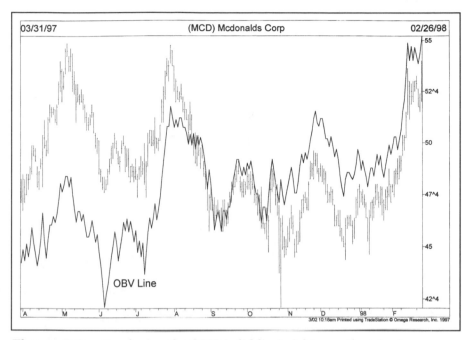

Figure 7.8   *Overlaying the OBV (solid line) right over the price bars makes for easier comparison between price and volume. This chart of McDonalds shows the OBV line leading the price higher and warning in advance of the bullish breakout.*

Even with these limitations, however, volume analysis can still be used in the futures markets, and the technical trader would be well advised to keep a watchful eye on volume indications.

INTERPRETATION OF OPEN INTEREST IN FUTURES

The rules for interpreting open interest changes are similar to those for volume, but require additional explanation.

1. With prices advancing in an uptrend and total open interest increasing, *new money is flowing into the market reflecting aggressive new buying, and is considered bullish.* (See Figure 7.9.)

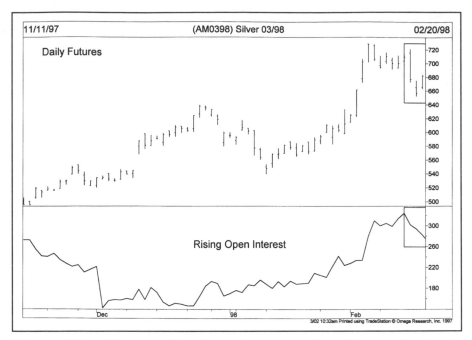

Figure 7.9   *The uptrend in silver prices was confirmed by a similar rise in the open interest line. The boxes to the right show some normal liquidation of outstanding contracts as prices start to correct downward.*

2. If, however, prices are rising and open interest declines, *the rally is being caused primarily by short covering* (holders of losing short positions being forced to cover those positions). *Money is leaving rather than entering the market.* This action is considered bearish because the uptrend will probably run out of steam once the necessary short covering has been completed. (See Figure 7.10.)

3. With prices in a downtrend and open interest rising, the technician knows that *new money is flowing into the market, reflecting aggressive new short selling.* This action increases the odds that the downtrend will continue and is considered bearish. (See Figure 7.11.)

4. If, however, total open interest is declining along with declining prices, *the price decline is being caused by discour-*

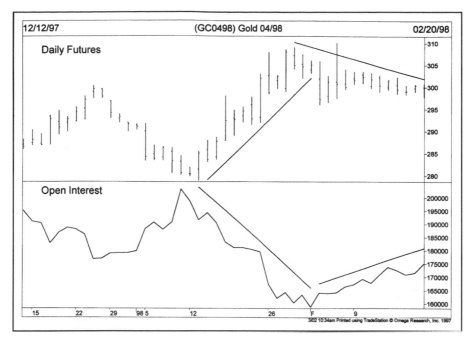

Figure 7.10 *An example of a weak price rebound in gold futures. The price rise is accompanied by falling open interest, while the price decline shows rising open interest. A strong trend would see open interest trending with price, not against it.*

aged or losing longs being forced to liquidate their positions. This action is believed to indicate a strengthening technical situation because the downtrend will probably end once open interest has declined sufficiently to show that most losing longs have completed their selling.

Let's summarize these four points:

1. *Rising open interest in an uptrend is bullish.*
2. *Declining open interest in an uptrend is bearish.*
3. *Rising open interest in a downtrend is bearish.*
4. *Declining open interest in a downtrend is bullish.*

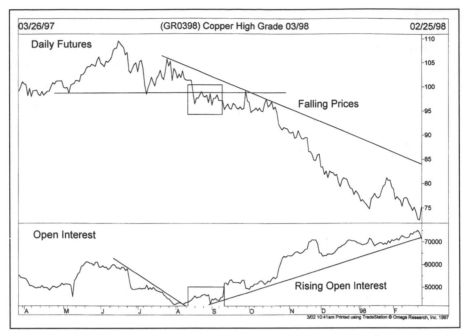

Figure 7.11   *The downturn in copper during the summer of 1997 and the subsequent price decline was accompanied by rising open interest. Rising open interest during a price decline is bearish because it reflects aggressive short selling.*

Other Situations Where Open Interest Is Important

In addition to the preceding tendencies, there are other market situations where a study of open interest can prove useful.

   1. Toward the end of major market moves, where open interest has been increasing throughout the price trend, *a leveling off or decline in open interest is often an early warning of a change in trend.*

   2. *A high open interest figure at market tops can be considered bearish if the price drop is very sudden.* This means that all of the new longs established near the end of the uptrend now have losing positions. Their forced liquidation will keep prices under pressure until the open interest has declined sufficiently. As an exam-

ple, let's assume that an uptrend has been in effect for some time. Over the past month, open interest has increased noticeably. Remember that every new open interest contract has one new long and one new short. Suddenly, prices begin to drop sharply and fall below the lowest price set over the past month. Every single new long established during that month now has a loss.

The forced liquidation of those longs keeps prices under pressure until they have all been liquidated. Worse still, their forced selling often begins to feed on itself and, as prices are pushed even lower, causes additional margin selling by other longs and intensifies the new price decline. As a corollary to the preceding point, *an unusually high open interest in a bull market is a danger signal.*

3. *If open interest builds up noticeably during a sideways consolidation or a horizontal trading range, the ensuing price move intensifies once the breakout occurs.* This only stands to reason. The market is in a period of indecision. No one is sure which direction the trend breakout will take. The increase in open interest, however, tells us that a lot of traders are taking positions in anticipation of the breakout. Once that breakout does occur, a lot of traders are going to be caught on the wrong side of the market.

Let's assume we've had a three month trading range and that the open interest has jumped by 10,000 contracts. This means that 10,000 new long positions and 10,000 new short positions have been taken. Prices then break out on the upside and new three month highs are established. Because prices are trading at the highest point in three months, every single short position (all 10,000 of them) initiated during the previous three months now shows a loss. The scramble to cover those losing shorts naturally causes additional upside pressure on prices, producing even more panic. Prices remain strong until all or most of those 10,000 short positions have been offset by buying into the market strength. If the breakout had been to the downside, then it would have been the longs doing the scrambling.

The early stage of any new trend immediately following a breakout is usually fueled by forced liquidation by those caught on the wrong side of the market. The more traders caught on the wrong side (manifested in the high open interest), the more severe the response to a sudden adverse market move. On a more positive note, the new trend is further aided by those on the right side of the market whose judgment has been vindicated, and who are now using accumulated paper profits to finance additional positions. It can be seen why *the greater the increase in open interest during a trading range (or any price formation for that matter), the greater the potential for the subsequent price move.*

4. *Increasing open interest at the completion of a price pattern is viewed as added confirmation of a reliable trend signal.* The breaking of the *neckline,* for example, of a *head and shoulders* bottom is more convincing if the breakout occurs on increasing open interest along with the heavier volume. The analyst has to be careful here. Because the impetus following the initial trend signal is often caused by those on the wrong side of the market, *sometimes the open interest dips slightly at the beginning of a new trend.* This initial dip in the open interest can mislead the unwary chart reader, and argues against focusing too much attention on the open interest changes over the very short term.

SUMMARY OF VOLUME AND OPEN INTEREST RULES

Let's summarize some of the more important elements of price, volume, and open interest.

1. Volume is used in all markets; open interest mainly in futures.
2. Only the *total* volume and open interest are used for futures.
3. Increasing volume (and open interest) indicate that the current price trend will probably continue.
4. Declining volume (and open interest) suggest that the price trend may be changing.
5. Volume precedes price. Changes in buying or selling pressure are often detected in volume before price.
6. On balance volume (OBV), or some variation thereof, can be used to more accurately measure the direction of volume pressure.

7. Within an uptrend, a sudden leveling off or decline in open interest often warns of a change in trend. (This applies only to futures.)

8. Very high open interest at market tops is dangerous and can intensify downside pressure. (This applies only to futures.)

9. A buildup in open interest during consolidation periods intensifies the ensuing breakout. (This applies only to futures.)

10. Increases in volume (and open interest) help confirm the resolution of price patterns or any other significant chart developments that signal the beginning of a new trend.

BLOWOFFS AND SELLING CLIMAXES

One final situation not covered so far that deserves mention is the type of dramatic market action that often takes place at tops and bottoms—*blowoffs* and *selling climaxes*. *Blowoffs* occur at major market tops and *selling climaxes* at bottoms. In futures, blowoffs are often accompanied by a drop in open interest during the final rally. In the case of a blowoff at market tops, prices suddenly begin to rally sharply after a long advance, accompanied by a large jump in trading activity and then peak abruptly. (See Figure 7.12.) In a selling climax bottom, prices suddenly drop sharply on heavy trading activity and rebound as quickly. (Refer back to Figure 4.22c.)

COMMITMENTS OF TRADERS REPORT

Our treatment of open interest would not be complete without mentioning the *Commitments of Traders (COT) Report,* and how it is used by futures technicians as a forecasting tool. The report is released by the Commodity Futures Trading Commission (CFTC) twice a month—a mid-month report and one at month's end. The

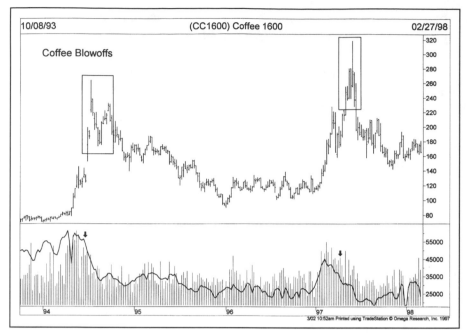

Figure 7.12 *A couple of blowoff tops in coffee futures. In both cases, prices rallied sharply on heavy volume. The negative warnings came from the decline in open interest (solid line) during both rallies (see arrows).*

report breaks down the open interest numbers into three categories—large hedgers, large speculators, and small traders. The large hedgers, also called commercials, use the futures markets primarily for hedging purposes. Large speculators include the large commodity funds, who rely primarily on mechanical trend-following systems. The final category of small traders includes the general public, who trade in much smaller amounts.

WATCH THE COMMERCIALS

The guiding principle in analyzing the Commitments Report is the belief that the large commercial hedgers are usually right, while the traders are usually wrong. That being the case, the idea is to place yourself in the same positions as the hedgers and in the opposite positions of the two categories of traders. For example, a bullish signal at a market bottom would occur when the commercials are heavily net long while the large and small traders are heavily net short. In a rising market, a warning signal of a possible top would take place when the large and small traders become heavily net long at the same time that the commercials are becoming heavily net short.

NET TRADER POSITIONS

It is possible to chart the trends of the three market groups, and to use those trends to spot extremes in their positions. One way to do that is to study the net trader positions published in *Futures Charts* (Published by Commodity Trend Service, PO Box 32309, Palm Beach Gardens, FL 33420). That charting service plots three lines that show the net trader positions for all three groups on a weekly price chart for each market going back four years. By providing four years of data, historical comparisons are easily done. Nick Van Nice, the publisher of that chart service, looks for situations where the commercials are at one extreme, and the two categories of traders at the other, to find buying and selling opportunities (as shown in Figures 7.13 and 7.14). Even if you don't use the COT Report as a primary input in your trading decisions, it's not a bad idea to keep an eye on what those three groups are doing.

OPEN INTEREST IN OPTIONS

Our coverage of open interest has concentrated on the *futures* markets. Open interest plays an important role in *options* trading as well. Open interest figures are published each day for *put* and *call* options on futures markets, stock averages, industry indexes, and individual stocks. While open interest in options may not be interpreted in exactly the same way as in futures, it tells us essentially the same thing—where the interest is and the liquidity. Some option traders compare *call* open interest (bulls) to *put* open interest (bears) in order to measure market sentiment. Others use option volume.

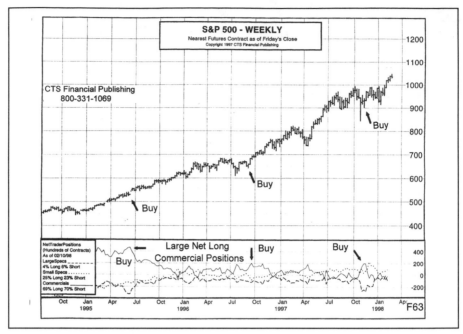

Figure 7.13 *This weekly chart of S&P 500 futures shows three buy signals (see arrows). The lines along the bottom show the commercials (solid line) heavily net long and the large speculators (dashed line) heavily net short at each buy signal.*

PUT/CALL RATIOS

Volume figures for the options markets are used essentially the same way as in futures and stocks—that is, they tell us the degree of buying or selling pressure in a given market. Volume figures in options are broken down into *call* volume (bullish) and *put* volume (bearish). By monitoring the volume in calls versus puts, we are able to determine the degree of bullishness or bearishness in a market. One of the primary uses of volume data in options trading is the construction of put/call volume ratios. When options traders are bullish, call volume exceeds put volume and the put/call ratio falls. A bearish attitude is reflected in heavier put volume and a higher put/call ratio. The put/call ratio is usually viewed as a contrary indicator. A very high ratio signals an oversold market. A very low ratio is a negative warning of an overbought market.

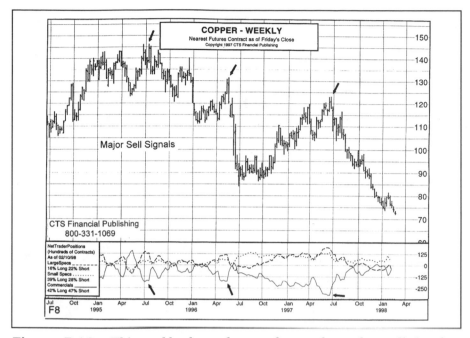

Figure 7.14 *This weekly chart of copper futures shows three sell signals marked by the arrows. Each sell signal shows net long positions by the two categories of speculators and a net short position by the commercials. The commercials were right.*

COMBINE OPTION SENTIMENT WITH TECHNICALS

Options traders use open interest and volume put/call figures to determine extremes in bullish or bearish sentiment. These sentiment readings work best when combined with technical measures such as support, resistance, and the trend of the underlying market. Since timing is so crucial in options, most option traders are technically oriented.

CONCLUSION

That concludes our coverage of volume and open interest, at least for now. Volume analysis is used in all financial markets—futures, options, and stocks. Open interest applies only to futures and options. But, since futures and options are traded on so many stock market vehicles, some understanding of how open interest works can be useful in all three financial arenas. In most of our discussions so far, we've concentrated on daily bar charts. The next step is to broaden our time horizon and to learn how to apply the tools we've learned to weekly and monthly charts in order to perform long range trend analysis. We'll accomplish that in the next chapter.

Long Term Charts

INTRODUCTION

Of all the charts utilized by the market technician for forecasting and trading the financial markets, the *daily* bar chart is by far the most popular. The daily bar chart usually covers a period of only six to nine months. However, because most traders confine their interest to relatively short term market action, daily bar charts have gained wide acceptance as the primary working tool of the chartist.

    The average trader's dependence on these daily charts, however, and the preoccupation with short term market behavior, cause many to overlook a very useful and rewarding area of price charting—*the use of weekly and monthly charts for longer range trend analysis and forecasting.*

    The daily bar chart covers a relatively short period of time in the life of any market. A thorough trend analysis of a market, however, should include some consideration of how the daily market price is moving in relation to its long range trend structure. To accomplish that task, *longer range charts must be employed.* Whereas on the daily bar chart each bar represents one day's price action, on the weekly and monthly charts each price bar represents one week's and one month's price action, respectively. *The purpose of weekly and monthly charts is to compress price action in such a way that the time horizon can be greatly expanded and much longer time periods can be studied.*

THE IMPORTANCE OF LONGER RANGE PERSPECTIVE

Long range price charts provide a perspective on the market trend that is impossible to achieve with the use of daily charts alone. During our introduction to the technical philosophy in Chapter 1, it was pointed out that one of the greatest advantages of chart analysis is the application of its principles to virtually any time dimension, including long range forecasting. We also addressed the fallacy, espoused by some, that technical analysis should be limited to short term "timing" with longer range forecasting left to the fundamental analyst.

The accompanying charts will demonstrate that the principles of technical analysis—including trend analysis, support and resistance levels, trendlines, percentage retracements, and price patterns—lend themselves quite well to the analysis of long range price movements. *Anyone who is not consulting these longer range charts is missing an enormous amount of valuable price information.*

CONSTRUCTION OF CONTINUATION CHARTS FOR FUTURES

The average futures contract has a trading life of about a year and a half before expiration. This *limited life* feature poses some obvious problems for the technician interested in constructing a long range chart going back several years. Stock market technicians don't have this problem. Charts are readily available for individual common stocks and the market averages from the inception of trading. How then does the futures technician construct longer range charts for contracts that are constantly expiring?

The answer is the *continuation* chart. Notice the emphasis on the word "continuation." The technique most commonly employed is simply to link a number of contracts together to provide continuity. When one contract expires, another one is used. In order to accomplish this, the simplest method, and the one used by most chart services, is to *always use the price of the nearest expiring contract.* When that nearest expiring contract stops trading, the next in line becomes the nearest contract and is the one plotted.

Other Ways to Construct Continuation Charts

The technique of linking prices of the nearest expiring contracts is relatively simple and does solve the problem of providing price continuity. However, there are some problems with that method. Sometimes the expiring contract may be trading at a significant premium or discount to the next contract, and the changeover to the new contract may cause a sudden price drop or jump on the chart. Another potential distortion is the extreme volatility experienced by some spot contracts just before expiration.

Futures technicians have devised many ways to deal with these occasional distortions. Some will stop plotting the nearest contract a month or two before it expires to avoid the volatility in the spot month. Others will avoid using the nearest contract altogether and will instead chart the second or third contract. Another method is to chart the contract with the highest open interest on the theory that that delivery month is the truest representation of market value.

Continuation charts can also be constructed by linking specific calendar months. For example, a November soybean continuation chart would combine only the historic data provided by each successive year's November soybean contract. (This technique of linking specific delivery months was favored by W.D. Gann.) Some chartists go even further by averaging the prices of several contracts, or constructing indices that attempt to smooth the changeover by making adjustments in the price premium or discount.

THE PERPETUAL CONTRACT™

An innovative solution to the problem of price continuity was developed by Robert Pelletier, president of Commodity Systems, Inc., a commodity and stock data service (CSI. 200 W. Palmetto Park Road, Boca Raton, FL 33422), called the *Perpetual Contract.*™ ("Perpetual Contract™ " is a registered trademark of that firm.)

The purpose of the Perpetual Contract™ is to provide years of futures price history in one continuous time series. That is accomplished by constructing a time series based on a constant forward time period. For example, the series would determine a value three months or six months into the future. The time period varies and can be chosen by the user. The Perpetual Contract™ is constructed by taking a weighted average of two futures contracts that surround the time period desired.

The value for the Perpetual Contract™ is not an actual price, but a weighted average of two other prices. The main advantage of the Perpetual Contract™ is that it eliminates the need for using only the nearest expiring contract and smoothes out the price series by eliminating the distortions that can take place during the transition between delivery months. For chart analysis purposes, the nearest-month continuation charts published by chart services are more than adequate. A continuous price series, however, is more useful for back-testing trading systems and indicators. A more complete explanation of ways to construct continuous futures contracts is provided by Greg Morris in Appendix D.

LONG TERM TRENDS DISPUTE RANDOMNESS

The most striking features of long range charts is that not only are trends very clearly defined, but that long range trends often last for years. Imagine making a forecast based on one of these long range trends, and not having to change that forecast for several years!

The persistence of long range trends raises another interesting question that should be mentioned—the question of randomness. While technical analysts do not subscribe to the theory that market action is random and unpredictable, it seems safe to observe that whatever randomness does exist in price action is probably a phenomenon of the very short term. *The persistence of existing trends over long periods of time, in many cases for years, is a compelling argument against the claims of Random Walk Theorists that prices are serially independent and that past price action has no effect on future price action.*

PATTERNS ON CHARTS: WEEKLY AND MONTHLY REVERSALS

Price patterns appear on the long range charts, which are interpreted in the same way as on the daily charts. *Double tops and bottoms* are very prominent on these charts, as are head and shoulder reversals. *Triangles,* which are usually continuation patterns, are frequently seen.

Another pattern that occurs quite frequently on these charts is the *weekly and monthly reversal.* For example, on the monthly chart, a new monthly high followed by a close below the previous month's close often represents a significant turning point, especially if it occurs near a major support or resistance area. Weekly reversals are quite frequent on the weekly charts. These patterns are the equivalent of the *key reversal day* on the daily charts, except that on the long range charts these reversals carry a great deal more significance.

LONG TERM TO SHORT TERM CHARTS

It's especially important to appreciate the order in which price charts should be studied in performing a thorough trend analysis. The proper order to follow in chart analysis is to begin with the long range and gradually work to the near term. The reason for this should become apparent as one works with the different time dimensions. If the analyst begins with only the near term picture, he or she is forced to constantly revise conclusions as more price data is considered. A thorough analysis of a daily chart may have to be completely redone after looking at the long range charts. By starting with the big picture, going back as far as 20 years, all data to be considered are already included in the chart and a proper perspective is achieved. Once the analyst knows where the market is from a longer range perspective, he or she gradually "zeros in" on the shorter term.

The first chart to be considered is the 20 year monthly chart. The analyst looks for the more obvious chart patterns, major trendlines, or the proximity of major support or resistance levels. He or she then consults the most recent five years on the weekly chart, repeating the same process. Having done that, the analyst narrows his or her focus to the last six to nine months of market action on the daily bar chart, thus going from the "macro" to the "micro" approach. If the trader wants to proceed further, intraday charts can then be consulted for an even more microscopic study of recent action.

WHY SHOULD LONG RANGE CHARTS BE ADJUSTED FOR INFLATION?

A question often raised concerning long term charts is whether or not historic price levels seen on the charts should be adjusted for inflation. After all, the argument goes, do these long range peaks and troughs have any validity if not adjusted to reflect the changes in the value of the U.S. dollar? This is a point of some controversy among analysts.

I do not believe that any adjustment is necessary on these long range charts for a number of reasons. The main reason is my belief that the markets themselves have already made the necessary adjustments. A currency declining in value causes commodities quoted in that currency to increase in value. The declining value of the dollar, therefore, would contribute to rising commodity prices. A rising dollar would cause the price of most commodities to fall.

The tremendous price gains in commodity markets during the 1970s and declining prices in the 1980s and 1990s are classic examples of inflation at work. To have suggested during the 1970s that commodity price levels that had doubled and tripled in price should then be adjusted to reflect rising inflation would make no sense at all. The rising commodity markets already were a manifestation of that inflation. Declining commodity markets since

187

the 1980s reflect a long period of disinflation. Should we take the price of gold, which is now worth less than half of its value in 1980, and adjust it to reflect the lower inflation rate? The market has already taken care of that.

The final point in this debate goes to the heart of the technical theory, which states that price action discounts everything, even inflation. All financial markets adjust to periods of inflation and deflation and to changes in currency values. The real answer to whether long range charts should be adjusted for inflation lies in the charts themselves. Many markets fail at historic resistance levels set several years earlier and then bounce off support levels not seen in several years. It's also clear that falling inflation since the early 1980s has helped support bull markets in bonds and stocks. It would seem that those markets have already made their own inflation adjustment. (See Figure 8.1.)

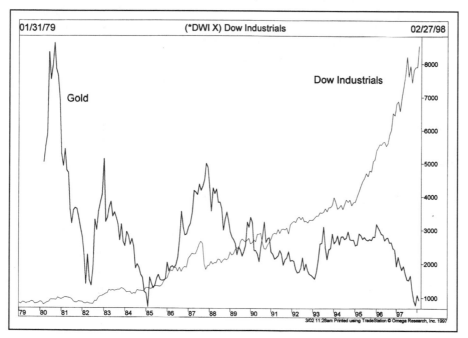

Figure 8.1 *The gold price peak in 1980 ushered in two decades of low inflation. Low inflation normally causes falling gold prices and rising stock prices as this chart shows. Why adjust the charts again for inflation? It's already been done.*

LONG TERM CHARTS NOT INTENDED FOR TRADING PURPOSES

Long term charts are not meant for trading purposes. A distinction has to be made between market *analysis* for forecasting purposes and the *timing* of market commitments. Long term charts are useful in the analytical process to help determine the major trend and price objectives. They are not suitable, however, for the timing of entry and exit points and should not be used for that purpose. For that more sensitive task, daily and intraday charts should be utilized.

EXAMPLES OF LONG TERM CHARTS

The following pages contain examples of long term weekly and monthly charts (Figures 8.2–8.12). The drawings on the charts are limited to long term support and resistance levels, trendlines, percentage retracements, weekly reversals, and an occasional price pattern. Be aware, however, that anything that can be done on a daily chart can also be done on a weekly or monthly. We'll show you later in the book how the application of various technical indicators to these long term charts is accomplished, and how signals on weekly charts become valuable filters for shorter term timing decisions. Remember also that *semilog* chart scaling becomes more valuable when studying long range price trends.

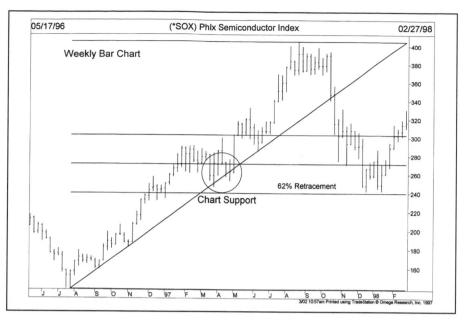

Figure 8.2 *This chart of semiconductor stocks shows the valuable perspective of a weekly chart. The late 1997 price fall stopped right at the 62% retracement level and bounced off chart support formed the previous spring (see circle).*

Figure 8.3 *The early 1998 bottom in General Motors began right at the trendline drawn along the 1995-1996 lows. That's why it's a good idea to track weekly charts.*

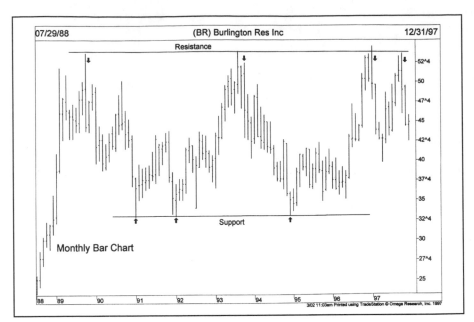

Figure 8.4 *This monthly chart shows the 1997 rally in Burlington Resources stopping right at the same level that stopped the 1989 and 1993 rallies. The 1995 bottom was at the same level as the 1991 bottom. Who says charts don't have a memory?*

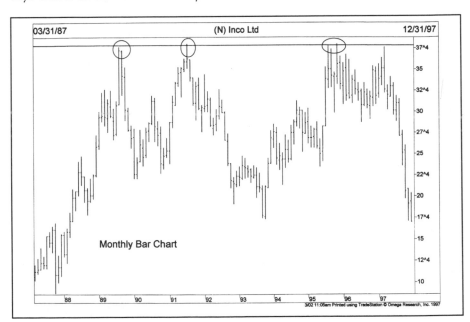

Figure 8.5 *An investor in Inco Ltd. during the 1997 rally could have benefited from the knowledge that the 1989, 1991, and 1995 tops occurred right at 38.*

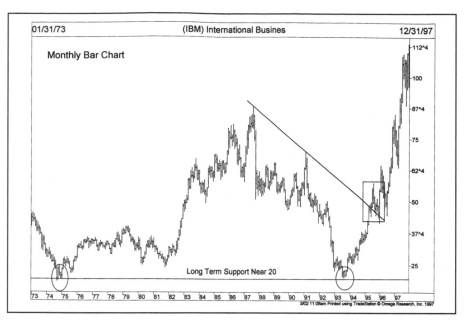

Figure 8.6 *Do long term charts matter? The 1993 bottom in IBM was at the same level as the bottom formed 20 years earlier in 1974. The break of an 8 year down trendline (see box) in 1995 confirmed the new major uptrend.*

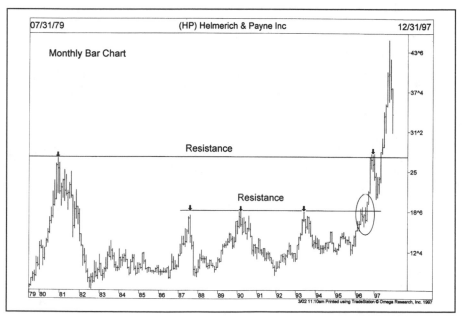

Figure 8.7 *Helmerich & Payne finally broke out above 19 in 1996 after failing in 1987, 1990, and 1993. The late 1996 pullback at 28 occurred near the 1980 peak.*

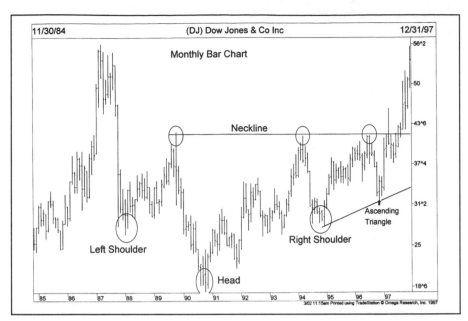

Figure 8.8 *This monthly chart of Dow Jones shows a head and shoulders bottom forming for 10 years from 1988 to 1997. The right shoulder also has the shape of a bullish ascending triangle. The breakout over the neckline at 42 completed the bottom.*

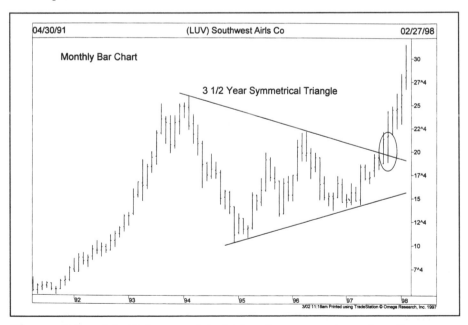

Figure 8.9 *A bullish symmetrical triangle was easy to spot on the monthly chart of Southwest Airlines. But you probably wouldn't have spotted it on a daily chart.*

Figure 8.10 *The 1994 bottom in the Dow Utilities bounced off a trend-line lasting 20 years. There are those who claim that past price action has no bearing on the future. If you still believe that, go back and look at these long term charts again.*

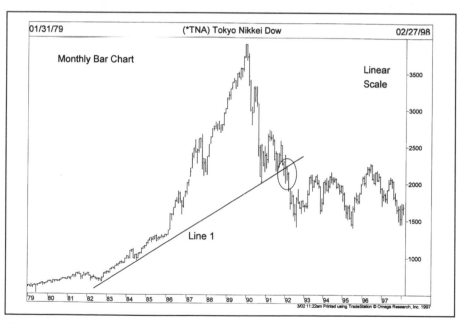

Figure 8.11 *On this linear-scaled chart of the Japanese stock market, the long term up trendline (line 1) drawn under the 1982 and 1984 lows was broken in early 1992 (see circle) near 22,000. That was two years after the actual peak.*

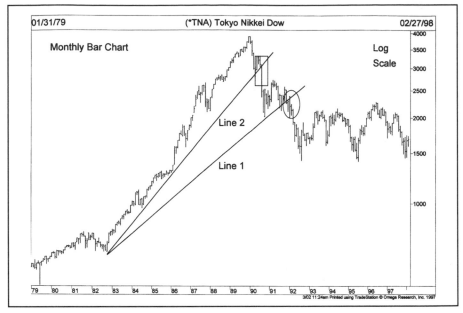

Figure 8.12 *The same Japanese chart from Figure 8.11 using log scaling. Line 1 is the trendline from the previous figure. The steeper line 2 was broken in mid-1990 (see box) at 30,000. Up trendlines on log charts are broken sooner than linear up trendlines.*

Moving Averages

INTRODUCTION

The *moving average* is one of the most versatile and widely used of all technical indicators. Because of the way it is constructed and the fact that it can be so easily quantified and tested, it is the basis for many mechanical trend-following systems in use today.

Chart analysis is largely subjective and difficult to test. As a result, chart analysis does not lend itself that well to computerization. Moving average rules, by contrast, can easily be programmed into a computer, which then generates specific buy and sell signals. While two technicians may disagree as to whether a given price pattern is a *triangle* or a *wedge*, or whether the volume pattern favors the bull or bear side, moving average trend signals are precise and not open to debate.

Let's begin by defining what a *moving average* is. As the second word implies, it is an *average* of a certain body of data. For example, if a 10 day average of closing prices is desired, the prices for the last 10 days are added up and the total is divided by 10. The term *moving* is used because only the latest 10 days' prices are used in the calculation. Therefore, the body of data to be averaged (the last 10 closing prices) moves forward with each new trading day. The most common way to calculate the moving average is to work from the total of the last 10 days' closing prices. Each day the new close is added to the total and the close 11 days back is subtracted. The new total is then divided by the number of days (10). (See Figure 9.1a.)

The above example deals with a simple 10 day moving average of closing prices. There are, however, other types of moving averages that are not simple. There are also many questions as to the best way to employ the moving average. For example, how many days should be averaged? Should a short term or a long term average be used? Is there a *best* moving average for all markets or for each individual market? Is the closing price the best price to average? Would it be better to use more than one average?

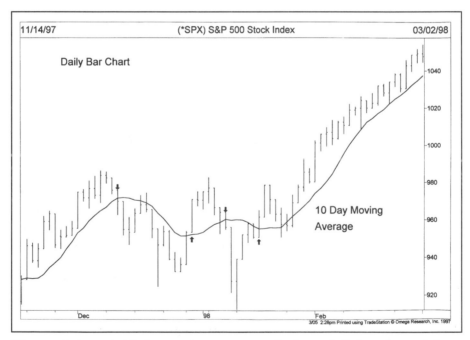

Figure 9.1a   *A 10 day moving average applied to a daily bar chart of the S&P 500. Prices crossed the average line several times (see arrows) before finally turning higher. Prices stayed above the average during the subsequent rally.*

Which type of average works better—a simple, linearly weighted or exponentially smoothed? Are there times when moving averages work better than others?

There are many questions to be considered when using moving averages. We'll address many of these questions in this chapter and show examples of some of the more common usages of the moving average.

THE MOVING AVERAGE: A SMOOTHING DEVICE WITH A TIME LAG

The *moving average* is essentially a trend following device. Its purpose is to identify or signal that a new trend has begun or that an old trend has ended or reversed. Its purpose is to track the progress of the trend. It might be viewed as a curving trendline. It does not, however, predict market action in the same sense that standard chart analysis attempts to do. The moving average is a follower, not a leader. It never anticipates; it only reacts. The moving average follows a market and tells us that a trend has begun, but only after the fact.

The moving average is a smoothing device. By averaging the price data, a smoother line is produced, making it much easier to view the underlying trend. By its very nature, however, the moving average line also lags the market action. A shorter moving average, such as a 20 day average, would hug the price action more closely than a 200 day average. The time lag is reduced with the shorter averages, but can never be completely eliminated. Shorter term averages are more sensitive to the price action, whereas longer range averages are less sensitive. In certain types of markets, it is more advantageous to use a shorter average and, at other times, a longer and less sensitive average proves more useful. (See Figure 9.1b.)

Which Prices to Average

We have been using the closing price in all of our examples so far. However, while the closing price is considered to be the most

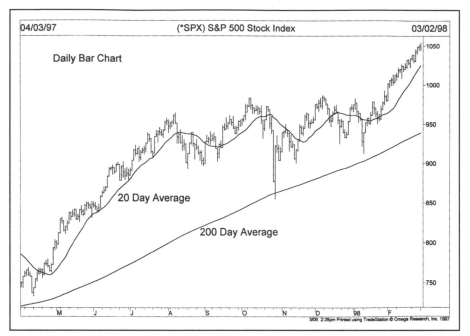

04/03/97   (*SPX) S&P 500 Stock Index   03/02/98

Daily Bar Chart

20 Day Average

200 Day Average

Figure 9.1b   *A comparison of a 20 day and a 200 day moving average. During the sideways period from August to January, prices crossed the shorter average several times. However, they remained above the 200 day average throughout the entire period.*

important price of the trading day and the price most commonly used in moving average construction, the reader should be aware that some technicians prefer to use other prices. Some prefer to use a *midpoint* value, which is arrived at by dividing the day's range by two.

Others include the closing price in their calculation by adding the high, low, and closing prices together and dividing the sum by three. Still others prefer to construct *price bands* by averaging the high and low prices separately. The result is two separate moving average lines that act as a sort of volatility buffer or neutral zone. Despite these variations, the closing price is still the price most commonly used for moving average analysis and is the price that we'll be focusing most of our attention on in this chapter.

The Simple Moving Average

The *simple moving average,* or the arithmetic mean, is the type used by most technical analysts. But there are some who question its usefulness on two points. The first criticism is that only the period covered by the average (the last 10 days, for example) is taken into account. The second criticism is that the simple moving average gives equal weight to each day's price. In a 10 day average, the last day receives the same weight as the first day in the calculation. Each day's price is assigned a 10% weighting. In a 5 day average, each day would have an equal 20% weighting. Some analysts believe that a heavier weighting should be given to the more recent price action.

The Linearly Weighted Moving Average

In an attempt to correct the weighting problem, some analysts employ a *linearly weighted moving average.* In this calculation, the closing price of the 10th day (in the case of a 10 day average) would be multiplied by 10, the ninth day by nine, the eighth day by eight, and so on. The greater weight is therefore given to the more recent closings. The total is then divided by the sum of the multipliers (55 in the case of the l0 day average: $10 + 9 + 8 + \ldots + 1$). However, the linearly weighted average still does not address the problem of including only the price action covered by the length of the average itself.

The Exponentially Smoothed
Moving Average

This type of average addresses both of the problems associated with the simple moving average. First, the exponentially smoothed average assigns a greater weight to the more recent data. Therefore, it is a weighted moving average. But while it assigns lesser importance to past price data, it does include in its calculation all of the data in the life of the instrument. In addition, the user is able to adjust the weighting to give greater or lesser weight to the most recent day's price. This is done by assigning a percentage value to the last day's price, which is added to a percentage of the previous day's value. The sum of both percentage values adds up to 100. For example, the last day's price could be assigned a value of 10% (.10), which is added to the previous day's value of 90% (.90). That gives the last day 10% of the total weighting. That would be the equivalent of a 20 day average. By giving the last day's price a smaller value of 5% (.05), lesser weight is given to the last day's data and the average is less sensitive. That would be the equivalent of a 40 day moving average. (See Figure 9.2.)

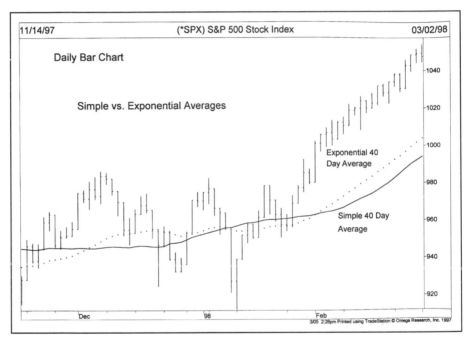

Figure 9.2 *The 40 day exponential moving average (dotted line) is more sensitive than the simple arithmetic 40 day moving average (solid line).*

The computer makes this all very easy for you. You just have to choose the number of days you want in the moving average—10, 20, 40, etc. Then select the type of average you want—simple, weighted, or exponentially smoothed. You can also select as many averages as you want—one, two, or three.

The Use of One Moving Average

The simple moving average is the one most commonly used by technicians, and is the one that we'll be concentrating on. Some traders use just one moving average to generate trend signals. The moving average is plotted on the bar chart in its appropriate trading day along with that day's price action. When the closing price moves above the moving average, a buy signal is generated. A sell signal is given when prices move below the moving average. For added confirmation, some technicians also like to see the moving average line itself turn in the direction of the price crossing. (See Figure 9.3.)

If a very short term average is employed (a 5 or 10 day), the average tracks prices very closely and several crossings occur. This

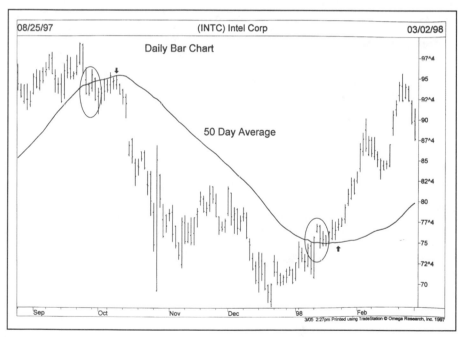

Figure 9.3 *Prices fell below the 50 day average during October (see left circle). The sell signal is stronger when the moving average also turns down (see left arrow). The buy signal during January was confirmed when the average itself turned higher.*

action can be either good or bad. The use of a very sensitive average produces more trades (with higher commission costs) and results in many false signals (whipsaws). If the average is too sensitive, some of the short term random price movement (or "noise") activates bad trend signals.

While the shorter average generates more false signals, it has the advantage of giving trend signals earlier in the move. It stands to reason that the more sensitive the average, the earlier the signals will be. So there is a tradeoff at work here. The trick is to find the average that is sensitive enough to generate early signals, but insensitive enough to avoid most of the random "noise." (See Figure 9.4.)

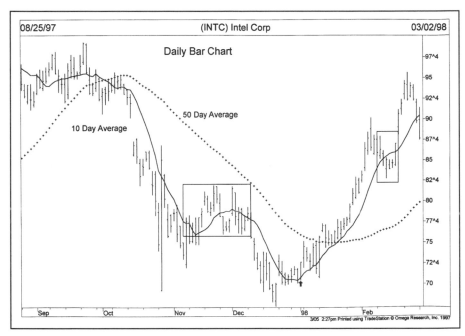

Figure 9.4   *A shorter average gives earlier signals. The longer average is slower, but more reliable. The 10 day turned up first at the bottom. But it also gave a premature buy signal during November and an untimely sell signal during February (see boxes).*

Let's carry the above comparison a step further. While the longer average performs better while the trend remains in motion, it "gives back" a lot more when the trend reverses. The very insensitivity of the longer average (the fact that it trailed the trend from a greater distance), which kept it from getting tangled up in short term corrections during the trend, works against the trader when the trend actually reverses. Therefore, we'll add another corollary here: The longer averages work better as long as the trend remains in force, but a shorter average is better when the trend is in the process of reversing.

It becomes clearer, therefore, that the use of one moving average alone has several disadvantages. It is usually more advantageous to employ two moving averages.

How to Use Two Averages to Generate Signals

This technique is called the *double crossover method.* This means that a buy signal is produced when the shorter average crosses above the longer. For example, two popular combinations are the 5 and 20 day averages and the 10 and 50 day averages. In the former, a buy signal occurs when the 5 day average crosses above the 20, and a sell signal when the 5 day moves below the 20. In the latter example, the 10 day crossing above the 50 signals an uptrend, and a downtrend takes place with the 10 slipping under the 50. This technique of using two averages together lags the market a bit more than the use of a single average but produces fewer whipsaws. (See Figures 9.5 and 9.6.)

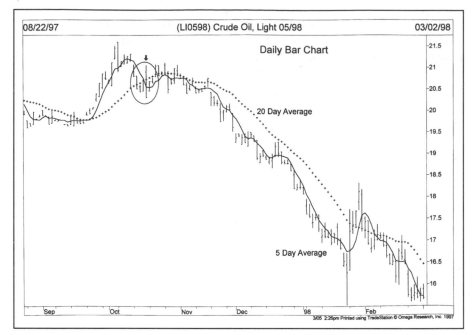

08/22/97   (LI0598) Crude Oil, Light 05/98   03/02/98

Daily Bar Chart

20 Day Average

5 Day Average

Figure 9.5   *The double crossover method uses two moving averages. The 5 and 20 day combination is popular with futures traders. The 5 day fell below the 20 day during October (see circle) and caught the entire downtrend in crude oil prices.*

The Use of Three Averages, or the Triple Crossover Method

That brings us to the *triple crossover method*. The most widely used triple crossover system is the popular *4-9-18-day moving average combination*. The 4-9-18 method is used mainly in futures trading. This concept was first mentioned by R.C. Allen in his 1972 book, *How to Build a Fortune in Commodities* and again later in a 1974 work by the same author, *How to Use the 4-Day, 9-Day and 18-Day Moving Averages to Earn Larger Profits from Commodities*. The 4-9-18-day system is a variation on the 5, 10, and 20 day moving average numbers, which are widely used in commodity circles. Many commercial chart services publish the 4-9-18-day moving averages. (Many charting software packages use the 4-9-18-day combination as their default values when plotting three averages.)

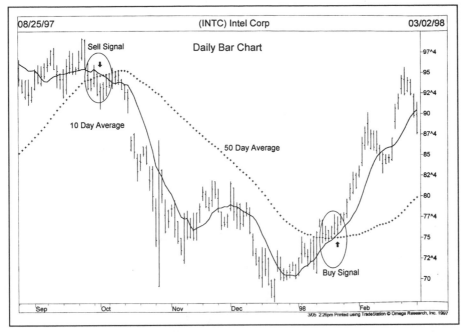

Figure 9.6 *Stock traders use 10 and 50 day moving averages. The 10 day fell below the 50 day in October (left circle), giving a timely sell signal. The bullish crossover in the other direction took place during January (lower circle).*

How to Use the 4-9-18-Day Moving Average System

It's already been explained that the shorter the moving average, the closer it follows the price trend. It stands to reason then that the shortest of the three averages—the 4 day—will follow the trend most closely, followed by the 9 day and then the 18. In an uptrend, therefore, the proper alignment would be for the 4 day average to be above the 9 day, which is above the 18 day average. In a downtrend, the order is reversed and the alignment is exactly the opposite. That is, the 4 day would be the lowest, followed by the 9 day and then the 18 day average. (See Figures 9.7a-b.)

A buying alert takes place in a downtrend when the 4 day crosses above both the 9 and the 18. A confirmed buy signal occurs when the 9 day then crosses above the 18. This places the

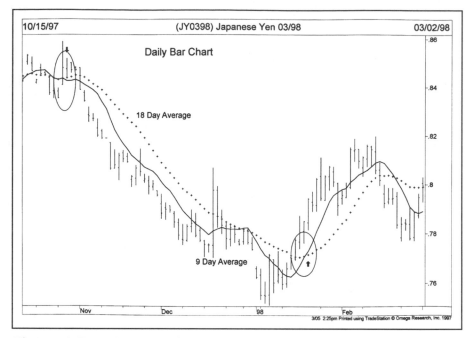

Figure 9.7a *Futures traders like the 9 and 18 day moving average combination. A sell signal was given in late October (first circle) when the 9 day fell below the 18. A buy signal was given in early 1998 when the 9 day crossed back above the 18 day.*

4 day over the 9 day which is over the 18 day. Some intermingling may occur during corrections or consolidations, but the general uptrend remains intact. Some traders may take profits during the intermingling process and some may use it as a buying opportunity. There is obviously a lot of room for flexibility here in applying the rules, depending on how aggressively one wants to trade.

When the uptrend reverses to the downside, the first thing that should take place is that the shortest (and most sensitive) average—the 4 day—dips below the 9 day and the 18 day. This is only a selling alert. Some traders, however, might use that initial crossing as reason enough to begin liquidating long positions. Then, if the next longer average—the 9 day—drops below the 18 day, a confirmed sell short signal is given.

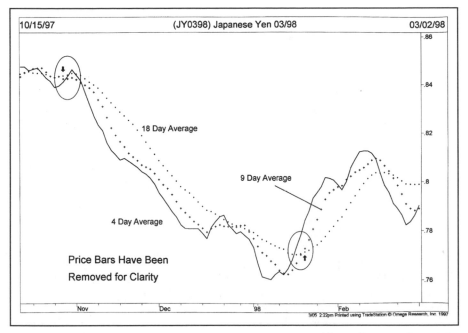

Figure 9.7b *The 4-9-18 day moving average combo is also popular with futures traders. At a bottom, the 4 day (solid line) turns up first and crosses the other two lines. Then the 9 day crosses over the 18 day (see circle), signaling a bottom.*

MOVING AVERAGE ENVELOPES

The usefulness of a single moving average can be enhanced by surrounding it with envelopes. *Percentage envelopes* can be used to help determine when a market has gotten overextended in either direction. In other words, they tell us when prices have strayed too far from their moving average line. In order to do this, the envelopes are placed at fixed percentages above and below the average. Shorter term traders, for example, often use 3% envelopes around a simple 21 day moving average. When prices reach one of the envelopes (3% from the average), the short term trend is considered to be overextended. For long range analysis, some possible combinations include 5% envelopes around a 10 week average or a 10% envelope around a 40 week average. (See Figures 9.8a-b.)

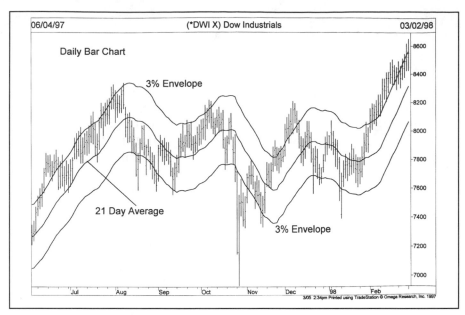

Figure 9.8a *3% envelopes placed around a 21 day moving average of the Dow. Moves outside the envelopes suggest an overextended stock market.*

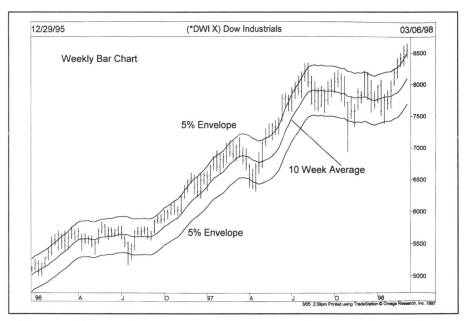

Figure 9.8b *For longer range analysis, 5% envelopes can be placed around a 10 week average. Moves outside the envelopes helped identify market extremes.*

BOLLINGER BANDS

This technique was developed by John Bollinger. Two trading bands are placed around a moving average similar to the envelope technique. Except that Bollinger Bands are placed two standard deviations above and below the moving average, which is usually 20 days. *Standard deviation* is a statistical concept that describes how prices are dispersed around an average value. Using two standard deviations ensures that 95% of the price data will fall between the two trading bands. As a rule, prices are considered to be overextended on the upside (overbought) when they touch the upper band. They are considered overextended on the downside (oversold) when they touch the lower band. (See Figures 9.9a-b.)

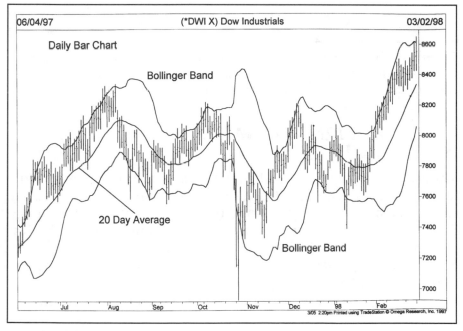

Figure 9.9a *Bollinger bands plotted around a 20 day moving average. During the sideways period from August to January, prices kept touching the outer bands. Once the uptrend resumed, prices traded between the upper band and 20 day average.*

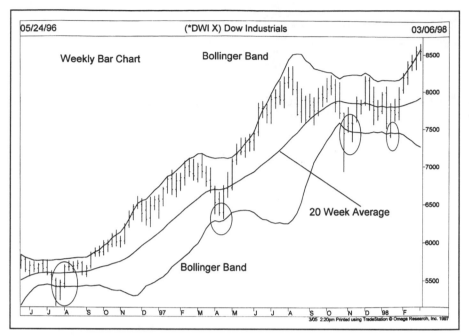

Figure 9.9b *Bollinger bands work on weekly charts as well, by using a 20 week average as the middle line. Each touch of the lower band (see circles) signaled an important market bottom and a buying opportunity.*

USING BOLLINGER BANDS AS TARGETS

The simplest way to use Bollinger Bands is to use the upper and lower bands as price targets. In other words, if prices bounce off the lower band and cross above the 20 day average, the upper band becomes the upper price target. A crossing below the 20 day average would identify the lower band as the downside target. In a strong uptrend, prices will usually fluctuate between the upper band and the 20 day average. In that case, a crossing below the 20 day average warns of a trend reversal to the downside.

BAND WIDTH
MEASURES VOLATILITY

Bollinger Bands differ from envelopes in one major way. Whereas the envelopes stay a *constant* percentage width apart, Bollinger Bands *expand* and *contract* based on the last 20 days' volatility. During a period of rising price volatility, the distance between the two bands will widen. Conversely, during a period of low market volatility, the distance between the two bands will contract. There is a tendency for the bands to alternate between expansion and contraction. When the bands are unusually far apart, that is often a sign that the current trend may be ending. When the distance between the two bands has narrowed too far, that is often a sign that a market may be about to initiate a new trend. Bollinger Bands can also be applied to weekly and monthly price charts by using 20 *weeks* and 20 *months* instead of 20 *days*. Bollinger Bands work best when combined with overbought/oversold oscillators that are explained in the next chapter. (See Appendix A for additional band techniques.)

Centering the Average

The more statistically correct way to plot a moving average is to *center* it. That means to place it in the middle of the time period it covers. A 10 day average, for example, would be placed five days back. A 20 day average would be plotted 10 days back in time. *Centering* the average, however, has the major flaw of producing much later trend change signals. Therefore, moving averages are usually placed at the end of the time period covered instead of the middle. The centering technique is used almost exclusively by cyclic analysts to isolate underlying market cycles.

MOVING AVERAGES TIED TO CYCLES

Many market analysts believe that *time cycles* play an important role in market movement. Because these time cycles are repetitive and can be measured, it is possible to determine the approximate times when market tops or bottoms will occur. Many different time cycles exist simultaneously, from a short term 5 day cycle to Kondratieff's long 54 year cycle. We'll delve more into this fascinating branch of technical analysis in Chapter 14.

The subject of cycles is introduced here only to make the point that there seems to be a relationship between the underlying cycles that affect a certain market and the correct moving averages to use. In other words, the moving averages can be adjusted to fit the dominant cycles in each market.

There appears to be a definite relationship between moving averages and cycles. For example, the *monthly cycle* is one of the best known cycles operating throughout the commodity markets. A month has 20-21 trading days. Cycles tend to be related to their next longer and shorter cycles *harmonically,* or by a factor of two. That means that the next longer cycle is double the length of a cycle and the next shorter cycle is half its length.

The monthly cycle, therefore, may explain the popularity of the 5, 10, 20, and 40 day moving averages. The 20 day cycle measures the monthly cycle. The 40 day average is double the 20 day. The 10 day average is half of 20 and the 5 day average is half again of 10.

Many of the more commonly used moving averages (including the 4, 9, and 18 day averages, which are derivatives of 5, 10, and 20) can be explained by cyclic influences and the harmonic relationships of neighboring cycles. Incidentally, the 4 week cycle may also help explain the success of the *4 week rule,* covered later in the chapter, and its shorter counterpart—the *2 week rule.*

FIBONACCI NUMBERS USED AS MOVING AVERAGES

We'll cover the Fibonacci number series in the chapter on Elliott Wave Theory. However, I'd like to mention here that this mysterious series of numbers—such as 13, 21, 34, 55, and so on—seem to lend themselves quite well to moving average analysis. This is true not only of daily charts, but for weekly charts as well. The *21 day moving average* is a Fibonacci number. On the weekly charts, the 13 week average has proven valuable in both stocks and commodities. We'll postpone a more in depth discussion of these numbers until Chapter 13.

MOVING AVERAGES APPLIED TO LONG TERM CHARTS

The reader should not overlook using this technique in longer range trend analysis. Longer range moving averages, such as 10 or 13 weeks, in conjunction with the 30 or 40 week average, have long been used in stock market analysis, but haven't been given as much attention in the futures markets. The 10 and 40 week moving averages can be used to help track the primary trend on weekly charts for futures and stocks. (See Figure 9.10.)

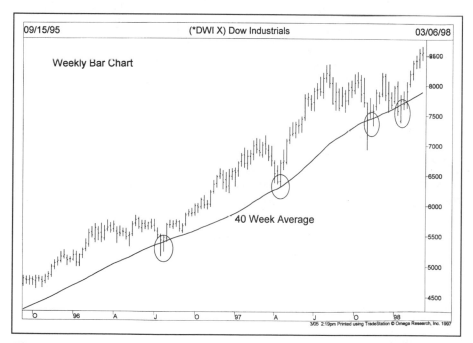

Figure 9.10 *Moving averages are valuable on weekly charts. The 40 week moving average should provide support during bull market corrections as it did here.*

Some Pros and Cons of the Moving Average

One of the great advantages of using moving averages, and one of
the reasons they are so popular as trend-following systems, is that
they embody some of the oldest maxims of successful trading.
They trade in the direction of the trend. They let profits run and
cut losses short. The moving average system forces the user to
obey those rules by providing specific buy and sell signals based
on those principles.

Because they are trend-following in nature, however, moving averages work best when markets are in a trending period.
They perform very poorly when markets get choppy and trade
sideways for a period of time. And that might be a third to a half
of the time.

The fact that they do not work that well for significant
periods of time, however, is one very compelling reason why it
is dangerous to rely too heavily on the moving average technique. In certain trending markets, the moving average can't be
beat. Just switch the program to automatic. At other times, a
nontrending method like the overbought–oversold oscillator is
more appropriate. (In Chapter 15, we'll show you an indicator
called ADX that tells you when a market is trending and when
it is not, and whether the market climate favors a trending
moving average technique or a nontrending oscillator
approach.)

Moving Averages As Oscillators

One way to construct an oscillator is to compare the difference
between two moving averages. The use of two moving averages
in the double crossover method, therefore, takes on greater significance and becomes an even more useful technique. We'll see
how this is done in Chapter 10. One method compares two exponentially smoothed averages. That method is called Moving
Average Convergence/Divergence (MACD). It is used partially as
an oscillator. Therefore, we'll postpone our explanation of that
technique until we deal with the entire subject of oscillators in
Chapter 10.

The Moving Average Applied to Other Technical Data

The moving average can be applied to virtually any technical data or indicator. It can be used on open interest and volume figures, including on balance volume. The moving average can be used on various indicators and ratios. It can be applied to oscillators as well.

THE WEEKLY RULE

There are other alternatives to the moving average as a trend-following device. One of the best known and most successful of these techniques is called the *weekly price channel* or, simply, *the weekly rule*. This technique has many of the benefits of the moving average, but is less time consuming and simpler to use.

With the improvements in computer technology over the past decade, a considerable amount of research has been done on the development of technical trading systems. These systems are mechanical in nature, meaning that human emotion and judgment are eliminated. These systems have become increasingly sophisticated. At first, simple moving averages were utilized. Then, double and triple crossovers of the averages were added. The averages were then linearly weighted and exponentially smoothed. These systems are primarily trend-following, which means their purpose is to identify and then trade in the direction of an existing trend.

With the increased fascination with fancier and more complex systems and indicators, however, there has been a tendency to overlook some of the simpler techniques that continue to work quite well and have stood the test of time. We're going to discuss one of the simplest of these techniques—the weekly rule.

In 1970, a booklet entitled the *Trader's Notebook* was published by Dunn & Hargitt's Financial Services in Lafayette, Indiana. The best known commodity trading systems of the day were computer-tested and compared. The final conclusion of all that research was that the most successful of all the systems tested was the *4 week rule,* developed by Richard Donchian. Mr.

Donchian has been recognized as a pioneer in the field of commodity trend trading using mechanical systems. (In 1983, *Managed Account Reports* chose Donchian as the first recipient of the Most Valuable Performer Award for outstanding contributions to the field of futures money management, and presents The Donchian Award to other worthy recipients.)

More recent work done by Louis Lukac, former research director at Dunn & Hargitt and currently president of Wizard Trading (a Massachusetts CTA) supports the earlier conclusions that breakout (or channel) systems similar to the weekly rule continue to show superior results. (Lukac et al.)*

Of the 12 systems tested from 1975-84, only 4 generated significant profits. Of those 4, 2 were channel breakout systems and one was a dual moving average crossover system. A later article by Lukac and Brorsen in *The Financial Review* (November 1990) published the results of a more extensive study done on data from 1976–86 that compared 23 technical trading systems. Once again, channel breakouts and moving average systems came out on top. Lukac finally concluded that a channel breakout system was his personal choice as the best starting point for all technical trading system testing and development.

The 4 Week Rule

The 4 week rule is used primarily for futures trading.

The system based on the 4 week rule is simplicity itself:

1. Cover short positions and buy long whenever the price exceeds the highs of the four preceding full calendar weeks.
2. Liquidate long positions and sell short whenever the price falls below the lows of the four preceding full calendar weeks.

The system, as it is presented here, is continuous in nature, which means that the trader always has a position, either long or short. As a general rule, continuous systems have a basic weakness. They stay in the market and get "whipsawed" during trendless market periods. It's already been stressed that trend-following systems do not work well when markets are in these sideways, or trendless phases.

* See Bibliography

The 4 week rule can be modified to make it noncontinuous. This can be accomplished by using a shorter time span—such as a one or two week rule—for liquidation purposes. In other words, a four week "breakout" would be necessary to initiate a new position, but a one or two week signal in the opposite direction would warrant liquidation of the position. The trader would then remain out of the market until a new four week breakout is registered.

The logic behind the system is based on sound technical principles. Its signals are mechanical and clearcut. Because it is trend following, it virtually guarantees participation on the right side of every important trend. It is also structured to follow the often quoted maxim of successful trading—"let profits run, while cutting losses short." Another feature, which should not be overlooked, is that this method tends to trade less frequently, so that commissions are lower. Another plus is that the system can be implemented with or without the aid of a computer.

The main criticism of the weekly rule is the same one leveled against all trend-following approaches, namely, that it does not catch tops or bottoms. But what trend-following system does? The important point to keep in mind is that the four week rule performs at least as well as most other trend-following systems and better than many, but has the added benefit of incredible simplicity.

Adjustments to the 4 Week Rule

Although we're treating the four week rule in its original form, there are many adjustments and refinements that can be employed. For one thing, the rule does not have to be used as a trading system. Weekly signals can be employed simply as another technical indicator to identify breakouts and trend reversals. Weekly breakouts can be used as a confirming filter for other techniques, such as moving average crossovers. One or 2 week rules function as excellent filters. A moving average crossover signal could be confirmed by a two week breakout in the same direction in order for a market position to be taken.

Shorten or Lengthen Time Periods for Sensitivity

The time period employed can be expanded or compressed in the interests of risk management and sensitivity. For example, the time period could be shortened if it is desirable to make the system more sensitive. In a relatively high priced market, where prices are trending sharply higher, a shorter time span could be chosen to make the system more sensitive. Suppose, for example, that a long position is taken on a 4 week upside breakout with a protective stop placed just below the low of the past 2 weeks. If the market has rallied sharply and the trader wishes to trail the position with a closer protective stop, a one week stopout point could be used.

In a trading range situation, where a trend trader would just as soon stay on the sidelines until an important trend signal is given, the time period could be expanded to eight weeks. This would prevent taking positions on shorter term and premature trend signals.

The 4 Week Rule Tied to Cycles

Earlier in the chapter reference was made to the importance of the monthly cycle in commodity markets. The 4 week, or 20 day, trading cycle is a dominant cycle that influences all markets. This may help explain why the 4 week time period has proven so successful. Notice that mention was made of 1, 2, and 8 week rules. The principle of *harmonics* in cyclic analysis holds that each cycle is related to its neighboring cycles (next longer and next shorter cycles) by 2.

In the previous discussion of moving averages, it was pointed out how the monthly cycle and harmonics explained the popularity of the 5, 10, 20, and 40 day moving averages. The same time periods hold true in the realm of weekly rules. Those daily numbers translated into weekly time periods are 1, 2, 4, and 8 weeks. Therefore, adjustments to the 4 week rule seem to work best when the beginning number (4) is divided or multiplied by 2. To shorten the time span, go from 4 to 2 weeks. If an even shorter time span is desired, go from 2 to 1. To lengthen, go from

4 to 8. Because this method combines price and time, there's no reason why the cyclic principle of harmonics should not play an important role. The tactic of dividing a weekly parameter by 2 to shorten it, or doubling it to lengthen it, does have cycle logic behind it.

The 4 week rule is a simple breakout system. The original system can be modified by using a shorter time period—a 1 or 2 week rule—for liquidation purposes. If the user desires a more sensitive system, a 2 week period can be employed for entry signals. Because this rule is meant to be simple, it is best addressed on that level. The 4 week rule is simple, but it works.(Charting packages allow you to plot *price channels* above and below current prices to spot channel breakouts. Price channels can be used on daily, weekly, or monthly charts. See Figures 9.11 and 9.12.)

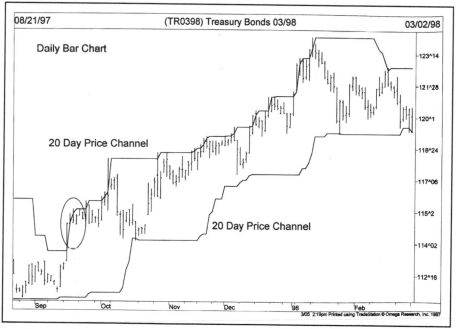

Figure 9.11 *A 20 day (4 week) price channel applied to Treasury Bond futures prices. A buy signal was given when prices closed above the upper channel (see circle). Prices have to close beneath the lower channel to reverse the signal.*

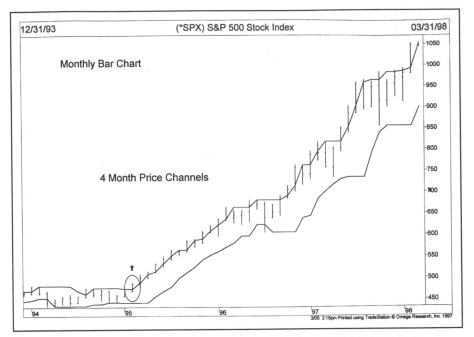

Figure 9.12 *A 4 month price channel applied to the S&P 500 Index. Prices crossed the upper channel in early 1995 (see circle) to give a buy signal which remains in effect 3 years later. A close beneath the lower line is needed to give a sell signal.*

TO OPTIMIZE OR NOT

The first edition of this book included the results of extensive research produced by Merrill Lynch, which published a series of studies on computerized trading techniques applied to the futures markets from 1978-82. Extensive testing of various moving average and channel breakout parameters was performed to find the best possible combinations in each futures market. The Merrill Lynch researchers produced a different set of optimized indicator values for each market.

Most charting packages allow you to optimize systems and indicators. Instead of using the same moving average in all markets, for example, you could ask the computer to find the moving average, or moving average combinations, that have worked the best in the past for that market. That could also be done for daily and weekly breakout systems and virtually all technical indicators included in this book. Optimization allows technical parameters to adapt to changing market conditions.

Some argue that optimization helps their trading results and others that it doesn't. The heart of the debate centers on how the data is optimized. Researchers stress that the correct procedure is to use only part of the price data to choose the best parameters, and another portion to actually test the results. Testing the optimized parameters on "out of sample" price data helps ensure that the final results will be closer to what one might experience from actual trading.

The decision to optimize or not is a personal one. Most evidence, however, suggests that optimization is not the Holy Grail some think it to be. I generally advise traders following only a handful of markets to experiment with optimization. Why should Treasury Bonds or the German mark have the exact same moving averages as corn or cotton? Stock market traders are a different story. Having to follow thousands of stocks argues against optimizing. If you specialize in a handful of markets, try optimizing. If you're a generalist who follows a large number of markets, use the same technical parameters for all of them.

SUMMARY

We've presented a lot of variations on the moving average approach. Let's try to simplify things a bit. Most technicians use a combination of two moving averages. Those two averages are usually simple averages. Although exponential averages have become popular, there's no real evidence to prove that they work any better than the simple average. The most commonly used daily moving average combinations in futures markets are 4 and 9, 9 and 18, 5 and 20, and 10 and 40. Stock traders rely heavily on a 50 day (or 10 week) moving average. For longer range stock market analysis, popular weekly moving averages are 30 and 40 weeks (or 200 days). Bollinger Bands make use of 20 day and 20 week moving averages. The 20 week average can be converted to daily charts by utilizing a 100 day average, which is another useful moving average. Channel breakout systems work extremely well in trending markets and can be used on daily, weekly, and monthly charts.

THE ADAPTIVE MOVING AVERAGE

One of the problems encountered with the moving average is choosing between a fast or a slow average. While one may work better in a trading range market, the other may be preferable in a trending market. The answer to the problem of choosing between the two may lie with an innovative approach called the "adaptive moving average."

Perry Kaufman presents this technique in his book *Smarter Trading*. The speed of Kaufman's "adaptive moving average" automatically adjusts to the level of noise (or volatility) in a market. The AMA moves more slowly when markets are trending sideways, but then moves more swiftly when the market is trending. That avoids the problem of using a faster moving average (and getting whipsawed more frequently) during a trading range, and using a slower average that trails too far behind a market when it is trending.

Kaufman does that by constructing an Efficiency Ratio that compares price direction with the level of volatility. When the Efficiency Ratio is high, there is more direction than volatility (favoring a faster average). When the ratio is low, there's more volatility than direction (favoring a slower average). By incorporating the Efficiency Ratio, the AMA automatically adjusts to the speed most suitable for the current market.

ALTERNATIVES TO THE MOVING AVERAGE

Moving averages don't work all of the time. They do their best work when the market is in a trending phase. They're not very helpful during trendless periods when prices trade sideways. Fortunately, there's another class of indicator that performs much better than the moving average during those frustrating trading ranges. They're called *oscillators* and we'll explain them in the next chapter.

10
Oscillators and Contrary Opinion

INTRODUCTION

In this chapter, we're going to talk about an alternative to trend-following approaches—the *oscillator*. The oscillator is extremely useful in nontrending markets where prices fluctuate in a horizontal price band, or trading range, creating a market situation where most trend-following systems simply don't work that well. The oscillator provides the technical trader with a tool that can enable him or her to profit from these periodic sideways and trendless market environments.

The value of the oscillator is not limited to horizontal trading ranges, however. Used in conjunction with price charts during trending phases, the oscillator becomes an extremely valuable ally by alerting the trader to short term market extremes, commonly referred to as *overbought* or *oversold* conditions. The oscillator can also warn that a trend is losing momentum before that situation becomes evident in the price action itself. Oscillators can signal that a trend may be nearing completion by displaying certain divergences.

   We'll begin by explaining first what an oscillator is and the basis for its construction and interpretation. We'll then discuss the meaning of momentum and its implications for market forecasting. Some of the more common oscillator techniques will be presented from the very simple to the more complicated. The important question of divergence will be covered. We'll touch on the value of coordinating oscillator analysis with underlying market cycles. Finally, we'll discuss how oscillators should be used as part of the overall technical analysis of a market.

OSCILLATOR USAGE IN CONJUNCTION WITH TREND

The oscillator is only a secondary indicator in the sense that it must be subordinated to basic trend analysis. As we go through the various types of oscillators used by technicians, the importance of trading in the direction of the overriding market trend will be constantly stressed. The reader should also be aware that there are times when oscillators are more useful than at others. For example, near the beginning of important moves, oscillator analysis isn't that helpful and can even be misleading. Toward the end of market moves, however, oscillators become extremely valuable. We'll address these points as we go along. Finally, no study of market extremes would be complete without a discussion of Contrary Opinion. We'll talk about the role of the contrarian philosophy and how it can be incorporated into market analysis and trading.

Interpretation of Oscillators

While there are many different ways to construct momentum oscillators, the actual interpretation differs very little from one technique to another. Most oscillators look very much alike. They are plotted along the bottom of the price chart and resemble a flat horizontal band. The oscillator band is basically flat while prices may be trading up, down, or sideways. However, the peaks and troughs in the oscillator coincide with the peaks and troughs on the price chart. Some oscillators have a midpoint value that divides the horizontal range into two halves, an upper and a lower. Depending on the formula used, this midpoint line is usually a *zero line*. Some oscillators also have upper and lower boundaries ranging from 0 to 100.

General Rules for Interpretation

As a general rule, when the oscillator reaches an extreme value in either the upper or lower end of the band, this suggests that the current price move may have gone too far too fast and is due for a correction or consolidation of some type. As another general rule, the trader should be buying when the oscillator line is in the lower end of the band and selling in the upper end. The crossing of the midpoint line is often used to generate buy and sell signals. We'll see how these general rules are applied as we deal with the various types of oscillators.

The Three Most Important Uses for the Oscillator

There are three situations when the oscillator is most useful. You'll see that these three situations are common to most types of oscillators that are used.

1. The oscillator is most useful when its value reaches an extreme reading near the upper or lower end of its boundaries. The market is said to be *overbought* when it is near the upper extreme and *oversold* when it is near the lower extreme. This warns that the price trend is overextended and vulnerable.
2. A divergence between the oscillator and the price action when the oscillator is in an extreme position is usually an important warning.
3. The crossing of the zero (or midpoint) line can give important trading signals in the direction of the price trend.

Figure 10.1a   *The 10 day momentum line fluctuates around a zero line. Readings too far above the zero line are overbought, while values too far below the line are oversold. Momentum should be used in conjunction with the trend of the market.*

MEASURING MOMENTUM

The concept of *momentum* is the most basic application of oscillator analysis. Momentum measures the velocity of price changes as opposed to the actual price levels themselves. Market momentum is measured by continually taking price differences for a fixed time interval. To construct a 10 day momentum line, simply subtract the closing price 10 days ago from the last closing price. This positive or negative value is then plotted around a zero line. The formula for momentum is:

$$M = V - V^x$$

where V is the latest closing price and V^x is the closing price x days ago.

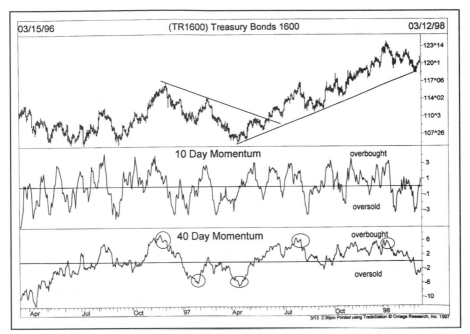

Figure 10.1b   *A comparison of 10 and 40 day momentum lines. The longer version is more helpful in catching major market turns (see circles).*

If the latest closing price is greater than that of 10 days ago (in other words, prices have moved higher), then a positive value would be plotted above the zero line. If the latest close is below the close 10 days earlier (prices have declined), then a negative value is plotted below the zero line.

While the 10 day momentum is a commonly used time period for reasons discussed later, any time period can be employed. (See Figure 10.1a.) A shorter time period (such as 5 days) produces a more sensitive line with more pronounced oscillations. A longer number of days (such as 40 days) results in a much smoother line in which the oscillator swings are less volatile. (See Figure 10.1b.)

Momentum Measures Rates of Ascent or Descent

Let's talk a bit more about just what this momentum indicator is measuring. By plotting price differences for a set period of time, the chartist is studying rates of ascent or descent. If prices are rising and the momentum line is above the zero line and rising, this means the uptrend is accelerating. If the up-slanting momentum line begins to flatten out, this means that the new gains being achieved by the latest closes are the same as the gains 10 days earlier. While prices may still be advancing, the rate of ascent (or the velocity) has leveled off. When the momentum line begins to drop toward the zero line, the uptrend in prices is still in force, but at a decelerating rate. The uptrend is losing momentum.

When the momentum line moves below the zero line, the latest 10 day close is now under the close of 10 days ago and a near term downtrend is in effect. (And, incidentally, the 10 day moving average also has begun to decline.) As momentum continues to drop farther below the zero line, the downtrend gains momentum. Only when the line begins to advance again does the analyst know that the downtrend is decelerating.

It's important to remember that momentum measures the differences between prices at two time intervals. In order for the line to advance, the price gains for the last day's close must be greater than the gains of 10 days ago. If prices advance by only the same amount as 10 days ago, the momentum line will be flat. If the last price gain is less than that of 10 days ago, the momentum line begins to decline even though prices are still rising. This is how the momentum line measures the acceleration or deceleration in the current advance or decline in the price trend.

The Momentum Line Leads the Price Action

Because of the way it is constructed, the momentum line is always a step ahead of the price movement. It leads the advance or decline in prices, then levels off while the current price trend is still in effect. It then begins to move in the opposite direction as prices begin to level off.

The Crossing of the Zero Line as a Trading Signal

The momentum chart has a *zero line*. Many technicians use the crossing of the zero line to generate buy and sell signals. A crossing above the zero line would be a buy signal, and a crossing below the zero line, a sell signal. It should be stressed here again, however, that basic trend analysis is still the overriding consideration. Oscillator analysis should not be used as an excuse to trade against the prevailing market trend. Buy positions should only be taken on crossings above the zero line if the market trend is up. Short positions should be taken on crossings below the zero line only if the price trend is down. (See Figures 10.2a and b.)

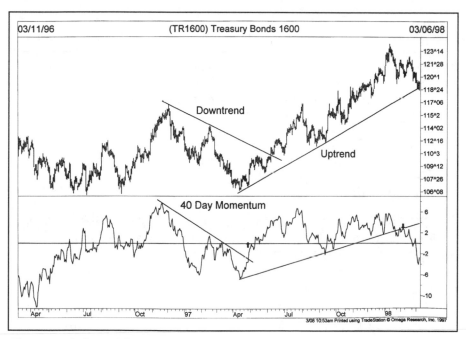

Figure 10.2a *The trendlines on the momentum chart are broken sooner than those on the price chart. The value of the momentum indicator is that it turns sooner than the market itself, making it a leading indicator.*

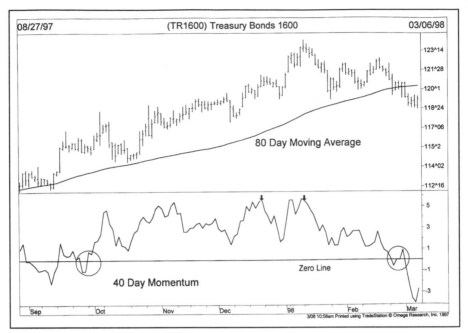

Figure 10.2b   *Some traders regard a crossing above the zero line as a buy signal and a crossing below the line as a sell signal (see circles). A moving average is helpful to confirm trend changes. The momentum line peaked before the price (see arrows).*

The Need for an Upper and Lower Boundary

One problem with the momentum line, as it is described here, is the absence of a fixed upper and lower boundary. It was stated earlier that one of the major values of oscillator analysis is being able to determine when markets are in extreme areas. But, how high is too high and how low is too low on the momentum line? The simplest way to solve this problem is by visual inspection. Check the back history of the momentum line on the chart and draw horizontal lines along its upper and lower boundaries. These lines will have to be adjusted periodically, especially after important trend changes have occurred. But it is the simplest and probably the most effective way of identifying the outer extremities. (See Figures 10.3 and 10.4.)

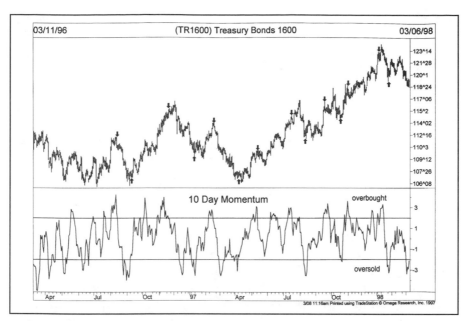

Figure 10.3 *By visual inspection, the analyst can find the upper and lower momentum boundaries that are suitable for each market (see horizontal lines).*

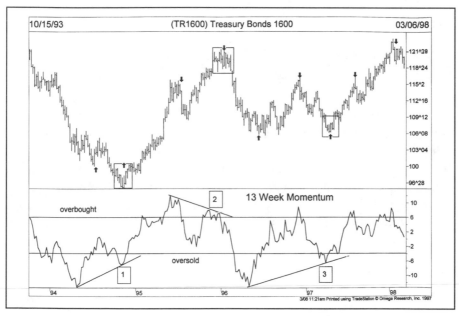

Figure 10.4 *A 13 week momentum line on a weekly chart of Treasury Bonds. The arrows mark the turning points from momentum extremes. The momentum line changed direction before the price at each major turn (points 1, 2, and 3).*

MEASURING RATE OF CHANGE (ROC)

To measure the *rate of change,* a ratio is constructed of the most recent closing price to a price a certain number of days in the past. To construct a 10 day rate of change oscillator, the latest closing price is divided by the close 10 days ago. The formula is as follows:

$$\text{Rate of change} = 100 \ (V/Vx)$$

where V is the latest close and Vx is the closing price x days ago.

In this case, the 100 line becomes the midpoint line. If the latest price is higher than the price 10 days ago (prices are rising), the resulting rate of change value will be above 100. If the last close is below 10 days ago, the ratio would be below 100. (Charting software sometimes uses variations of the preceding formulas for momentum and rate of change. While the construction techniques may vary, the interpretation remains the same.)

CONSTRUCTING AN OSCILLATOR USING TWO MOVING AVERAGES

Chapter 9 discussed two moving averages being used to generate buy and sell signals. The crossing of the shorter average above or below the longer average registered buy and sell signals, respectively. It was mentioned at that time that these dual moving average combinations could also be used to construct oscillator charts. This can be done by plotting the difference between the two averages as a histogram. These histogram bars appear as a plus or minus value around a centered zero line. This type of oscillator has three uses:

1. To help spot divergences.

2. To help identify short term variations from the long term trend, when the shorter average moves too far above or below the longer average.

3. To pinpoint the crossings of the two moving averages, which occur when the oscillator crosses the zero line.

The shorter average is divided by the longer. In both cases, however, the shorter average oscillates around the longer average, which is in effect the zero line. If the shorter average is above the longer, the oscillator would be positive. A negative reading would be present if the shorter average were under the longer. (See Figures 10.5-10.7.)

When the two moving average lines move too far apart, a market extreme is created calling for a pause in the trend. (See Figure 10.6.) Very often, the trend remains stalled until the shorter average line moves back to the longer. When the

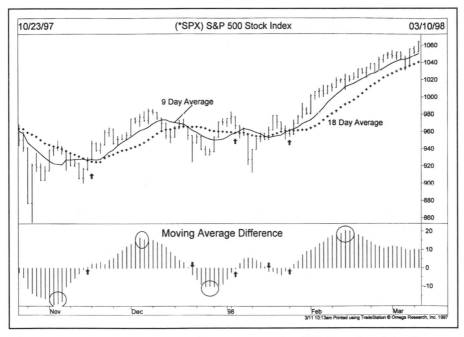

Figure 10.5   *The histogram lines measure the difference between the two moving averages. Crossing above and below the zero line give buy and sell signals (see arrows). Notice that the histogram turns well before the actual signals (see circles).*

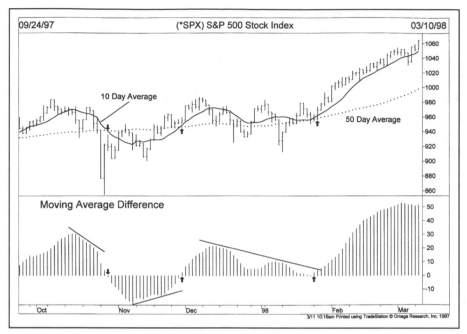

Figure 10.6 *A histogram measuring the difference between the 10 and 50 day averages. The histogram always turns well before the zero line crossover. In an uptrend, the histogram will find support at the zero line and turn up again (third arrow).*

shorter line approaches the longer, a critical point is reached. In an uptrend, for example, the shorter line dips back to the longer average, but should bounce off it. This usually represents an ideal buying area. It's much like the testing of an up trendline. If the shorter average crosses below the longer average, however, a trend reversal is signaled.

In a downtrend, a rise in the shorter average to the longer usually represents an ideal selling area unless the longer line is crossed, in which case a trend reversal signal would be registered. The relationships between the two averages can be used, therefore, not only as an excellent trend-following system, but also to help identify short term overbought and oversold conditions.

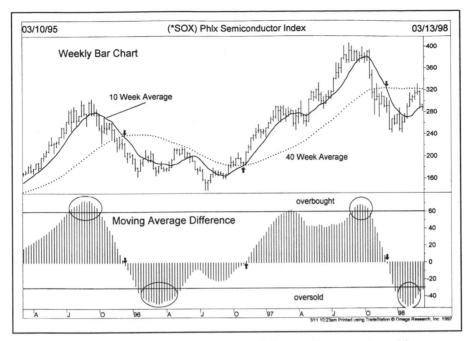

Figure 10.7 *A histogram plotting the difference between 2 weekly averages. The histogram turned in the direction of the new price trend weeks before the actual zero line crossings on the histogram. Notice how easily the overbought and oversold levels are seen.*

COMMODITY CHANNEL INDEX

It is possible to normalize an oscillator by dividing the values by a constant divisor. In the construction of his Commodity Channel Index (CCI), Donald R. Lambert compares the current price with a moving average over a selected time span—usually 20 days. He then normalizes the oscillator values by using a divisor based on mean deviation. As a result, the CCI fluctuates in a constant range from +100 on the upside to –100 on the downside. Lambert recommended long positions in those markets with values over +100. Markets with CCI values below –100 were candidates for short sales.

It seems, however, that most chartists use CCI simply as an overbought/oversold oscillator. Used in that fashion readings over +100 are considered overbought and under –100 are oversold. While the Commodity Channel Index was originally developed for commodities, it is also used for trading stock index futures and options like the S&P 100 (OEX). Although 20 days is the common default value for CCI, the user can vary the number to adjust its sensitivity. (See Figures 10.8 and 10.9.)

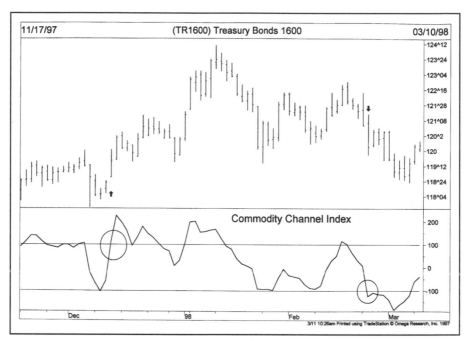

Figure 10.8 *A 20 day Commodity Channel Index. The original intent of this indicator was to buy moves above +100 and sell moves below –100 as shown here.*

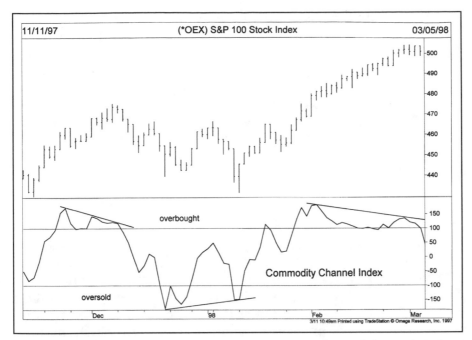

Figure 10.9 *The Commodity Channel Index can be used for stock index-es like this one and can also be used like any other oscillator to measure market extremes. Notice that the CCI turns before prices at each top and bottom. The default length is 20 days.*

THE RELATIVE STRENGTH INDEX (RSI)

The RSI was developed by J. Welles Wilder, Jr. and presented in his 1978 book, *New Concepts in Technical Trading Systems*. We're only going to cover the main points here. A reading of the original work by Wilder himself is recommended for a more in-depth treatment. Because this particular oscillator is so popular among traders, we'll use it to demonstrate most of the principles of oscillator analysis.

As Wilder points out, one of the two major problems in constructing a momentum line (using price differences) is the erratic movement often caused by sharp changes in the values being dropped off. A sharp advance or a decline 10 days ago (in the case of a 10 day momentum line) can cause sudden shifts in the momentum line even if the current prices show little change. Some smoothing is therefore necessary to minimize these distortions. The second problem is that there is the need for a constant range for comparison purposes. The RSI formula not only provides the necessary smoothing, but also solves the latter problem by creating a constant vertical range of 0 to 100.

The term "relative strength," incidentally, is a misnomer and often causes confusion among those more familiar with that term as it is used in stock market analysis. *Relative strength* generally means a ratio line comparing two different entities. A ratio of a stock or industry group to the S&P 500 Index is one way of gauging the *relative strength* of different stocks or industry groups against one objective benchmark. We'll show you later in the book how useful *relative strength* or *ratio* analysis can be. Wilder's *Relative Strength Index* doesn't really measure the relative strength between different entities and, in that sense, the name is somewhat misleading. The RSI, however, does solve the problem of erratic movement and the need for a constant upper and lower boundary. The actual formula is calculated as follows:

$$RSI = 100 - \frac{100}{1 + RS}$$

$$RS = \frac{\text{Average of } x \text{ days' up closes}}{\text{Average of } x \text{ days' down closes}}$$

Fourteen days are used in the calculation; 14 weeks are used for weekly charts. To find the average up value, add the total points gained on up days during the 14 days and divide that total by 14. To find the average down value, add the total number of points lost during the down days and divide that total by 14. Relative strength (RS) is then determined by dividing the *up* average by the *down* average. That RS value is then inserted into the formula for RSI. The number of days can be varied by simply changing the value of *x*.

Wilder originally employed a 14 day period. *The shorter the time period, the more sensitive the oscillator becomes and the wider its amplitude.* RSI works best when its fluctuations reach the upper and lower extremes. Therefore, if the user is trading on a very short term basis and wants the oscillator swings to be more pronounced, the time period can be shortened. The time period is lengthened to make the oscillator smoother and narrower in amplitude. The amplitude in the 9 day oscillator is therefore greater than the original 14 day. While 9 and 14 day spans are the most common values used, technicians experiment with other periods. Some use shorter lengths, such as 5 or 7 days, to increase the volatility of the RSI line. Others use 21 or 28 days to smooth out the RSI signals. (See Figures 10.10 and 10.11.)

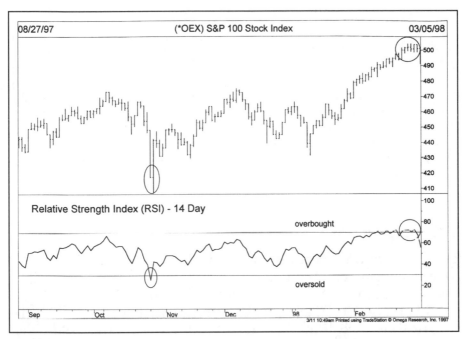

Figure 10.10 *The 14 day Relative Strength Index becomes overbought over 70 and oversold below 30. This chart shows the S&P 100 being oversold in October and overbought during February.*

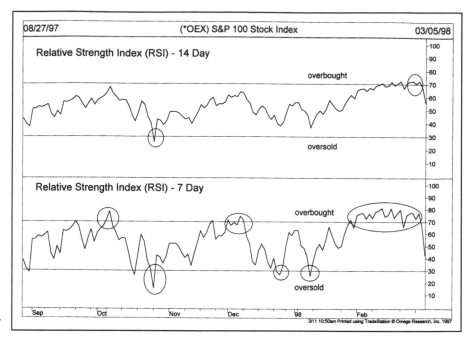

Figure 10.11 *The amplitude of the RSI line can be widened by shortening the time period. Notice that the 7 day RSI reaches the outer extremes more frequently than the 14 day RSI. That makes the 7 day RSI more useful to short term traders.*

Interpreting RSI

RSI is plotted on a vertical scale of 0 to 100. Movements above 70 are considered overbought, while an oversold condition would be a move under 30. Because of shifting that takes place in bull and bear markets, the 80 level usually becomes the overbought level in bull markets and the 20 level the oversold level in bear markets.

"Failure swings," as Wilder calls them, occur when the RSI is above 70 or under 30. A *top failure swing* occurs when a peak in the RSI (over 70) fails to exceed a previous peak in an uptrend, followed by a downside break of a previous trough. A *bottom failure swing* occurs when the RSI is in a downtrend (under 30), fails to set a new low, and then proceeds to exceed a previous peak. (See Figures 10.12a–b.)

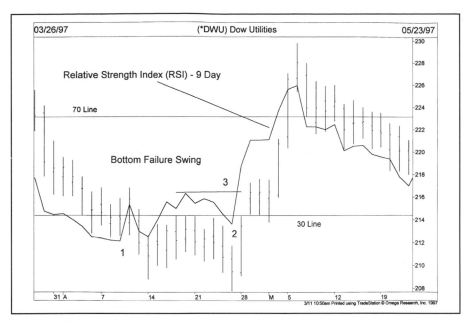

Figure 10.12a *A bottom failure swing in the RSI line. The second RSI trough (point 2) is higher than the first (point 1) while it is below 30 and prices are still falling. The upside penetration of the RSI peak (point 3) signals a bottom.*

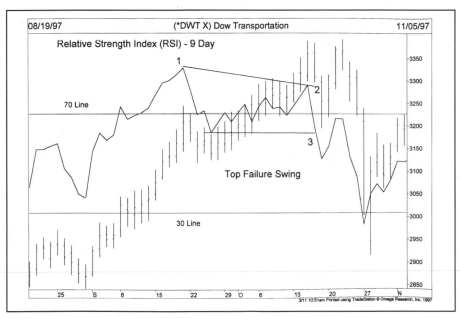

Figure 10.12b *A top failure swing. The second peak (2) is lower than the first (1) while the RSI line is over 70 and prices are still rallying. The break by the RSI line below the middle trough (point 3) signals the top.*

Divergence between the RSI and the price line, when the RSI is above 70 or below 30, is a serious warning that should be heeded. Wilder himself considers divergence "the single most indicative characteristic of the Relative Strength Index" [Wilder, p. 70].

Trendline analysis can be employed to detect changes in the trend of the RSI. Moving averages can also be used for the same purpose. (See Figure 10.13.)

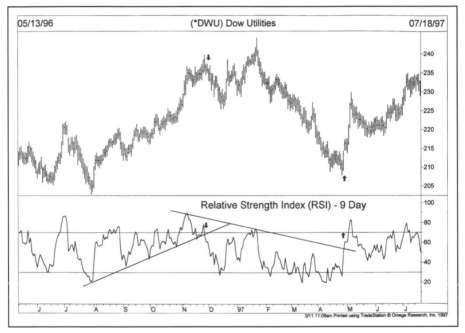

Figure 10.13   *Trendlines work very effectively on the RSI line. The breaking of the two RSI trendlines gave timely buy and sell signals on this chart (see arrows).*

In my own personal experience with the RSI oscillator, its greatest value lies in failure swings or divergences that occur when the RSI is over 70 or under 30. Let's clarify another important point on the use of oscillators. Any strong trend, either up or down, usually produces an extreme oscillator reading before too long. In such cases, claims that a market is overbought or oversold are usually premature and can lead to an early exit from a profitable trend. In strong uptrends, overbought markets can stay overbought for some time. Just because the oscillator has moved into the upper region is not reason enough to liquidate a long position (or, even worse, short into the strong uptrend).

The first move into the overbought or oversold region is usually just a warning. The signal to pay close attention to is the second move by the oscillator into the *danger zone*. If the second move fails to confirm the price move into new highs or new lows (forming a double top or bottom on the oscillator), a possible divergence exists. At that point, some defensive action can be taken to protect existing positions. If the oscillator moves in the opposite direction, breaking a previous high or low, then a divergence or failure swing is confirmed.

The 50 level is the RSI midpoint value, and will often act as support during pullbacks and resistance during bounces. Some traders treat RSI crossings above and below the 50 level as buying and selling signals respectively.

USING THE 70 AND 30 LINES TO GENERATE SIGNALS

Horizontal lines appear on the oscillator chart at the 70 and 30 values. Traders often use those lines to generate buy and sell signals. We already know that a move under 30 warns of an oversold condition. Suppose the trader thinks a market is about to bottom and is looking for a buying opportunity. He or she watches the oscillator dip under 30. Some type of divergence or double bottom may develop in the oscillator in that oversold region. A crossing back above the 30 line at that point is taken by many traders as a confirmation that the trend in the oscillator has turned up. Accordingly, in an overbought market, a crossing back under the 70 line can often be used as a sell signal. (See Figure 10.14.)

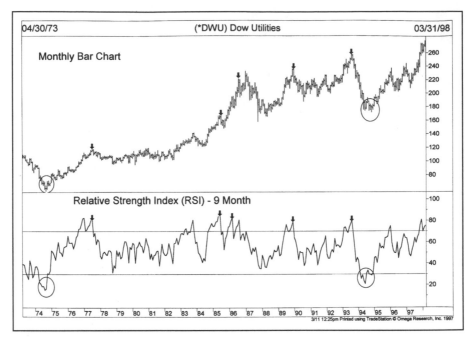

Figure 10.14   *The RSI oscillator can be used on monthly charts. Notice the two major oversold buy signals in 1974 and 1994. The overbought peaks in the RSI line did a pretty good job of pinpointing important tops in the utilities.*

STOCHASTICS (K%D)

The *Stochastic* oscillator was popularized by George Lane (president of Investment Educators, Inc., Watseka, IL). It is based on the observation that as prices increase, closing prices tend to be closer to the upper end of the price range. Conversely, in downtrends, the closing price tends to be near the lower end of the range. Two lines are used in the Stochastic Process—the %K line and the %D line. The %D line is the more important and is the one that provides the major signals.

The intent is to determine where the most recent closing price is in relation to the price range for a chosen time period. Fourteen is the most common period used for this oscillator. To determine the K line, which is the more sensitive of the two, the formula is:

$$\%K = 100\,[(C - L14) / (H14 - L14)]$$

where C is the latest close, L14 is the lowest low for the last 14 periods, and H14 is the highest high for the same 14 periods (14 periods can refer to days, weeks, or months).

The formula simply measures, on a percentage basis of 0 to 100, where the closing price is in relation to the total price range for a selected time period. A very high reading (over 80) would put the closing price near the top of the range, while a low reading (under 20) near the bottom of the range.

The second line (%D) is a 3 period moving average of the %K line. This formula produces a version called *fast* stochastics. By taking another 3 period average of %D, a smoother version called *slow* stochastics is computed. Most traders use the *slow* stochastics because of its more reliable signals.*

These formulas produce two lines that oscillate between a vertical scale from 0 to 100. The K line is a faster line, while the D line is a slower line. The major signal to watch for is a divergence between the D line and the price of the underlying market when the D line is in an overbought or oversold area. The upper and lower extremes are the 80 and 20 values. (See Figure 10.15.)

A bearish divergence occurs when the D line is over 80 and forms two declining peaks while prices continue to move higher. A bullish divergence is present when the D line is under 20 and forms two rising bottoms while prices continue to move lower. Assuming all of these factors are in place, the actual buy or sell signal is triggered when the faster K line crosses the slower D line.

There are other refinements in the use of Stochastics, but this explanation covers the more essential points. Despite the higher level of sophistication, the basic oscillator interpretation remains the same. An alert or set-up is present when the %D line is in an extreme area and diverging from the price action. The actual signal takes place when the D line is crossed by the faster K line.

The Stochastic oscillator can be used on weekly and monthly charts for longer range perspective. It can also be used effectively on intraday charts for shorter term trading. (See Figure 10.16.)

One way to combine daily and weekly stochastics is to use weekly signals to determine market direction and daily signals for timing. It's also a good idea to combine stochastics with RSI. (See Figure 10.17.)

---

* The second smoothing produces 3 lines. Fast stochastics uses the first 2 lines. Slow stochastics uses the last 2 lines.

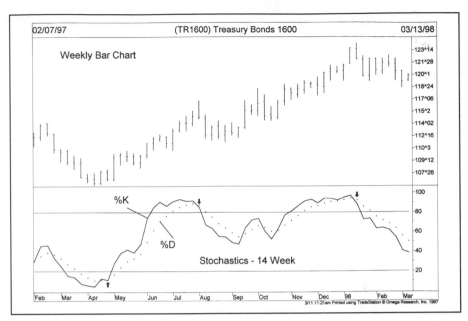

Figure 10.15   *The down arrows show two sell signals which occur when the faster %K line crosses below the slower %D line from above the 80 level. The %K line crossing above the %D line below 20 is a buy signal (up arrow).*

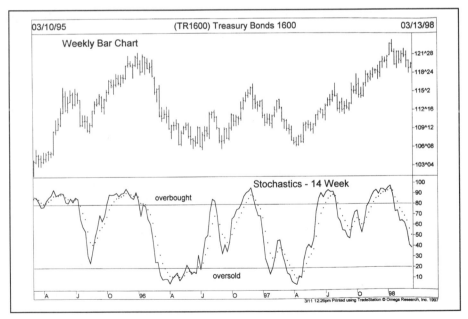

Figure 10.16   *Turns in the 14 week stochastics from above 80 and below 20 did a nice job of anticipating major turns in the Treasury Bond market. Stochastics charts can be constructed for 14 days, 14 weeks, or 14 months.*

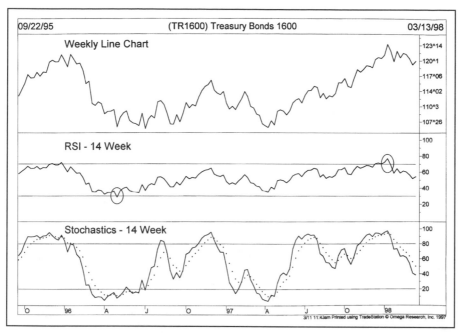

Figure 10.17 *A comparison of the 14 week RSI and stochastics. The RSI line is less volatile and reaches extremes less frequently than stochastics. The best signals occur when both oscillators are in overbought or oversold territory.*

LARRY WILLIAMS %R

Larry Williams %R is based on a similar concept of measuring the latest close in relation to its price range over a given number of days. Today's close is subtracted from the price high of the range for a given number of days and that difference is divided by the total range for the same period. The concepts already discussed for oscillator interpretation are applied to %R as well, with the main factors being the presence of divergences in overbought or oversold areas. (See Figure 10.18.) Since %R is subtracted from the high, it looks like an upside down stochastics. To correct that, charting packages plot an inverted version of %R.

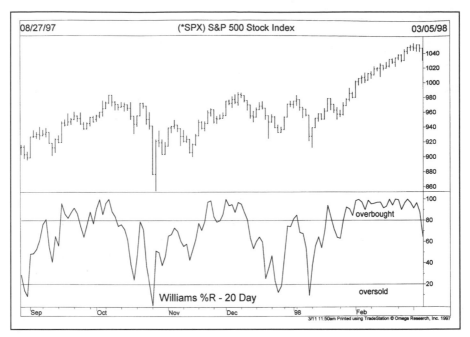

Figure 10.18   *Larry Williams %R oscillator is used in the same fashion as other oscillators. Readings over 80 or under 20 identify market extremes.*

Choice of Time Period Tied to Cycles

Oscillator lengths can be tied to underlying market cycles. A time period of $1/2$ the cycle length is used. Popular time inputs are 5, 10, and 20 days based on calendar day periods of 14, 28, and 56 days. Wilder's RSI uses 14 days, which is half of 28. In the previous chapter, we discussed some reasons why the numbers 5, 10, and 20 keep cropping up in moving average and oscillator formulations, so we won't repeat them here. Suffice it to mention here that 28 calendar days (20 trading days) represent an important dominant monthly trading cycle and that the other numbers are related harmonically to that monthly cycle. The popularity of the 10 day momentum and the 14 day RSI lengths are based largely on the 28 day trading cycle and measure $1/2$ of the value of that dominant trading cycle. We'll come back to the importance of cycles in Chapter 14.

THE IMPORTANCE OF TREND

In this chapter, we've discussed the use of the oscillator in market analysis to help determine near term overbought and oversold conditions, and to alert traders to possible divergences. We started with the momentum line. We discussed another way to measure rates of change (ROC) by using price ratios instead of differences. We then showed how two moving averages could be compared to spot short term extremes and crossovers. Finally, we looked at RSI and Stochastics and considered how oscillators should be synchronized with cycles.

Divergence analysis provides us with the oscillator's greatest value. However, the reader is cautioned against placing too much importance on divergence analysis to the point where basic trend analysis is either ignored or overlooked. Most oscillator buy signals work best in uptrends and oscillator sell signals are most profitable in downtrends. The place to start your market analysis is always by determining the general trend of the market. If the trend is up, then a buying strategy is called for. Oscillators can then be used to help time market entry. Buy when the market is oversold in an uptrend. Sell short when the market is overbought in a downtrend. Or, buy when the momentum oscillator crosses back above the zero line when the major trend is bullish and sell a crossing under the zero line in a bear market.

The importance of trading in the direction of the major trend cannot be overstated. The danger in placing too much importance on oscillators by themselves is the temptation to use divergence as an excuse to initiate trades contrary to the general trend. This action generally proves a costly and painful exercise. The oscillator, as useful as it is, is just one tool among many others and must always be used as an aid, not a substitute, for basic trend analysis.

WHEN OSCILLATORS ARE MOST USEFUL

There are times when oscillators are more useful than at others. During choppy market periods, as prices move sideways for several weeks or months, oscillators track the price movement very closely. The peaks and troughs on the price chart coincide almost exactly with the peaks and troughs on the oscillator. Because both price and oscillator are moving sideways, they look very much alike. At some point, however, a price breakout occurs and a new uptrend or downtrend begins. By its very nature, the oscillator is already in an extreme position just as the breakout is taking place. If the breakout is to the upside, the oscillator is already overbought. An oversold reading usually accompanies a downside breakout. The trader is faced with a dilemma. Should he or she buy the bullish breakout in the face of an overbought oscillator reading? Should the downside breakout be sold into an oversold market?

In such cases, the oscillator is best ignored for the time being and the position taken. The reason for this is that in the early stages of a new trend, following an important breakout, oscillators often reach extremes very quickly and stay there for awhile. Basic trend analysis should be the main consideration at such times, with oscillators given a lesser role. Later on, as the trend begins to mature, the oscillator should be given greater weight. (We'll see in Chapter 13, that the fifth and final wave in Elliott Wave analysis is often confirmed by bearish oscillator divergences.) Many dynamic bull moves have been missed by traders who saw the major trend signal, but decided to wait for their oscillators to move into an oversold condition before buying. To summarize, give less attention to the oscillator in the early stages of an important move, but pay close attention to its signals as the move reaches maturity.

MOVING AVERAGE CONVERGENCE/ DIVERGENCE (MACD)

We mentioned in the previous chapter an oscillator technique that uses 2 exponential moving averages and here it is. The Moving Average Convergence/Divergence indicator, or simply MACD, was developed by Gerald Appel. What makes this indicator so useful is that it combines some of the oscillator principles we've already explained with a dual moving average crossover approach. You'll see only two lines on your computer screen although three lines are actually used in its calculation. The faster line (called the MACD line) is the difference between two exponentially smoothed moving averages of closing prices (usually the last 12 and 26 days or weeks). The slower line (called the signal line) is usually a 9 period exponentially smoothed average of the MACD line. Appel originally recommended one set of numbers for buy signals and another for sell signals. Most traders, however, utilize the default values of 12, 26, and 9 in all instances. That would include daily and weekly values. (See Figure 10.19a.)

The actual buy and sell signals are given when the two lines cross. A crossing by the faster MACD line above the slower signal line is a buy signal. A crossing by the faster line below the slower is a sell signal. In that sense, MACD resembles a dual moving average crossover method. However, the MACD values also fluctuate above and below a zero line. That's where it begins to resemble an oscillator. An overbought condition is present when

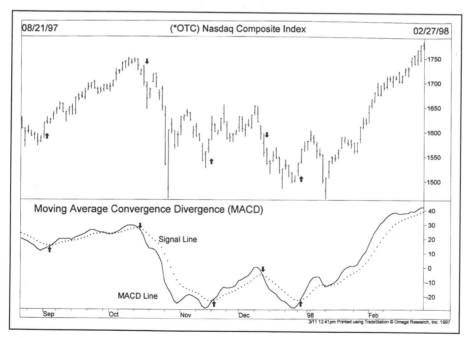

Figure 10.19a   *The Moving Average Convergence Divergence system shows two lines. A signal is given when the faster MACD line crosses the slower signal line. The arrows show five trading signals on this chart of the Nasdaq Composite Index.*

the lines are too far above the zero line. An oversold condition is present when the lines are too far below the zero line. The best buy signals are given when prices are well below the zero line (oversold). Crossings above and below the zero line are another way to generate buy and sell signals respectively, similar to the momentum technique we discussed previously.

Divergences appear between the trend of the MACD lines and the price line. A negative, or bearish, divergence exists when the MACD lines are well above the zero line (overbought) and start to weaken while prices continue to trend higher. That is often a warning of a market top. A positive, or bullish, divergence exists when the MACD lines are well below the zero line (oversold) and start to move up ahead of the price line. That is often an early sign of a market bottom. Simple trendlines can be drawn on the MACD lines to help identify important trend changes. (See Figure 10.19b.)

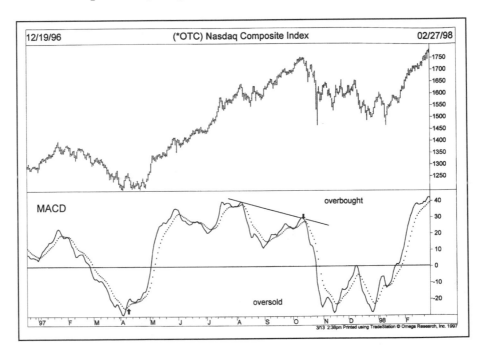

Figure 10.19b   *The MACD lines fluctuate around a zero line, giving it the quality of an oscillator. The best buy signals occur below the zero line. The best sell signals come from above. Notice the negative divergence given in October (see down arrow).*

MACD HISTOGRAM

We showed you earlier in the chapter how a histogram could be constructed that plots the difference between two moving average lines. Using that same technique, the two MACD lines can be turned into an MACD histogram. The histogram consists of vertical bars that show the difference between the two MACD lines. The histogram has a zero line of its own. When the MACD lines are in positive alignment (faster line over the slower), the histogram is above its zero line. Crossings by the histogram above and below its zero line coincide with actual MACD crossover buy and sell signals.

The real value of the histogram is spotting when the spread between the two lines is widening or narrowing. When the histogram is over its zero line (positive) but starts to fall toward the zero line, the uptrend is weakening. Conversely, when the histogram is below its zero line (negative) and starts to move upward toward the zero line, the downtrend is losing its momentum. Although no actual buy or sell signal is given until the histogram crosses its zero line, the histogram turns provide earlier warnings that the current trend is losing momentum. Turns in the histogram back toward the zero line always precede the actual crossover signals. Histogram turns are best used for spotting early exit signals from existing positions. It's much more dangerous to use the histogram turns as an excuse to initiate new positions against the prevailing trend. (See Figure 10.20a.)

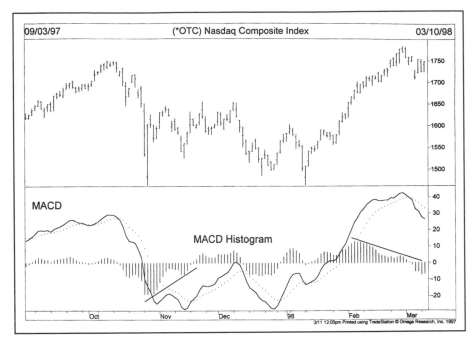

Figure 10.20a *The MACD histogram plots the difference between the two MACD lines. Signals are given on the zero line crossings. Notice that the histogram turns earlier than the crossover signals, giving the trader some advanced warning.*

COMBINE WEEKLIES AND DAILIES

As with all technical indicators, signals on weekly charts are always more important than those on daily charts. The best way to combine them is to use weekly signals to determine market direction and the daily signals to fine-tune entry and exit points. A daily signal is followed only when it agrees with the weekly signal. Used in that fashion, the weekly signals become trend filters for daily signals. That prevents using daily signals to trade against the prevailing trend. Two crossover systems in which this principle is especially true are MACD and Stochastics. (See Figure 10.20b.)

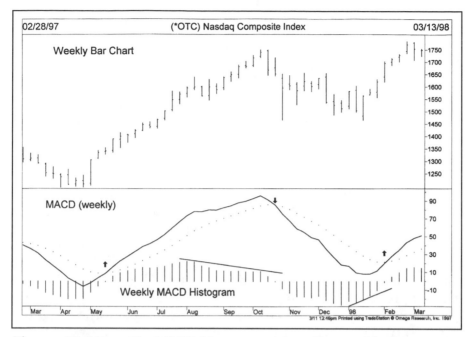

Figure 10.20b *The MACD histogram works well on weekly charts. At the middle peak, the histogram turned down 10 weeks before the sell signal (down arrow). At the two upturns, the histogram turned up 2 and 4 weeks before the buy signals (up arrows).*

THE PRINCIPLE OF CONTRARY OPINION IN FUTURES

Oscillator analysis is the study of market extremes. One of the most widely followed theories in measuring those market extremes is the principle of Contrary Opinion. At the beginning of the book, two principal philosophies of market analysis were identified—fundamental and technical analysis. Contrary Opinion, although it is generally listed under the category of technical analysis, is more aptly described as a form of psychological analysis. Contrary Opinion adds the important third dimension to market analysis—the psychological—by determining the degree of bullishness or bearishness among participants in the various financial markets.

The principle of *Contrary Opinion* holds that when the vast majority of people agree on anything, they are generally wrong. A true contrarian, therefore, will first try to determine what the majority are doing and then will act in the opposite direction.

Humphrey B. Neill, considered the dean of contrary thinking, described his theories in a 1954 book entitled, *The Art of Contrary Thinking.* Ten years later, in 1964, James H. Sibbet began to apply Neill's principles to commodity futures trading by creating the Market Vane advisory service, which includes the Bullish Consensus numbers (Market Vane, P.O. Box 90490, Pasadena, CA 91109). Each week a poll of market letters is taken to determine the degree of bullishness or bearishness among commodity professionals. The purpose of the poll is to quantify market sentiment into a set of numbers that can be analyzed and used in the market forecasting process. The rationale behind this approach is that most futures traders are influenced to a great extent by market advisory services. By monitoring the views of the professional market letters, therefore, a reasonably accurate gauge of the attitudes of the trading public can be obtained.

Another service that provides an indication of market sentiment is the "Consensus Index of Bullish Market Opinion," published by *Consensus National Commodity Futures Weekly* (Consensus, Inc., 1735 McGee Street, Kansas City, MO 64108). These numbers are published each Friday and use 75% as an overbought and 25% as an oversold measurement.

Interpreting Bullish Consensus Numbers

Most traders seem to employ a fairly simple method of analyzing these weekly numbers. If the numbers are above 75%, the market is considered to be overbought and means that a top may be near. A reading below 25% is interpreted to warn of an oversold condition and the increased likelihood that a market bottom is near.

Contrary Opinion Measures Remaining Buying or Selling Power

Consider the case of an individual speculator. Assume that speculator reads his or her favorite newsletter and becomes convinced that a market is about to move substantially higher. The more bullish the forecast, the more aggressively that trader will approach the market. Once that individual speculator's funds are fully committed to that particular market, however, he or she is overbought—meaning there are no more funds to commit to the market.

Expanding this situation to include all market participants, if 80-90% of market traders are bullish on a market, it is assumed that they have already taken their market positions. Who is left to buy and push the market higher? This then is one of the keys to understanding Contrary Opinion. If the overwhelming sentiment of market traders is on one side of the market, there simply isn't enough buying or selling pressure left to continue the present trend.

Contrary Opinion Measures Strong Versus Weak Hands

A second feature of this philosophy is its ability to compare strong versus weak hands. Futures trading is a zero sum game. For every long there is also a short. If 80% of the traders are on the long side of a market, then the remaining 20% (who are holding short positions) must be well financed enough to absorb the longs held by the other 80%. The shorts, therefore, must be holding much larger positions than the longs (in this case, 4 to 1).

This means further that the shorts must be well capitalized and are considered to be strong hands. The 80%, who are holding much smaller positions per trader, are considered to be weaker hands who will be forced to liquidate those longs on any sudden turn in prices.

Some Additional Features of the Bullish Consensus Numbers

Let's consider a few additional points that should be kept in mind when using these numbers. The norm or equilibrium point is at 55%. This allows for a built-in bullish bias on the part of the general public. The upper extreme is considered to be 90% and the lower extreme, 20%. Here again, the numbers are shifted upward slightly to allow for the bullish bias.

A contrarian position can usually be considered when the bullish consensus numbers are above 90% or under 20%. Readings over 75% or under 25% are also considered warning zones and suggest that a turn may be near. However, it is generally advisable to await a change in the trend of the numbers before taking action against the trend. A change in the direction of the Bullish Consensus numbers, especially if it occurs from one of the danger zones, should be watched closely.

The Importance of Open Interest (Futures)

Open interest also plays a role in the use of Bullish Consensus numbers. In general, the higher the open interest figures are, the better the chance that the contrarian positions will prove profitable. A contrarian position should not be taken, however, while open interest is still increasing. A continued rise in open interest numbers increases the odds that the present trend will continue. Wait for the open interest numbers to begin to flatten out or to decline before taking action.

Study the Commitments of Traders Report to ensure that hedgers hold less than 50% of the open interest. Contrary Opinion works better when most of the open interest is held by speculators, who are considered to be weaker hands. It is not advisable to trade against large hedging interests.

Watch the Market's Reaction to Fundamental News

Watch the market's reaction to fundamental news very closely. The failure of prices to react to bullish news in an overbought area is a clear warning that a turn may be near. The first adverse news is usually enough to quickly push prices in the other direction. Correspondingly, the failure of prices in an oversold area (under 25%) to react to bearish news can be taken as a warning that all the bad news has been fully discounted in the current low price. Any bullish news will push prices higher.

Combine Contrarian Opinion with Other Technical Tools

As a general rule, trade in the same direction as the trend of the consensus numbers until an extreme is reached, at which time the numbers should be monitored for a sign of a change in trend. It goes without saying that standard technical analytical tools can and should also be employed to help identify market turns at these critical times. The breaking of support or resistance levels, trendlines, or moving averages can be utilized to help confirm that the trend is in fact turning. Divergences on oscillator charts are especially useful when the Bullish Consensus numbers are overbought or oversold.

INVESTOR SENTIMENT READINGS

Each weekend *Barron's* includes in its Market Laboratory section a set of numbers under the heading "Investor Sentiment Readings." In that space, four different investor polls are included to gauge the degree of bullishness and bearishness in the stock market. The figures are given for the latest week and the period two and three weeks back for comparison purposes. Here's a random sample of what the latest week's figures might look like. Remember that these numbers are contrary indicators. Too much bullishness is bad. Too much bearishness is good.

Investor's Intelligence	
Bulls	48%
Bears	27
Correction	*24*

Consensus Index	
Bullish Opinion	77%

AAII Index *(American Association of* *Individual Investors* *625 N. Michigan Ave.* *Chicago, IL 60611)*	
Bullish	53%
Bearish	13
Neutral	34

Market Vane	
Bullish Consensus	66%

INVESTORS INTELLIGENCE NUMBERS

Investors Intelligence (30 Church Street, New Rochelle, NY 10801) takes a weekly poll of investment advisors and produces three numbers—the percent of investment advisors that are bullish, those that are bearish, and those that are expecting a market correction. Bullish readings over 55% warn of too much optimism and are potentially negative for the market. Bullish readings below 35% reflect too much pessimism and are considered positive for the market. The correction figure represents advisers who are bullish but expecting short term weakness.

Investors Intelligence also publishes figures each week that measure the number of stocks that are above their 10 and 30 week moving averages. Those numbers can also be used in a contrary fashion. Readings above 70% suggest an overbought stock market. Readings below 30% suggest an oversold market. The 10 week readings are useful for measuring short to intermediate market turns. The 30 week numbers are more useful for measuring major market turns. The actual signal of a potential change in trend takes place when the numbers rise back above 30 or fall back below 70.

Point and Figure Charting

INTRODUCTION

The first charting technique used by stock market traders before the turn of the century was point and figure charting. The actual name "point and figure" has been attributed to Victor deVilliers in his 1933 classic, *The Point and Figure Method of Anticipating Stock Price Movements*. The technique has had various names over the years. In the 1880s and 1890s, it was known as the "book method." This was the name Charles Dow gave it in a July 20, 1901 editorial of *The Wall Street Journal*.

Dow indicated that the book method had been used for about 15 years, giving it a starting date of 1886. The name "figure charts" was used from the 1920s until 1933 when "point and figure" became the accepted name for this technique of tracking market movement. R.D. Wyckoff also published several works dealing with the point and figure method in the early 1930s.

The Wall Street Journal started publishing daily high, low, and closing stock prices in 1896, which is the first reference to the more commonly known bar chart. Therefore, it appears that the point and figure method predates bar charting by at least 10 years.

We're going to approach point and figure charting in two steps. We'll look at the original method that relies on intraday price moves. Then we'll show you a simpler version of point and figure charting that can be constructed by using only the high and low prices for any market.

THE POINT AND FIGURE VERSUS THE BAR CHART

Let's begin with some of the basic differences between point and figure charting and bar charting and look at a couple of chart examples.

The point and figure chart is a study of pure price movement. That is to say, it does not take time into consideration while plotting the price action. A bar chart, by contrast, combines both price and time. Because of the way the bar chart is constructed, the vertical axis is the price scale and the horizontal axis, a time scale. On a daily chart, for example, each successive day's price action moves one space or bar to the right. This happens even if prices saw little or no change for that day. Something must always be placed in the next space. On the point and figure chart, only the price changes are recorded. If no price change occurs, the chart is left untouched. During active market periods, a considerable amount of plotting may be required. During quiet market conditions, little or no plotting will be needed.

An important difference is the treatment of volume. Bar charts record volume bars under the day's price action. Point and figure charts ignore volume numbers, as a separate entity. This last phrase, "as a separate entity," is an important one. Although the volume numbers are not recorded on the point and figure chart, it does not necessarily follow that volume, or trading activity, is totally lost. On the contrary, since intraday point and figure charts record all price change activity, the heavier or lighter volume is reflected in the amount of price changes recorded on the chart. Because volume is one of the more important ingredients in determining the potency of support and resistance levels, point and figure charts become especially useful in determining at which price levels most of the trading activity took place and, hence, where the important support and resistance numbers are.

Figure 11.1 compares a bar chart and a point and figure chart covering the same time span. In one sense, the charts look similar, but, in another sense, quite different. The general price and trend picture is captured on both charts, but the method of recording prices is different. Notice in Figure 11.2 the alternating columns of x's and o's. The *x columns* represent rising prices, while the *o columns* show declining prices. Each time a column of x's moves one box above a previous column of x's, an upside breakout occurs. (See arrows in Figure 11.2.)

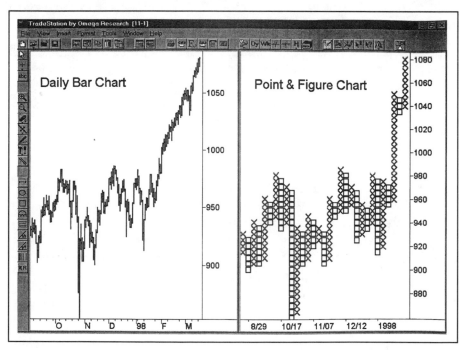

Figure 11.1   *A comparison of a daily bar chart for the S&P 500 Index (left) and a point and figure chart (right) for the same time period. The point and figure chart uses x columns for rising prices and o columns for declining prices.*

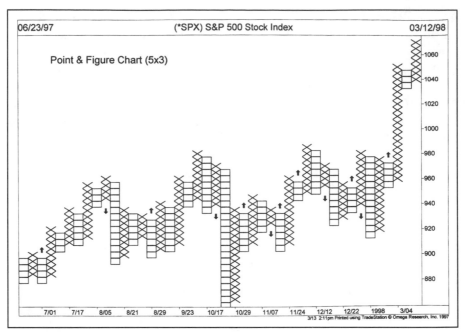

Figure 11.2   *A buy signal is given when one x column rises above the top of a previous x column (see up arrows). A sell signal is given when a column of o's falls below a previous o column (see down arrows). Signals are more precise on point and figure charts.*

Correspondingly, when a column of o's declines one box under a previous column of o's, a downside breakout occurs. Notice how much more precise these breakouts are than those on the bar chart. These breakouts can, of course, be used as buy and sell signals. We'll have more to say on buy and sell signals a bit later. But the charts demonstrate one of the advantages of the point and figure chart, mainly the greater precision and ease in recognizing trend signals.

Figures 11.3 and 11.4 reveal another major advantage of the point and figure chart: flexibility. While all three of the p&f charts cover the same price action, we can make them look very different to serve different purposes. One way to change the p&f chart is to vary the *reversal criteria* (let's say from a 3 box reversal to a 5 box reversal). The larger the number of boxes required for a reversal, the

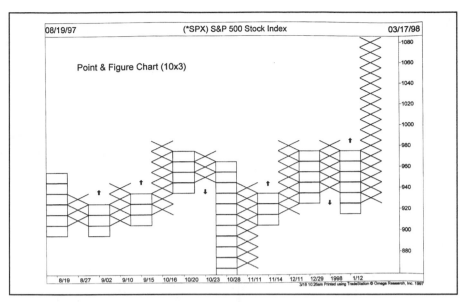

Figure 11.3 *Increasing the box size from 5 points to 10 makes the point and figure chart less sensitive and fewer signals are given. This is more suitable for a long term investor.*

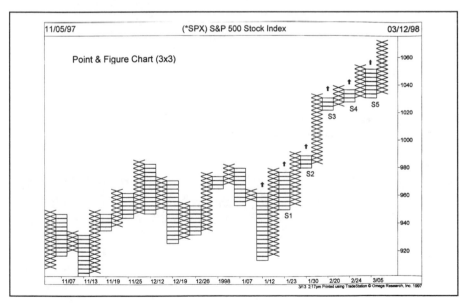

Figure 11.4 *Reducing the box size to 3 points produces more signals. This is better for shorter term trading. The last rally from 920 to 1060 produced 6 different buy signals. Protective sell stops can be placed under the highest column of o's (see S1-S5).*

less sensitive the chart becomes. The second way to vary the chart is to change the *box size* . Figure 2 uses a box size of 5 points. Figure 11.3 changes the box size from 5 points to 10 points. The number of columns has been reduced from 44 in the 5×3 chart in Figure 11.2 to only 16 columns in Figure 11.3. By using the larger box size in Figure 11.3, fewer signals are given. That allows the investor to concentrate on the major trend of a market by avoiding all the short term sell signals that are eliminated from the less sensitive chart.

Figure 11.4 reduces the box size from 5 to 3. That increases the sensitivity of the chart. Why would anyone want to do that? Because it's better for shorter term trading. Compare the last rally from 920 to 1060 in all three charts. The 10×3 chart (Figure 11.3) shows the last column as a series of x's with no o columns. The 5×3 chart (Figure 11.2) shows the last upleg in 5 columns—3 x columns and 2 o columns. The 3×3 chart (Figure 11.4) breaks the last upleg into 11 columns—6 x columns and 5 o columns. By increasing the number of corrections during the uptrend (by increasing the number of o columns), more repeat buy signals are given either for later entry or for adding to winning positions. It also allows the trader to raise protective sell stops below the latest columns of o's. The bottom line is that you can alter the look of the point and figure chart to adjust its sensitivity to suit your own needs.

CONSTRUCTION OF THE INTRA-DAY POINT AND FIGURE CHART

We've already stated that the intraday chart was the original type used by point and figure chartists. The technique was originally used to track stock market movement. The intent was to capture and record on paper each one point move of the stocks under consideration. It was felt that accumulation (buying) and distribution (selling) could be better detected in this manner. Only whole numbers were employed. Each box was given a value of one point and each one point move in either direction was recorded. Fractions were largely ignored. When the technique was later adopted to commodity markets, the value of the box had to be adjusted to fit each different commodity market. Let's construct an intraday chart using some actual price data.

The following numbers describe 9 actual days of trading in a Swiss franc futures contract. The box size is 5 points. Therefore, every 5 point swing in either direction is plotted. We'll start with a 1 box reversal chart.

4/29	4875 4880 4860 4865 4850 4860 4855
5/2	4870 4860 4865 4855 4860 4855 4860 4855 4860 4855 4865 4855
5/3	4870 4865 4870 4860 4865 4860 4870 4865
5/4	4885 4880 4890 4885 4890 4875
5/5	4905 4900 4905 4900 4905
5/6	4885 4900 4890 4930 4920 4930 4925 4930 4925
5/9	4950 4925 4930 4925 4930 4925 4935 4925 4930 4925 4935 4930 4940 4935
5/10	4940 4915 4920 4905 4925 4920 4930 4925 4935 4930 4940 4935 4940
5/11	4935 4950 4945 4950 4935 4940 4935 4945 4940 4965 4960 4965 4955 4960 4955 4965 4960 4970

Figure 11.5a is what the previously listed numbers would look like on the chart. Let's begin on the left side of the chart. First the chart is scaled to reflect a 5 point increment for every box.

Column 1: Put a dot at 4875. Because the next number—4880—is higher, fill in the next box up to 4880.

Column 2: The next number is 4860. Move 1 column to the right, go down 1 box, and fill in all the o's down to 4860.

Column 3: The next number is 4865. Move 1 column to the right, move up 1 box and put an x at 4865. Stop here. So far you have only 1 x marked in column 3 because prices have only moved up 1 box. On a 1 box reversal chart, there must always be at least 2 boxes filled in each column. Notice that the next number is 4850, calling for o's down to that number. Do you go to the next column to record the column of declining o's? The answer is no because that would leave only 1 mark, the x, in column 3. Therefore, in the column with the lone x (column 3) fill in o's down to 4850.

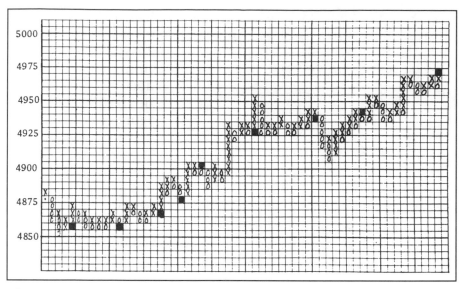

Figure 11.5a   *A 5×1 point and figure chart of a Deutsche mark contract is shown in the upper chart. The blackened boxes show the end of each day's trading. Figure 11.5b shows the same price data with a 3 box reversal. Notice the compression. Figure 11.5c shows a 5 box reversal.*

Column 4:   The next number is 4860. Move to the next column, move 1 box up, and plot in the x's up to 4860.

Column 5:   The next number is 4855. Because this is a move down, go to the next column, move down a box, and fill the o at 4860. Notice on the table that this is the last price of the day. Let's do one more.

Column 6:   The first number on 5/2 is 4870. So far, you only have one o in column 5. You must have at least 2 marks in each column. Therefore, fill in x's (because prices are advancing) up to 4870. But notice that the last price on the previous day is blacked out. This is to help keep track of time. By blacking in the last price each day, it's much easier to keep track of the separate days' trading.

Feel free to continue through the remainder of the chart to sharpen your understanding of the plotting process. Notice that this chart has several columns where both x's and o's are present. This situation will only develop on the 1 point reversal chart and is caused by the necessity of having at least 2 boxes filled in each column. Some purists might argue with combining the x's and o's. Experience will show, however, that this method of plotting prices makes it much easier to follow the order of the transactions.

Figure 11.5b takes the same data from Figure 11.5a and transforms it into a 3 box reversal chart. Notice that the chart is condensed and a lot of data is lost. Figure 11.5c shows a 5 box reversal. These are the 3 reversal criteria that have traditionally been used—the 1, 3, and 5 box reversal. The 1 box reversal is generally used for very short term activity and the 3 box for the study of the intermediate trend. The 5 box reversal, because of its severe condensation, is generally used for the study of long term trends. The correct order to use is the one shown here, that is, begin with the 1 point reversal chart. The 3 and 5 box reversals can then be constructed right off the first chart. For obvious reasons, a 1 point reversal chart could not possibly be constructed from a 3 or 5 box reversal.

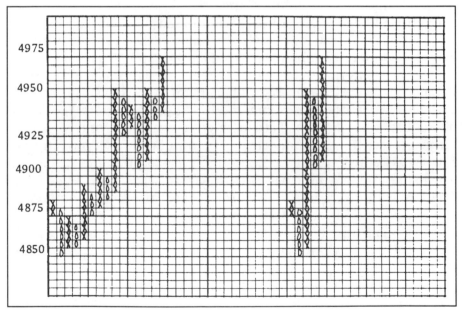

Figure 11.5b   **Figure 11.5c**

THE HORIZONTAL COUNT

One principal advantage of the intraday 1 box reversal chart is the ability to obtain price objectives through use of the *horizontal count*. If you think back to our coverage of bar charts and price patterns, the question of price objectives was discussed. However, virtually all methods of obtaining price objectives off bar charts were based on what we call *vertical measurements*. This meant measuring the height of a pattern (the volatility) and projecting that distance upward or downward. For example, the head and shoulders pattern measured the distance from the head to the neckline and swung that objective from the break of that neckline.

Point and Figure Charts Allow
Horizontal Measurement

The principle of the horizontal count is based on the premise that there is a direct relationship between the width of a congestion area and the subsequent move once a breakout occurs. If the *congestion area* represents a basing pattern, some estimate can be made of the upside potential once the base is completed. Once the uptrend has begun, subsequent congestion areas can be used to obtain additional counts which can be utilized to confirm the original counts from the base. (See Figure 11.6.)

The intent is to measure the width of the pattern. Remember we're talking here of intraday 1 box reversal charts. The technique requires some modifications for other types of charts that we'll come back to later. Once a topping or basing area has been identified, simply count the number of columns in that top or base. If there are 20 columns, for example, the upside or downside target would be 20 boxes from the measuring point. The key is to determine which line to measure from. Sometimes this is easy and, at other times, more difficult.

Usually, the horizontal line to count across is near the middle of the congestion area. A more precise rule is to use the line that has the least number of empty boxes in it. Or put the other way, the line with the most number of filled in x's and o's. Once you find the correct line to count across, it's important that you include every column in your count, even the ones that are

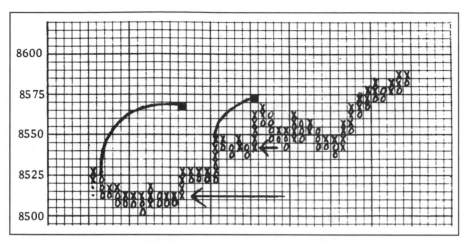

Figure 11.6 *By counting the number of columns across the horizontal congestion area, price objectives can be determined. The wider the congestion area, the greater the objective.*

empty. Count the number of columns in the congestion area and then project that number up or down from the line that was used for the count.

PRICE PATTERNS

Pattern identification is also possible on point and figure charts. Figure 11.7 shows the most common types.

As you can see, they're not much different from ones already discussed on bar charting. Most of the patterns are variations on the double and triple tops and bottoms, head and shoulders, V's and inverted V's, and saucers. The term "fulcrum" shows up quite a bit in the point and figure literature. Essentially, the *fulcrum* is a well defined congestion area, occurring after a significant advance or decline, that forms an accumulation base or a distribution top. In a base, for example, the bottom of the area is subjected to repeated tests, interrupted by intermittent rally attempts. Very often, the fulcrum takes on the appearance of a double or triple bottom. The basing pattern is completed when a breakout (catapult) occurs over the top of the congestion area.

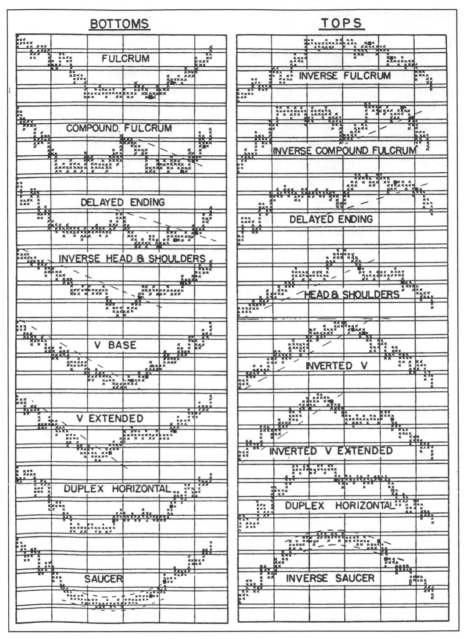

Figure 11.7 *Reversal patterns. (Source: Alexander H. Wheelan,* Study Helps in Point and Figure Technique *[New York, NY: Morgan, Rogers and Roberts, Inc., 1954] p. 25.) Reprinted in 1990 by Traders Press, P.O. Box 6206, Greenville, SC 29606.]*

Those reversal patterns with the most pronounced horizontal ranges obviously lend themselves quite well to the taking of count measurements. The V base, in contrast, because of the absence of a significant horizontal price area, would not be amenable to the taking of a horizontal count. The blackened boxes in the chart examples in Figure 11.7 represent suggested buying and selling points. Notice that those entry points generally coincide with the retesting of support areas in a base or resistance areas in a top, breakout points, and the breaking of trendlines.

Trend Analysis and Trendlines

The price patterns in Figure 11.7 show trendlines drawn as part of those patterns. Trendline analysis on intraday charts is the same as that applied to bar charts. Up trendlines are drawn under successive lows and down trendlines are drawn over successive peaks. This is not true of the simplified point and figure chart, which we're going to study next. It utilizes 45 degree lines and plots them differently.

3 BOX REVERSAL POINT AND FIGURE CHARTING

In 1947, a book on point and figure was written by A.W. Cohen entitled, *Stock Market Timing.* The following year, when the *Chartcraft Weekly Service* was started, the book's name was changed to *The Chartcraft Method of Point & Figure Trading.* Several revised editions have been published since then to include commodities and options. In 1990, Michael Burke wrote *The All New Guide to the Three-Point Reversal Method of Point & Figure Construction and Formations* (Chartcraft, New Rochelle, NY).

The original 1 box reversal method of plotting markets required intraday prices. The 3 box reversal was a condensation of the 1 box and was meant for intermediate trend analysis. Cohen reasoned that because so few 3 box reversals occurred in stocks during the day that it was not necessary to use intraday prices to construct the 3 box reversal chart. Hence the decision to use only the high and low prices, which were readily available in most financial newspapers. This modified technique, which is the basis of the Chartcraft service, greatly simplified point and figure charting and made it accessible to the average trader.

CONSTRUCTION OF THE 3 POINT REVERSAL CHART

The construction of the chart is relatively simple. First, the chart must be scaled in the same way as the intraday chart. A value must be assigned to each box. These tasks are performed for subscribers to the *Chartcraft* service because the charts are already constructed and the box values assigned. The chart shows a series of alternating columns with x's representing rising prices and the o columns showing falling prices. (See Figure 11.8.)

The actual plotting of the x's and o's requires only the high and low prices for the day. If the last column is an x column (showing rising prices), then look at the high price for the day. If the daily high permits the filling in of 1 or more x's, then fill in those boxes and stop. That's all you do for that day. Remember that the entire value of the box must be filled. Fractions or partial filling of the box don't count. Repeat the same process the next day, looking only at the high price. As long as prices continue to rise, permitting the plotting of at least one x, continue to fill in the boxes with x's, ignoring the low price.

The day finally comes when the daily high price is not high enough to fill the next x box. At that point, look at the low price to determine if a 3 box reversal has occurred in the other direction. If so, move one column to the right, move down one box, and fill the next 3 boxes with o's to signify a new down column. Because you are now in a down column, the next day consult the low price to see if that column of o's can be continued. If one or more o's can be filled in, then do so. Only when the daily low does not permit the filling in of any more o's do you look at the daily high to see if a 3 box reversal has occurred to the upside. If so, move 1 column to the right and begin a new x column.

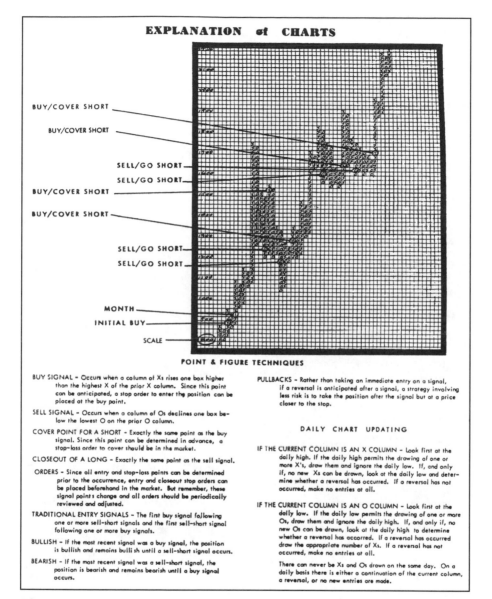

Figure 11.8 *Source: Courtesy of Chartcraft, Inc., New Rochelle, NY.*

Chart Patterns

Figure 11.9 shows 16 price patterns most common to this type of point and figure chart—8 buy signals and 8 sell signals.

Let's take a look at the patterns. Since column 2, showing signals S-1 through S-8, is just a mirror image of column 1, we'll concentrate on the buy side. The first 2 signals, B-1 and B-2, are simple formations. All that is required for the *simple bullish buy signal* is 3 columns, with the second column of x's moving 1 box above the previous column of x's. B-2 is similar to B-1 with one minor difference—there are now 4 columns, with the bottom of the second column of o's higher than the first. B-1 shows a simple breakout through resistance. B-2 shows the same bullish breakout but with the added bullish feature of rising bottoms. B-2 is a slightly stronger pattern than B-1 for that reason.

The third pattern (B-3), *breakout of a triple top,* begins the complex formations. Notice that the simple bullish buy signal is a part of each complex formation. Also, as we move down the page, these formations become increasingly stronger. The triple top breakout is stronger because there are 5 columns involved and 2 columns of x's have been penetrated. Remember that the wider the base, the greater the upside potential. The next pattern (B-4), *ascending triple top,* is stronger than B-3 because the tops and bottoms are both ascending. The *spread triple top* (B-5) is even stronger because there are 7 columns involved, and 3 columns of x's are exceeded.

The *upside breakout above a bullish triangle* (B-6) combines two signals. First, a simple buy signal must be present. Then the upper trendline must be cleared. (We'll cover the drawing of trendlines on these charts in the next section). Signal B-7, *upside breakout above a bullish resistance line,* is self-explanatory. Again, two things must be present. A buy signal must have already been given; and the upper channel line must be completely cleared. The final pattern, the *upside breakout above a bearish resistance line* (B-8), also requires two elements. A simple buy signal must be combined with a clearing of the down trendline. Of course, everything we've said regarding patterns B-1 through B-8 applies equally to patterns S-1 through S-8 except that, in the latter case, prices are headed down instead of up.

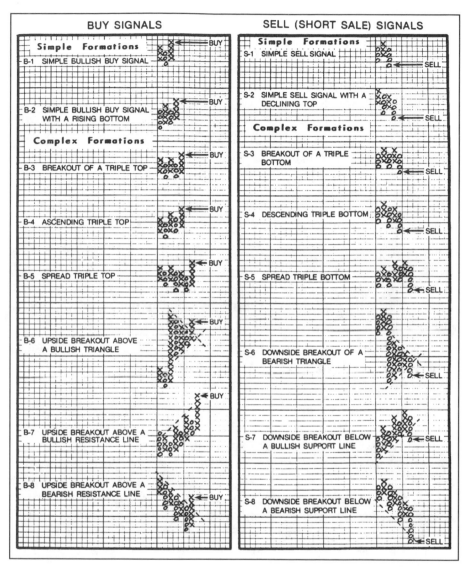

Figure 11.9 *Source: K.C. Zieg, Jr., and P.J. Kaufman,* Point and Figure Commodity Trading Techniques *(New Rochelle, NY: Investors Intelligence)* p. 73.

There is a difference between how these patterns are applied to commodity markets as opposed to common stocks. In general, all 16 signals can be used in stock market trading. However, because of the rapid movement so characteristic of the futures markets, the *complex* patterns are not as common in the commodity markets. Much greater emphasis is therefore placed on the *simple* signals. Many futures traders utilize the simple signals alone. If the trader chooses to wait for the more complex and stronger patterns, many profitable trading opportunities will be missed.

THE DRAWING OF TRENDLINES

In our discussion of intraday charts, it was pointed out that trendlines were drawn in the conventional way. This is not the case on these 3 point reversal charts. Trendlines on these charts are drawn at 45 degree angles. Also, trendlines do not necessarily have to connect previous tops or bottoms.

The Basic Bullish Support Line and Bearish Resistance Line

These are your basic up and down trendlines. Because of the severe condensation on these charts, it would be impractical to try to connect rally tops or reaction lows. The 45 degree line is, therefore, used. In an uptrend, the *bullish support line* is drawn at a *45 degree angle* upward to the right from under the lowest column of o's. As long as prices remain above that line, the major trend is considered to be bullish. In a downtrend, the bearish resistance line is drawn at a 45 degree angle downward to the right from the top of the highest column of x's. As long as prices remain below that down trendline, the trend is bearish. (See Figures 11.10-11.12.)

At times, those lines may have to be adjusted. For example, sometimes a correction in an uptrend breaks below the rising support line after which the uptrend resumes. In such cases, a new support line must be drawn at a 45 degree angle from the bottom of that reaction low. Sometimes a trend is so strong that the orig-

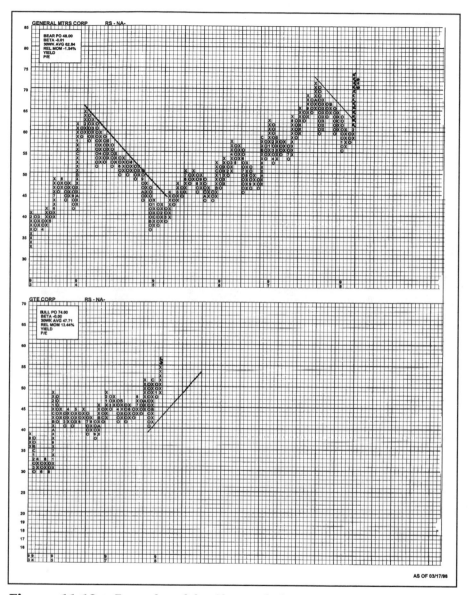

Figure 11.10 *Examples of the Chartcraft three point reversal stock charts. Notice that the trendlines are drawn at 45 degree angles. (Source: Courtesy of Chartcraft, New Rochelle, NY.)*

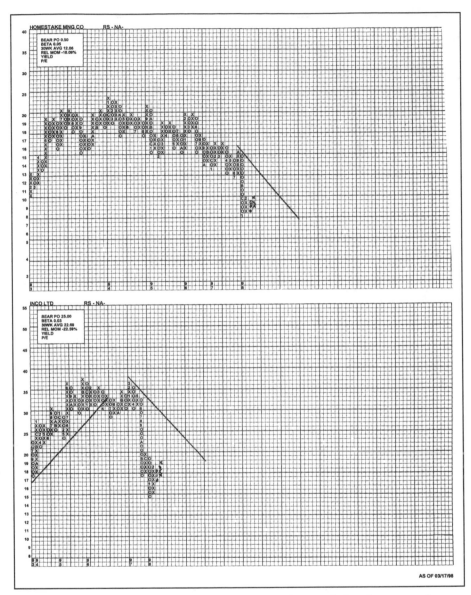

Figure 11.11   *Two more examples of the Chartcraft 3 point reversal method of point and figure charting. Trendlines on these charts are drawn at 45 degree angles. (Source: Courtesy of Chartcraft, New Rochelle, NY.)*

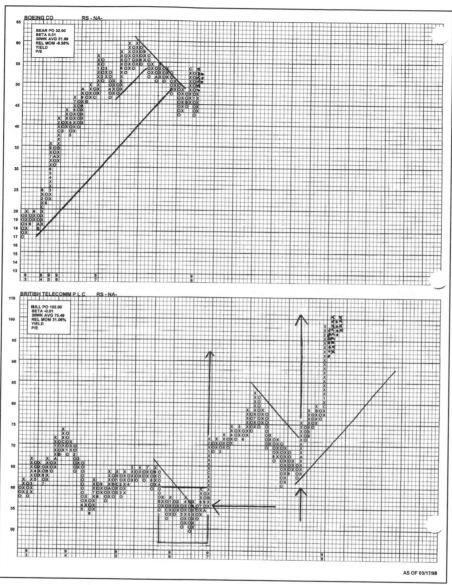

Figure 11.12 *The box to the bottom left shows a horizontal target to 92 in British Telecomm PLC arrived at by tripling the base and adding to 50. To the right, a vertical target to 102 is arrived at by tripling the x column and adding to 63. (Source: Courtesy of Chartcraft, New Rochelle, NY.)*

inal up trendline is simply too far away from the price action. In that case, a tighter trendline should be drawn in an attempt to arrive at a "best fitting" support line.

MEASURING TECHNIQUES

Three point reversal charts allow the use of two different measuring techniques—the *horizontal* and the *vertical*. For the horizontal, count the number of columns in a bottom or topping pattern. That number of columns must then be multiplied by the value of the reversal or the number of boxes needed for a reversal. For example, let's assign a $1.00 box value to a chart with a 3 box reversal. We count the number of boxes across a base and come up with 10. Because we're using a 3 box reversal, the value of that reversal is $3.00 (3×$1.00). Multiply the 10 columns across the base by $3 for a total of $30. That number is then added to the bottom of the basing pattern or subtracted from the top of a topping pattern to arrive at the price objective.

    The *vertical* count is a bit simpler. Measure the number of boxes in the first column of the new trend. In an uptrend, measure the first up column of x's. In a downtrend, measure the first down column of o's. Multiply that value by 3 and add that total to the bottom or subtract it from the top of the column. What you're doing in effect with a 3 box reversal chart is tripling the size of the first leg. If a double top or bottom occurs on the chart, use the second column of o's or x's for the vertical count. (See Figure 11.12.)

TRADING TACTICS

Let's look at the various ways that these point and figure charts can be used to determine specific entry and exit points.

1. A simple buy signal can be used for the covering of old shorts and/or the initiation of new longs.
2. A simple sell signal can be used for the liquidation of old longs and/or the initiation of new shorts.

3. The simple signal can be used only for liquidation purposes with a complex formation needed for a new commitment.

4. The trendline can be used as a filter. Long positions are taken above the trendline and short positions below the trendline.

5. For stop protection, always risk below the last column of o's in an uptrend and over the last column of x's in a downtrend.

6. The actual entry point can be varied as follows:

   a. Buy the actual breakout in an uptrend.

   b. Buy a 3 box reversal after the breakout occurs to obtain a lower entry point.

   c. Buy a 3 box reversal in the direction of the original breakout after a correction occurs. Not only does this require the added confirmation of a positive reversal in the right direction, but a closer stop point can now be used under the latest column of o's.

   d. Buy a second breakout in the same direction as the original breakout signal.

   As you can readily see from the list, there are many different ways that the point and figure chart can be used. Once the basic technique is understood, there is almost unlimited flexibility as to how to best enter and exit a market using this approach.

Adjusting Stops

The actual buy or sell signal occurs on the first signal. However, as the move continues, several other signals appear on the chart. These repeat buy or sell signals can be used for additional positions. Whether or not this is done, the protective stop point can be raised to just below the latest o column in an uptrend and lowered to just over the latest x column in a downtrend. This use of a *trailing stop* allows the trader to stay with the position and protect accumulated profits at the same time.

What to Do After a Prolonged Move

Intermittent corrections against the trend allow the trader to adjust stops once the trend has resumed. How is this accomplished, however, if no 3 box reversals occur during the trend? The trader is then faced with a long column of x's in an uptrend or o's in a downtrend. This type of market situation creates what is called a *pole,* that is, a long column of x's and o's without a correction. The trader wants to stay with the trend but also wants some technique to protect profits. There is at least one way to accomplish this. After an uninterrupted move of 10 or more boxes, place a protective stop at the point where a 3 box reversal would occur. If the position does get stopped out, reentry can be done on another 3 box reversal in the direction of the original trend. In that case, an added advantage is the placement of the new stop under the most recent column of o's in an uptrend or over the latest column of x's in a downtrend.

ADVANTAGES OF POINT AND FIGURE CHARTS

Let's briefly recap some of the advantages of point and figure charting.

1. By varying the box and reversal sizes, these charts can be adapted to almost any need. There are also many different ways these charts can be used for entry and exit points.

2. Trading signals are more precise on point and figure charts than on bar charts.

3. By following these specific point and figure signals, better trading discipline can be achieved. (See Figures 11.13-11.18.)

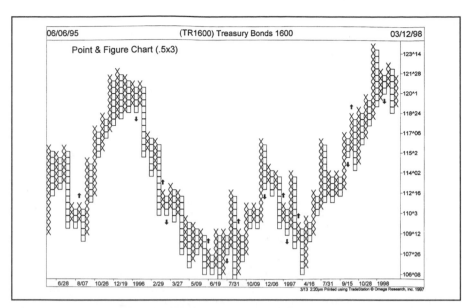

Figure 11.13 *This chart of Treasury Bond futures prices covers more than two years. The arrows mark the buy and sell signals. Most of the signals captured the market trend very well. Even when a bad signal is given, the chart quickly corrects itself.*

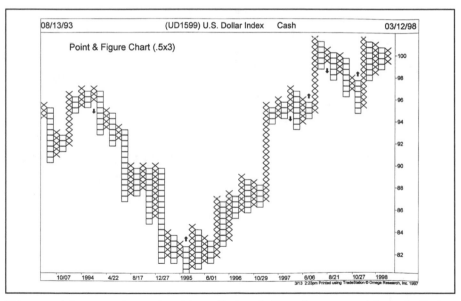

Figure 11.14 *The early 1994 sell signal (first down arrow) lasted all the way through 1994. The buy signal at the start of 1995 (first up arrow) lasted for two years until 1997. A sell signal in mid-1997 turned into a buy at the start of 1998.*

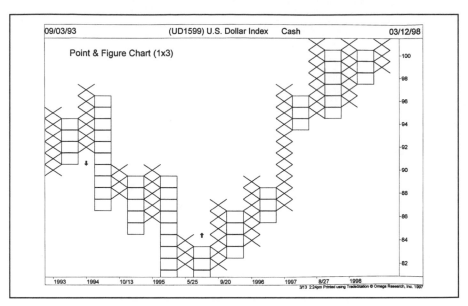

Figure 11.15 *This chart condenses the previous dollar chart by doubling the box size. Only two signals are given on this less sensitive version. The last signal was a buy (see up arrow) in mid-1995 near 85, which has lasted for almost three years.*

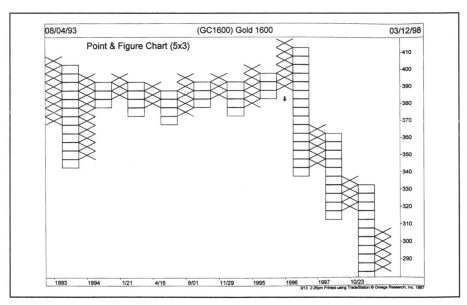

Figure 11.16 *This point and figure chart of gold gave a sell signal (see down arrow) near $380 during 1996. Gold prices fell another $100 over the next two years.*

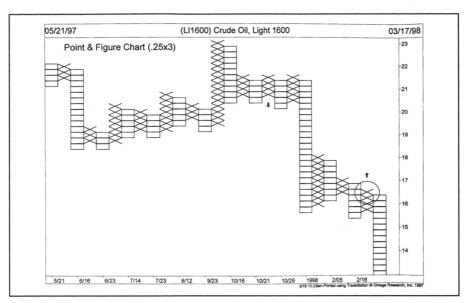

Figure 11.17   *The crude oil point and figure chart gave a sell signal (see down arrow) near $20 during October 1997 and caught the subsequent $6 tumble. Crude oil prices would have to rise above the last x column at 16.50 to reverse the downtrend.*

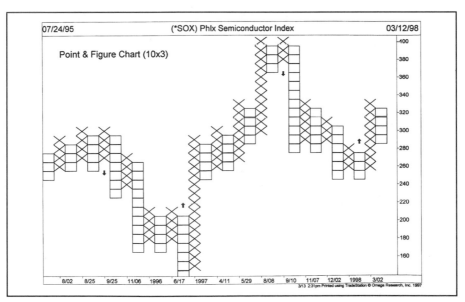

Figure 11.18   *This point and figure chart of the Semiconductor Index gave four signals over a period of two and a half years. The down arrows mark two timely sell signals in 1995 and 1997. The buy signal during 1996 (first up arrow) caught most of the ensuing rally.*

P&F TECHNICAL INDICATORS

In his 1995 book, *Point & Figure Charting* (John Wiley & Sons), Thomas J. Dorsey espouses the Chartcraft method of 3 point reversal charting of stocks. He also discusses point and figure application to commodity and options trading. In addition to explaining how to construct and read the charts, Dorsey also shows how the P&F technique can be applied to relative strength analysis, sector analysis, and in the construction of an NYSE Bullish Percent Index. He shows how p&f charts can be constructed for the NYSE advance decline line, the NYSE High-Low Index, and the percentage of stocks over their 10 and 30 week averages. Dorsey credits Michael Burke, the publisher of Chartcraft, (Chartcraft, Inc., Investors Intelligence, 30 Church Street, New Rochelle, N.Y. 10801) with the actual development of these innovative p&f indicators which are available in that chart service.

COMPUTERIZED P&F CHARTING

Computers have taken the drudgery out of point and figure charting. The days of laboriously constructing columns of x's and o's are gone. Most charting software packages do the charting for you. In addition, you can vary the box and reversal sizes with a keystroke to adjust the chart for shorter or longer term analysis. You can construct p&f charts from real-time (intraday) and end of day data, and you can apply them to any market you want. But you can do a lot more with a computer.

Kenneth Tower (CMT), technical analyst for UST Securities Corporation, (5 Vaughn Drive, CN5209, Princeton, N.J. 08543) uses a logarithmic method of point and figure charting. A screening process that measures the volatility of a stock over the last 3 years determines the right percentage box size for each stock. Figures 11.19 and 11.20 show examples of Tower's logarithmic p&f charts applied to America Online and Intel. The box size for AOL in Figure 11.19 is 3.6%. A 1 box reversal, therefore, would require a retracement of 3.6%. Since that happens to be a 2 box reversal chart, prices would have to retrace 7.2% to start a new column. Each box size for the Intel chart shown in Figure 11.20 is worth 3.2%.

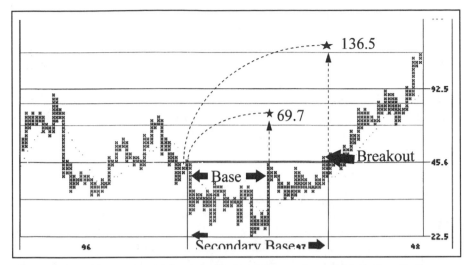

Figure 11.19 *A logarithmic point and figure chart of America Online. The reversal criteria is based on percentages. Each box is worth 3.6%. Since this is a two box reversal chart, a reversal is worth 7.2%. Notice the horizontal upside counts to 69.7 and 136.5 (see arcs). (Chart courtesy of UST Securities Corp.)*

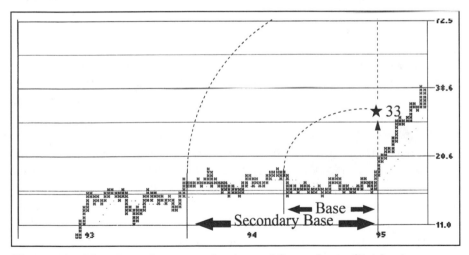

Figure 11.20 *A one box reversal point and figure chart of Intel using percentages. A reversal of 3.2% is needed to move into the next column. Measuring horizontally from right to left along the base, upside counts can be made to 33 and then to 87.6 (see arcs). (Chart courtesy of UST Securities Corp.)*

The arcs you see on both charts are examples of using horizontal price counts across a price base to arrive at short and long
term price objectives. The Intel chart, for example, shows a short
term objective to 33, arrived at by measuring halfway across the
price base (lower arc). The larger arc, which measures to 87.6, is
arrived at by measuring across the entire price base and projecting
that distance upward. If you look closely at Figures 11.19 and
11.20, you'll also see price dots trailing the price action. Those
dots happen to be moving averages.

P&F MOVING AVERAGES

Moving averages are usually applied to bar charts. But here they
are on point & figure charts, courtesy of Ken Tower and UST
Securities. Tower uses two moving averages on his charts, a 10 column and a 20 column moving average. The dots you see in
Figures 11.19 and 11.20 are 10 column averages. These moving
averages are constructed by first finding an average price for each
column. That is done by simply adding up the prices in each column and dividing the total by the number of x's or o's in that column. The resulting numbers are then averaged over 10 and 20
columns. The moving averages are used in the same way as on bar
charts.

Figure 11.21 shows two point and figure charts of the same
stock with 10 column averages (dots) and 20 column averages
(dashes). The bottom chart is a 2.7% reversal logarithmic chart of
Royal Dutch Petroleum going back to 1992. Notice that the faster
moving average stayed above the slower moving average from
1993 to the 1997 during the four year uptrend. You can see the
two moving averages coming together during the second half of
1997 in what turned out to be a consolidation year for that stock.
To the far right, you can see that Royal Dutch may be on the verge
of resuming its major uptrend. A closer look at that potential
upside breakout is seen in the upper chart in Figure 11.21.

The upper chart is a traditional one point reversal linear
chart of the same stock. The time frame covered in the linear
chart is much shorter than the long chart. But you get a closer
look at the late 1997 and early 1998 price action and can see the

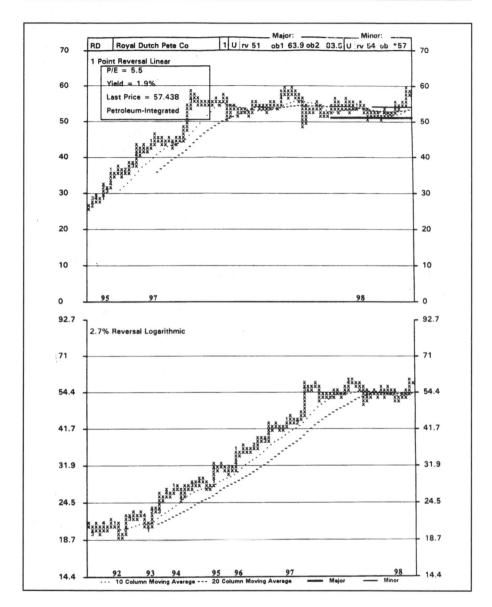

Figure 11.21 *Two point and figure versions of Royal Dutch Petroleum. The bottom chart is a log chart spanning several years. The upper chart is a linear chart for one year. The dots and dashes represent 10 and 20 column moving averages, respectively. (Prepared by UST Securities Corp. Updated through March 26, 1998.)*

short term upside breakout at the start of 1998. The stock still needs to close through 60 to confirm a major bullish breakout. The moving averages haven't been much help during the trading range (they never are), but should begin to trend higher once again if the bullish breakout materializes. By adding moving averages to point and figure charts, Ken Tower brings another valuable technical indicator to p&f charting. The use of logarithmic charts also adds a modern wrinkle to this old charting method.

CONCLUSION

Point and figure charting isn't the oldest technique in the world. That credit goes to the Japanese candlestick chart, which has been used in that country for centuries. In the next chapter Greg Morris, author of two books on candlesticks, will introduce that ancient technique that has gained new popularity in recent years among Western technical analysts.

Japanese Candlesticks*

INTRODUCTION

While the Japanese have used this charting and analysis technique for centuries, only in recent years has it become popular in the West. The term, candlesticks, actually refers to two different, but related subjects. First, and possibly the more popular, is the method of displaying stock and futures data for chart analysis. Secondly, it is the art of identifying certain combinations of candlesticks in defined and proven combinations. Fortunately, both techniques can be used independently or in combination.

CANDLESTICK CHARTING

Charting market data in candlestick form uses the same data available for standard bar charts; open, high, low, and close prices. While using the exact same data, candlestick charts offer a much

*This chapter was contributed by Gregory L. Morris.

more visually appealing chart. Information seems to jump off the page (computer screen). The information displayed is more easily interpreted and analyzed. The box below is a depiction of of a single day of prices showing the difference between the bar (left) and the candlestick(s). (See Figure 12.1.)

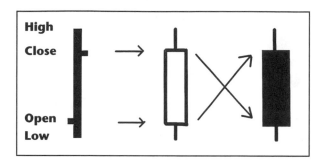

Figure 12.1

You can see how the name "candlesticks" came about. They look somewhat like a candle with a wick. The rectangle represents the difference between the open and close price for the day, and is called the *body*. Notice that the body can be either black or white. A *white body* means that the close price was greater (higher) than the open price. Actually, the body is not white, but open (not filled), which makes it work better with computers. This is so that it will print correctly when printing charts on a computer. This is one of the adaptations that have occurred in the West; the Japanese use red for the open body. The *black body* means that the close price was lower than the open price. The open and close prices are given much significance in Japanese candlesticks. The small lines above and below the body are referred to as *wicks* or *hairs* or *shadows*. Many different names for these lines appear in Japanese reference literature, which is odd since they represent the high and low prices for the day and are normally not considered vital in the analysis by the Japanese. (See Figure 12.2.)

Figure 12.2 shows the same data in both the popular bar chart and in a Japanese candlestick format. You can quickly see that information not readily available on the bar chart seems to jump from the page (screen) on the candlestick chart. Initially, it takes some getting use to, but after a while you may prefer it.

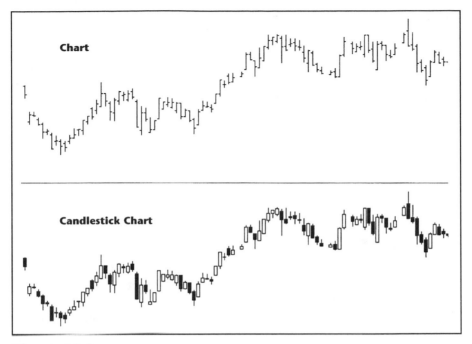

Figure 12.2

The different shapes for candlesticks have different meanings. The Japanese have defined different primary candlesticks, based upon the relationship of open, high, low, and close prices. Understanding these basic candlesticks is the beginning of candlestick analysis.

BASIC CANDLESTICKS

Different body/shadow combinations have different meanings. Days in which the difference between the open and close prices is great are called *Long Days*. Likewise, days in which the difference between the open and close price is small, are called *Short Days*. Remember, we are only talking about the size of the body and no reference is made to the high and/or low prices. (See Figure 12.3.)

Spinning Tops are days in which the candlesticks have small bodies with upper and lower shadows that are of greater length

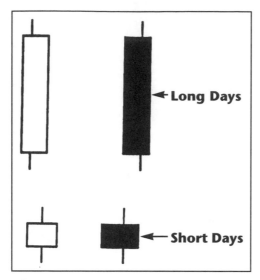

Figure 12.3

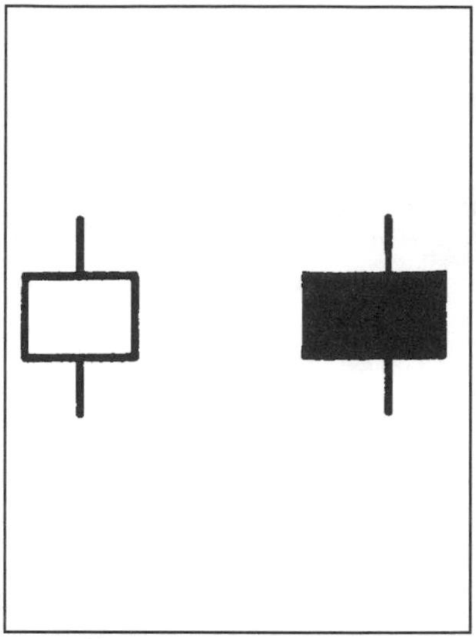

Figure 12.4   *Spinning tops.*

than that of the body. The body color is relatively unimportant in spinning top candlesticks. These candlesticks are considered as days of indecision. (See Figure 12.4.)

When the open price and the close price are equal, they are called Doji lines. *Doji candlesticks* can have shadows of varying length. When referring to Doji candlesticks, there is some consideration as to whether the open and close price must be exactly equal. This is a time when the prices must be almost equal, especially when dealing with large price movements.

There are different Doji candlesticks that are important. The Long-legged Doji has long upper and lower shadows and reflects considerable indecision on the part of market participants. The Gravestone Doji has only a long upper shadow and no lower shadow. The longer the upper shadow, the more bearish the interpretation.

Figure 12.5   *Doji candlesticks.*

The Dragonfly Doji is the opposite of the Gravestone Doji, the lower shadow is long and there is no upper shadow. It is usually considered quite bullish. (See Figure 12.5.)

The single candlestick lines are essential to Japanese candlestick analysis. You will find that all Japanese candle patterns are made from combinations of these basic candlesticks.

CANDLE PATTERN ANALYSIS

A Japanese candle pattern is a psychological depiction of traders' mentality at the time. It vividly shows the actions of the traders as time unfolds in the market. The mere fact that humans react consistently during similar situations makes candle pattern analysis work.

A Japanese candle pattern can consist of a single candlestick line or be a combination of multiple lines, normally never more than five. While most candle patterns are used to determine reversal points in the market, there are a few that are used to determine trend continuation. They are referred to as reversal and continuation patterns. Whenever a reversal pattern has bullish implications, an inversely related pattern has bearish meaning. Similarly, whenever a continuation pattern has bullish implications, an opposite pattern gives bearish meaning. When there is a pair of patterns that work in both bullish and bearish situations, they usually have the same name. In a few cases, however, the bullish pattern and its bearish counterpart have completely different names.

Reversal Patterns

A *reversal candle pattern* is a combination of Japanese candlesticks that normally indicate a reversal of the trend. One serious consideration that must be used to help identify patterns as being either bullish or bearish is the trend of the market preceding the pattern. You cannot have a bullish reversal pattern in an uptrend. You can have a series of candlesticks that resemble the bullish pattern, but if the trend is up, it is not a bullish Japanese candle pattern. Likewise, you cannot have a bearish reversal candle pattern in a downtrend.

This presents one of the age-old problems when analyzing markets: What is the trend? You must determine the trend, before you can utilize Japanese candle patterns effectively. While volumes have been written on the subject of trend determination, the use of a moving average will work quite well with Japanese candle patterns. Once the short term (ten periods or so) trend has been determined, Japanese candle patterns will significantly assist in identifying the reversal of that trend.

Japanese literature consistently refers to approximately forty reversal candle patterns. These vary from single candlestick lines to more complex patterns of up to five candlestick lines. There are many good references on candlesticks, so only a few of the more popular patterns will be discussed here.

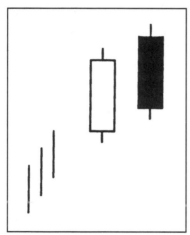

Figure 12.6 *Dark cloud cover –.*

Dark Cloud Cover.   This is a two day reversal pattern that only has bearish implications. (See Figure 12.6.) This is also one of the times when the pattern's counterpart exists but has a different name (see Piercing Line). The first day of this pattern is a long white candlestick. This reflects the current trend of the market and helps confirm the uptrend to traders. The next day opens above the high price of the previous day, again adding to the bullishness. However, trading for the rest of the day is lower with a close price at least below the midpoint of the body of the first day. This is a significant blow to the bullish mentality and will force many to exit the market. Since the close price is below the open price on the second day, the body is black. This is the dark cloud referred to in the name.

Piercing Line.   The opposite of the Dark Cloud Cover, the Piercing Line, has bullish implications. (See Figure 12.7.) The scenario is quite similar, but opposite. A downtrend is in place, the

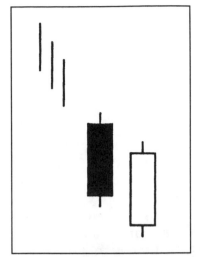

Figure 12.7 *Piercing line +.*

first candlestick is a long black day which solidifies traders' confidence in the downtrend. The next day, prices open at a new low and then trade higher all day and close above the midpoint of the first candlestick's body. This offers a significant change to the downtrend mentality and many will reverse or exit their positions.

Evening Star and Morning Star. The Evening Star and its cousin, the Morning Star, are two powerful reversal candle patterns. These are both three day patterns that work exceptionally well. The scenario for understanding the change in trader psychology for the Evening Star will be thoroughly discussed here since the opposite can be said for the Morning Star. (See Figures 12.8 and 12.9.)

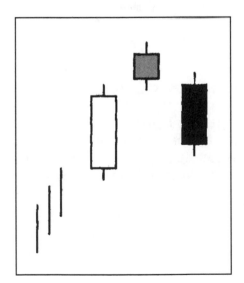

Figure 12.8 *Evening star –.*

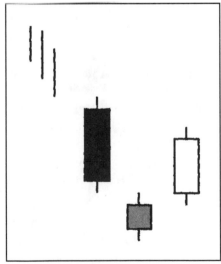

Figure 12.9 *Morning star +.*

The Evening Star is a bearish reversal candle pattern, as its name suggests. The first day of this pattern is a long white candlestick which fully enforces the current uptrend. On the open of the second day, prices gap up above the body of the first day. Trading on this second day is somewhat restricted and the close price is near the open price while remaining above the body of the first day. The body for the second day is small. This type of day following a long day is referred to as a Star pattern. A Star is a small body day that gaps away from a long body day. The third and last day of this pattern opens with a gap below the body of the star and closes lower with the close price below the midpoint of the first day.

The previous explanation was the perfect scenario. Many references will accept as valid, an Evening Star which does not meet each detail exactly. For instance, the third day might not gap down or the close on the third day might not be quite below the midpoint of the first day's body. These details are subjective when viewing a candlestick chart, but not when using a computer program to automatically identify the patterns. That is because computer programs require explicit instructions to read the candle chart, and don't allow for subjective interpretation.

Continuation Patterns

Each trading day, a decision needs to be made, whether it is to exit a trade, enter a trade, or remain in a trade. A candle pattern that helps identify the fact that the current trend is going to continue is more valuable than may first appear. It helps answer the question as to whether or not you should remain in a trade. Japanese literature refers to 16 continuation candle patterns. One continuation pattern and its related opposite cousin are particularly good at trend continuation identification.

Rising and Falling Three Methods.   The Rising Three Methods continuation candle pattern is the bullish counterpart to this duo and will be the subject of this scenario building. A bullish continuation pattern can only occur in an uptrend and a bearish continuation pattern can only occur in a downtrend. This restates the required relationship to the trend that is so necessary in candle pattern analysis. (See Figures 12.10 and 12.11.)

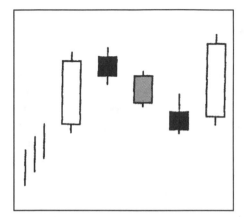

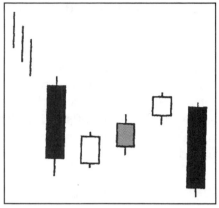

Figure 12.10 *Rising Three Methods +.*

Figure 12.11 *Falling Three Methods –.*

The first day of the Rising Three Methods pattern is a long white day which fully supports the uptrending market. However, over the course of the next three trading periods, small body days occur which, as a group, trend downward. They all remain within the range of the first day's long white body and at least two of these three small-bodied days have black bodies. This period of time when the market appears to have gone nowhere is considered by the Japanese as a "period of rest." On the fifth day of this pattern, another long white day develops which closes at a new high. Prices have finally broken out of the short trading range and the uptrend will continue.

A five day pattern such as the Rising Three Methods requires a lot of detail in its definition. The above scenario is the perfect example of the Rising Three Methods pattern. Flexibility can be applied with some success and this only comes with experience. For example, the three small reaction days could remain within the first day's high-low range instead of the body's range. The small reaction days do not always have to be predominantly black. And finally, the concept of the "period of rest" could be expanded to include more than three reaction days. Don't ignore the Rising and Falling Three Methods pattern; it can give you a feeling of comfort when worrying about protecting profits in a trade.

Using Computers for Candle
Pattern Identification

A personal computer with software designed to recognize candle patterns is a great way to remove emotion, especially during a trade. However, there are a couple of things to keep in mind when viewing candlesticks on a computer screen. A computer screen is made up of small light elements called pixels. There are only so many pixels on your computer screen, with the amount based upon the resolution of your video card/monitor combination. If you are viewing price data that has a large range of prices in a short period of time, you may think that you are seeing many Doji days (open and close price are equal) when in fact, you are not. With a large range of prices on the screen, each pixel element will have a price range of its own. A computer software program that identifies patterns based on a mathematical relationship will overcome this visual anomaly. Hopefully, the above explanation will keep you from thinking that your software isn't working.

FILTERED CANDLE PATTERNS

A revolutionary concept developed by Greg Morris in 1991, called candle pattern filtering, provides a simple method to improve the overall reliability of candle patterns. While the short term trend of the market must be identified before a candle pattern can exist, determination of overbought and oversold markets using traditional technical analysis will enhance a candle pattern's predictive ability. Concurrently, this technique helps eliminate bad or premature candle patterns.

One must first grasp how a traditional technical indicator responds to price data. In this example, Stochastics %D will be used. The stochastic indicator oscillates between 0 and 100, with 20 being oversold and 80 being overbought. The primary interpretation for this indicator is when %D rises above 80 and then falls below 80, a sell signal has been generated. Similarly, when it drops below 20 and then rises above 20, a buy signal is given. (See Chapter 10 for more on Stochastics.)

Here is what we know about stochastics %D: When it enters the area above 80 or below 20, it will eventually generate a signal. In other words, it is just a matter of time until a signal is given. The area above 80 and below 20 is called the presignal area and represents the area that %D must get to before it can give a trading signal of its own. (See Figure 12.12.)

Figure 12.12

The filtered candle pattern concept uses this presignal area. Candle patterns are considered *only* when %D is in its presignal area. If a candle pattern occurs when stochastics %D is at, say 65, the pattern is ignored. Also, only reversal candle patterns are considered using this concept.

Candle pattern filtering is not limited to using stochastics %D. Any technical oscillator that you might normally use for analysis can be used to filter candle patterns. Wilder's RSI, Lambert's CCI, and Williams' %R are a few that will work equally as well. (These oscillators are explained in Chapter 10.)

CONCLUSION

Japanese candlestick charting and candle pattern analysis are essential tools for making market timing decisions. One should use Japanese candle patterns in the same manner as any other technical tool or technique; that is, to study the psychology of market participants. Once you become used to seeing your price charts using candlesticks, you may not want to use bar charts again. Japanese candle patterns, used in conjunction with other technical indicators in the filtering concept, will almost always offer a trading signal prior to using other price-based indicators.

CANDLE PATTERNS

The candle patterns listed below comprise the library that is used to identify candlestick signals. The number in parentheses at the end of each name represents the number of candles that are used to define that particular pattern. The bullish and bearish patterns are divided into two groups signifying either reversal or continuation patterns.

Bullish Reversals
Long White Body (1)
Hammer (1)
Inverted Hammer (1)
Belt Hold (1)
Engulfing Pattern (2)
Harami (2)
Harami Cross (2)
Piercing Line (2)
Doji Star (2)
Meeting Lines (2)
Three White Soldiers (3)
Morning Star (3)
Morning Doji Star (3)
Abandoned Baby (3)
Tri-Star (3)
Breakaway (5)
Three Inside Up (3)
Three Outside Up (3)
Kicking (2)
Unique Three Rivers Bottom (3)
Three Stars in the South (3)
Concealing Swallow (4)
Stick Sandwich (3)
Homing Pigeon (2)
Ladder Bottom (5)
Matching Low (2)

Bearish Reversals
Long Black Body (1)
Hanging Man (1)
Shooting Star (1)
Belt Hold (1)
Engulfing Pattern (2)
Harami (2)
Harami Cross (2)
Dark Cloud Cover (2)
Doji Star (2)
Meeting Lines (2)
Three Black Crows (3)
Evening Star (3)
Evening Doji Star (3)
Abandoned Baby (3)
Tri-Star (3)
Breakaway (5)
Three Inside Down (3)
Three Outside Down (3)
Kicking (2)
Latter Top (5)
Matching High (2)
Upside Gap Two Crows (3)
Identical Three Crows (3)
Deliberation (3)
Advance Block (3)
Two Crows (3)

Bullish Continuation
Separating Lines (2)
Rising Three Methods (5)
Upside Tasuki Gap (3)
Side by Side White Lines (3)
Three Line Strike (4)
Upside Gap Three Methods (3)
On Neck Line (2)
In Neck Line (2)

Bearish Continuation
Separating Lines (2)
Falling Three Methods (5)
Downside Tasuki Gap (3)
Side by Side White Lines (3)
Three Line Strike (4)
Downside Gap Three Methods (3)
On Neck Line (2)
In Neck Line (2)

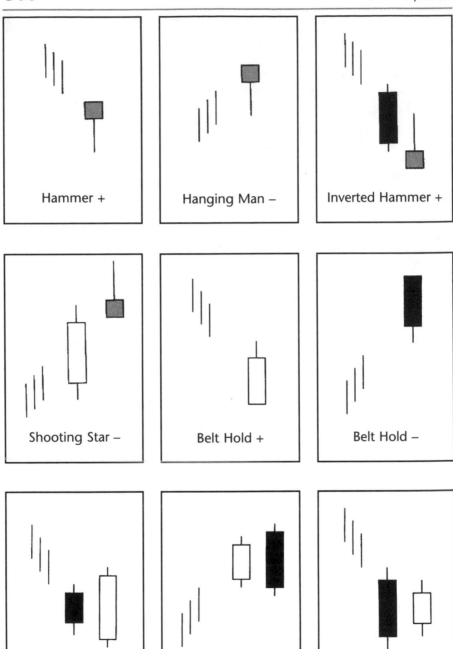

Hammer +

Hanging Man −

Inverted Hammer +

Shooting Star −

Belt Hold +

Belt Hold −

Engulfing +

Engulfing −

Harami +

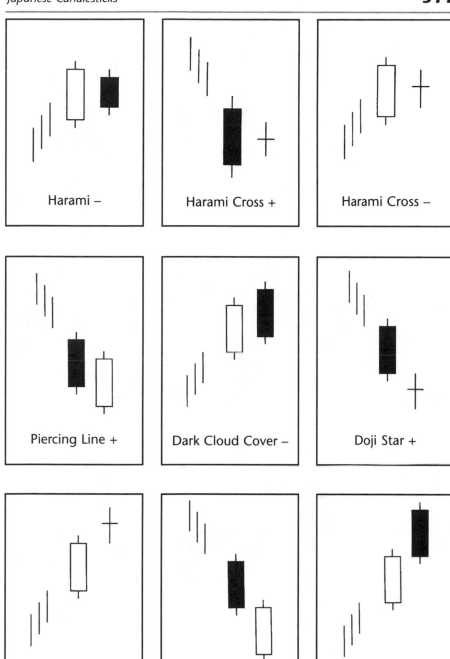

Harami –	Harami Cross +	Harami Cross –
Piercing Line +	Dark Cloud Cover –	Doji Star +
Doji Star –	Meeting Line +	Meeting Line –

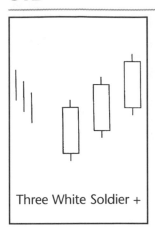

Three White Soldier +

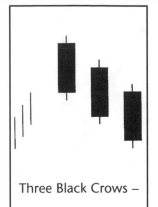

Three Black Crows −

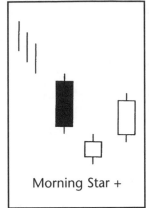

Morning Star +

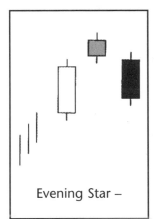

Evening Star −

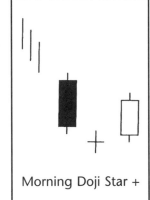

Morning Doji Star +

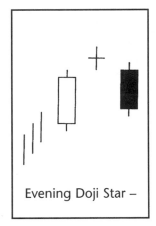

Evening Doji Star −

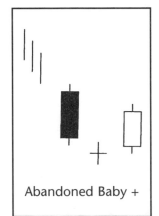

Abandoned Baby +

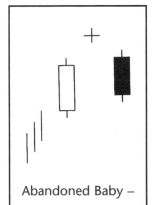

Abandoned Baby −

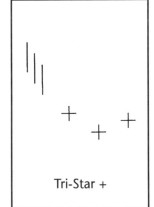

Tri-Star +

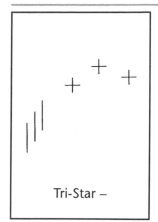

Tri-Star –

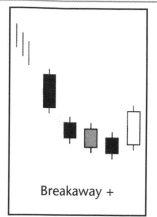

Breakaway +

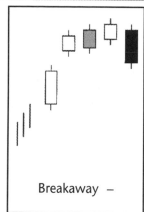

Breakaway –

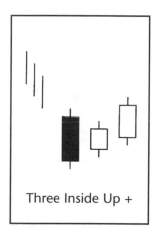

Three Inside Up +

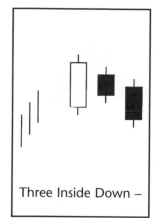

Three Inside Down –

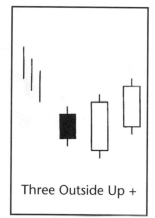

Three Outside Up +

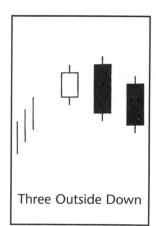

Three Outside Down

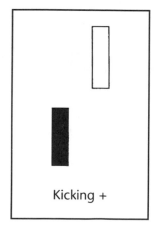

Kicking +

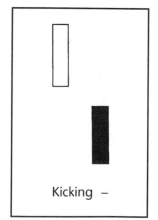

Kicking –

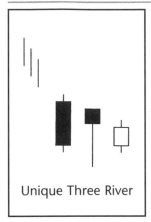

Unique Three River

Three Stars in the
South +

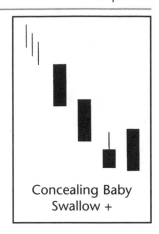

Concealing Baby
Swallow +

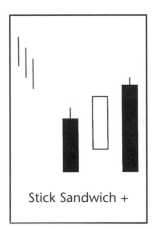

Stick Sandwich +

Identical Three
Crows –

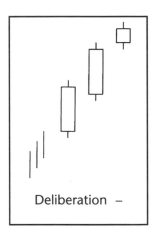

Deliberation –

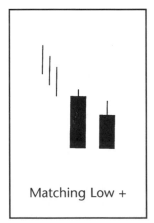

Matching Low +

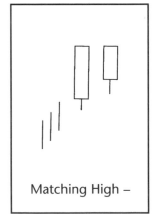

Matching High –

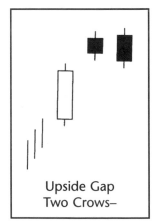

Upside Gap
Two Crows–

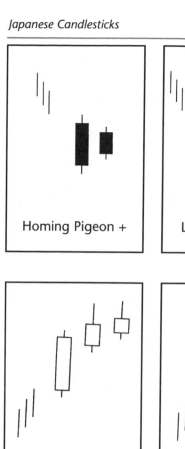

Homing Pigeon +

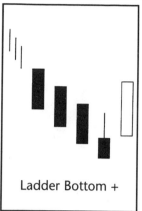

Ladder Bottom +

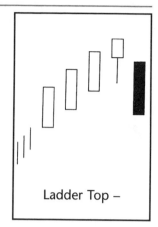

Ladder Top –

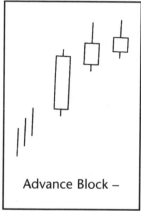

Advance Block –

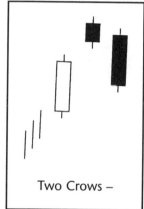

Two Crows –

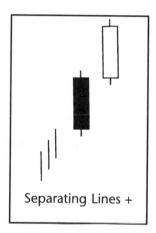

Separating Lines +

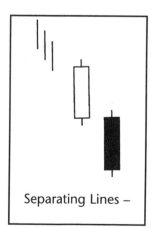

Separating Lines –

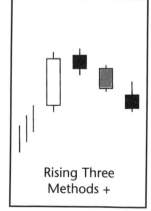

Rising Three
Methods +

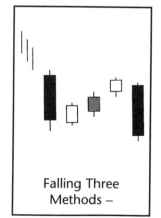

Falling Three
Methods –

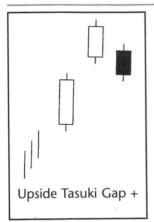

Upside Tasuki Gap +

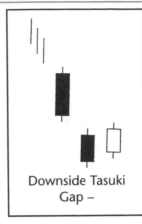

Downside Tasuki
Gap –

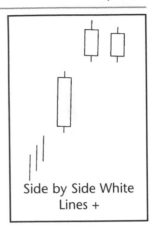

Side by Side White
Lines +

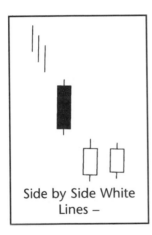

Side by Side White
Lines –

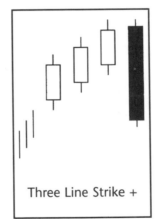

Three Line Strike +

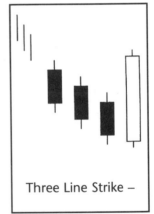

Three Line Strike –

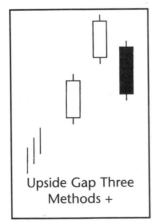

Upside Gap Three
Methods +

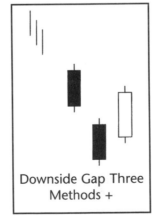

Downside Gap Three
Methods +

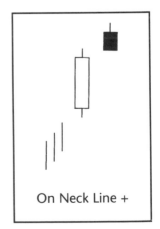

On Neck Line +

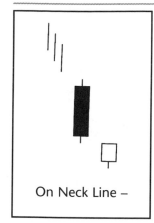

On Neck Line –

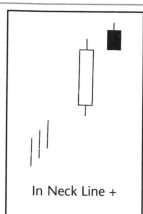

In Neck Line +

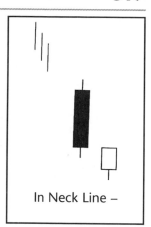

In Neck Line –

13
Elliott Wave Theory

HISTORICAL BACKGROUND

In 1938, a monograph entitled *The Wave Principle* was the first published reference to what has come to be known as the *Elliott Wave Principle.* The monograph was published by Charles J. Collins and was based on the original work presented to him by the founder of the Wave Principle, Ralph Nelson (R.N.) Elliott.

Elliott was very much influenced by the Dow Theory, which has much in common with the Wave Principle. In a 1934 letter to Collins, Elliott mentioned that he had been a subscriber to Robert Rhea's stock market service and was familiar with Rhea's book on Dow Theory. Elliott goes on to say that the Wave Principle was "a much needed complement to the Dow Theory."

In 1946, just two years before his death, Elliott wrote his definitive work on the Wave Principle, *Nature's Law—The Secret of the Universe.*

Elliott's ideas might have faded from memory if A. Hamilton Bolton hadn't decided in 1953 to publish the *Elliott Wave Supplement* to the *Bank Credit Analyst,* which he did annually for 14 years, until his death in 1967. A.J. Frost took over the Elliott Supplements and collaborated with Robert Prechter in 1978 on the *Elliott Wave Principle.* Most of the diagrams in this chapter are taken from Frost and Prechter's book. Prechter went a step further and in 1980 published *The Major Works of R.N. Elliott,* making available the original Elliott writings that had long been out of print.

BASIC TENETS OF THE ELLIOTT WAVE PRINCIPLE

There are three important aspects of wave theory—*pattern, ratio, and time*—in that order of importance. *Pattern* refers to the wave patterns or formations that comprise the most important element of the theory. *Ratio analysis* is useful in determining retracement points and price objectives by measuring the relationships between the different waves. Finally, *time* relationships also exist and can be used to confirm the wave patterns and ratios, but are considered by some Elliotticians to be less reliable in market forecasting.

Elliott Wave Theory was originally applied to the major stock market averages, particularly the Dow Jones Industrial Average. In its most basic form, the theory says that the stock market follows a repetitive rhythm of a five wave advance followed by a three wave decline. Figure 13.1 shows one complete cycle. If you count the waves, you will find that one complete cycle has eight waves—five up and three down. In the advancing portion of the cycle, notice that each of the five waves are numbered. Waves 1, 3, and 5—called *impulse* waves—are rising waves, while waves 2 and 4 move against the uptrend. Waves 2 and 4 are called *corrective* waves because they correct waves 1 and 3. After the five wave numbered advance has been completed, a three wave correction begins. The three corrective waves are identified by the letters a, b, c.

Along with the constant form of the various waves, there is the important consideration of degree. There are many different degrees of trend. Elliott, in fact, categorized nine different degrees of trend (or magnitude) ranging from a *Grand Supercycle*

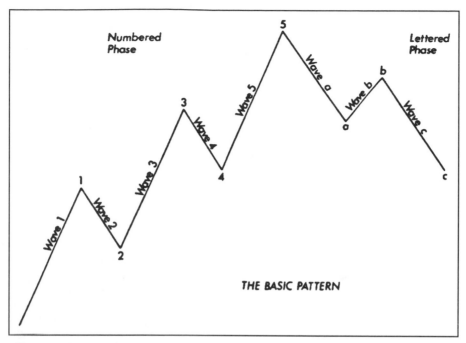

Figure 13.1   *The Basic Pattern. (A.J. Frost and Robert Prechter,* Elliott Wave Principle *[Gainesville, GA: New Classics Library, 1978], p. 20. Copyright © 1978 by Frost and Prechter.)*

spanning two hundred years to a *subminuette* degree covering only a few hours. The point to remember is that the basic eight wave cycle remains constant no matter what degree of trend is being studied.

Each wave subdivides into waves of one lesser degree that, in turn, can also be subdivided into waves of even lesser degree. It also follows then that each wave is itself part of the wave of the next higher degree. Figure 13.2 demonstrates these relationships. The largest two waves—1 and 2—can be subdivided into eight lesser waves that, in turn, can be subdivided into 34 even lesser waves. The two largest waves—1 and 2—are only the first two waves in an even larger five wave advance. Wave 3 of that next higher degree is about to begin. The 34 waves in Figure 13.2 are subdivided further to the next smaller degree in Figure 13.3, resulting in 144 waves.

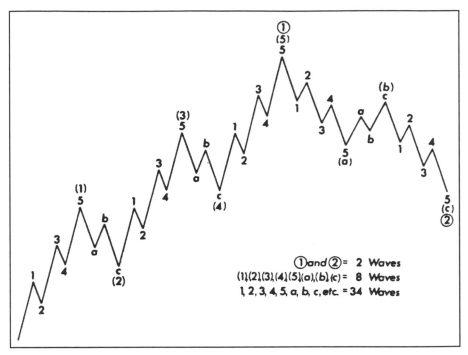

Figure 13.2   *(Frost and Prechter, p. 21. Copyright © 1978 by Frost and Prechter.)*

The numbers shown so far 1,2,3,5,8,13,21,34,55,89,144—are not just random numbers. They are part of the *Fibonacci number sequence,* which forms the mathematical basis for the Elliott Wave Theory. We'll come back to them a little later. For now, look at Figures 13.1-13.3 and notice a very significant characteristic of the waves. Whether a given wave divides into five waves or three waves is determined by the direction of the next larger wave. For example, in Figure 13.2, waves (1), (3), and (5) subdivide into five waves because the next larger wave of which they are part—wave 1—is an advancing wave. Because waves (2) and (4) are moving against the trend, they subdivide into only three waves. Look more closely at corrective waves (a), (b), and (c), which comprise the larger corrective wave 2. Notice that the two declining waves—(a) and (c)—each break down into five waves. This is

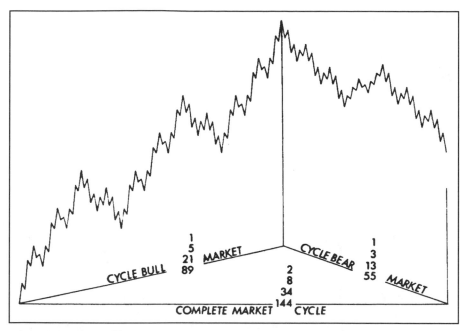

Figure 13.3 *(Frost and Prechter, p. 22. Copyright © 1978 by Frost and Prechter.)*

because they are moving in the same direction as the next larger wave 2. Wave (b) by contrast only has three waves, because it is moving against the next larger wave 2.

Being able to determine between threes and fives is obviously of tremendous importance in the application of this approach. That information tells the analyst what to expect next. A completed five wave move, for example, usually means that only part of a larger wave has been completed and that there's more to come (unless it's a fifth of a fifth). *One of the most important rules to remember is that a correction can never take place in five waves.* In a bull market, for example, if a five wave decline is seen, this means that it is probably only the first wave of a three wave (a-b-c) decline and that there's more to come on the downside. In a bear market, a three wave advance should be followed by resumption of the downtrend. A five wave rally would warn of a more substantial move to the upside and might possibly even be the first wave of a new bull trend.

CONNECTION BETWEEN ELLIOTT WAVE AND DOW THEORY

Let's take a moment here to point out the obvious connection between Elliott's idea of five advancing waves and Dow's three advancing phases of a bull market. It seems clear that Elliott's idea of three up waves, with two intervening corrections, fits nicely with the Dow Theory. While Elliott was no doubt influenced by Dow's analysis, it also seems clear that Elliott believed he had gone well beyond Dow's theory and had in fact improved on it. It's also interesting to note the influence of the sea on both men in the formulation of their theories. Dow compared the major, intermediate, and minor trends in the market with the tides, waves, and ripples on the ocean. Elliott referred to "ebbs and flows" in his writing and named his theory the "wave" principle.

CORRECTIVE WAVES

So far, we've talked mainly about the impulse waves in the direction of the major trend. Let's turn our attention now to the corrective waves. In general, corrective waves are less clearly defined and, as a result, tend to be more difficult to identify and predict. One point that is clearly defined, however, is that corrective waves can never take place in five waves. Corrective waves are threes, never fives (with the exception of triangles). We're going to look at three classifications of corrective waves—zig-zags, flats, and triangles.

Zig-Zags

A zig-zag is a three wave corrective pattern, against the major trend, which breaks down into a 5-3-5 sequence. Figures 13.4 and 13.5 show a bull market zig-zag correction, while a bear market rally is shown in Figures 13.6 and 13.7. Notice that the middle wave B falls short of the beginning of wave A and that wave C moves well beyond the end of wave A.

A less common variation of the zig-zag is the double zig-zag shown in Figure 13.8. This variation sometimes occurs in larger corrective patterns. It is in effect two different 5-3-5 zig-zag patterns connected by an intervening a-b-c pattern.

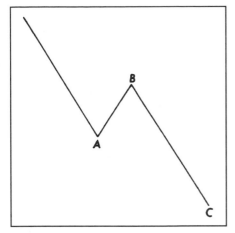

Figure 13.4   *Bull Market Zig-Zag (5-3-5). (Frost and Prechter, p. 36. Copyright © 1978 by Frost and Prechter.)*

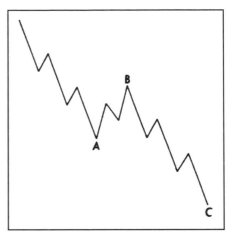

Figure 13.5   *Bull Market Zig-Zag (5-3-5). (Frost and Prechter, p. 36. Copyright © 1978 by Frost and Prechter.)*

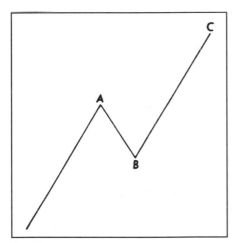

Figure 13.6   *Bear Market Zig-Zag (5-3 5). (Frost and Prechter, p. 36. Copyright © 1978 by Frost and Prechter.)*

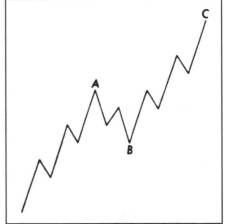

Figure 13.7   *Bear Market Zig-Zag (5-3-5). (Frost and Prechter, p. 36 Copyright © 1978 by Frost and Prechter.)*

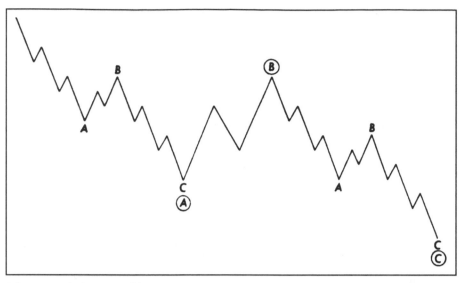

Figure 13.8 *Double Zig-Zag. (Frost and Prechter, p. 37. Copyright ©
1978 by Frost and Prechter.)*

Flats

What distinguishes the flat correction from the zig-zag correction
is that the flat follows a 3-3-5 pattern. Notice in Figures 13.10 and
13.12 that the A wave is a 3 instead of a 5. In general, the flat is
more of a consolidation than a correction and is considered a sign
of strength in a bull market. Figures 13.9-13.12 show examples of
normal flats. In a bull market, for example, wave B rallies all the
way to the top of wave A, showing greater market strength. The
final wave C terminates at or just below the bottom of wave A in
contrast to a zig-zag, which moves well under that point.

There are two "irregular" variations of the normal *flat* correction. Figures 13.13-13.16 show the first type of variation.
Notice in the bull market example (Figures 13.13 and 13.14) that
the top of wave B exceeds the top of A and that wave C violates
the bottom of A.

Another variation occurs when wave B reaches the top of A,
but wave C fails to reach the bottom of A. Naturally, this last pattern denotes greater market strength in a bull market. This variation is shown in Figures 13.17-13.20 for bull and bear markets.

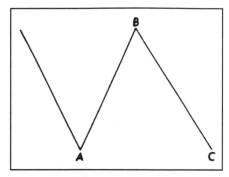

Figure 13.9 *Bull Market Flat (3-3-5), Normal Correction. (Frost and Prechter, p. 38. Copyright © 1978 by Frost and Prechter.)*

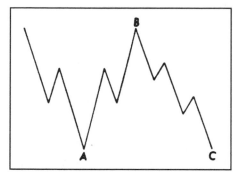

Figure 13.10 *Bull Market Flat (3-3-5), Normal Correction. (Frost and Prechter, p. 38. Copyright © 1978 by Frost and Prechter.)*

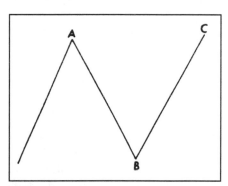

Figure 13.11 *Bear Market Flat (3-3-5), Normal Correction. (Frost and Prechter, p. 38. Copyright © 1978 by Frost and Prechter.)*

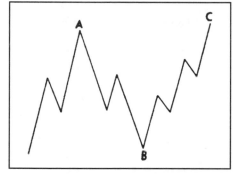

Figure 13.12 *Bear Market Flat (3-3-5), Normal Correction. (Frost and Prechter, p. 38. Copyright © 1978 by Frost and Prechter.)*

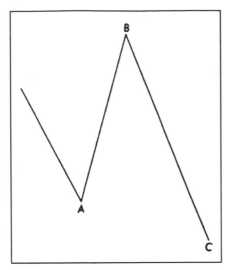

Figure 13.13 *Bull Market Flat (3-3-5), Irregular Correction. (Frost and Prechter,p. 39. Copyright © 1978 by Frost and Prechter.)*

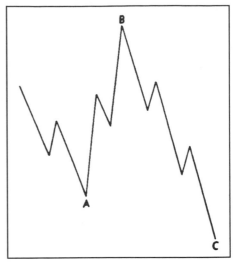

Figure 13.14 *Bull Market Flat (3-3-5), Irregular Correction. (Frost and Prechter, p. 39. Copyright © 1918 by Frost and Prechter.)*

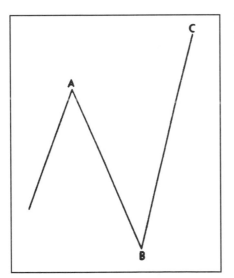

Figure 13.15 *Bear Market Flat (3-3-5), Irregular Correction. (Frost and Prechter, p. 39. Copyright © 1978 by Frost and Prechter.)*

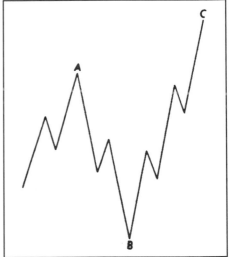

Figure 13.16 *Bear Market Flat (3-3-5), Irregular Correction. (Frost and Prechter, p. 39. Copyright © 1978 by Frost and Prechter.)*

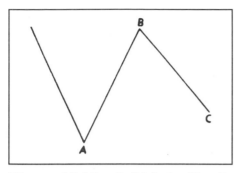

Figure 13.17 *Bull Market Flat (3-3-5), Inverted Irregular Correction. (Frost and Prechter, p. 40. Copyright © 1978 by Frost and Prechter.)*

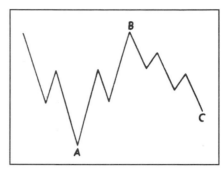

Figure 13.18 *Bull Market Flat (3-3-5), Inverted Irregular Correction. (Frost and Prechter, p. 40. Copyright © 1978 by Frost and Prechter.)*

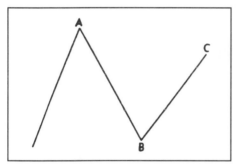

Figure 13.19 *Bear Market Flat (3-3-5), Inverted Irregular Correction. (Frost and Prechter, p. 40. Copyright © 1978 by Frost and Prechter.)*

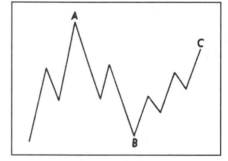

Figure 13.20 *Bear Market Flat (3-3-5), Inverted Irregular Correction. (Frost and Prechter, p. 40. Copyright © 1978 by Frost and Prechter.)*

Triangles

Triangles usually occur in the fourth wave and precede the final move in the direction of the major trend. (They can also appear in the b wave of an a-b-c correction.) In an uptrend, therefore, it can be said that triangles are both bullish and bearish. They're bullish in the sense that they indicate resumption of the uptrend. They're bearish because they also indicate that after one more wave up, prices will probably peak. (See Figure 13.21.)

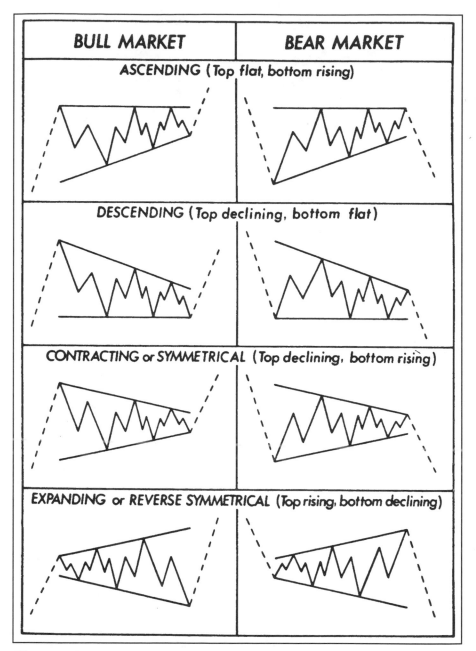

Figure 13.21   *Corrective Wave (Horizontal) Triangles. (Frost and Prechter, p. 43. Copyright © 1978 by Frost and Prechter.)*

Elliott's interpretation of the triangle parallels the classical use of the pattern, but with his usual added precision. Remember from Chapter 6 that the triangle is usually a continuation pattern, which is exactly what Elliott said. Elliott's triangle is a sideways consolidation pattern that breaks down into five waves, each wave in turn having three waves of its own. Elliott also classifies four different kinds of triangles—*ascending, descending, symmetrical,* and *expanding*—all of which were seen in Chapter 6. Figure 13.21 shows the four varieties in both uptrends and downtrends.

Because chart patterns in commodity futures contracts sometimes don't form as fully as they do in the stock market, it is not unusual for triangles in the futures markets to have only three waves instead of five. (Remember, however, that the minimum requirement for a triangle is still four points—two upper and two lower—to allow the drawing of two converging trendlines.) Elliott Wave Theory also holds that the fifth and last wave within the triangle sometimes breaks its trendline, giving a false signal, before beginning its "thrust" in the original direction.

Elliott's measurement for the fifth and final wave after completion of the triangle is essentially the same as in classical charting—that is, the market is expected to move the distance that matches the widest part of the triangle (its height). There is another point worth noting here concerning the timing of the final top or bottom. According to Prechter, the apex of the triangle (the point where the two converging trendlines meet) often marks the timing for the completion of the final fifth wave.

THE RULE OF ALTERNATION

In its more general application, this rule or principle holds that the market usually doesn't act the same way two times in a row. If a certain type of top or bottom occurred the last time around, it will probably not do so again this time. The rule of alternation doesn't tell us exactly what will happen, but tells us what probably won't. In its more specific application, it is most generally used to tell us what type of corrective pattern to expect. Corrective patterns tend to alternate. In other words, if corrective wave 2 was a simple a-b-c pattern, wave 4 will probably be a complex pattern, such as a triangle. Conversely, if wave 2 is complex, wave 4 will probably be simple. Figure 13.22 gives some examples.

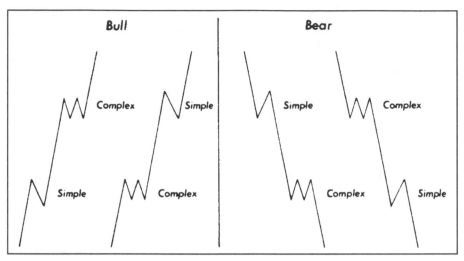

Figure 13.22 *The Rule of Alternation. (Frost and Prechter, p. 50. Copyright © 1978 by Frost and Prechter.)*

CHANNELING

Another important aspect of wave theory is the use of *price channels*. You'll recall that we covered trend channeling in Chapter 4. Elliott used price channels as a method of arriving at price objectives and also to help confirm the completion of wave counts. Once an uptrend has been established, an initial trend channel is constructed by drawing a basic up trendline along the bottoms of waves 1 and 2. A parallel channel line is then drawn over the top of wave 1 as shown in Figure 13.23. The entire uptrend will often stay within those two boundaries.

If wave 3 begins to accelerate to the point that it exceeds the upper channel line, the lines have to be redrawn along the top of wave 1 and the bottom of wave 2 as shown in Figure 13.23. The final channel is drawn under the two corrective waves—2 and 4—and usually above the top of wave 3 as shown in Figure 13.24. If wave 3 is unusually strong, or an extended

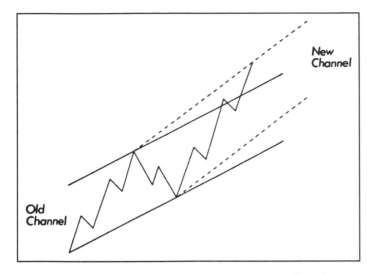

Figure 13.23
Old and New Channels. (Frost and Prechter, p. 62. Copyright © 1978 by Frost and Prechter.)

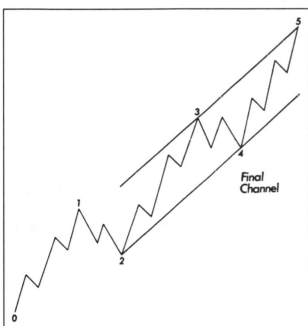

Figure 13.24
Final Channel. (Frost and Prechter, p. 63. Copyright © 1978 by Frost and Prechter.)

wave, the upper line may have to be drawn over the top of wave 1. The fifth wave should come close to the upper channel line before terminating. For the drawing of channel lines on long term trends, it's recommended that semilog charts be employed along with arithmetic charts.

WAVE 4 AS A SUPPORT AREA

In concluding our discussion of wave formations and guidelines, one important point remains to be mentioned, and that is the significance of wave 4 as a support area in subsequent bear markets. Once five up waves have been completed and a bear trend has begun, that bear market will usually not move below the previous fourth wave of one lesser degree; that is, the last fourth wave that was formed during the previous bull advance. There are exceptions to that rule, but usually the bottom of the fourth wave contains the bear market. This piece of information can prove very useful in arriving at a maximum downside price objective.

FIBONACCI NUMBERS AS THE BASIS OF THE WAVE PRINCIPLE

Elliott stated in *Nature's Law* that the mathematical basis for his Wave Principle was a number sequence discovered by Leonardo Fibonacci in the thirteenth century. That number sequence has become identified with its discoverer and is commonly referred to as the *Fibonacci numbers*. The number sequence is 1, 1, 2, 3, 5, 8, 13, 21, 34, 55, 89, 144, and so on to infinity.

The sequence has a number of interesting properties, not the least of which is an almost constant relationship between the numbers.

1. The sum of any two consecutive numbers equals the next higher number. For example, 3 and 5 equals 8, 5 and 8 equals 13, and so on.
2. The ratio of any number to its next higher number approaches .618, after the first four numbers. For example,

1/1 is 1.00, 1/2 is .50, 2/3 is .67, 3/5 is .60, 5/8 is .625, 8/13 is .615, 13/21 is .619, and so on. Notice how these early ratio values fluctuate above and below .618 in narrowing amplitude. Also, notice the values of 1.00, .50, .67. We'll comment further on these values when we talk more about ratio analysis and percentage retracements.

3. The ratio of any number to its next lower number is approximately 1.618, or the inverse of .618. For example, 13/8 is 1.625, 21/13 is 1.615, 34/21 is 1.619. The higher the numbers become, the closer they come to the values of .618 and 1.618.

4. The ratios of alternate numbers approach 2.618 or its inverse, .382. For example, 13/34 is .382, 34/13 is 2.615.

FIBONACCI RATIOS AND RETRACEMENTS

It was already stated that wave theory is comprised of three aspects—wave form, ratio, and time. We've already discussed wave form, which is the most important of the three. Let's talk now about the application of the *Fibonacci ratios and retracements*. These relationships can apply to both price and time, although the former is considered to be the more reliable. We'll come back later to the aspect of time.

First of all, a glance back at Figures 13.1 and 13.3 shows that the basic wave form always breaks down into Fibonacci numbers. One complete cycle comprises eight waves, five up and three down—all Fibonacci numbers. Two further subdivisions will produce 34 and 144 waves—also Fibonacci numbers. The mathematical basis of the wave theory on the Fibonacci sequence, however, goes beyond just wave counting. There's also the question of proportional relationships between the different waves. The following are among the most commonly used Fibonacci ratios:

1. One of the three impulse waves sometimes extends. The other two are equal in time and magnitude. If wave 5 extends, waves 1 and 3 should be about equal. If wave 3 extends, waves 1 and 5 tend toward equality.

2. A minimum target for the top of wave 3 can be obtained by multiplying the length of wave 1 by 1.618 and adding that total to the bottom of 2.

3. The top of wave 5 can be approximated by multiplying wave 1 by 3.236 (2×1.618) and adding that value to the top or bottom of wave 1 for maximum and minimum targets.

4. Where waves 1 and 3 are about equal, and wave 5 is expected to extend, a price objective can be obtained by measuring the distance from the bottom of wave 1 to the top of wave 3, multiplying by 1.618, and adding the result to the bottom of 4.

5. For corrective waves, in a normal 5-3-5 zig-zag correction, wave c is often about equal to the length of wave a.

6. Another way to measure the possible length of wave c is to multiply .618 by the length of wave a and subtract that result from the bottom of wave a.

7. In the case of a flat 3-3-5 correction, where the b wave reaches or exceeds the top of wave a, wave c will be about 1.618 the length of a.

8. In a symmetrical triangle, each successive wave is related to its previous wave by about .618.

Fibonacci Percentage Retracements

The preceding ratios help to determine price objectives in both impulse and corrective waves. Another way to determine price objectives is by the use of *percentage retracements*. The most commonly used numbers in retracement analysis are 61.8% (usually rounded off to 62%), 38%, and 50%. Remember from Chapter 4 that markets usually retrace previous moves by certain predictable percentages—the best known ones being 33%, 50%, and 67%. The Fibonacci sequence refines those numbers a bit further. In a strong trend, a minimum retracement is usually around 38%. In a weaker trend, the maximum percentage retracement is usually 62%. (See Figures 13.25 and 13.26.)

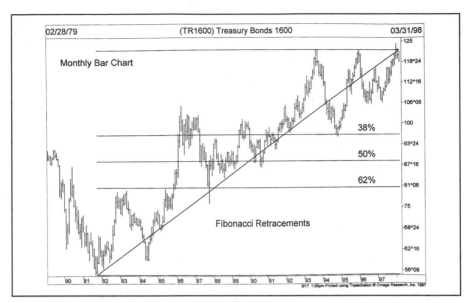

Figure 13.25 *The three horizontal lines show Fibonnaci retracement levels of 38%, 50%, and 62% measured from the 1981 bottom to the 1993 peak in Treasury Bonds. The 1994 correction in bond prices stopped right at the 38% retracement line.*

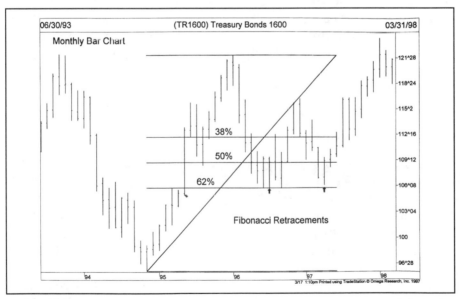

Figure 13.26 *The three Fibonacci percentage lines are measured from the 1994 bottom in bond prices to the early 1996 top. Bond prices corrected to the 62% line.*

It was pointed out earlier, that the Fibonacci ratios approach .618 only after the first four numbers. The first three ratios are 1/1 (100%), 1/2 (50%), and 2/3 (66%). Many students of Elliott may be unaware that the famous 50% retracement is actually a Fibonacci ratio, as is the two-thirds retracement. A complete retracement (100%) of a previous bull or bear market also should mark an important support or resistance area.

FIBONACCI TIME TARGETS

We haven't said too much about the aspect of time in wave analysis. Fibonacci time relationships exist. It's just that they're harder to predict and are considered by some Elliotticians to be the least important of the three aspects of the theory. Fibonacci time targets are found by counting forward from significant tops and bottoms. On a daily chart, the analyst counts forward the number of trading days from an important turning point with the expectation that future tops or bottoms will occur on Fibonacci days—that is, on the 13th, 21st, 34th, 55th, or 89th trading day in the future. The same technique can be used on weekly, monthly, or even yearly charts. On the weekly chart, the analyst picks a significant top or bottom and looks for weekly time targets that fall on Fibonacci numbers. (See Figures 13.27 and 13.28.)

COMBINING ALL THREE ASPECTS
OF WAVE THEORY

The ideal situation occurs when wave form, ratio analysis, and time targets come together. Suppose that a study of waves reveals that a fifth wave has been completed, that wave 5 has gone 1.618 times the distance from the bottom of wave 1 to the top of wave 3, and that the time from the beginning of the trend has been 13 weeks from a previous low and 34 weeks from a previous top. Suppose further that the fifth wave has lasted 21 days. Odds would be pretty good that an important top was near.

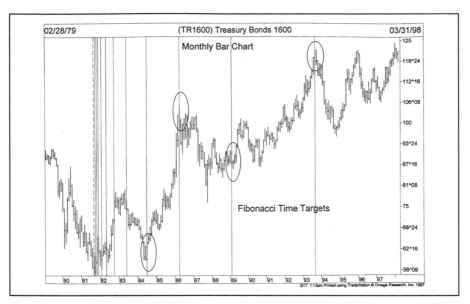

Figure 13.27 *Fibonacci time targets measured in months from the 1981 bottom in Treasury Bonds. It may be coincidence, but the last four Fibonacci time targets (vertical bars) coincided with important turns in bond prices.*

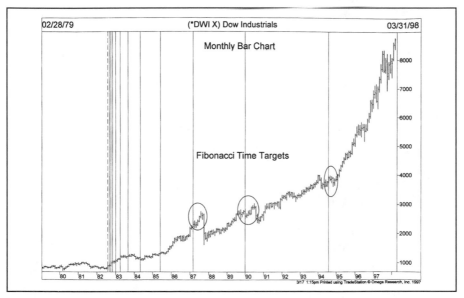

Figure 13.28 *Fibonacci time targets in months from the 1982 bottom in the Dow. The last three vertical bars coincide with bear market years in stocks—1987, 1990, and 1994. The 1987 peak was 13 years from the 1982 bottom—a Fibonacci number.*

A study of price charts in both stocks and futures markets reveals a number of Fibonacci time relationships. Part of the problem, however, is the variety of possible relationships. Fibonacci time targets can be taken from top to top, top to bottom, bottom to bottom, and bottom to top. These relationships can always be found after the fact. It's not always clear which of the possible relationships are relevant to the current trend.

ELLIOTT WAVE APPLIED TO STOCKS VERSUS COMMODITIES

There are some differences in applying wave theory to stocks and commodities. For example, wave 3 tends to extend in stocks and wave 5 in commodities. The unbreakable rule that wave 4 can never overlap wave 1 in stocks is not as rigid in commodities. (Intraday penetrations can occur on futures charts.) Sometimes charts of the cash market in commodities give a clearer Elliott pattern than the futures market. The use of continuation charts in commodity futures markets also produces distortions that may affect long term Elliott patterns.

Possibly the most significant difference between the two areas is that major bull markets in commodities can be "contained," meaning that bull market highs do not always exceed previous bull market highs. It is possible in commodity markets for a completed five wave bull trend to fall short of a previous bull market high. The major tops formed in many commodity markets in the 1980 to 1981 period failed to exceed major tops formed seven and eight years earlier. As a final comparison between the two areas, it appears that the best Elliott patterns in commodity markets arise from breakouts from long term extended bases.

It is important to keep in mind that wave theory was originally meant to be applied to the stock market averages. It doesn't work as well in individual common stocks. It's quite possible that it doesn't work that well in some of the more thinly traded futures markets as well because mass psychology is one of the important foundations on which the theory rests. Gold, as an illustration, is an excellent vehicle for wave analysis because of its wide following.

SUMMARY AND CONCLUSIONS

Let's briefly summarize the more important elements of wave theory and then try to put it into proper perspective.

1. A complete bull market cycle is made up of eight waves, five up waves followed by three down waves.

2. A trend divides into five waves in the direction of the next longer trend.

3. Corrections always take place in three waves.

4. The two types of simple corrections are zig-zags (5-3-5) and flats (3-3-5).

5. Triangles are usually fourth waves, and always precede the final wave. Triangles can also be B corrective waves.

6. Waves can be expanded into longer waves and subdivided into shorter waves.

7. Sometimes one of the impulse waves extends. The other two should then be equal in time and magnitude.

8. The Fibonacci sequence is the mathematical basis of the Elliott Wave Theory.

9. The number of waves follows the Fibonacci sequence.

10. Fibonacci ratios and retracements are used to determine price objectives. The most common retracements are 62%, 50%, and 38%.

11. The rule of alternation warns not to expect the same thing twice in succession.

12. Bear markets should not fall below the bottom of the previous fourth wave.

13. Wave 4 should not overlap wave 1 (not as rigid in futures).

14. The Elliott Wave Theory is comprised of wave forms, ratios, and time, in that order of importance.

15. The theory was originally applied to stock market averages and does not work as well on individual stocks.

16. The theory works best in those commodity markets with the largest public following, such as gold.

17. The principal difference in commodities is the existence of contained bull markets.

The Elliott Wave Principle builds on the more classical approaches, such as Dow Theory and traditional chart patterns. Most of those price patterns can be explained as part of the Elliott Wave structure. It builds on the concept of "swing objectives" by using Fibonacci ratio projections and percentage retracements. The Elliott Wave Principle takes all of these factors into consideration, but goes beyond them by giving them more order and increased predictability.

Wave Theory Should Be Used in Conjunction with Other Technical Tools

There are times when Elliott pictures are clear and other times when they are not. Trying to force unclear market action into an Elliott format, and ignoring other technical tools in the process, is a misuse of the theory. The key is to view Elliott Wave Theory as a partial answer to the puzzle of market forecasting. Using it in conjunction with all of the other technical theories in this book will increase its value and improve your chances for success.

REFERENCE MATERIAL

Two of the best sources of information on Elliott Wave Theory and the Fibonacci numbers are *The Major Works of R.N. Elliott,* (Prechter, Jr.) and the *Elliott Wave Principle* (Frost and Prechter). All of the diagrams used in Figures 13.1-13.24 are from the *Elliott Wave Principle* and are reproduced in this chapter through the courtesy of New Classics Library.

A primer booklet on the Fibonacci numbers, *Understanding Fibonacci Numbers* by Edward D. Dobson, is available from Traders Press (P.O. Box 6206, Greenville, S.C. 29606 (800-927-8222).

Time Cycles

14

INTRODUCTION

Our main focus up to this point has been on price movement, and not too much has been said about the importance of *time* in solving the forecasting puzzle. The question of time has been present by implication throughout our entire coverage of technical analysis, but has generally been relegated to secondary consideration. In this chapter, we're going to view the problem of forecasting through the eyes of cyclic analysts who believe that *time cycles* hold the ultimate key to understanding why markets move up or down. In the process, we're going to add the important dimension of time to our growing list of analytical tools. Instead of just asking ourselves *which way* and *how far* a market will go, we'll start asking *when* it will arrive there or even *when* the move will begin.

Consider the standard daily bar chart. The vertical axis gives the price scale. But that's only half of the relevant data. The horizontal scale gives the time horizon. Therefore, the bar chart is really a time and price chart. Yet, many traders concentrate solely on price data to the exclusion of time considerations. When we study chart patterns, we're aware that there is a relationship between the amount of time it takes for those patterns to form and the potential for subsequent market moves. The longer a trendline or a support or resistance level remains in effect, the more valid it becomes. Moving averages require input as to the proper time period to use. Even oscillators require some decision as to how many days to measure. In the previous chapter, we considered the usefulness of Fibonacci time targets.

It seems clear then that all phases of technical analysis depend to some extent on time considerations. Yet those considerations are not really applied in a consistent and dependable manner. That's where time cycles come into play. Instead of playing a secondary or supporting role in market movement, cyclic analysts hold that time cycles are the determining factor in bull and bear markets. Not only is time the dominant factor, but all other technical tools can be improved by incorporating cycles. Moving averages and oscillators, for example, can be optimized by tying them to dominant cycles. Trendline analysis can be made more precise with cyclic analysis by determining which are valid trendlines and which are not. Price pattern analysis can be enhanced if combined with cyclic peaks and troughs. By the use of "time windows," price movement can be filtered in such a way that extraneous action can be ignored and primary emphasis placed only on such times when important cycle tops and bottoms are due to occur.

CYCLES

The most intriguing book I've ever read on the subject of cycles was written by Edward R. Dewey, one of the pioneers of cyclic analysis, with Og Mandino entitled *Cycles: The Mysterious Forces That Trigger Events*. Thousands of seemingly unrelated cycles were isolated spanning hundreds and, in some cases, thousands of years. Everything from the 9.6 year cycle in Atlantic salmon abundance to the 22.20 year cycle in international battles from 1415 to 1930 was tracked. An average cycle of sunspot activity since 1527 was found to be 11.11 years. Several economic cycles, including the 18.33 year cycle in real estate activity and a 9.2 year stock market cycle, were presented. (See Figures 14.1 and 14.2.)

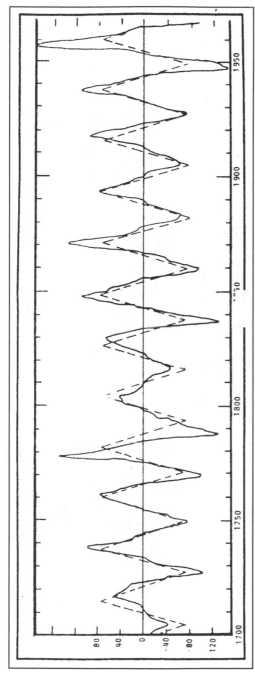

Figure 14.1 *The 22.2 year cycle of incidence of sunspots. Drought often follows two years after the sunspot minima which last occurred in the early 1970s, and is due again in the mid 1990s. In the chart, the dotted line is the "ideal" cycle, and the solid line is the actual detrended data. (Courtesy of the Foundation for the Study of Cycles, Wayne, PA.)*

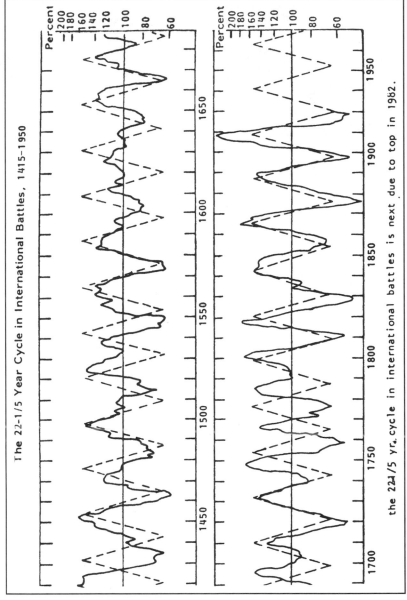

Figure 14.2 *The 22.2 year cycle in international battles was due to top in 1982. In the chart, the dotted line is the "ideal" cycle, and the solid line is the actual detrended data. (Courtesy of the Foundation for the Study of Cycles, Wayne, PA.*

Two startling conclusions are discussed by Dewey. First, that many of the cycles of seemingly unrelated phenomena clustered around similar periods. On p. 188 of his book, Dewey listed 37 different examples of the 9.6 year cycle, including caterpillar abundance in New Jersey, coyote abundance in Canada, wheat acreage in the U.S., and cotton prices in the U.S. Why should such unrelated activities show the same cycles?

The second discovery was that these similar cycles acted in synchrony, that is, they turned at the same time. Figure 14.3

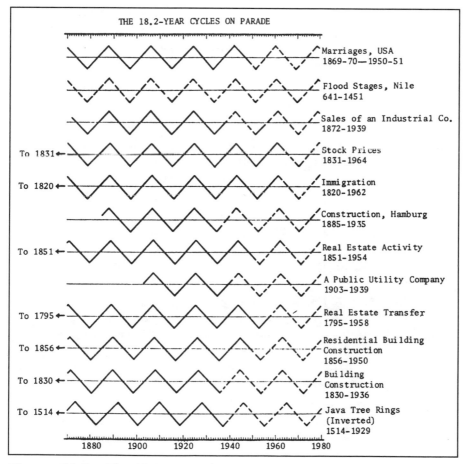

Figure 14.3 *The 18.2 year cycles on parade. (Source: Dewey, Edward R.,* Cycles: The Mysterious Forces That Trigger Events *(New York: Manor Books, 1973.)*

shows 12 different examples of the 18.2 year cycle including mar-
riages, immigration, and stock prices in the U.S. Dewey's startling
conclusion was that something "out there" in the universe must
be causing these cycles; that there seemed to be a sort of *pulse* to
the universe that accounted for the pervasive presence of these
cycles throughout so many areas of human existence.

In 1941, Dewey organized the Foundation for the Study of
Cycles (900 W. Valley Rd., Suite 502, Wayne, PA 19087). It is the
oldest organization engaged in cycles research and the recognized
leader in the field. The Foundation publishes *Cycles* magazine,
which presents research in many different areas including eco-
nomics and business. It also publishes a monthly report, *Cycle
Projections,* which applies cyclical analysis to stocks, commodities,
real estate and the economy.

Basic Cyclic Concepts

In 1970, J.M. Hurst authored *The Profit Magic of Stock Transaction
Timing.* Although it deals mainly with stock market cycles, this
book represents one of the best explanations of cycle theory available in print, and is highly recommended reading. The following
diagrams are derived from Hurst's original work.

First, let's see what a cycle looks like and discuss its three
main characteristics. Figure 14.4 shows two repetitions of a price
cycle. The cycle bottoms are called *troughs* and the tops referred to
as *crests.* Notice that the two waves shown here are measured from
trough to trough. *Cyclic analysts prefer to measure cycle lengths from
low to low.* Measurements can be taken between crests, but they are
not considered to be as stable or reliable as those taken between the
troughs. Therefore, common practice is to measure the beginning
and end of a cyclic wave at a low point, as shown in this example.

The three qualities of a cycle are *amplitude, period,* and *phase.*
Amplitude measures the height of the wave as shown in Figure
14.5, and is expressed in dollars, cents, or points. The period of a
wave, as shown in Figure 14.6, is the time between troughs. In this
example, the period is 20 days. The phase is a measure of the time
location of a wave trough. In Figure 14.7, the phase difference
between two waves is shown. Because there are several different

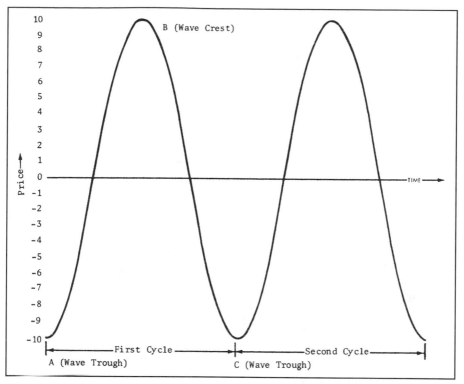

Figure 14.4 *Two cycles of a price wave. A simple, single price wave of the kind that combines to form stock and commodity price action. Only two cycles of this wave are shown, but the wave itself extends infinitely far to the left and to the right. Such waves repeat themselves cycle after cycle. As a result, once the wave is identified, its value can be determined at any past or future time. It is this characteristic of waves that provides a degree of predictability for equity price action.*

cycles occurring at the same time, *phasing* allows the cyclic analyst to study the relationships between the different cycle lengths. Phasing is also used to identify the date of the last cycle low. If, for example, a 20 day cycle bottomed 10 days earlier, the date of the next cycle low can be determined. Once the amplitude, period, and phase of a cycle are known, the cycle can theoretically be extrapolated into the future. Assuming the cycle remains fairly constant, it can then be used to estimate future peaks and troughs. That is the basis of the cyclic approach in its simplest form.

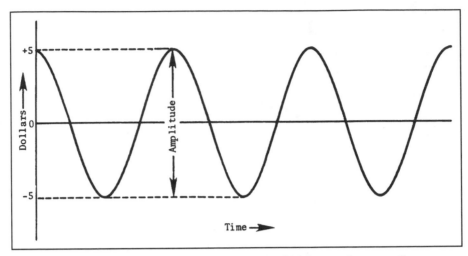

Figure 14.5   *The amplitude of a wave. In this figure, the wave has an amplitude of ten dollars (from minus five dollars to plus five dollars). Amplitude is always measured from wave trough to wave crest.*

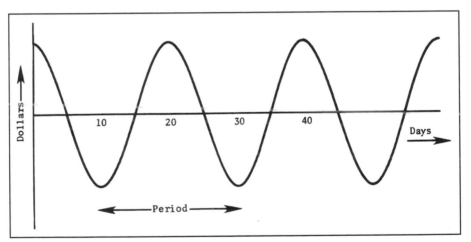

Figure 14.6   *The period of a wave. In this figure, the wave has a period of 20 days, which is shown measured between two consecutive wave troughs. The period could just as well have been measured between wave crests. But in the case of price waves, the wave troughs are usually more clearly defined than the wave crests for reasons that will be discussed later. Consequently, price wave periods are most often measured from trough to trough.*

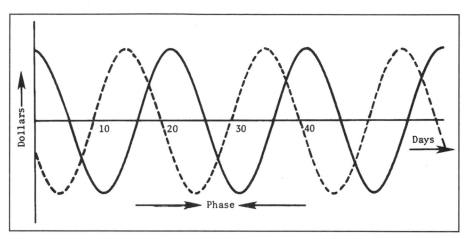

Figure 14.7 *The phase difference between two waves. The phase difference between the two waves shown is 6 days. This phase difference is measured between the troughs of the two waves because, again, wave troughs are the most convenient points to identify in the case of price waves.*

Cyclic Principles

Let's take a look now at some of the principles that underlie the cyclic philosophy. The four most important ones are the Principles of Summation, Harmonicity, Synchronicity, and Proportionality.

The Principle of Summation holds that all price movement is the simple addition of all active cycles. Figure 14.8 demonstrates how the price pattern on the top is formed by simply adding together the two different cycles at the bottom of the chart. Notice, in particular, the appearance of the double top in composite wave C. Cycle theory holds that all price patterns are formed by the interaction of two or more different cycles. We'll come back to this point again. The Principle of Summation gives us an important insight into the rationale of cyclic forecasting. Let's assume that all price action is just the sum of different cycle lengths. Assume further that each of those individual cycles could be isolated and measured. Assume also that each of those cycles will continue to fluctuate into the future. Then by simply continuing each cycle into the future and summing them back together again, the future price trend should be the result. Or, so the theory goes.

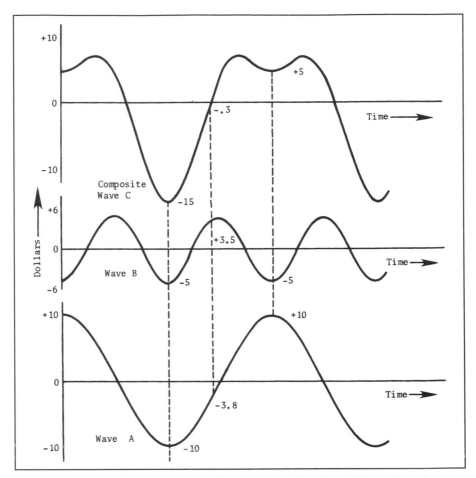

Figure 14.8 *The summation of two waves. The dotted lines show how, at each point in time, the value of wave A is added to the value of wave B to produce the value of composite wave C.*

The Principle of Harmonicity simply means that neighboring waves are usually related by a small, whole number. That number is usually *two*. For example, if a 20 day cycle exists, the next shorter cycle will usually be half its length, or 10 days. The next longer cycle would then be 40 days. If you'll remember back to the discussion on the 4 *week rule* (Chapter 9), the principle of harmonics was invoked to explain the validity of using a shorter 2 week rule and a longer 8 weeks.

The Principle of Synchronicity refers to the strong tendency for waves of differing lengths to bottom at about the same time. Figure 14.9 is meant to show both harmonicity and synchronicity. Wave B at the bottom of the chart is half the length of wave A. Wave A includes two repetitions of the smaller wave B, showing harmonicity between the two waves. Notice also that when wave A bottoms, wave B tends to do the same, demonstrating synchronicity between the two. Synchronicity also means that similar cycle lengths of different markets will tend to turn together.

The Principle of Proportionality describes the relationship between cycle period and amplitude. Cycles with longer periods (lengths) should have proportionally wider amplitudes. The amplitude, or height, of a 40 day cycle, for example, should be about double that of a 20 day cycle.

The Principles of Variation and Nominality

There are two other cyclic principles that describe cycle behavior in a more general sense—*The Principles of Variation and Nominality.*

The Principle of Variation, as the name implies, is a recognition of the fact that all of the other cyclic principles already mentioned—summation, harmonicity, synchronicity, and proportionality—are just strong tendencies and not hard and fast rules. Some "variation" can and usually does occur in the real world.

The Principle of Nominality is based on the premise that, despite the differences that exist in the various markets and allowing for some variation in the implementing of cyclic principles, there seems to be a nominal set of harmonically related cycles that affect all markets. And that nominal model of cycle lengths can be used as a starting point in the analysis of any market. Figure 14.10 shows a simplified version of that nominal model. The model begins with an 18 year cycle and proceeds to each successively lower cycle *half* its length. The only exception is the relationship between 54 and 18 months which is a *third* instead of a *half.*

When we discuss the various cycle lengths in the individual markets, we'll see that this nominal model does account for most cyclic activity. For now, look at the "Days" column. Notice

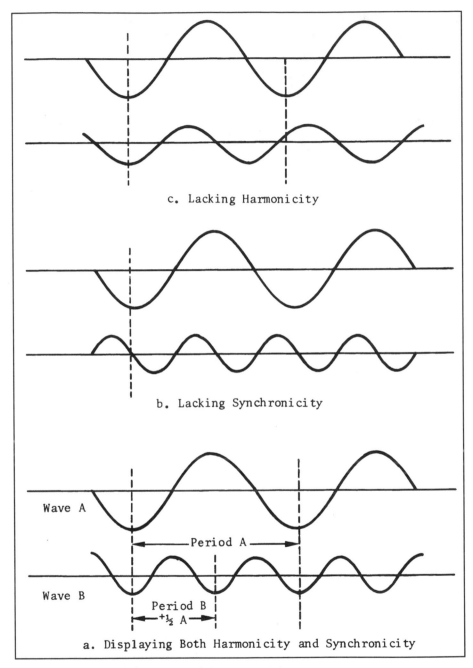

c. Lacking Harmonicity

b. Lacking Synchronicity

Wave A

Period A

Wave B

Period B

+½ A

a. Displaying Both Harmonicity and Synchronicity

Figure 14.9   *Harmonicity and synchronicity.*

Years	Months	Weeks	Days
18			
9			
	54		
	18		
		40	
		20	
			80
			40
			20
			10
			5

Figure 14.10 *The simplified nominal model.*

40, 20, 10, and 5 days. You'll recognize immediately that these numbers account for most of the popular moving average lengths. Even the well known 4, 9, and 18 day moving average technique is a variation of the 5, 10, and 20 day numbers. Many oscillators use 5, 10, and 20 days. Weekly rule breakouts use the same numbers translated into 2, 4, and 8 weeks.

HOW CYCLIC CONCEPTS HELP EXPLAIN CHARTING TECHNIQUES

Chapter 3 in Hurst's book explains in great detail how the standard charting techniques—trendlines and channels, chart patterns, and moving averages—can be better understood and used to greater advantage when coordinated with cyclic principles. Figure 14.11 helps explain the existence of trendlines and channels. The flat cycle wave along the bottom becomes a rising price channel when it is summed with a rising line representing the long term uptrend. Notice how much the horizontal cycle along the bottom of the chart resembles an oscillator.

Figure 14.12 from the same chapter shows how a *head and shoulders* topping pattern is formed by combining two cycle

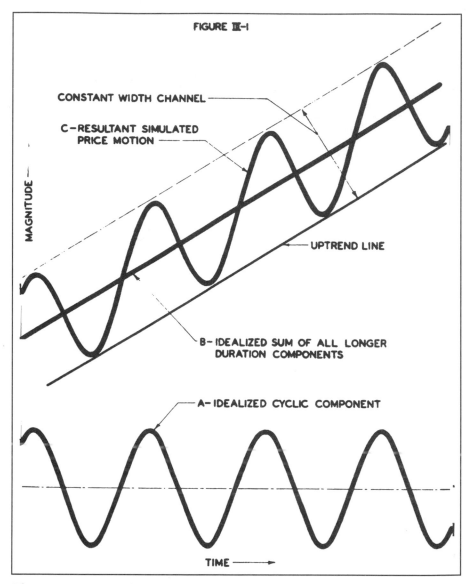

Figure 14.11 *Channel formation. (Source: Hurst, J.M.,* The Profit Magic of Stock Transaction Timing *[Englewood Cliffs, N.J.: Prentice-Hall, Inc., 1970].)*

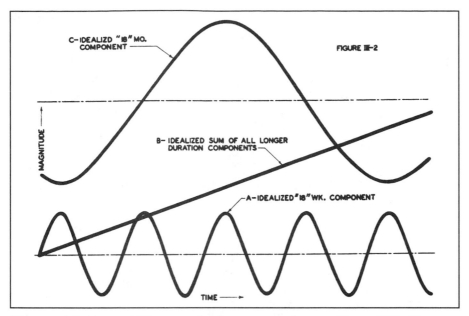

Figure 14.12a *Adding another component. (Source: Hurst, J.M., The Profit Magic of Stock Transaction Timing [Englewood Cliffs, N.J.: Prentice-Hall, Inc., 1970].)*

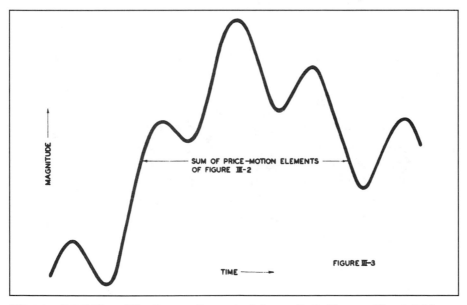

Figure 14.12b *The Summation principle applied. (Source: Hurst, J.M., The Profit Magic of Stock Transaction Timing [Englewood Cliffs, N.J.: Prentice Hall. Inc., 19701].)*

lengths with a rising line representing the sum of all longer duration components. Hurst goes on to explain double tops, triangles, flags, and pennants through the application of cycles. The "V" top or bottom, for example, occurs when an intermediate cycle turns at the exact same time as its next longer and next shorter duration cycles.

Hurst also addresses how moving averages can be made more useful if their lengths are synchronized with dominant cycle lengths. Students of traditional charting techniques should gain additional insight into how these popular chart pictures form and maybe even why they work by reading Hurst's chapter, entitled "Verify Your Chart Patterns."

DOMINANT CYCLES

There are many different cycles affecting the financial markets. The only ones of real value for forecasting purposes are the *dominant cycles*. Dominant cycles are those that consistently affect prices and that can be clearly identified. Most futures markets have at least five dominant cycles. In an earlier chapter on the use of long term charts, it was stressed that all technical analysis should begin with the long term picture, gradually working toward the shorter term. That principle holds true in the study of cycles. The proper procedure is to begin

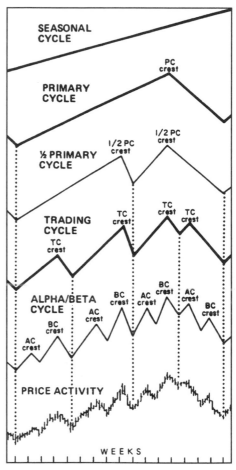

Figure 14.13   *(Source: The Power of Oscillator/Cycle Combinations by Walt Bressert.)*

the analysis with a study of long term dominant cycles, which can span several years; then work toward the intermediate, which can be several weeks to several months; finally, the very short term cycles, from several hours to several days, can be used for timing of entry and exit points and to help confirm the turning points of the longer cycles.

Classification of Cycles

The general categories are: *long term cycles* (2 or more years in length), the *seasonal cycle* (1 year), the *primary or intermediate cycle* (9 to 26 weeks), and the *trading cycle* (4 weeks). The trading cycle breaks down into two shorter *alpha* and *beta* cycles, which average 2 weeks each. (The labels Primary, Trading, Alpha, and Beta are used by Walt Bressert to describe the various cycle lengths.) (See Figure 14.13.)

The Kondratieff Wave

There are even longer range cycles at work. Perhaps the best known is the approximate 54 year Kondratieff cycle. This controversial long cycle of economic activity, first discovered by a Russian economist in the 1920s by the name of Nikolai D. Kondratieff, appears to exert a major influence on virtually all stock and commodity prices. In particular, a 54 year cycle has been identified in interest rates, copper, cotton, wheat, stocks, and wholesale commodity prices. Kondratieff tracked his "long wave" from 1789 using such factors as commodity prices, pig iron production, and wages of agricultural workers in England. (See Figure 14.14.) The Kondratieff cycle has become a popular subject of discussion in recent years, primarily owing to the fact that its last top occurred in the 1920s, and its next top is long overdue. Kondratieff himself paid a heavy price for his cyclic view of capitalistic economies. He is believed to have died in a Siberian labor camp. For more information, see *The Long Wave Cycle* (Kondratieff), translated by Guy Daniels. (Two other books on the subject are *The K Wave* by David Knox Barker and *The Great Cycle* by Dick Stoken.)

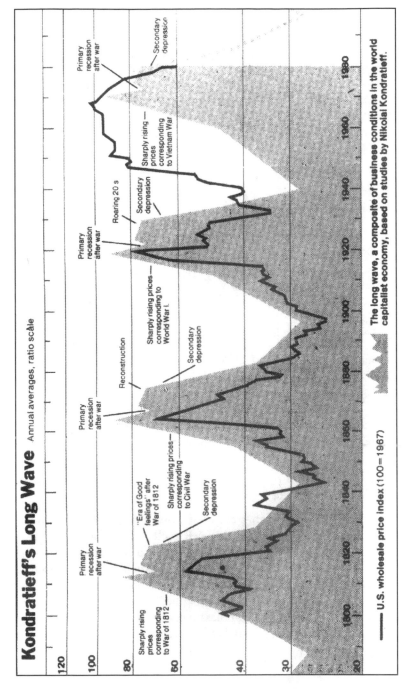

Figure 14.14 *Kondratieff's long wave. For more information, see* The Long Wave Cycle *by Nikolai Kondratieff, translated by Guy Daniels (New York: Richardson and Snyder, 1984). That translation is the first ever from the original Russian text. (Copyright ©1984 by The New York Times Company. Reprinted by permission [May 27, 1984, p. F11.])*

COMBINING CYCLE LENGTHS

As a general rule, long term and seasonal cycles determine the major trend of a market. Obviously, if a two year cycle has bottomed, it can be expected to advance for at least a year, measured from its trough to its crest. Therefore, the long term cycle exerts major influence on market direction. Markets also have annual seasonal patterns, meaning that they tend to peak or trough at certain times of the year. Grain markets, for example, usually hit their low point around harvest time and rally from there. Seasonal moves usually last for several months.

For trading purposes, *the weekly primary cycle is the most useful*. The 3 to 6 month primary cycle is the equivalent of the intermediate trend, and generally determines which side of a market to trade. The next shorter cycle, the 4 week trading cycle, is used to establish entry and exit points in the direction of the primary trend. If the primary trend is up, troughs in the trading cycle are used for purchases. If the primary trend is down, crests in the trading cycles should be sold short. The 10 day *alpha* and *beta* cycles can be used for further fine tuning. (See Figure 14.13.)

THE IMPORTANCE OF TREND

The concept of trading in the direction of the trend is stressed throughout the body of technical analysis. In an earlier chapter, it was suggested that short term dips should be used for purchases if the intermediate trend was up, and that short term bulges be sold in downtrends. In the chapter on Elliott Wave Theory, it was pointed out that five wave moves only take place in the direction of the next larger trend. Therefore, it is necessary when using any short term trend for timing purposes to first determine the direction of the next longer trend and then trade in the direction of that longer trend. That concept holds true in cycles. *The trend of each cycle is determined by the direction of its next longer cycle.* Or stated the other way, once the trend of a longer cycle is established, the trend of the next shorter cycle is known.

The 28 Day Trading Cycle in Commodities

There is one important short term cycle that tends to influence most commodity markets—*the 28 day trading cycle.* In other words, most markets have a tendency to form a trading cycle low every 4 weeks. One possible explanation for this strong cyclic tendency throughout all commodity markets is the *lunar cycle.* Burton Pugh studied the 28 day cycle in the wheat market in the 1930s (*Science and Secrets of Wheat Trading,* Lambert-Gann, Pomeroy, WA, 1978, orig., 1933) and concluded that the moon had some influence on market turning points. His theory was that wheat should be bought on a full moon and sold on a new moon. Pugh acknowledged, however, that the lunar effects were mild and could be overridden by the effects of longer cycles or important news events.

Whether or not the moon has anything to do with it, the average 28 day cycle does exist and explains many of the numbers used in the development of shorter term indicators and trading systems. First of all, the 28 day cycle is based on calendar days. Translated into actual trading days, the number becomes 20. We've already commented on how many popular moving averages, oscillators, and weekly rules are based on the number 20 and its harmonically related shorter cycles, 10 and 5. The 5, 10, and 20 day moving averages are widely used along with their derivatives, 4, 9, and 18. Many traders use 10 and 40 day moving averages, with the number 40 being the next harmonically related longer cycle at twice the length of 20.

In Chapter 9, we discussed the profitability of the 4 week rule developed by Richard Donchian. Buy signals were generated when a market set new 4 week highs and a sell signal when a 4 week low was established. Knowledge of the existence of a 4 week trading cycle gives a better insight into the significance of that number and helps us to understand why the 4 week rule has worked so well over the years. When a market exceeds the high of the previous 4 weeks, cycle logic tells us that, at the very least, the next longer cycle (the 8 week cycle) has bottomed and turned up.

LEFT AND RIGHT TRANSLATION

The concept of translation may very well be the most useful aspect of cycle analysis. Left and right translation refers to the shifting of the cycle peaks either to the left or the right of the ideal cycle midpoint. For example, a 20 day trading cycle is measured from low to low. The ideal peak should occur 10 days into the cycle, or at the halfway point. That would allow for a 10 day advance followed by a 10 day decline. Ideal cycle peaks, however, rarely occur. Most variations in cycles occur at the peaks (or crests) and not at the troughs. That's why cycle troughs are considered more reliable and are used to measure cycle lengths.

The cycle crests act differently depending on the trend of the next longer cycle. If the trend is up, the cycle crest shifts to the right of the ideal midpoint, causing right translation. If the longer trend is down, the cycle crest shifts to the left of the midpoint, causing left translation. Therefore, right translation is bullish and left translation is bearish. Stop to think about it. All we're saying here is that in a bull trend, prices will spend more time going up than down. In a bear trend, prices spend more time going down than up. Isn't that the basic definition of a trend? Only, in this case, we're talking about time instead of price. (See Figure 14.15.)

HOW TO ISOLATE CYCLES

In order to study the various cycles affecting any given market, it is necessary to first isolate each dominant cycle. There are various ways of accomplishing this task. The simplest is by visual inspection. By studying daily bar charts, for example, it is possible to identify obvious tops and bottoms in a market. By taking the average time periods between those cyclic tops and bottoms, certain average lengths can be found.

There are tools available to make that task a bit easier. One such tool is the *Ehrlich Cycle Finder,* named after its inventor, Stan Ehrlich (ECF, 112 Vida Court, Novato, CA 94947 [415] 892-1183). The Cycle Finder is an accordion-like device that can be placed on the price chart for visual inspection. The distance between the points is always equidistant and can be expanded or contracted to fit any cycle length. By plotting a distance between any two obvious cycle lows, it can be quickly determined if other cycle lows of

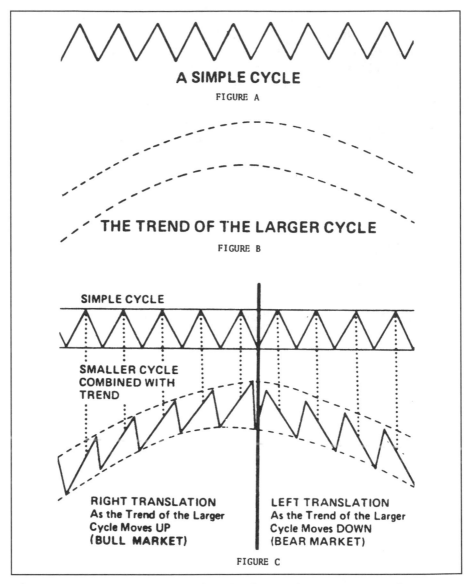

Figure 14.15 *Example of left and right translation. Figure A shows a simple cycle. Figure B shows the trend of the larger cycle. Figure C shows the combined effect. When the longer trend is up, the midpeak shifts to the right. When the longer trend is down, the midpeak shifts to the left. Right translation is bullish, left translation is bearish. (Source: The Power of Oscillator/Cycle Combination by Walt Bressert.)*

the same length exist. An electronic version of that device, called the *Ehrlich Cycle Forecaster,* is now available as an analysis technique on Omega Research's Trade Station and Super Charts (#Omega Research, 8700 West Flagler Street, Suite 250, Miami, FL 33174, [305] 551-9991, www.omegaresearch.com). (See Figures 14.16-14.18.)

Computers can help you find cycles by visual inspection. The user first puts a price chart on the screen. The next step is to pick a prominent bottom on the chart as a starting point. Once that is done, vertical lines (or arcs) appear every 10 days (the default value). The cycle periods can be lengthened, shortened, or moved left or right to find the right cycle fit on the chart. (See Figures 14.19 and 14.20.)

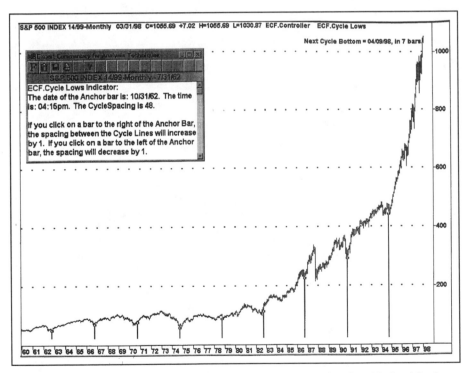

Figure 14.16 *The 4 year presidential cycle is clearly identified with the Ehrlich Cycle Forecaster (see vertical lines). If the cycle is still working, the next major low would be expected to occur during 1998.*

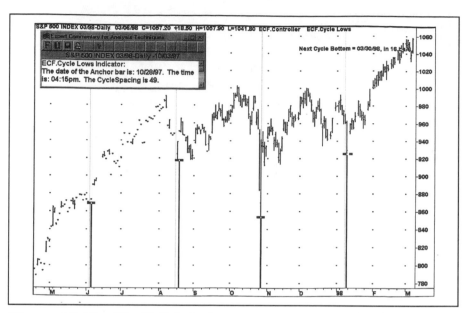

Figure 14.17 *The Ehrlich Cycle Forecaster has identified a 49 day trading cycle in S&P 500 futures prices (see vertical lines). The ECF estimates that the next cycle low will be formed 49 days from the last cycle low, which would be on March 30, 1998.*

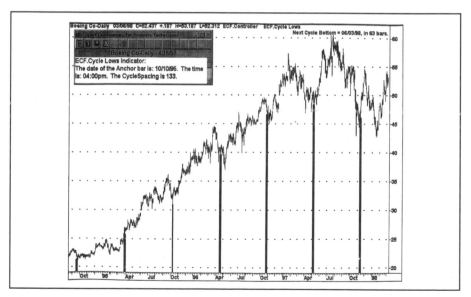

Figure 14.18 *The ECF has uncovered a 133 day cycle in Boeing (see vertical lines). Since the last cycle low occurred during November, 1997, the ECF estimates that the next cycle low is due to occur 133 days later on June 3, 1998.*

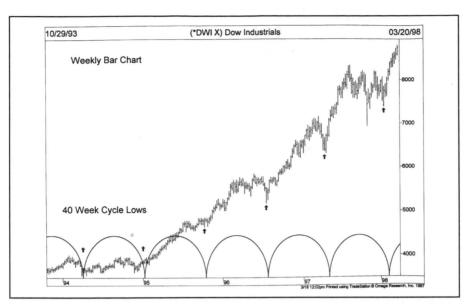

Figure 14.19a *The bottoms in the cycle arcs coincide with important reaction lows in the Dow when spaced 40 weeks apart. That suggests a 40 week cycle in the Dow. The last two cycle troughs were in the spring of 1997 and the start of 1998 (see arrows).*

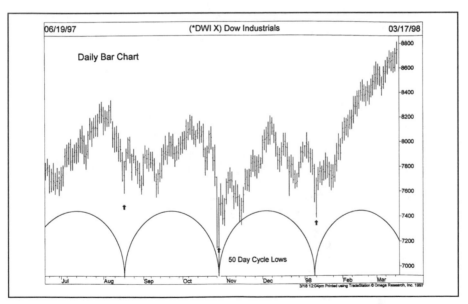

Figure 14.19b *The daily cycle arcs reveal the presence of 50 day cycle bottoms in the Dow during the second half of 1997 and the start of 1998. The idea is to shift the arcs until their lows coincide with a number of reaction lows on the price chart.*

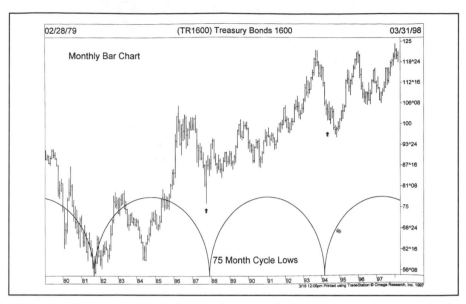

Figure 14.20a *Beginning with the major bottom in 1981, the cycle finder arcs reveal that bonds have shown a tendency to form important bottoms every 75 months (6.25 years). These numbers may shift with time, but still provide useful trading information.*

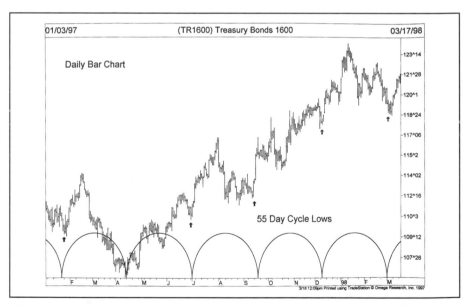

Figure 14.20b *Applied to this daily chart, the cycle arcs showed a tendency for bond prices to bottom every 55 trading days during this time span (see arrows).*

SEASONAL CYCLES

All markets are affected to some extent by an annual seasonal cycle. The seasonal cycle refers to the tendency for markets to move in a given direction at certain times of the year. The most obvious seasonals involve the grain markets where seasonal lows usually occur around harvest time when supply is most plentiful. In soybeans, for example, most seasonal tops occur between April and June with seasonal bottoms taking place between August and October. (See Figure 14.21.) One well known seasonal pattern is the "February Break" where grain and soybean prices usually drop from late December or early January into February.

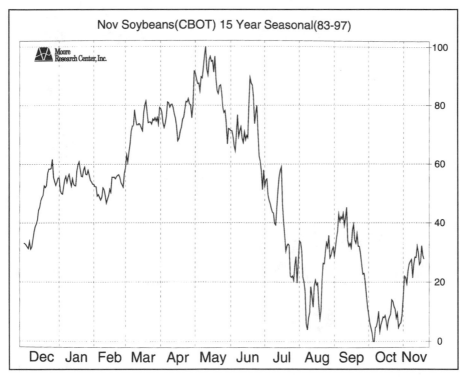

Figure 14.21 *Soybeans usually peak in May and bottom in October.*

Although the reasons for seasonal tops and bottoms are more obvious in the agricultural markets, virtually all markets experience seasonal patterns. Copper, for example, shows a strong seasonal uptrend from the January/February period with a tendency to top in March or April. (See Figure 14.22.) Silver has a low in January with higher prices into March. Gold shows a tendency to bottom in August. Petroleum products have a tendency to peak during October and usually don't bottom until the end of the winter. (See Figure 14.23.) Financial markets also have seasonal patterns.

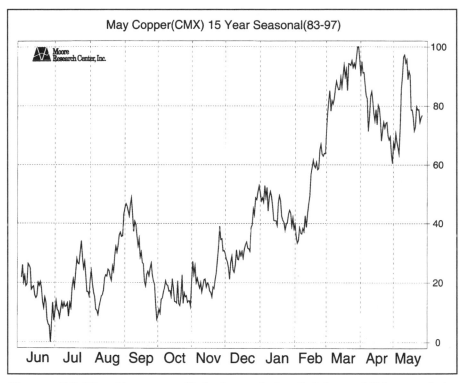

Figure 14.22 *Copper usually bottoms during October and February, but peaks during the April-May period.*

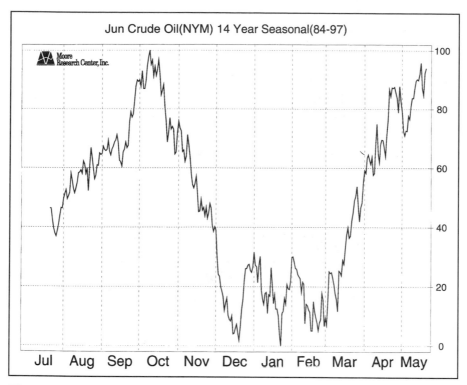

Figure 14.23 *Crude oil prices peak during October and turn up during March.*

The U.S. Dollar has a tendency to bottom during January. (See Figure 14.24.) Treasury Bond prices usually hit important highs during January. Over the entire year, Treasury Bond prices are usually weaker during the first half of the year and stronger during the second half. (See Figure 14.25.) The examples of seasonal charts are provided by the Moore Research Center (Moore Research Center, 321 West 13th Avenue, Eugene, OR 97401, (800) 927-7259), which specializes in seasonal analysis of futures markets.

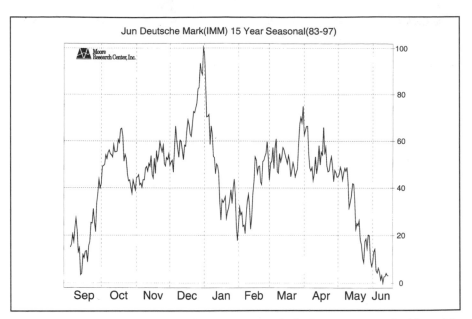

Figure 14.24 *The peak in the German mark during January coincides with a lowpoint in the U.S. dollar that usually occurs at the start of the new year.*

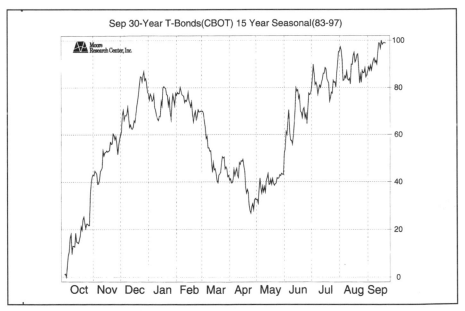

Figure 14.25 *Treasury Bonds prices usually peak around the new year, and then remain weak for most of the first half. The second half of the year is better for bond bulls.*

STOCK MARKET CYCLES

Did you know that the strongest three month span for the stock market is November through January? February is then weaker, but is followed by a strong March and April. After a soft June, the market turns strong during July (the start of the traditional summer rally). The weakest month of the year is September. The strongest month is December (ending with the well known Santa Claus rally just after Christmas). That information, and a whole lot more about stock market cycles, can be found in Yale Hirsch's annual *Stock Trader's Almanac* (The Hirsch Organization, 184 Central Avenue, Old Tappen, NJ 07675).

THE JANUARY BAROMETER

According to Hirsch: "as January goes, so goes the year." The well known January Barometer holds that what the S&P 500 does during January will determine what kind of year the market as a whole will have. Another variation on that theme is the belief that the direction of the S&P 500 during the first 5 trading days of the year gives some hint of what's ahead for the year. The January Barometer shouldn't be confused with the January Effect, which is the tendency for smaller stocks to outperform larger stocks during January.

THE PRESIDENTIAL CYCLE

Another well known cycle that affects stock market behavior is the 4 year cycle, also called the Presidential Cycle, because it coincides with the elected term of U.S. presidents. Each of the 4 years has a different historical return. The election year (1) is normally strong. The postelection and midyears (2 and 3) are normally weak. The preelection year (4) is normally strong. According to Hirsch's *Trader's Almanac,* election years since 1904 have seen averages gains of 224%; postelection years, gains of 72%; midterm years, gains of 63%; and preelection years, gains of 217%. (See Figure 14.16.)

COMBINING CYCLES WITH OTHER TECHNICAL TOOLS

Two of the most promising areas of overlap between cycles and traditional technical indicators are in the use of moving averages and oscillators. It is believed that the usefulness of both indicators can be enhanced if the time periods used are tied to each market's dominant cycles. Let's assume that a market has a dominant 20 day trading cycle. Normally, when constructing an oscillator, it's best to use half the length of the cycle. In this case, the oscillator period would be 10 days. To trade a 40 day cycle, use a 20 day oscillator. Walt Bressert discusses in his book, *The Power of Oscillator/Cycle Combinations*, how cycles can be used to adjust time spans for the Commodity Channel Index, the Relative Strength Index, Stochastics, and Moving Average Convergence Divergence (MACD).

Moving averages can also be tied to cycles. You could use different moving averages to track different cycle lengths. To generate a moving average crossover system for a 40 day cycle, you could use a 40 day moving average in conjunction with a 20 day average (one-half of the 40 day cycle) or a 10 day average (one-quarter of the 40 day cycle). The main problem with this approach is determining what the dominant cycles are at a particular point in time.

MAXIMUM ENTROPY SPECTRAL ANALYSIS

The search for the right dominant cycles in any market is complicated by the belief that cycle lengths aren't static; in other words, they keep changing over time. What worked a month ago may not work a month from now. In his book, *MESA and Trading Market Cycles*, John Ehlers uses a statistical approach called Maximum Entropy Spectral Analysis (MESA). Ehlers explains that one of the main advantages of MESA is its high-resolution measurement of cycles with relatively small time periods, which is crucial for shorter term trading. Ehlers also explains how cycles can be used to optimize moving average lengths and many of the oscillator-type indicators we've already mentioned. Uncovering cycles allows for the dynamic adjusting of technical indicators to fit current market conditions. Ehlers also addresses the problem of distinguishing between a market in a *cycle* mode versus one that is in a *trend* mode. When a market is in a trend mode, a trend-following indicator like a moving average is needed to implement trades. A cycle mode would favor the use of oscillator-type indicators. Cycle measurement can help determine which mode the market is currently in, and which type of technical indicator is more appropriate to use for trading strategies.

CYCLE READING AND SOFTWARE

Most of the books referred to in this chapter on cycles can be obtained through mail order firms like Traders Press (see reference in previous chapter) or Traders' Library, P.O. Box 2466, Ellicott City, MD 21041, [800] 272-2855). There's also a lot more software to help you perform cycle analysis with your computer. The *Ehrlich Cycle Forecaster* and Walt Bressert's *CycleTrader* are both available as add-on options to run with charting software provided by Omega Research. Bressert's *CycleTrader* integrates the concepts he describes in his book, *The Power of Oscillator/Cycle Combinations*. (Bressert Marketing Group, 100 East Walton, Suite 200, Chicago, IL 60611 (312) 867-8701). More information on the MESA computer program can be gotten from John Ehlers (Box 1801, Goleta, CA 93116 (805) 969-6478). For ongoing cycle research and analysis, don't forget the Foundation for the Study of Cycles.

15

Computers and Trading Systems

INTRODUCTION

The computer has played an increasingly important role in the field of technical analysis. In this chapter, we'll see how the computer can make the technical trader's task a good deal easier by providing quick and easy access to an arsenal of technical tools and studies that would have required an enormous amount of work just a few years earlier. This assumes, of course, that the trader knows how to use these tools, which brings us to one of the disadvantages of the computer.

The trader not properly schooled in the concepts that underlie the various indicators, and who is not comfortable with how each indicator is interpreted, may find him- or herself overwhelmed with the vast array of computer software currently available. Even worse, the amount of impressive technical data at one's fingertips sometimes fosters a false sense of security and competence. Traders mistakenly assume that they are automatically better simply because they have access to so much computer power.

The theme emphasized in this discussion is that the computer is an extremely valuable tool in the hands of a technically oriented trader who has already done his or her basic homework. When we review many of the routines available in the computer, you'll see that a fair number of the tools and indicators are quite basic and have already been covered in previous chapters. There are, of course, more sophisticated tools that require more advanced charting software.

Much of the work involved in technical analysis can be performed without the computer. Certain functions can be more easily performed with a simple chart and ruler than with a computer printout. Some types of longer range analysis don't require a computer. As useful as it is, the computer is only a tool. It can make a good technical analyst even better. It won't, however, turn a poor technician into a good one.

Charting Software

Several of the technical routines available in charting software have been covered in previous chapters. We'll review some of the tools and indicators currently available. We'll then address some additional features such as the ability to automate the various functions chosen by the user. In addition to providing us with the various technical studies, the computer also enables us to test various studies for profitability, which may be the most valuable feature of the program. Some software allows the user, with little or no programming background, to construct indicators and systems.

Welles Wilder's Directional Movement and Parabolic Systems

We'll take a close look at a couple of Welles Wilder's more popular systems, the *Directional Movement System* and the *Parabolic System*. We'll use those two systems in our discussion of the relative merits of relying on mechanical trading systems. It will be demonstrated that mechanical trend following systems only work well in certain types of market environments. It will also be shown how a mechanical system can be incorporated into one's market analysis and used simply as a confirming technical indicator.

Too Much of a Good Thing

It may strike you that there are *too many* indicators from which to choose. Instead of simplifying our lives, has the computer only served to complicate things by giving us so much more to look at? Charting packages offer 80 different studies that are available to the technician. How does one possibly reach any conclusions (and find the time to trade) with so much data to contend with? We'll say a few words about some work being done in that direction.

SOME COMPUTER NEEDS

Charting software can be applied to virtually any financial market. Most software is user-friendly, meaning that it can be easily implemented by choosing from successive lists of available routines. The place to start is with a charting software package that works for the computer you already own or are thinking of buying. Bear in mind that most charting software has been written for IBM-compatible computers.

Charting packages do not provide daily market data. The user must obtain that data elsewhere. Data can be collected automatically from a data service over telephone lines (requiring a phone modem). Charting packages provide the names of various data vendors from which to choose. These data vendors provide all the software and instructions needed to set up and collect the data files.

When first starting out, the user must collect historical data going back for at least several months to have something to work with. After that, data should be collected daily. It is possible to analyze "on line" data during the trading day by hooking up to a quote service. However, in our use of daily data, we will be referring to end-of-day data, which is available after the markets close. The final piece of equipment you might want is a printer to obtain a copy of whatever appears on the terminal screen. CD-Rom capability is highly recommended since some software vendors provide you with several years of historical data on a CD-Rom disk to get you started. There are some data vendors that also provide charting capability, which simplifies your task even more. One such service is Telescan (5959 Corporate Drive, Suite 2000, Houston, TX 77036, (800) 324-8246, www.telescan.com).

GROUPING TOOLS AND INDICATORS

The following list groups some of the chart and indicator options.

- *Basic Charts:* Bar, line, point and figure, and candlesticks
- *Chart Scales:* Arithmetic and semilogarithmic
- *Bar Chart:* Price, volume, and open interest (for futures)
- *Volume:* Bars, on balance, and Demand Index
- *Basic Tools:* Trendlines and channels, percentage retracements, moving averages, and oscillators
- *Moving Averages:* Reference envelopes, Bollinger Bands
- *Oscillators:* Commodity Channel Index, momentum, rate of change, MACD, Stochastic, Williams %R, RSI
- *Cycles:* Cycle Finder
- *Fibonacci Tools:* Fan lines, arcs, time zones and retracements
- *Wilder:* RSI, Commodity Selection Index, Directional Movement, Parabolic, Swing Index, ADX line

USING THE TOOLS AND INDICATORS

How does one cope with so much from which to choose? A suggestion is to first use the basic tools such as price, volume, trendlines, percentage retracements, moving averages, and oscillators. Notice the large number of oscillators available. Pick one or two that you are most comfortable with and go with them. Use such things as cycles and Fibonacci tools as secondary inputs unless you have a special interest in those areas. Cycles can help fine tune moving average and oscillator lengths, but require study and practice. For mechanical trading systems, Wilder's Parabolic and DMI are especially noteworthy.

WELLES WILDER'S PARABOLIC AND DIRECTIONAL MOVEMENT SYSTEMS

We're going to spend some time on two studies that are especially useful. Both studies were developed by J. Welles Wilder Jr. and discussed in his book, *New Concepts in Technical Trading Systems*. Three of Wilder's other studies included on the computer menu— Commodity Selection Index, Relative Strength Index, and the Swing Index—are also included in the same book.

Parabolic System (SAR)

Wilder's Parabolic system (SAR) is a time/price reversal system that is always in the market. The letters "SAR" stand for "stop and reverse," meaning that the position is reversed when the protective stop is hit. It is a trend-following system. It gets its name from the shape assumed by the trailing stops that tend to curve like a parabola. (See Figures 15.1-15.4. Notice that as prices trend higher, the rising dots below the price action (the stop and reverse points) tend to start out slower and then accelerate with the trend. In a downtrend, the same thing happens but in the opposite direction (the dots are above the price action). The SAR numbers are calculated and available to the user for the following day.

Wilder built an acceleration factor into the system. Each day the stop moves in the direction of the new trend. At first, the movement of the stop is relatively slow to allow the trend time to become established. As the acceleration factor increases, the SAR begins to move faster, eventually catching up to the price action. If the trend falters, or fails to materialize, the result is usually a stop and reverse signal. As the accompanying charts show, the Parabolic system works extremely well in trending markets. Notice that while the trending portions were captured well, the system whipsawed constantly during the sideways, nontrending periods.

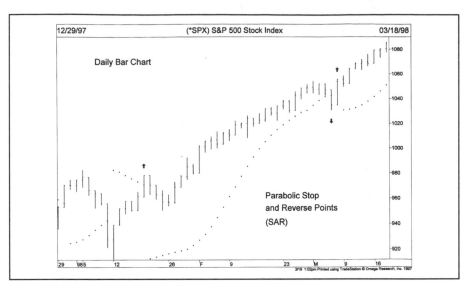

Figure 15.1 *The Parabolic SARs look like dots on the chart. A buy signal was given when the upper SAR was hit (first arrow). Notice how the SARs accelerated upward during the rally and caught most of the uptrend. A small whipsaw occurred to the upper right, which was quickly corrected. This system works when a trend is present.*

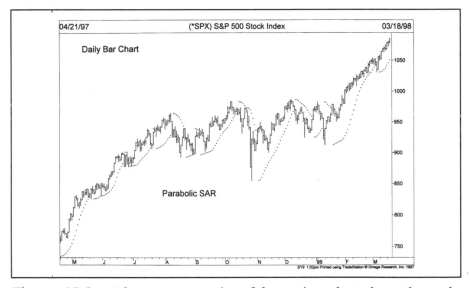

Figure 15.2 *A longer range version of the previous chart shows the good and bad aspects of Parabolics and any trend-following system. They work during trending periods (to the left and right of the chart). But are useless during the type of trading range that occurred from August to January.*

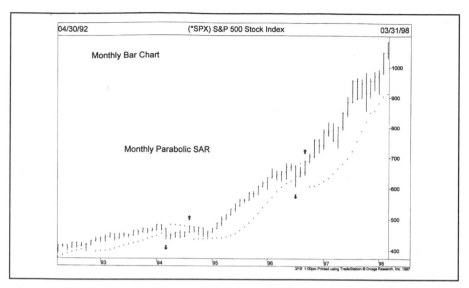

Figure 15.3 *Parabolics can be used on a monthly chart to track the primary trend. A sell signal in early 1994 was followed by a buy in late summer. Except for one whipsaw during 1996, this system has stayed positive for almost four years.*

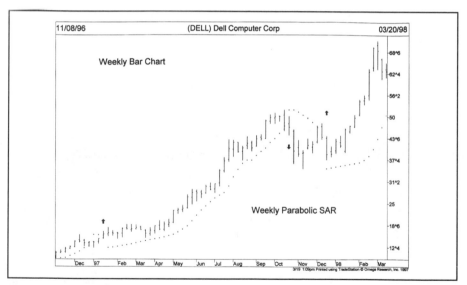

Figure 15.4 *Parabolics applied to weekly chart of Dell Computer. After staying positive through most of 1997, a sell signal was given during October. That sell signal was reversed and a buy signal given as 1997 ended.*

That demonstrates both the strength and weakness of most trend-following systems. They work well during strong trending periods, which Wilder himself estimates occur only about 30% of the time. If that estimate is even close to reality, then a trend-following system will not work for about 70% of the time. How then does one deal with this problem?

DMI and ADX

One possible solution is to use some type of filter or a device to determine if the market is in a trending mode. Wilder's ADX line rates the directional movement of the various markets on a scale of 0 to 100. A rising ADX line means the market is trending and a better candidate for a trend-following system. A falling ADX line indicates a nontrending environment, which would not be suitable for a trend-following approach. (See Figure 15.5.)

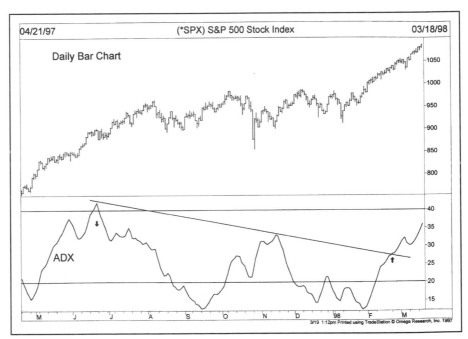

Figure 15.5 *The ADX line measures the degree of directional movement. A downturn from above 40 (left arrow) signaled the onset of a trading range. The upturn from below 20 (right arrow) signaled the resumption of a trending phase.*

Because the ADX line is on a scale from 0 to 100, the trend trader could simply trade those markets with the highest trend ratings. Nontrending systems (oscillators, for example) could be utilized on markets with low directional movement.

Directional Movement can be used either as a system on its own or as a filter on the Parabolic or any other trend-following system. Two lines are generated in the DMI study, +DI and –DI. The first line measures positive (upward) movement and the second number, negative (downward) movement). Figure 15.6 shows the two lines. The darker line is + DI and the lighter line –DI. A buy signal is given when the +DI line crosses over the – DI line and a sell signal when it crosses below the – DI line.

Figure 15.6 also shows both the Parabolic and Directional Movement systems. The Parabolic is clearly a more sensitive sys-

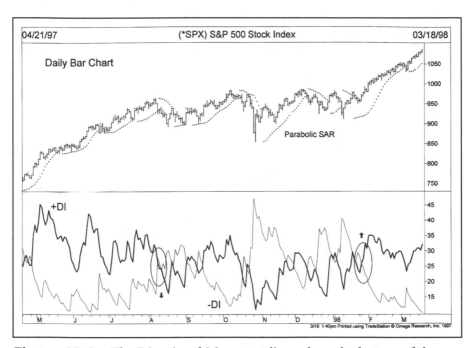

Figure 15.6 *The Directional Movement lines along the bottom of the chart can be used as a filter on Parabolics (upper chart). When the +DI line is above the –DI line (far left and far right of chart), all Parabolic sell signals can be ignored. That would have eliminated several whipsaws during the rally phases.*

tem, meaning that more frequent and earlier signals are given. However, by using the Directional Movement as a filter, several of the bad signals in the Parabolic could be avoided by following only those signals in the same direction as the Directional Movement lines. It appears then that the Parabolic and Directional Movement systems should be used together, with Directional Movement acting as a screen or filter on the more sensitive Parabolic.

The best time to use a trending system is when the ADX line is rising. (See Figures 15.7 and 15.8.) Be forewarned, however, that when the ADX line starts to drop from above the 40 level, that is an early sign that the trend is weakening. A rise back above the 20 level is often a sign of the start of a new trend. (The ADX line is essentially a smoothed difference between the +DI and –DI lines.)

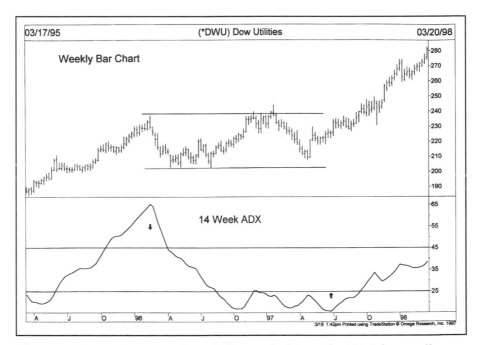

Figure 15.7   *The 14 week ADX line peaked in early 1996 from well over 40, and initiated an 18 month trading range in utilities. The ADX upturn during the summer of 1997 from below 20 signaled that utilities were starting to trend.*

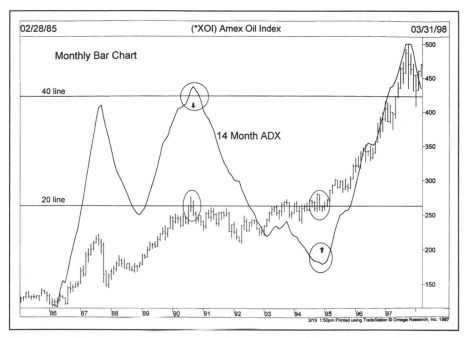

Figure 15.8 *An ADX line overlaid over a monthly chart of the AMEX Oil Index (XOI). The ADX peaked above 40 in 1990, ending the oil stock rally. The upturn in the ADX line from below 20 at the start of 1995 signaled the end of a 4 year trading range in oil stocks, and correctly spotted the start of a new upleg.*

PROS AND CONS OF SYSTEM TRADING

Advantages of Mechanical Systems

1. Human emotion is eliminated.
2. Greater discipline is achieved.
3. More consistency is possible.
4. Trades are taken in the direction of the trend.
5. Participation is virtually guaranteed in the direction of every important trend.
6. Profits are allowed to run.
7. Losses are minimized.

Disadvantages of Mechanical Systems

1. Most mechanical systems are trend-following.
2. Trend-following systems rely on major trends in order to be profitable.
3. Trend-following systems are generally nonprofitable when markets are not trending.
4. There are long periods of time when markets are not trending and, therefore, not suitable for a trending approach.

The major problem is the failure of the system to recognize when the market is not trending and its inability to turn itself off. The measure of a good system is not only its ability to make money in trending markets, but its ability to preserve capital during nontrending periods. It is this inability of the system to monitor itself that is its greatest weakness. This is where some overriding filtering device, such as Welles Wilder's Directional Movement system or the ADX line could prove especially useful by allowing the trader to determine which markets are most suitable for a trending system.

Another drawback is that no allowance is generally made for anticipating market reversals. Trend-following systems ride with the trend until it turns. They don't recognize when a market has reached a long term support or resistance level, when oscillator divergences are being given, or when an Elliott Wave fifth pattern is clearly visible. Most traders would get more defensive at that point, and begin taking some profits. The system, however, will stay with the position until well after the market has changed direction. Therefore, it's up to the trader to determine how best to employ the system. That is to say, whether it should be followed blindly or whether it should be incorporated into a trading plan with other technical factors. That brings us to our next section on how a mechanical system can be used as just another technical input into the forecasting and trading process.

Using System Signals as a Disciplining Device

The system signals can be used simply as a mechanical confirmation along with other technical factors. Even if the system is not being traded mechanically, and other technical factors are being employed, the signals could be used as a disciplined way to keep the trader on the right side of the major trend. No short positions would be taken as long as the computer trend was up. No longs would be taken in a computer downtrend. (This would be a simple way for fundamentally oriented traders to use a technical device as a filter or trigger on their own trading ideas.) Trend direction can be a matter of judgment. The computer signals relieve the trader of some degree of uncertainty. They can prevent him or her from falling into the trap of "top and bottom picking."

Using Signals as Alerts

System signals can also be used as an excellent screening device to alert the trader to recent trend changes. The trader can simply glance at the trend signals and instantly has several trading candidates. The same information could be found by studying all of the charts. The computer just makes that task quicker, easier, and more authoritative. The ability of the computer to automate system signals and then alert the trader when signals are triggered is an enormous asset, especially when the universe of financial markets has grown so large.

NEED EXPERT HELP?

One of the products offered by Omega Research called TradeStation offers a variety of Expert Features (Omega Research, Miami, FL 33174, (305) 551-9991). You can call up its Expert Commentary, which interprets indicators for you based on current market conditions. Omega's Expert Analyst will determine which indicators should work best in the current market and interpret them for you. In addition, it has two Expert Tools. The Trendlines Automatic Indicator actually draws trendlines for you. The Candlestick Patterns Indicator reads the more common candlestick chart patterns.

TEST SYSTEMS OR CREATE YOUR OWN

Omega Research also includes a library of the most popular trading systems used by traders. You can test them, change them, or create your own if you wish. All of Omega's charting tools, indicators, and trading systems are written in a relatively simple language called EasyLanguage. EasyLanguage takes trading ideas that you have described in plain language and converts them into the machine code needed to run the program. It's hard to overestimate the value of being able to develop, test, optimize if you wish, and then automate your own trading ideas—without being a computer programmer. The computer will even generate the appropriate trading orders for you and alert you via your alphanumeric pager that signals have been triggered. (In Appendix C, we'll use Omega Research's EasyLanguage and TradeStation to show you how to go about creating a trading system of your own.)

CONCLUSION

This chapter introduced a couple more of Welles Wilder's systems to you—Parabolics and Directional Movement (DMI). Parabolics can generate useful trading signals, but probably shouldn't be used alone. The two Dl lines can be used as a filter on Parabolics or any other sensitive trend-following trading system. The ADX line, which is part of the DMI system, provides one way to determine which type of market you're dealing with—a trending or a trading market. A rising ADX line suggests a trend and favors moving averages. A falling ADX line suggests a trading range and favors oscillators. We also used the Parabolic examples to show the good and bad sides of most trend-following systems. They work well when a trend is present. They're useless during a trading range. You have to be able to tell the difference. We also touched on the merits of mechanical trading systems. These systems remove human emotion and can be very helpful in the right market climate. They can also be used as technical alerts and used in conjunction with fundamental analysis. (See Appendix C for more on system trading.)

There's no question that the computer has revolutionized financial market analysis and trading. While our interest is primarily in technical analysis, software programs also allow you to blend fundamental analysis with the technical. When the first edition of this book was published in 1986, it cost about $5,000 to outfit yourself with the necessary computer hardware to perform serious technical analysis. The leading software package of the day cost close to $2,000. How things have changed. You can now obtain incredibly powerful computers for less than $2,000. Most software packages can be had for less than $300. The better ones provide you with up to 20 years of historical price data on a CD-Rom disk at little or no additional cost.

Another big benefit is the amount of educational help that you can obtain with those software packages. The user manuals alone are the size of a book and include technical formulas and all kinds of useful explanations. The screening and alert capabilities of today's computer are especially helpful to those monitoring global bond and stock markets and thousands of individual common stocks, not to mention mutual funds. In Chapter 17, we'll talk about an even more sophisticated use of computer technology for developing *neural networks*. But the message to you is clear. If you are serious about investing or trading financial markets, get a computer and learn how to use it. You'll be glad you did.

16

Money Management and Trading Tactics

INTRODUCTION

The previous chapters presented the major technical methods used to forecast and trade financial markets. In this chapter, we'll round out the trading process by adding to the task of *market forecasting* the crucial elements of *trading tactics* (or timing) and the often overlooked aspect of *money management.* No trading program can be complete without all three elements.

THE THREE ELEMENTS OF SUCCESSFUL TRADING

Any successful trading program must take into account three important factors: price forecasting, timing, and money management.

1. *Price forecasting* indicates which way a market is expected to trend. It is the crucial first step in the trading decision. The forecasting process determines whether the trader is bullish or bearish. It provides the answer to the basic question of whether to enter the market from the long or short side. If the price forecast is wrong, nothing else that follows will work.

2. *Trading tactics,* or timing, determines specific entry and exit points. Timing is especially crucial in futures trading. Because of the low margin requirements and the resulting high leverage, there isn't much room for error. It's quite possible to be correct on the direction of the market, but still lose money on a trade if the timing is off. Timing is almost entirely technical in nature. Therefore, even if the trader is fundamentally oriented, technical tools must be employed at this point to determine specific entry and exit points.

3. *Money management* covers the allocation of funds. It includes such areas as portfolio makeup, diversification, how much money to invest or risk in any one market, the use of stops, reward-to-risk ratios, what to do after periods of success or adversity, and whether to trade conservatively or aggressively.

The simplest way to summarize the three different elements is that price forecasting tells the trader *what* to do (buy or sell), timing helps decide *when* to do it, and money management determines *how much* to commit to the trade. The subject of price forecasting has been covered in the previous chapters. We'll deal with the other two aspects here. We'll discuss money management first because that subject should be taken into consideration when deciding on the appropriate trading tactics.

MONEY MANAGEMENT

After having spent many years in the research department of a major brokerage firm, I made the inevitable switch to managing money. I quickly discovered the major difference between recommending trading strategies to others and implementing them myself. What surprised me was that the most difficult part of the transition had little to do with market strategies. The way I went about analyzing the markets and determining entry and exit points didn't change much. What did change was my perception of the importance of money management. I was amazed at the impact such things as the size of the account, the portfolio mix, and the amount of money committed to each trade could have on the final results.

Needless to say, I am a believer in the importance of money management. The industry is full of advisors and advisory services telling clients *what* to buy or sell and *when* to do it. Very little is said about *how much* of one's capital to commit to each trade.

Some traders believe that money management is the most important ingredient in a trading program, even more crucial than the trading approach itself. I'm not sure I'd go that far, but I don't think it's possible to survive for long without it. Money management deals with the question of survival. It tells the trader how to handle his or her money. Any good trader should win in the long run. Money management increases the odds that the trader will survive to reach the long run.

Some General Money Management Guidelines

Admittedly, the question of portfolio management can get very complicated, requiring the use of advanced statistical measures. We'll approach it here on a relatively simple level. The following are some general guidelines that can be helpful in allocating one's funds and in determining the size of one's trading commitments. These guidelines refer primarily to futures trading.

1. *Total invested funds should be limited to 50% of total capital.* The balance is placed in Treasury Bills. This means that at any one time, no more than half of the trader's capital should be committed to the markets. The other half acts as a reserve during periods of adversity and drawdown. If, for example, the size of the account is $100,000, only $50,000 would be available for trading purposes.

2. *Total commitment in any one market should be limited to 10-15% of total equity.* Therefore, in a $100,000 account, only $10,000 to $15,000 would be available for margin deposit in any one market. This should prevent the trader from placing too much capital in any one trade.

3. *The total amount risked in any one market should be limited to 5% of total equity.* This 5% refers to how much the trader is willing to lose if the trade doesn't work. This is an important consideration in deciding how many contracts to trade and how far away a protective stop should be placed. A $100,000 account, therefore, should not risk more than $5,000 on a single trade.

4. *Total margin in any market group should be limited to 20-25% of total equity.* The purpose of this criteria is to protect against getting too heavily involved in any one market group. Markets within groups tend to move together. Gold and silver are part of the precious metals group and usually trend in the same direction. Putting on full positions in each market in the same group would frustrate the principle of diversification. Market commitments in the same group should be controlled.

These guidelines are fairly standard in the futures industry, but can be modified to the trader's needs. Some traders are more aggressive than others and take bigger positions. Others are more conservative. The important consideration is that some form of diversification be employed that allows for preservation of capital and some measure of protection during losing periods. (Although these guidelines relate to futures trading, the general principles of money management and asset allocation can be applied to all forms of investing.)

Diversification Versus Concentration

While diversification is one way to limit risk exposure, it can be overdone. If a trader has trading commitments in too many markets at the same time, a few profitable trades may be diluted by a larger number of losing trades. A tradeoff exists and the proper balance must be found. Some successful traders concentrate their trading in a handful of markets. That's fine as long as those markets are the ones that are trending at that time. The more negative correlation between the markets, the more diversification is achieved. Holding long positions in four foreign currency markets at the same time would not be a good example of diversification, since foreign currencies usually trend in the same direction against the U.S. dollar.

Using Protective Stops

I strongly recommend the use of protective stops. Stop placement, however, is an art. The trader must combine technical factors on the price chart with money management considerations. We'll show how this is done later in the chapter in the section on tactics. The trader must consider the volatility of the market. The more volatile the market is, the looser the stop that must be employed. Here again, a tradeoff exists. The trader wants the protective stop to be close enough so that losing trades are as small as possible. Protective stops placed too close, however, may result in unwanted liquidation on short term market swings (or "noise"). Protective stops placed too far away may avoid the noise factor, but will result in larger losses. The trick is to find the right middle ground.

REWARD TO RISK RATIOS

The best futures traders make money on only 40% of their trades. That's right. Most trades wind up being losers. How then do traders make money if they're wrong most of the time? Because futures contracts require so little margin, even a slight move in the wrong direction results in forced liquidation. Therefore, it may be necessary for a trader to probe a market several times before catching the move he or she is looking for.

     This brings us to the question of reward-to-risk ratios. Because most trades are losers, the only way to come out ahead is to ensure that the dollar amount of the winning trades is greater than that of the losing trades. To accomplish this, most traders use a reward-to-risk ratio. For each potential trade, a profit objective is determined. That profit objective (the reward) is then balanced against the potential loss if the trade goes wrong (the risk). A commonly used yardstick is a 3 to 1 reward-to-risk ratio. The profit potential must be at least three times the possible loss if a trade is to be considered.

"Letting profits run and cutting losses short" is one of the oldest maxims of trading. Large profits in trading are achieved by staying with persistent trends. Because only a relative handful of trades during the course of a year will generate large profits, it's necessary to maximize those few big winners. Letting profits run is the way that is done. The other side of the coin is to keep losing trades as small as possible. You'd be surprised how many traders do just the opposite.

TRADING MULTIPLE POSITIONS: TRENDING VERSUS TRADING UNITS

Letting profits run isn't as easy as it sounds. Picture a situation where a market starts to trend, producing large profits in a relatively short period of time. Suddenly, the trend stalls, the oscillators show an overbought situation and there's some resistance visible on the chart. What to do? You believe the market has much higher potential, but you're worried about losing your paper profits if the market should fail. Do you take profits or ride out a possible correction?

One way to resolve that problem is to always trade in multiple units. Those units can be divided into *trading* and *trending* positions. The trending portion of the position is held for the long pull. Loose protective stops are employed and the market is given plenty of room to consolidate or correct itself. These are the positions that produce the largest profits in the long run.

The trading portion of the portfolio is earmarked for shorter term in-and-out trading. If the market reaches a first objective, is near resistance and overbought, some profits could be taken or a tight protective stop utilized. The purpose is to lock up or protect profits. If the trend then resumes, any liquidated positions can be reinstated. It's best to avoid trading only one unit at a time. The increased flexibility that is achieved from trading multiple units makes a big difference in overall trading results.

WHAT TO DO AFTER PERIODS OF SUCCESS AND ADVERSITY

What does a trader do after a losing or a winning streak? Suppose your trading equity is down by 50%. Do you change your style of trading? If you've already lost half of your money, you now have to double what you have remaining just to get back to where you were in the first place. Do you get more selective choosing trades, or keep doing the same things you were doing before? If you become more conservative, it will be that much harder to win back your losses.

A more pleasant dilemma occurs after a winning streak. What do you do with your winnings? Suppose you've doubled your money. One alternative is to put your money to maximum use by doubling the size of your positions. If you do that, however, what will happen during the inevitable losing period that's sure to follow? Instead of giving back 50% of your winnings, you'll wind up giving it all back. So the answers to these two questions aren't as simple or obvious as they might first appear.

Every trader's track record is a series of peaks and troughs, much like a price chart. The trend of the equity chart should be pointing upward if the trader is making money on balance. The worst time to increase the size of one's commitments is after a winning streak. That's much like buying into an overbought market in an uptrend. The wiser thing to do (which goes against basic human nature) is to begin increasing one's commitments after a dip in equity. This increases the odds that the heavier commitments will be made near the equity troughs instead of the peaks.

TRADING TACTICS

Upon completion of the market analysis, the trader should know whether he or she wants to buy or sell the market. By this time, money management considerations should have dictated the level of involvement. The final step is the actual purchase or sale. This can be the most difficult part of the process. The final decision as to how and where to enter the market is based on a combination of technical factors, money management parameters, and the type of trading order to employ. Let's consider them in that order.

Using Technical Analysis in Timing

There's nothing really new in applying the technical principles discussed in previous chapters to the timing process. The only real difference is that timing covers the very short term. The time frame that concerns us here is measured in days, hours, and minutes as opposed to weeks and months. But the technical tools employed remain the same. Rather than going through all of the technical methods again, we'll limit our discussion to some general concepts.

1. Tactics on breakouts
2. The breaking of trendlines
3. The use of support and resistance
4. The use of percentage retracements
5. The use of gaps

Tactics on Breakouts: Anticipation or Reaction?

The trader is forever faced with the dilemma of taking a position in anticipation of a breakout, taking a position on the breakout itself, or waiting for the pullback or reaction after the breakout occurs. There are arguments in favor of each approach or all three combined. If the trader is trading several units, one unit can be taken in each instance. If the position is taken in anticipation of an upside breakout, the payoff is a better (lower) price if the anticipated breakout takes place. The odds of making a bad trade, however, are increased. Waiting for the actual breakout increases the odds of success, but the penalty is a later (higher) entry price. Waiting for the pullback after the breakout is a sensible compromise, providing the pullback occurs. Unfortunately, many dynamic markets (usually the most profitable ones) don't always give the patient trader a second chance. The risk involved in waiting for the pullback is the increased chance of missing the market.

This situation is an example of how trading multiple positions simplifies the dilemma. The trader could take a small position in anticipation of the breakout, buy some more on the breakout, and add a little more on the corrective dip following the breakout.

The Breaking of Trendlines

This is one of the most useful early entry or exit signals. If the trader is looking to enter a new position on a technical sign of a trend change or a reason to exit an old position, the breaking of a tight trendline is often an excellent action signal. Other technical factors must, of course, always be considered. Trendlines can also be used for entry points when they act as support or resistance. Buying against a major up trendline or selling against a down trendline can be an effective timing strategy.

Using Support and Resistance

Support and resistance are the most effective chart tools to use for entry and exit points. The breaking of resistance can be a signal for a new long position. Protective stops can then be placed under the nearest support point. A closer protective stop could be placed just below the actual breakout point, which should now function as support. Rallies to resistance in a downtrend or declines to support in an uptrend can be used to initiate new positions or add to old profitable ones. For purposes of placing protective stops, support and resistance levels are most valuable.

Using Percentage Retracements

In an uptrend, pullbacks that retrace 40-60% of the prior advance can be utilized for new or additional long positions. Because we're talking primarily about timing, percentage retracements can be applied to very short term action. A 40% pullback after a bullish breakout, for example, might provide an excellent buying point. Bounces of 40-60% usually provide excellent shorting opportunities in downtrends. Percentage retracements can be used on intraday charts also.

Using Price Gaps

Price gaps on bar charts can be used effectively in the timing of purchases or sales. After an upmove, for example, underlying gaps usually function as support levels. Buy a dip to the upper end of the gap or a dip into the gap itself. A protective stop can be placed below the gap. In a bear move, sell a rally to the lower end of the gap or into the gap itself. A protective stop can be kept over the gap.

Combining Technical Concepts

The most effective way to use these technical concepts is to combine them. Remember that when we're discussing timing, the basic decision to buy or sell has already been made. All we're doing here is fine tuning the entry or exit point. If a buy signal has been given, the trader wants to get the best price possible. Suppose prices dip into the 40-60% buying zone, show a prominent support level in that zone, and/or have a potential support gap. Suppose further that a significant up trendline is nearby.

All of these factors used together would improve the timing of the trade. The idea is to buy near support, but to exit quickly if that support is broken. Violation of a tight down trendline drawn above the highs of a downside reaction could also be used as a buying signal. During a bounce in a downtrend, the breaking of a tight up trendline could be a shorting opportunity.

COMBINING TECHNICAL FACTORS AND MONEY MANAGEMENT

Besides using chart points, money management guidelines should play a role in how protective stops are set. Assuming an account size of $100,000, and using the 10% criteria for maximum commitment, only $10,000 is available for the trade. The maximum risk is 5%, or $5,000. Therefore, protective stops on the total position must be placed in such a way that no more than $5,000 would be lost if the trade doesn't work.

A closer protective stop would permit the taking of larger positions. A looser stop would reduce the size of the position. Some traders use only money management factors in determining where to place a protective stop. It's critically important, however, that the protective stop be placed over a *valid* resistance point for a short position or below a *valid* support point for a long position. The use of intraday charts can be especially effective in finding closer support or resistance levels that have some validity.

TYPES OF TRADING ORDERS

Choosing the right type of trading order is a necessary ingredient in the tactical process. We'll concern ourselves only with some of the more common types of orders: market, limit, stop, stop limit, and market-if-touched (M.I.T.).

1. The *market order* simply instructs your broker to buy or sell at the current market price. This is usually preferable in fast market conditions or when the trader wants to ensure that a position is taken and to protect against missing a potentially dynamic market move.

2. The *limit order* specifies a price that the trader is willing to pay or accept. A *buy limit* order is placed below the current market price and states the highest price the trader is willing to pay for a purchase. A *sell limit* order is placed over the current market price and is the lowest price the seller is

willing to accept. This type of resting order is used, for example, after a bullish breakout when the buyer wants to buy a downside reaction closer to support.

3. A *stop order* can be used to establish a new position, limit a loss on an existing position, or protect a profit. A stop order specifies a price at which an order is to be executed. A *buy stop* is placed over the market and a *sell stop* under the market (which is the opposite of the limit order). Once the stop price is hit, the order becomes a *market* order and is executed at the best price possible. On a long position, a sell stop is placed below the market to limit a loss. After the market moves higher, the stop can be raised to protect the profit (a trailing stop). A buy stop could be placed above resistance to initiate a long position on a bullish breakout. Since the stop order becomes a market order, the actual "fill" price may be beyond the stop price, especially in a fast market.

4. A *stop limit order* combines both a stop and a limit order. This type of order specifies both a stop price where the trade is activated and a limit price. Once the stop is elected, the order becomes a limit order. This type of order is useful when the trader wants to buy or sell a breakout, but wants to control the price paid or received.

5. The *market-if-touched (M.I.T.) order* is similar to a limit order, except that it becomes a market order when the limit price is touched. An M.I.T. order to buy would be placed under the market like a limit order. When the limit price is hit, the trade is made at the market. This type of trade has one major advantage over the limit order. The buy limit order placed under the market does not guarantee a fill even if the limit price is touched. Prices may bounce sharply from the limit price, leaving the order unfilled. An M.I.T. order is most useful when the trader wants to buy the dip, but doesn't want to risk missing the market after the limit price is hit.

Each of these orders is appropriate at certain times. Each has its own strong and weak points. Market orders guarantee a position, but may result in "chasing" the market. Limit orders provide more control and better prices, but risk missing the market. Stop limit orders also risk missing the market if prices gap beyond the limit price. Stop prices are strongly recommended to limit losses and protect profits. However, the use of a buy or sell stop to initiate new positions may result in bad fills. The market-if-touched order is particularly useful, but is not allowed on some exchanges. Familiarize yourself with the different types of orders and learn their strengths and weaknesses. Each of them has a place in your trading plan. Be sure to find out which types of orders are permitted on the various financial exchanges.

FROM DAILY CHARTS TO INTRADAY PRICE CHARTS

Because timing deals with very short term market action, intraday price charts are especially useful. Intraday charts are indispensable for day trading purposes, although that's not our focus here. We're mainly interested in how intraday activity can be used to aid the trader in the timing of purchases and sales once the basic decision to enter or exit a market has been made.

It bears repeating that the trading process must begin with a long range view and then gradually work toward the shorter term. Analysis begins with monthly and weekly charts for long term perspective. Then the daily chart is consulted, which is the basis for the actual trading decision. The intraday chart is the last one viewed for even greater precision. The long term chart gives a telescopic view of a market. The intraday chart allows more microscopic study. The technical principles already discussed are clearly visible on these very sensitive charts. (See Figures 16.1-16.3.)

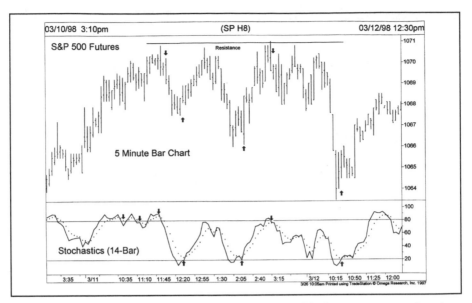

Figure 16.1 *A 5 minute bar chart of an S&P 500 futures contract showing a day and a half of trading. The last five stochastic signals (see arrows) worked pretty well. Intraday charts are used for very short term trading purposes.*

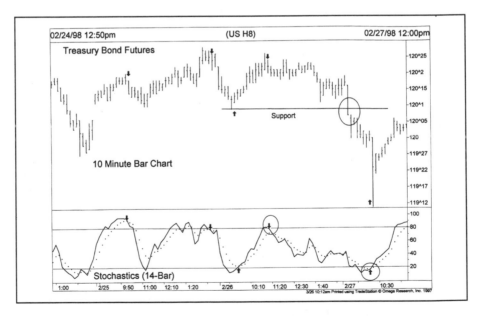

Figure 16.2 *A 10 minute bar chart of a Treasury Bond futures contract showing three days of trading. The last two stochastic signals show a sell just after 10:10 on the morning of 2/26 and then a buy signal the following morning around the same time.*

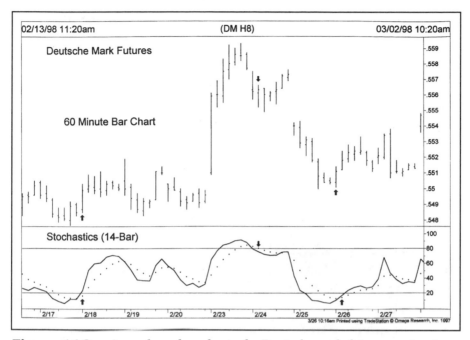

Figure 16.3 *A one hour bar chart of a Deutschemark futures contract showing ten trading days. Three stochastic signals are shown (see arrows). A buy signal on 2/17 turned to a sell on 2/24 and then another buy on 2/26.*

THE USE OF INTRADAY PIVOT POINTS

In order to achieve earlier entry with even tighter protective stops, some traders try to anticipate where a market will close by the use of pivot points. This technique combines seven key price levels with four time periods. The seven pivot points are the previous day's high, low, and close and the current day's open, high, low, and close. The four time periods are applied to the current trading day. They are the open, 30 minutes after the open, midday (about 12:30 New York time), and 35 minutes before the close.

These are average times and can be adjusted to the individual markets. The idea is to use pivot points only as a timing device when the trader believes a market is topping or bottoming. Buy or sell signals are given as the pivot points are broken during the day. The later in the day the signal is given, the stronger it is.

As an illustration of a buy signal, if the market opens above the previous day's close, but is below the previous day's high, a buy stop is placed above the previous day's high. If the buy stop is elected, a protective sell stop is placed below the current day's low. At 35 minutes before the close, if no position has been taken, a buy stop is placed above the current day's high, with a protective stop under today's open. No action is generally taken during the first 30 minutes of trading. As the day progresses, the pivot points are narrowed as are the protective stops. As a final requirement on a buy signal, prices must close above both the previous day's closing price and today's opening price.

SUMMARY OF MONEY MANAGEMENT AND TRADING GUIDELINES

The following list pulls together most of the more important elements of money management and trading.

1. Trade in the direction of the intermediate trend.
2. In uptrends, buy the dips; in downtrends, sell bounces.
3. Let profits run, cut losses short.
4. Use protective stops to limit losses.
5. Don't trade impulsively; have a plan.
6. Plan your work and work your plan.
7. Use money management principles.
8. Diversify, but don't overdo it.
9. Employ at least a 3 to 1 reward-to-risk ratio.
10. When pyramiding (adding positions), follow these guidelines.
    a. Each successive layer should be smaller than before.
    b. Add only to winning positions.
    c. Never add to a losing position.
    d. Adjust protective stops to the breakeven point.
11. Never meet a margin call; don't throw good money after bad.

12. Close out losing positions before the winning ones.
13. Except for very short term trading, make decisions away from the market, preferably when the markets are closed.
14. Work from the long term to the short term.
15. Use intraday charts to fine-tune entry and exit.
16. Master interday trading before trying intraday trading.
17. Try to ignore conventional wisdom; don't take anything said in the financial media too seriously.
18. Learn to be comfortable being in the minority. If you're right on the market, most people will disagree with you.
19. Technical analysis is a skill that improves with experience and study. Always be a student and keep learning.
20. Keep it simple; more complicated isn't always better.

APPLICATION TO STOCKS

The trading tactics that we've covered in this chapter (and the analytical tools in preceding chapters) also apply to the stock market, with some minor adjustments. While futures traders focus on short to intermediate trends, stock investors are more concerned with intermediate to longer term trends. Stock trading places less emphasis on the very short term and makes less use of intraday charts. But the general principles remain the same for analyzing and trading markets—whether they're in the futures pits of Chicago or on the floor of the New York Stock Exchange.

ASSET ALLOCATION

The money management guidelines presented in this chapter refer mainly to futures trading. However, many of the principles included in that discussion relate to the need for proper diversification in one's investment portfolio and touches on the subject of asset allocation. Asset allocation refers to how a person's portfolio is divided among stocks, bonds, and cash (usually in the form of a money market fund or Treasury Bills). It can also refer to how much of one's portfolio should be allocated to foreign markets. Asset allocation also refers to how one's stockholdings are spread among the various market sectors and industry groups. And, more recently, it deals with how much of one's portfolio should be allocated to traditional commodity markets.

MANAGED ACCOUNTS AND MUTUAL FUNDS

Managed accounts have been available in the futures markets for several years and have provided a vehicle for those wishing to put some money into futures but lacked the expertise to do so themselves. Managed accounts have provided a sort of mutual fund approach to futures. Even though managed futures accounts invest in all futures markets—including currencies, commodities, bonds, and stock index futures—they still provide some measure of diversification from bonds and stocks. Part of the diversification is due to their practice of trading from both the long and the short side. Another part comes from the commodity portion itself. However, the ability to devote some of one's assets to commodities was made even easier during 1997.

Oppenheimer Real Assets, launched in March 1997, is the first mutual fund devoted exclusively to commodity investing. By investing in commodity-linked notes, the fund is able to fashion a commodity portfolio that tracks the Goldman Sachs Commodity Index, which includes 22 commodity markets. Since commodities often trend in opposite directions to bonds and stocks, they provide an excellent diversification vehicle. Proper diversification requires spreading one's assets among market groups or classes that have a low correlation to each other—in other words, they don't always trend in the same direction. Commodities certainly fit that criteria.

We point these things out for two reasons. One is to show that the areas of money management and asset allocation are very much intertwined. The second is to show that the markets themselves are very much intertwined. In the next two chapters, you'll see how closely linked the futures and stock markets really are, and why it's important that stock investors keep informed of what's going on in the futures markets. Chapter 17 will introduce you to intermarket technical analysis.

MARKET PROFILE

We couldn't leave the subject of intraday charts without introducing one of the most innovative approaches to intraday trading called *Market Profile*. This trading technique was developed by J. Peter Steidlmayer, a former floor trader on the Chicago Board of Trade. Mr. Steidlmayer's approach has gained an enthusiastic following over the past decade, especially in the futures markets. Market Profile can, however, be applied to common stocks as well. It's not an easy approach to grasp. But those traders that have done so give it very high marks. Dennis Hynes, an expert in Market Profile trading, explains the approach in Appendix B.

The Link Between Stocks and Futures: Intermarket Analysis

When the first edition of this book was published in 1986 the separation of the commodity futures world from the more traditional world of stocks and bonds was already starting to break down. Twenty years ago, commodities referred to such things as corn, soybeans, porkbellies, gold, and oil. These were traditional commodities that could be grown, mined, or refined. Dramatic changes took place from 1972 to 1982 with the introduction of futures contracts on currencies, Treasury Bonds, and stock index futures. The term "commodities" gave way to "futures" since bonds and stocks were hardly commodities. But they were futures contracts. Since then, the world of futures trading has blended with that of traditional stocks and bonds to the point that they can hardly be separated. As a result, the technical analysis methods used to analyze the different financial markets have become more universally applied.

On any given day, quotes are readily available for dollar futures, bond futures, and stock index futures—and they often move in sync with one another. The direction those three markets move is often affected by what happens in the commodity pits. *Program trading,* which occurs when the price of the S&P 500 futures contract is out of line with the S&P 500 cash index, is a day-to-day reality. For those reasons, it seems clear that the more understanding you have about the world of futures trading, the more insight you will gain into the entire financial marketplace.

It has become clear that action in the futures markets can have an important influence on the stock market itself. Early warnings signs of inflation and interest rate trends are usually spotted in the futures pits first, which often determine the direction stock prices will take at any given time. Trends in the dollar tell us a lot about the strength or weakness of the American economy, which also has a major impact on corporate earnings and the valuation of stock prices. But the linkage goes even deeper than that. The stock market is divided into sectors and industry groups. Rotation into and out of those groups is often dictated by action in futures. With the tremendous growth in mutual funds, and sector funds in particular, the ability to capitalize on sector rotation into winning groups and out of losing ones has become much simpler.

In this chapter, we'll deal with the broader subject of intermarket analysis as it deals with the interplay between currencies, commodities, bonds, and stocks. Our primary message is how closely the four markets are linked. We'll show how to use the futures markets in the process of sector and industry group rotation within the stock market itself.

INTERMARKET ANALYSIS

In 1991, I wrote a book entitled *Intermarket Technical Analysis.* That book described the interrelationships between the various financial markets, which are universally accepted today. The book provided a guide, or blueprint, to help explain the sequence that develops among the various markets and to show how interdependent they really are. The basic premise of intermarket analysis is that all financial markets are linked in some way. That includes international markets as well as domestic ones. Those relationships may shift on occasion, but they are always present in one form or another. As a result, a complete understanding of what's going on in one market—such as the stock market—isn't possible without some understanding of what's going on in other markets. Because the markets are now so intertwined, the technical analyst has an enormous advantage. The technical tools described in this book can be applied to all markets, which greatly facilitates the application of intermarket analysis. You'll also see why the ability to follow the charts of so many markets is a tremendous advantage in today's complex marketplace.

PROGRAM TRADING: THE ULTIMATE LINK

Nowhere is the close link between stocks and futures more obvious than in the relationship between the S&P 500 cash index and the S&P 500 futures contract. Normally, the futures contract trades at a premium to the cash index. The size of that premium is determined by such things as the level of short term interest rates, the yield on the S&P 500 index itself, and the number of days until the futures contract expires. The premium (or spread) between S&P 500 futures over the cash index diminishes as the futures contract approaches expiration. (See Figure 17.1.) Each day, institutions calculate what the actual premium should be—called *fair value*. That fair value remains constant throughout the trading day, but changes gradually with each new day. When the futures premium moves above its fair value to the cash index by some predetermined amount, an arbitrage trade is automatically activated—called *program buying*. When the futures are too high relative to the cash index, program traders sell the futures contract and buy a basket of stocks in the S&P 500 to bring the two entities back into line. The result of program buying is positive for the stock market since it pushes the S&P 500 cash index higher. Program selling is just the opposite and occurs when the premium of the futures over the cash narrows too far below its fair value. In that case, *program selling* is activated which results in the buying of S&P 500 futures and

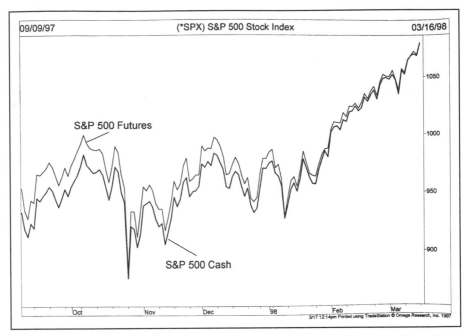

| 09/09/97 | (*SPX) S&P 500 Stock Index | 03/16/98 |

Figure 17.1 *S&P 500 futures normally trade at a premium to the cash index as shown in this chart. Notice that the premium narrows as the March contract nears expiration.*

selling of the basket of stocks. Program selling is negative for the market. Most traders understand this relationship between the two related markets. What they don't always understand is that the sudden moves in the S&P 500 futures contract, which activate the program trading, are often caused by sudden moves in other futures markets—like bonds.

THE LINK BETWEEN BONDS AND STOCKS

The stock market is influenced by the direction of interest rates. The direction of interest rates (or yield) can be monitored on a minute-to-minute basis by tracking the movements in the Treasury Bond futures contract. Bond prices move in the opposite direction of interest rates or yields. Therefore, when bond prices are rising, yields are falling. That is normally considered positive for stocks.* Falling bond prices, or rising yields, are considered negative for stocks. From a technician's point of view, it is very easy to compare the charts of Treasury Bond futures with the charts of either the S&P 500 cash index or its related futures contract. You'll see that they have generally trended in the same direction. (See Figure 17.2.) On a short term basis, sudden changes in trend in the S&P 500 futures contract are often influenced by sudden changes in the Treasury Bond futures contract. On a longer range basis, changes in the trend of the Treasury Bond contract often warn of similar turns in the S&P 500 cash index itself. In that sense, bond futures can be viewed as a leading indicator for the stock market. Bond futures, in turn, are usually influenced by trends in the commodity markets.

* In a deflationary environment, bonds and stocks usually decouple. Bond prices rise while stock prices fall.

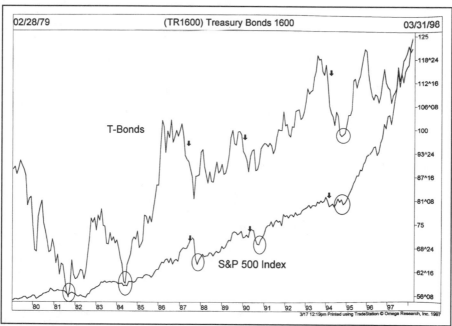

Figure 17.2 *Rising bond prices are usually good for stock prices. The bond market bottoms in 1981, 1984, 1988, 1991, and 1995 led to major upturns in stocks. Bond peaks in 1987, 1990, and 1994 warned of bad stock market years.*

THE LINK BETWEEN BONDS
AND COMMODITIES

Treasury Bond prices are influenced by expectations for inflation. Commodity prices are considered to be leading indicators of inflationary trends. As a result, commodity prices usually trend in the opposite direction of bond prices. If you study the market's history since the 1970s, you'll see that sudden upturns in commodity markets (signaling higher price inflation) have usually been associated with corresponding declines in Treasury Bond prices. The flip side of that relationship is that strong Treasury Bond gains have normally corresponded with falling commodity prices. (See Figure 17.3). Commodity prices, in turn, are impacted by the direction of the U.S. dollar.

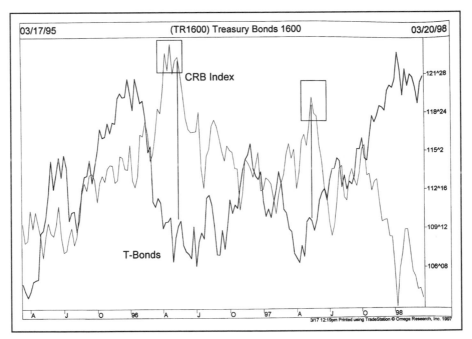

Figure 17.3   *Commodity prices and bond prices normally trend in opposite directions as shown here. The bond bottoms in the spring of 1996 and 1997 coincided with major peaks in commodity prices (see boxes).*

THE LINK BETWEEN COMMODITIES AND THE DOLLAR

A rising U.S. dollar normally has a depressing effect on most commodity prices. In other words, a rising dollar is normally considered to be noninflationary. (See Figure 17.4.) One of the commodities most effected by the dollar is the gold market. If you study their relationship over time, you'll see that the prices of gold and the U.S. dollar usually trend in opposite directions. (See Figure 17.5.) The gold market, in turn, usually acts as a leading indicator for other commodity markets. So, if you're analyzing the gold market, it's necessary to know what the dollar is doing. If you're studying the commodity price trend in general (using

Figure 17.4 *A rising dollar normally has a depressing effect on commodity markets. In 1980, the dollar bottom coincided with a major peak in commodities. The dollar bottom in 1995 contributed to a sharp decline in commodities a year later.*

Figure 17.5 *The U.S. Dollar and gold prices usually trend in opposite directions as shown in this example. Gold prices, in turn, usually lead other commodities.*

one of the better known commodity price indexes), it's necessary to know what the gold market is doing. The fact of the matter is that all four markets are linked—the dollar influences commodities, which influence bonds, which influence stocks. To fully comprehend what's happening in any one asset class, it's necessary to know what's happening in the other three. Fortunately, that's easily done by simply looking at their respective price charts.

STOCK SECTORS AND INDUSTRY GROUPS

An understanding of these intermarket relationships also sheds light on the interaction between the various stock market sectors and industry groups. The stock market is divided into market sectors which are then subdivided into industry groups. These market categories are influenced by what's happening on the intermarket scene. For example, when bonds are strong and commodities weak, interest rate-sensitive stock groups—such as the utilities, financial stocks, and consumer staples—usually do well relative to the rest of the stock market. At the same time, inflation-sensitive stock groups—like gold, energy, and cyclical stocks—usually underperform. When commodity markets are strong relative to bonds, the opposite is the case. By monitoring the relationship between Treasury Bond prices and commodity prices, you can determine which sectors or industry groups will do better at any given time.

Since there is such a close relationship between stock market sectors and their related futures markets, they can be used in conjunction with each other. Utility stocks, for example, are closely linked to Treasury Bond prices. (See Figure 17.6.) Gold

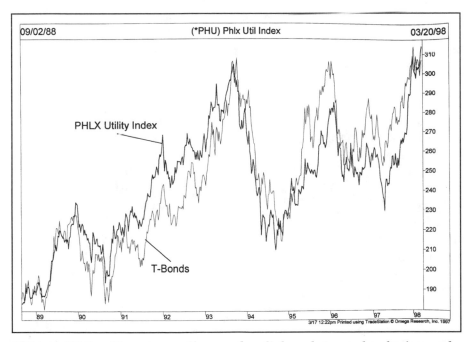

Figure 17.6 *There is usually very close linkage between bond prices and utilities. In addition, utilities often make their turns a little before bonds.*

mining shares are closely linked to the price of gold. What's more, the related stock groups often tend to lead their respective futures markets. As a result, utility stocks can be used as leading indicators for Treasury Bonds. Gold mining shares can be used as leading indicators for gold prices. Another example of intermarket influence is the impact of the trend of oil prices on energy and airline stocks. Rising oil prices help energy shares but hurt airlines. Falling oil prices have the opposite effect.

THE DOLLAR AND LARGE CAPS

Another intermarket relationship involves how the dollar affects large and small cap stocks. Large multinational stocks can be negatively impacted by a very strong dollar, which may make their products too expensive in foreign markets. By contrast, the more domestically oriented small cap stocks are less affected by dollar movements and may actually do better than larger stocks in a strong dollar environment. As a result, a stronger dollar may favor smaller stocks (like those in the Russell 2000), while a weaker dollar may benefit the large multinationals (like those in the Dow Industrial Average.)

INTERMARKET ANALYSIS AND MUTUAL FUNDS

It should be obvious that some understanding of these intermarket relationships can go a long way in mutual fund investing. The direction of the U.S. dollar, for example, might influence your commitment to small cap funds versus large cap funds. It may also help determine how much money you might want to commit to gold or natural resource funds. The availability of so many sector-oriented mutual funds actually complicates the decision of which ones to emphasize at any given time. That task is made a good deal easier by comparing the relative performance of the futures markets and the various stock market sectors and industry groups. That is easily accomplished by a simple charting approach called *relative strength* analysis.

RELATIVE STRENGTH ANALYSIS

This is an extremely simple but effective charting tool. All you do is divide one market entity by another—in other words, plot a ratio of two market prices. When the ratio line is rising, the numerator price is stronger than the denominator. When the ratio line is declining, the denominator market is stronger. Consider some examples of what you can do with this simple indicator. Divide a commodity index (such as the CRB Futures Price Index) by Treasury Bond futures prices. (See Figure 17.7.) When the ratio line is rising, commodity prices are outperforming bonds. In that scenario, futures traders would be buying commodity markets and selling bonds. At the same time, stock traders would be buying inflation sensitive stocks and selling interest-rate sensitive stocks. When the ratio line

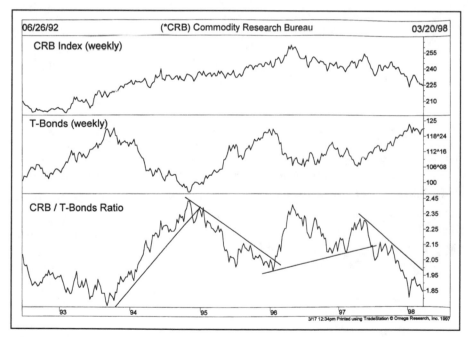

Figure 17.7 *The CRB Index/Treasury Bond ratio tells us which asset class is stronger. 1994 favored commodities, while 1995 favored bonds. The ratio took a sharp downturn in mid-1997 owing to the Asian crisis and fears of deflation.*

is falling, they would be doing the opposite. That is, they would sell commodities and buy bonds. At the same time, stock investors would be selling the golds, the oils, and the cyclicals, while buying the utilities, the financials, and consumer staples. (See Figure 17.8.)

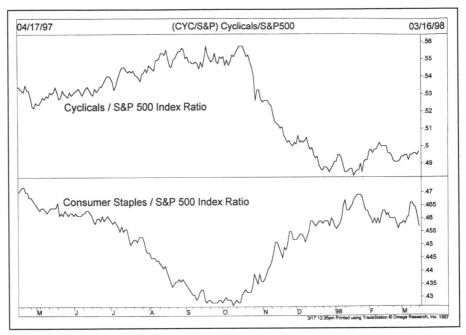

Figure 17.8 *During October 1997, the Asian crisis caused funds to flow out of cyclicals and into consumer staples, which coincided with a falling CRB/Bond ratio in Figure 17.7.*

RELATIVE STRENGTH AND SECTORS

Many exchanges now trade index options on various stock market sectors. The Chicago Board Options Exchange has the greatest selection and includes such diverse groups as automotive, computer software, environmental, gaming, real estate, healthcare, retail, and transportation. The American and Philadelphia Stock Exchanges offer popular index options on banks, gold, oil, pharmaceuticals, semiconductors, technology, and utilities. All of these index options can be charted and analyzed like any other market. The best way to use relative strength analysis on them is to divide their price by some industry benchmark such as the S&P 500. You can then determine which are outperforming the overall market (a rising RS line) or underperforming (a falling RS line). Employing some simple charting tools like trendlines and moving averages on the relative strength lines themselves will help you spot important changes in their trend. (See Figure 17.9.) The general idea is to rotate your funds into those sectors of the market whose relative strength lines are just turning up, and to rotate out of those market groups whose relative strength lines are just turning down. Those moves can be implemented either with the index options themselves or through mutual funds that match the various market sectors and industry groups.

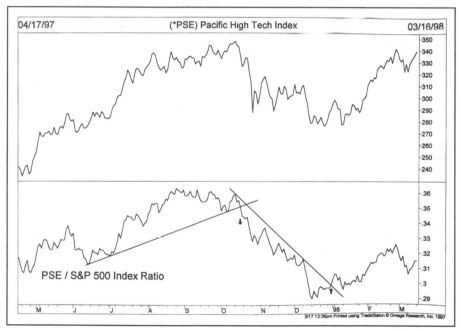

Figure 17.9 *A relative strength (ratio) comparison of the PSE High Tech Index to the S&P 500. Simple trendline analysis helped spot the downturn in technology stocks during October 1997 and the upturn at year-end.*

RELATIVE STRENGTH AND INDIVIDUAL STOCKS

Investors have two ways to go at that point. They can simply rotate their funds out of one market group into another and stop there. Or, if they wish, they can continue on to choose individual stocks within those groups. *Relative strength* analysis plays a role here as well. Once the desired index has been chosen, the next step is to divide each of the individual stocks within the index by the index itself. In that way, you can easily spot the individual stocks that are showing the greatest relative strength. (See Figure 17.10.) You can purchase the stocks showing the strongest ratio lines, or you can buy a cheaper stock whose ratio line may just be turning up. The idea, however, is to avoid stocks whose relative strength (ratio) lines are still falling.

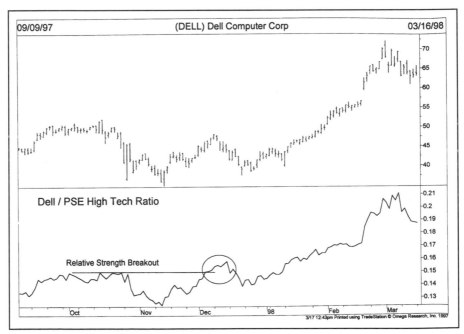

Figure 17.10 *A ratio analysis of Dell Computer versus the PSE High Tech Index at the end of 1997 showed Dell to be one of the better stock picks in the tech sector.*

TOP-DOWN MARKET APPROACH

What we've described here is a *top down* market approach. You begin by studying the major market averages to determine the trend of the overall market. Then you select those market sectors or industry groups that are showing the best relative strength. Then you select individual stocks within those groups that are also showing the best relative strength. By incorporating intermarket principles into your decision making process, you can also determine whether the current market climate favors bonds, commodities, or stocks which can play a role in your asset allocation decisions. The same principles can also be applied to international investing by simply comparing the relative strength of the various global stock markets. And, finally, all of these technical tools described herein can be applied to charts of mutual funds as a final check on your analysis. All of this work is easily done with price charts and a computer. Imagine trying to apply fundamental analysis to so many markets at the same time.

DEFLATION SCENARIO

The intermarket principles described herein are based on market trends since 1970. The 1970s saw runaway inflation which favored commodity assets. The decades of the 1980s and 1990s have been characterized by falling commodities (disinflation) and strong bull markets in bonds and stocks. During the second half of 1997, a severe downturn in Asian currency and stock markets was especially damaging to markets like copper, gold, and oil. For the first time in decades, some market observers expressed concern that a beneficial disinflation (prices rising at a slower level) might turn into a harmful deflation (falling prices). To add to the concerns, producer prices fell on an annual basis for the first time in more than a decade. As a result, the bond and stock markets began to decouple. For the first time in four years, investors were switching out of stocks and putting more money into bonds and rate-sensitive stock groups like utilities. The reason for that asset allocation adjustment is that deflation changes the intermarket scenario. The inverse relationship between bond prices and commodities is maintained. Commodities fall while bond prices rise. The difference is that the stock market can react negatively in that environment. We point this out because it's been a long time since the financial markets had to deal with the problem of price deflation. If and when deflation does occur, intermarket relationships will still be present but in a different way. Disinflation is bad for commodities, but good for bonds and stocks. Deflation is good for bonds and bad for commodities, but may also be bad for stocks.

The deflationary trend that started in Asia in mid-1997 spread to Russia and Latin America by mid-1998 and began to hurt all global equity markets. A plunge in commodity prices had an especially damaging impact on commodity exporters like Australia, Canada, Mexico, and Russia. The deflationary impact of falling commodity and stock prices had a positive impact on Treasury bond prices, which hit record highs. Market events of 1998 were a dramatic example of the existence of global intermarket linkages and demonstrated how bonds and stocks can decouple in a deflationary world.

INTERMARKET CORRELATION

Two markets that normally trend in the same direction, such as bonds and stocks, are positively correlated. Markets that trend in opposite directions, like bonds and commodities, are negatively correlated. Charting software allows you to measure the degree of correlation between different markets. A high positive reading suggests a strong positive correlation. A high negative reading suggests a strong negative correlation. A reading near zero suggests little or no correlation between two markets. By measuring the degree of correlation, the trader is able to establish how much emphasis to place on a particular intermarket relationship. More weight should be placed on those with higher correlations, and less weight on those closer to zero. (See Figure 17.11.)

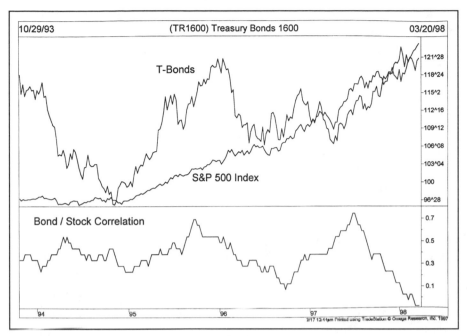

Figure 17.11   *The line along the bottom shows the positive correlation between T-bond prices and the S&P500. During the second half of 1997, the Asian crisis caused an unusual decoupling. Investors bought bonds and sold stocks.*

In his book, *Cybernetic Trading Strategies*, Murray Ruggiero, Jr. presents creative work on the subject of intermarket correlations. He also shows how to use intermarket filters on trading systems. He demonstrates, for example, how a moving-average crossover system in the bond market can be used as a filter for stock index trading. Ruggiero explores the application of state-of-the-art artificial intelligence methods like chaos theory, fuzzy logic, and neural networks to the development of technical trading systems. He also explores the application of neural networks to the field of intermarket analysis.

INTERMARKET NEURAL NETWORK SOFTWARE

One major problem with the study of intermarket relationships is that there are so many of them—and they're all interacting at the same time. That's where neural networks come into play. Neural networks provide a more quantitative framework for identifying and tracking the complex relationships that exist among the financial markets. Louis Mendelsohn, president of Market Technologies Corporation (25941 Apple Blossom Lane, Wesley Chapel, FL 33544; e-mail address: *45141@ProfitTaker.com;* website URL: www.ProfitTaker.com/45141), was the first person to develop intermarket analysis software in the financial industry during the 1980s. Mendelsohn is the leading pioneer in the application of microcomputer software and neural networks to intermarket analysis. His VantagePoint software, first introduced in 1991, uses intermarket principles to trade interest rate markets, stock indexes, currency markets, and energy futures. VantagePoint uses neural network technology to detect the hidden patterns and correlations that exist between related markets.

CONCLUSION

This chapter summarizes the main points included in my book, *Intermarket Technical Analysis.* It discusses the ripple effect that flows from the dollar to commodities to bonds to stocks. Intermarket work also recognizes the existence of global linkages. What happens in Asia, Europe, and Latin America has an impact on U.S. markets and vice versa. Intermarket analysis sheds light on sector rotation within the stock market. Relative strength analysis is helpful for seeking out asset classes, market sectors, or individual stocks that are likely to outperform the general market. In his book, *Leading Indicators for the 1990s,* Dr. Geoffrey Moore shows how the interaction between commodity prices, bond prices, and stock prices follows a sequential pattern that tracks the business cycle. Dr. Moore substantiates the intermarket rotation within the three asset classes, and argues for their use in economic forecasting. In doing so, Dr. Moore elevates intermarket work and technical analysis in general into the realm of economic forecasting. Finally, technical analysis can be applied to mutual funds like any other market (with some minor modifications). That being the case, all of the techniques discussed in this book can be applied right on the mutual fund charts themselves. Even better, the lower degree of volatility in mutual fund charts make them excellent vehicles for chart analysis. My latest book, *The Visual Investor,* deals more extensively with the subject of sector analysis and trading, and shows how mutual funds can be charted and then used to implement various trading strategies. (See Figure 17.12.)

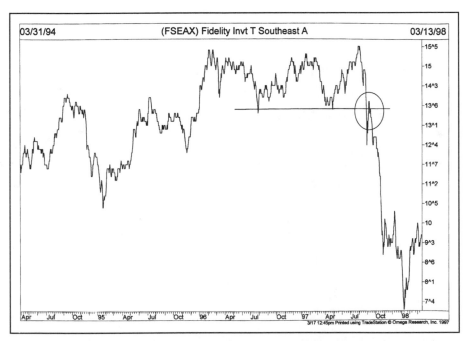

Figure 17.12 *Chart analysis can be done on mutual fund charts. You didn't have to be a chart expert to see that Asia was headed for trouble by tracking this mutual fund.*

18

Stock Market Indicators

MEASURING MARKET BREADTH

In the previous chapter, we described the top-down approach that is most commonly employed in stock market analysis. With that approach, you begin your analysis with a study of the health of the overall market. Then you work down to market sectors and industry groups. The final step is the study of individual stocks. Your goal is to pick the best stocks in the best groups in an environment when the stock market is technically healthy. The study of market sectors and individual stocks can be accomplished with the technical tools employed throughout this book—including chart patterns, volume analysis, trendlines, moving averages, oscillators, etc. Those same indicators can also be applied to the major market averages. But there's another class of market indicators widely employed in stock market analysis whose purpose is to determine the health of the overall stock market by measuring market breadth. The data used in their construction are advancing versus declining issues, new highs versus new lows, and up volume versus down volume.

SAMPLE DATA

If you check the Stock Market Data Bank section of *The Wall Street Journal* (Section C, page 2) each day, you'll find the following data for the previous trading day. The numbers shown are based on an actual day's trading results.

Diaries	
NYSE	*Monday*
Issues Traded	3,432
Advances	1,327
Declines	1,559
Unchanged	546
New highs	78
New lows	43
Adv vol (000)	248,215
Decl vol (000)	279,557
Total vol (000)	553,914
Closing tick	−135
Closing Arms (trin)	.96

The above figures are derived from New York Stock Exchange (NYSE) data. A similar breakdown is also shown for the NASDAQ and the American Stock Exchange. We'll concentrate on the NYSE in this discussion. It just so happens that on that particular day the Dow Jones Industrial Average had gained 12.20 points. So the market was up as measured by the Dow. However, there were more declining stocks (1,559) than advancing stocks (1,327), suggesting that the broader market didn't fare as well as the Dow. There was also more declining volume than advancing volume. Those two sets of figures suggest that market breadth was actually negative for that particular day—even though the Dow itself closed higher. The other figures present a more mixed picture. The number of stocks hitting new 52 week highs (78) was greater than those hitting new lows (43) suggesting a positive market environment. However, the closing tick (the number of stocks that closed on an uptick versus a downtick) was a negative, –135. That meant that 135 more stocks closed on a downtick than an uptick, a short term negative factor. The negative closing tick, however, is offset by a closing Arms (Trin) reading of .96 which is mildly positive. We'll explain why that is later in the chapter. All of these internal market readings have one intended purpose—to give us a more accurate reading on the health of the overall market that isn't always reflected in the movement of the Dow itself.

COMPARING MARKET AVERAGES

Another way to study the breadth of the market is to compare the performance of the stock averages themselves. Using the same day's trading as an example, the following data lists the relative performance of the major stock averages:

Dow Industrials	+12.20 (+.16%)
S&P 500	–.64 (–.07%)
Nasdaq Composite	–14.47 (–.92%)
Russell 2000	–3.80 (–.89%)

The first thing that is clear is that the Dow Industrials was the only market average to gain on the day. On all the TV news programs that night, investors were told that the market (represented by the Dow) was up for the day. Yet all the other measures were actually down. Notice also that the broader the average (the more stocks included) the worse it did. Compare the percentage changes. The 30 stock Dow gained .16%. The S&P 500 lost .07%. The Nasdaq Composite, which includes more than 5,000 stocks, was the day's worst performer and lost .92%. Almost as bad as the Nasdaq was the Russell 2000 (–.89%), which is a measure of 2000 small cap stocks. The message in this brief comparison is that even though the Dow gained on the day, the overall market lost ground as measured by the more broader based stock averages. We'll revisit the idea of comparing market averages again. But first, let's show the different ways market technicians can analyze the market's breadth numbers.

THE ADVANCE-DECLINE LINE

This is the best known of the breadth indicators. The construction of the advance decline line is extremely simple. Each day's trading on the New York Stock Exchange produces a certain number of stocks that advanced, a number that declined, and a number that remained unchanged. These figures are reported each day in *The Wall Street Journal* and *Investor's Business Daily*, and are used to construct a daily advance-decline (AD) line. The most common way to calculate the AD line is to take the difference between the number of advancing issues and the number of declining issues. If there are more advances than declines, the AD number for that day is positive. If there are more declines than advances, the AD line for that day is negative. That positive or negative daily number is then added to the cumulative AD line. The AD line displays a trend of its own. The idea is to make sure the AD line and the market averages are trending in the same direction. (See Figure 18.1.)

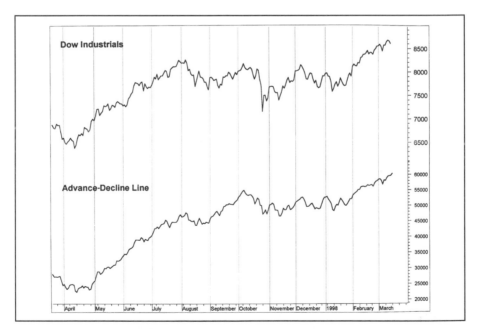

Figure 18.1   *The NYSE advance-decline line versus the Dow Industrials. In a healthy market, both lines should be trending upward together as they are here.*

AD DIVERGENCE

What does the advance-decline line measure? The advance-decline line tells us whether or not the broader universe of 3500 NYSE stocks is advancing in line with the most widely followed stock averages, which include only the 30 Dow Industrials or the 500 stocks in the S&P 500. To paraphrase a Wall Street maxim: the advance-decline line tells us if the "troops" are keeping up with the "generals." As long as the AD line is advancing with the Dow Industrials, for example, the breadth or health of the market is good. The danger appears when the AD line begins to diverge from the Dow. In other words, when you have a situation where the Dow Industrials are hitting new highs while the broader market (measured by the AD line) isn't following, technicians begin to worry about "bad market breadth" or an AD divergence. Historically, the AD line peaks out well ahead of the market averages, which is why it's watched so closely.

DAILY VERSUS WEEKLY AD LINES

The daily AD line, which we have described herein, is better used for short to intermediate comparisons with the major stock averages. It is less useful for comparisons going back several years. A weekly advance-decline line measures the number of advancing versus declining stocks for the entire week. Those figures are published in *Barron's* each weekend. A weekly advance-decline line is considered more useful for trend comparisons spanning several years. While a negative divergence in the daily AD line may warn of short to intermediate problems in the market, it's necessary to also show a similar divergence in the weekly AD line to confirm that a more serious problem is developing.

VARIATIONS IN AD LINE

Since the number of stocks traded on the NYSE has grown over the years, some market analysts believe the method of subtracting the number of declining issues from the number of advancing issues gives greater weight to the more recent data. To combat that problem, many technicians prefer to use an advance/decline ratio which divides the number of advancing issues by the number of declining issues. Some also believe that there's value in including the number of unchanged issues in the calculation. Whichever way the AD line is calculated, its use is always the same—that is, to measure the direction of the broader market and to ensure it's moving in the same direction as the more narrowly constructed, but popular market averages. Advance decline lines can also be constructed for the American Stock Exchange and the Nasdaq Market. Market technicians like to construct overbought/oversold oscillators on the AD lines to help measure short to intermediate term market extremes in the breadth figures themselves. One of the better known examples is the McClellan Oscillator.

McCLELLAN OSCILLATOR

Developed by Sherman McClellan, this oscillator is constructed by taking the difference between two exponential moving averages of the daily NYSE advance-decline figures. The McClellan Oscillator is the difference between the 19 day (10% trend) and the 39 day (5% trend) exponential moving averages of the daily net advance decline figures. The oscillator fluctuates around a zero line with its upper and lower extremes ranging from +100 and –100. A McClellan Oscillator reading above +100 is a signal of an overbought stock market. A reading below –100 is considered an oversold stock market. Crossings above and below the zero line are also interpreted as short to intermediate term buying and selling signals respectively. (See Figure 18.2.)

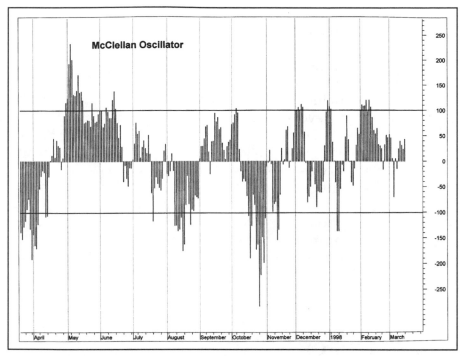

Figure 18.2 *The McClellan oscillator shown as a histogram. Crossings above the zero line are positive signals. Readings above +100 are overbought, while readings below –100 are oversold. Notice the extreme oversold reading during October of 1997.*

McCLELLAN SUMMATION INDEX

The Summation Index is simply a longer range version of the McClellan Oscillator. The McClellan Summation Index is a cumulative sum of each day's positive or negative readings in the McClellan Oscillator. Whereas the McClellan Oscillator is used for short to intermediate trading purposes, the Summation Index provides a longer range view of market breadth and is used to spot major market turning points. (See Figure 18.3.)

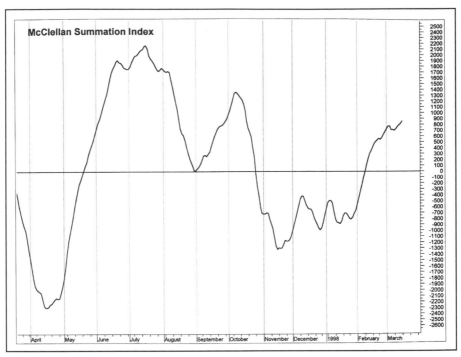

Figure 18.3   *The McClellan Summation Index is simply a longer range version of the McClellan Oscillator. The Summation Index is used for major trend analysis. Crossings below zero are negative. The February 1998 signal was positive.*

NEW HIGHS VERSUS NEW LOWS

In addition to the number of advancing and declining stocks, the financial press also publishes the number of stocks hitting new 52 week highs or new 52 week lows. Here again, these figures are available on a daily and weekly basis. There are two ways to show these figures. One way is to plot the two lines separately. Since the daily values can sometimes be erratic, moving averages (usually 10 days) are plotted to present a smoother picture of the two lines. (See Figure 18.4.) In a strong market, the number of new highs should be much greater than the number of new lows. When the number of new highs start to decline, or the number of new lows start to expand, a caution signal is given. A negative market signal is activated when the moving average of new lows crosses above

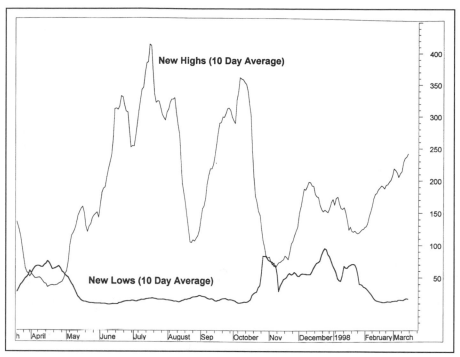

Figure 18.4 *A 10 day average of new highs versus a 10 day average of new lows. A healthy market should see more stocks hitting new highs than new lows. During October 1997, the two lines almost crossed before reasserting their bullish alignment.*

the moving average of new highs. It can also be shown that whenever the new highs reach an extreme, the market has a topping tendency. Similarly, whenever new lows reach an extreme, the market is near a bottom. Another way to use the new highs versus new lows numbers is to plot the difference between the two lines.

NEW HIGH-NEW LOW INDEX

The advantage of a New High-New Low index is that it can be directly compared to one of the major market averages. In that way, the high-low line can be used just like an advance-decline line. (See Figure 18.5.) The trend of the high-low line can be chart-

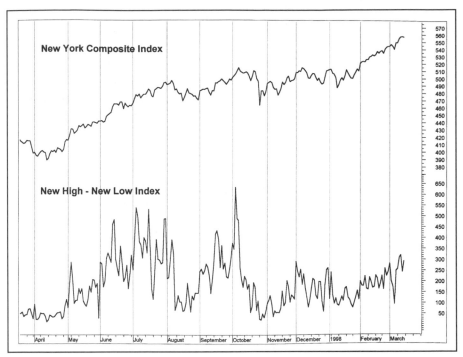

Figure 18.5 *The New High-New Low Index versus the NYSE Composite Index. This line plots the difference between the number of stocks hitting new highs and new lows. A rising line is positive. Notice the sharp drop during October of 1997.*

ed and it can be used to spot market divergences. A new high in the Dow, for example, that is not matched by a corresponding new high in the high-low line could be a sign of weakness in the broader market. Trendline and moving-average analysis can be applied to the line itself. But its major value is in either confirming or diverging from the major stock trends and giving early warning of potential trend changes in the overall market. Dr. Alexander Elder describes the New High-New Low index as "probably the best leading indicator of the stock market" *Trading for a Living,* (Wiley).

Elder suggests plotting the indicator as a histogram with a horizontal reference point at its zero line, making divergences easier to spot. He points out that crossings above and below the zero line also reflect bullish and bearish shifts in market psychology.

UPSIDE VERSUS DOWNSIDE VOLUME

This is the third and final piece of data that is utilized to measure the breadth of the market. The New York Stock Exchange also provides the level of volume in both the advancing and declining issues. That data is also available the next day in the financial press. It is then possible to compare the upside volume versus the downside volume to measure which is dominant at any given time. (See Figure 18.6.) The upside volume and downside volume can be shown as two separate lines (just as we did with the new highs and new lows figures) or the difference can be shown as a single line. Either way, the interpretation is always the same. When the upside volume is domi-

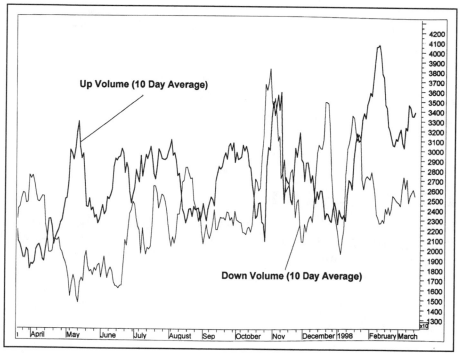

Figure 18.6 *A 10 day average of stock market upside volume (dark line) versus downside volume. A strong market should have more upside than downside volume.*

nant, the market is strong. When downside volume is greater, the market is weak. It's possible to combine the number of advancing and declining issues with advancing and declining volume. That's what Richard Arms did in the creation of the Arms Index.

THE ARMS INDEX

The Arms Index, named after its creator Richard Arms, is a ratio of a ratio. The numerator is the ratio of the number of advancing issues divided by the number of declining issues. The denominator is the advancing volume divided by declining volume. The purpose of the Arms Index is to gauge whether there's more volume in rising or falling stocks. A reading below 1.0 indicates more volume in rising stocks and is positive. A reading above 1.0 reflects more volume in declining issues and is negative. On an intraday basis, a very high Arms Index reading is positive, while a very low reading is negative. The Arms Index, therefore, is a contrary indicator that trends in the opposite direction of the market. It can be used for intraday trading by tracking its direction and for spotting signs of short term market extremes. (See Figure 18.7.)

TRIN VERSUS TICK

The Arms Index (TRIN) can be used in conjunction with the TICK indicator for intraday trading. TICK measures the difference between the number of stocks trading on an uptick versus the number trading on a downtick. The TICK is a minute-by-minute version of the daily advance-decline line and is used for the same purpose. When combining the two during the day, a rising TICK indicator and a falling Arms Index (TRIN) are positive, while a falling TICK indicator and a rising Arms Index (TRIN) are negative. The Arms Index, however, can also be used for longer range analysis.

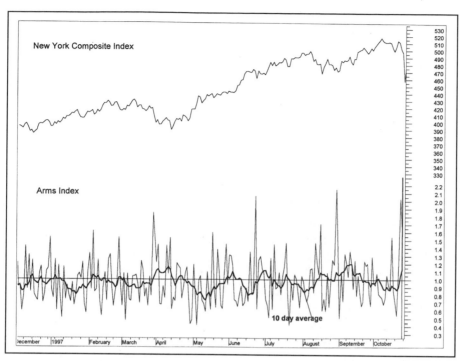

Figure 18.7 *The Arms Index (also called TRIN) trends in the opposite direction of the market. Exceptionally high spikes usually signal market bottoms. A 10-day moving average of the Arms Index is a popular way to view this contrary indicator.*

SMOOTHING THE ARMS INDEX

While the Arms Index is quoted throughout the trading day and has some short term forecasting value, most traders use a 10 day moving average of its values. According to Arms himself, a 10 day average of the Arms Index above 1.20 is considered oversold, while a 10 day Arms value below .70 is overbought, although those numbers may shift depending on the overall trend of the market. Arms expresses a preference for Fibonacci numbers as well. He suggests using a 21 day Arms Index in addition to the 10 day version. He also utilizes 21 day and 55 day moving-average crossovers of the Arms Index to generate good intermediate term trades. For more in-depth treatment, read *The Arms Index (TRIN)* by Richard W. Arms, Jr.

OPEN ARMS

In calculating the 10 day Arms Index, each day's closing value is determined using the four inputs and that final value is smoothed with a 10 day moving average. In the "Open" version of the Arms Index, each of the four components in the formula is averaged separately over a period of 10 days. The Open Arms Index is then calculated from those four different averages. Many analysts prefer the Open Arms version to the original version. Different moving average lengths, like 21 and 55 days, can also be applied to the Open Arms version. (See Figure 18.8.)

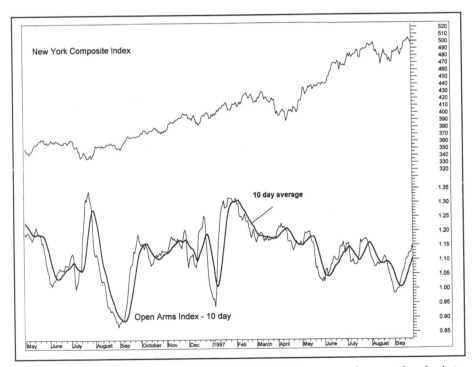

Figure 18.8 *The 10 day Open Arms Index gives a much smoother look to this indicator, but still trends in the opposite direction of the market. A crossing of its 10-day moving average (darker line) often signals turning points.*

EQUIVOLUME CHARTING

Although Arms is best known for creating the Arms Index, he has also pioneered other ways of combining price and volume analysis. In doing so, he created an entirely new form of charting called Equivolume. In the traditional bar chart, the day's trading range is shown on the price bar with the volume bar plotted at the bottom of the chart. Since technical analysts combine price and volume analysis, they have to look at both parts of the chart at the same time. On the Equivolume chart, each price bar is shown as a rectangle. The height of the rectangle measures the day's trading range. The width of the rectangle is determined by that day's volume. Heavier volume days produce a wider rectangle. Lighter volume days are reflected in a narrower rectangle. (See Figure 18.9.)

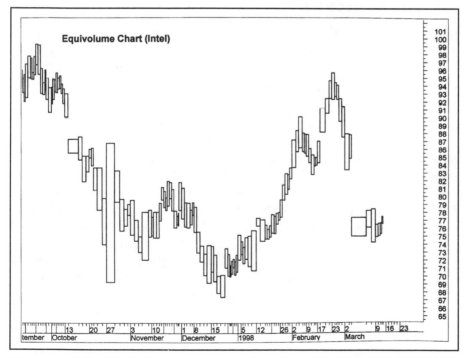

Figure 18.9 *Equivolume charts combine price and volume. The width of each rectangle (daily bar) is determined by the volume. Wider rectangles show heavier volume. The rectangles started to widen during Intel's last sell-off—a negative sign.*

As a rule, a bullish price breakout should always be accompanied by a burst of trading activity. On an Equivolume chart, therefore, a bullish price breakout should be accompanied by a noticeably wider rectangle. Equivolume charting combines price and volume analysis into one chart and makes for much easier comparisons between price and volume. In an uptrend, for example, up days should see wider rectangles while down days should see narrower rectangles. Equivolume charting can be applied to market averages as well as individual stocks and can be plotted for both daily and weekly charts. For more information, consult *Volume Cycles in the Stock Market* by Richard Arms (Dow Jones-Irwin, 1983).

CANDLEPOWER

In Chapter 12, Greg Morris explained candlestick charting. In a 1990 article published in *Technical Analysis of Stocks and Commodities* magazine entitled "East Meets West: CandlePower Charting," Morris proposed combining candlestick charts with Arms' Equivolume charting method. Morris' version shows the candlestick chart in an Equivolume format. In other words, the width of the candlestick is determined by the volume. The greater the volume, the wider the candlestick. Morris called the combination CandlePower charting. Quoting from the article: ". . . the CandlePower chart offers similar if not better information than Equivolume or candlestick charting and is as visually appealing as either of them." Morris' CandlePower technique is available on Metastock charting software (published by Equis International, 3950 S. 700 East, Suite 100, Salt Lake City, UT 84107 [800] 882-3040, www.equis.com). However its name has been changed to Candlevolume. (See Figure 18.10.)

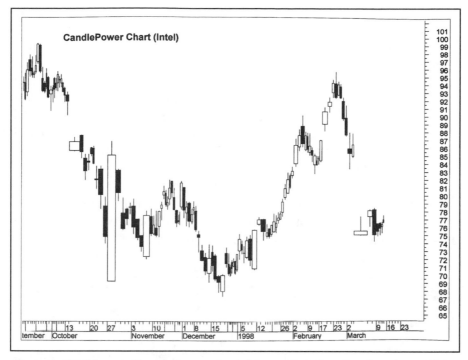

Figure 18.10 *A CandlePower chart (also called Candlevolume) combines equivolume and candlesticks. The width of each candle (daily bar) is determined by volume.*

COMPARING MARKET AVERAGES

At the start of the chapter, we mentioned that another way to gauge market breadth was to compare the different market averages themselves. We're talking here primarily about the Dow Industrials, the S&P 500, the New York Stock Exchange Index, the Nasdaq Composite, and the Russell 2000. Each measures a slightly different portion of the market. The Dow and the S&P 500 capture the trends of a relatively small number of large capitalization stocks. The NYSE Composite Index includes all stocks traded on the New York Stock Exchange, and gives a slightly broader perspective. Breakouts in the Dow Industrials should, as a rule, be confirmed by similar breakouts in both the S&P 500 and the NYSE Composite Index if the breakout is to have staying power.

Most important divergences involve the Nasdaq and the Russell 2000. The Nasdaq Composite has the largest number of stocks (5000). However, since the Nasdaq is a capitalization-weighted index, it is usually dominated by the one hundred largest technology stocks like Intel and Microsoft. Because of that, the Nasdaq is more often a measure of the direction of the technology sector. The Russell 2000 is a truer measure of the smaller stock universe. Both indexes, however, should be trending upward along with the Dow and the S&P 500 if the trend of the market is truly healthy.

Relative strength (RS) analysis plays a useful role here. A ratio of the Nasdaq to the S&P 500 tells us whether the technology stocks are leading or lagging. It's usually better for the market if they're leading and the ratio line is rising. (See Figure 18.11.) A

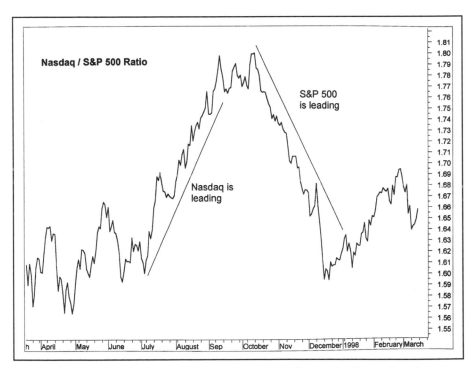

Figure 18.11   *The Nasdaq/S&P 500 ratio tells us whether technology stocks are leading or lagging the market. It's usually better for the market when the ratio line is rising.*

comparison of the Russell 2000 and the S&P 500 tells us whether the "troops" are following the "generals." When the small stocks are showing poor relative strength, or are lagging too far behind the large stocks, that's often a warning that market breadth is weakening. (See Figure 18.12.)

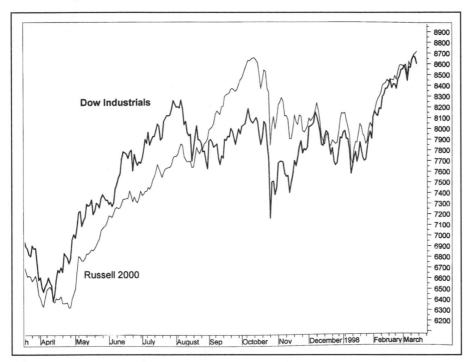

Figure 18.12 *An overlay comparison of the small cap Russell 2000 and the large cap Dow. It's usually better when both lines are rising together.*

CONCLUSION

Another example of comparing two market averages for signs of confirmation or divergence involves the Dow Theory. In Chapter 2, we discussed the importance of the relationship between the Dow Industrials and the Dow Transports. A Dow Theory buy signal is present when both averages hit new highs. When one diverges from the other, a caution signal is given. It can be seen then that the study of market breadth, and the related issues of confirmation and divergence, can take many forms. The general rule to follow is that the greater the number of stock market averages that are trending in the same direction, the greater the chances are for that trend continuing. In addition, be sure to check the advance-decline line, the new highs-new lows line, and the upside-downside volume lines to make sure that they're also trending in the same direction.

19

Pulling It All Together— A Checklist

As this book has demonstrated, technical analysis is a blend of many approaches. Each approach adds something to the analyst's knowledge of the market. Technical analysis is much like putting together a giant jigsaw puzzle. Each technical tool holds a piece of the puzzle. My approach to market analysis is to combine as many techniques as possible. Each works better in certain market situations. The key is knowing which tools to emphasize in the current situation. That comes with knowledge and experience.

All of these approaches overlap to some extent and complement one another. The day the user sees these interrelationships, and is able to view technical analysis as the sum of its parts, is the day that person deserves the title of technical analyst. The following checklist is provided to help the user touch all the bases, at least in the early going. Later on, the checklist becomes second nature. The checklist is not all-inclusive, but does have most of the more important factors to keep in mind. Sound market analysis seldom consists of doing the obvious. The technician is constantly seeking clues to future market movement. The final clue that leans the trader in one direction or the other is often some minor factor that has gone largely unnoticed by others. The more factors the analyst considers, the better the chances of finding that right clue.

TECHNICAL CHECKLIST

1. What is the direction of the overall market?
2. What is the direction of the various market sectors?
3. What are the *weekly* and *monthly* charts showing?
4. Are the major, intermediate, and minor *trends* up, down, or sideways?
5. Where are the important *support* and *resistance* levels?
6. Where are the important *trendlines* or *channels?*
7. Are *volume* and *open interest* confirming the price action?
8. Where are the 33%, 50%, and 66% *retracements?*
9. Are there any price gaps and what type are they?
10. Are there any *major reversal patterns* visible?
11. Are there any *continuation patterns* visible?
12. What are the *price objectives* from those patterns?
13. Which way are the *moving averages* pointing?
14. Are the *oscillators* overbought or oversold?
15. Are any *divergences* apparent on the oscillators?
16. Are *contrary opinion* numbers showing any extremes?
17. What is the *Elliot Wave* pattern showing?
18. Are there any obvious *3 or 5 wave patterns?*
19. What about *Fibonacci* retracements or projections?
20. Are there any *cycle* tops or bottoms due?
21. Is the market showing *right or left translation?*

22. Which way is the *computer trend* moving: up, down, or sideways?

23. What are the *point and figure* charts or *candlesticks* showing?

After you've arrived at a bullish or bearish conclusion, ask yourself the following questions.

1. Which way will this market trend over the next several months?

2. Am I going to buy or sell this market?

3. How many units will I trade?

4. How much am I prepared to risk if I'm wrong?

5. What is my profit objective?

6. Where will I enter the market?

7. What type of order will I use?

8. Where will I place my protective stop?

Going through the checklist won't guarantee the right conclusions. It's only meant to help you ask the right questions. Asking the right questions is the surest way of finding the right answers. The keys to successful trading are knowledge, discipline, and patience. Assuming that you have the knowledge, the best way to achieve discipline and patience is doing your homework and having a plan of action. The final step is putting that plan of action to work. Even that won't guarantee success, but it will greatly increase the odds of winning in the financial markets.

HOW TO COORDINATE TECHNICAL AND FUNDAMENTAL ANALYSIS

Despite the fact that technicians and fundamentalists are often at odds with one another, there are ways they can work together for mutual benefit. Market analysis can be approached from either direction. While I believe that technical factors do lead the known fundamentals, I also believe that any important market move must be caused by underlying fundamental factors. Therefore, it simply makes sense for a technician to have some awareness of the fundamental condition of a market. If nothing else, the technician can inquire from his or her fundamental counterpart as to what would have to happen fundamentally to justify a significant market move identified on a price chart. In addition, seeing how the market reacts to fundamental news can be used as an excellent technical indication.

The fundamental analyst can use technical factors to confirm an analysis or as an alert that something important may be happening. The fundamentalist can consult a price chart or use a computer trend-following system as a filter to prevent him or her from assuming a position opposite an existing trend. Some unusual action on a price chart can act as an alert for the fundamental analyst and cause him or her to examine the fundamental situation a bit closer. During my years in the technical analysis department of a major brokerage firm, I often approached our fundamental department to discuss some market move that seemed imminent on the price charts. I often received responses like "that can never happen" or "no way." Very often, that same person was scrambling a couple of weeks later to find fundamental reasons to explain a sudden and "unexpected" market move. There's obviously room for much more coordination and cooperation in this area.

CHARTERED MARKET TECHNICIAN (CMT)

A lot of people use technical analysis and offer opinions on the technical condition of the various markets. But are they really qualified to do so? How would you know? After all, you wouldn't go to a doctor who didn't have a medical degree on the wall. Nor would you consult a lawyer who hadn't passed the bar exam. Your accountant is undoubtedly a CTA. If you asked a security analyst for an assessment on a common stock, you would certainly make sure that he or she was a Chartered Financial Analyst (CFA). Why wouldn't you take the same precautions with a technical analyst?

The Market Technicians Association (MTA) resolved this question by instituting a Chartered Market Technician (CMT) program. The CMT program is a three step examination process that qualifies the analyst to carry the CMT letters after his or her name. Most professional technical analysts have gone through the program. The next time someone offers you his or her technical opinion, ask to see the CMT.

MARKET TECHNICIANS ASSOCIATION (MTA)

The Market Technicians Association (MTA) is the oldest and best known technical society in the world. It was founded in 1972 to encourage the exchange of technical ideas, educate the public and the investment community, and establish a code of ethics and professional standards among technical analysts. (On March 11, 1998 the MTA celebrated the 25th birthday of its incorporation. The event was highlighted by a special presentation at the New York monthly meeting by three of the organization's founding members—Ralph Acampora, John Brooks, and John Greeley.) MTA membership includes full-time technical analysts and other interested parties (called affiliates). Monthly meetings are held in New York (Market Technicians Association, Inc., One World Trade Center, Suite 4447, New York, NY 10048 (212) 912-0995, e-mail: shelleymta@aol.com), and an annual seminar is held each May at various locations around the country. Members have access to the MTA library and a computer bulletin board. A monthly newsletter and a periodic MTA Journal are published. Some regional chapters have even been formed. MTA members also become colleagues of the International Federation of Technical Analysts (IFTA).

THE GLOBAL REACH OF TECHNICAL ANALYSIS

During the fall of 1985, a meeting was held in Japan with technical representatives of several different countries to draft a constitution for the International Federation of Technical Analysts (IFTA, Post Office Box 1347, New York, NY 10009 USA). Since then, the organization has grown to include technical analysis organizations from more than twenty countries. One of the nice things about being a member is that annual meetings are held in places like Australia, Japan, Paris, and Rome since a different national organization hosts each seminar. I'm proud to say that in 1992 I received the first award ever given at an IFTA conference for "outstanding contribution to global technical analysis."

TECHNICAL ANALYSIS BY ANY NAME

After a century of use in this country (and 300 years in Japan), technical analysis is more popular than ever. Of course, it's not always called technical analysis. In my book, *The Visual Investor,* I called it *visual* analysis. That was simply an attempt to get people beyond the intimidating title of technical analysis and to get them to examine this valuable approach more closely. Whatever you want to call it, technical analysis is practiced under many names. A lot of financial organizations employ analysts whose job it is to number-crunch market prices to find stocks or stock groups that are expensive (overbought) or cheap (oversold). They're called quantitative analysts, but the numbers they crunch are often the same ones the technicians are crunching. The financial press has written about a "new" class of trader called "momentum" players. These traders move funds out of stocks and stock groups that are showing poor momentum and into those that are showing good momentum. They use a technique called relative strength. Of course, we recognize "momentum" and "relative strength" as technical terms.

Then there are the brokerage firms' "fundamental" upgrades and downgrades. Have you noticed how often these "fundamental" changes take place the day after a significant "chart" breakout or breakdown? Economists, who certainly don't consider themselves technical analysts, use charts all the time to measure the direction of inflation, interest rates, and all sorts of economic indicators. And they talk about the "trend" of those charts. Even fundamental tools like the price/earnings ratio have a technical side to them. Anytime you introduce price into the equation, you're moving into the realm of technical analysis. Or when security analysts say the dividend yield of the stock market is too low, aren't they saying prices are too high? Isn't that the same thing as saying a market is overbought?

Finally, there are the academics who have reinvented technical analysis under the new name of *Behavioral Finance*. For years, the academics espoused the Efficient Market Hypothesis to prove that technical analysis simply didn't work. No less an authority than the Federal Reserve Board has thrown some doubt on those ideas.

FEDERAL RESERVE FINALLY APPROVES

During August of 1995, the Federal Reserve Bank of New York published a Staff Report under the title: "Head and Shoulders: Not Just a Flaky Pattern." The report was intended to examine the validity of the head and shoulders pattern in foreign exchange trading. (The first edition of this book was cited as one of the primary sources on technical analysis.) The opening sentence in the introduction reads:

> Technical analysis, the prediction of price movements based on past price movements, has been shown to generate statistically significant profits despite its incompatibility with most economists' notions of "efficient markets." (Federal Reserve Bank of New York, C.L. Osler and P.H. Kevin Chang, Staff Report No. 4, August 1995.)

A more recent report, published in the fall of 1997 by the Federal Reserve Bank of St. Louis, also addresses the use of technical analysis and the relative merits of the Efficient Market Hypothesis. (*Technical Analysis of the Futures Markets* was again cited as a primary source of information on technical analysis.) Under the paragraph titled, "Rethinking the Efficient Markets Hypothesis," the author writes:

> The success of technical trading rules shown in the previous section is typical of a number of later studies showing that the simple efficient market hypothesis fails in important ways to describe how the foreign exchange market actually functions. While these results did not surprise market practitioners, they have helped persuade economists to examine features of the market ... that might explain the profitability of technical analysis. (Neely)

CONCLUSION

If imitation is the sincerest form of flattery, then market technicians should feel very flattered. *Technical analysis* is practiced under many different names, and often by those who may not realize they're using it. But it *is* being practiced. Technical analysis has also evolved. The introduction of *intermarket* analysis, for example, has changed the focus away from "single market" analysis to a more interdependent view of the financial markets. The idea that all global markets are linked isn't questioned much anymore either. That's why the universal language of technical analysis makes it especially useful in a world where the financial markets, here and abroad, have become so intertwined. In a world where computer technology and lightning-fast communications require quick responses, the ability to read the market's signals is more crucial than ever. And reading market signals is what technical analysis is all about. Charles Dow introduced technical analysis at the start of the twentieth century. As the twentieth century draws to a close, Mr. Dow would be proud of what he started.

APPENDICES

Appendix A: Advanced Technical Indicators*

This appendix introduces several more advanced technical methods that can be used by themselves or with other technical studies. As with any technical approach, it is always recommended that investors do their own independent testing and research before actually investing.

DEMAND INDEX (DI)

Most technicians will agree that volume analysis is an important ingredient in determining a market's direction. The *Demand Index* (DI) is one of the early volume indicators that was developed in the 1970s by James Sibbett. The formula is quite complex (see end of this appendix). The Demand Index is the ratio of buying pres-

*This Appendix was prepared by Thomas E. Aspray.

sure to selling pressure. When the buying pressure is greater than the selling pressure, the DI is above the zero line, which is positive. Greater selling pressure means the DI is below zero, which implies prices will move lower. Most traders also look for divergences between the DI and prices.

Figure A.1 is a weekly chart of T-Bond futures from early 1994 until late 1997. From April to November 1994, the DI was mostly below the zero line as bonds declined from 104 to the 96 area. While prices made lower lows (line A), the DI formed higher lows (line B). This is a classic positive, or bullish divergence, which suggested that bond prices were bottoming. The divergence was confirmed when the DI moved above the zero line at point 1. The DI reached its highest level for this rally in late May 1995 at point 2, and then dropped for the next six weeks before

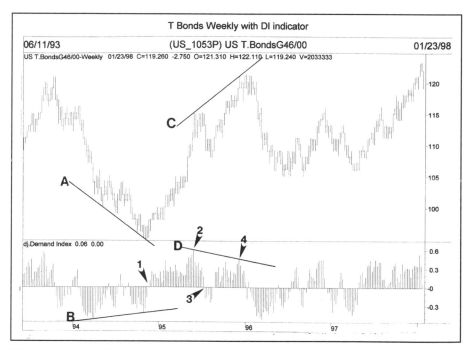

Figure A.1 *The Demand Index (DI), which incorporates price and volume, is shown here as a histogram. Values above zero are positive; below zero they are negative. Notice the bullish divergence in late 1994 and the bearish divergence in late 1995. (Courtesy MetaStock Equis International.)*

crossing below the zero line at point 3. It stayed negative for five weeks before it again turned positive. On the next rally the DI formed a significantly lower high in late November at point 4. While the DI was lower (line D), the bond contract was almost six points higher (line C). This negative or bearish divergence warned of a price peak.

This indicator can also be used with stocks. The weekly chart of General Motors (Figure A.2) shows the DI plotted as a line rather than a histogram. This allows for trendlines to more easily be drawn on the indicator. I have personally found trendline analysis of indicators to be quite valuable. Indicator trendlines are often broken ahead of price trendlines. This was the case in late 1995 as the downtrend in the DI (line A) was broken

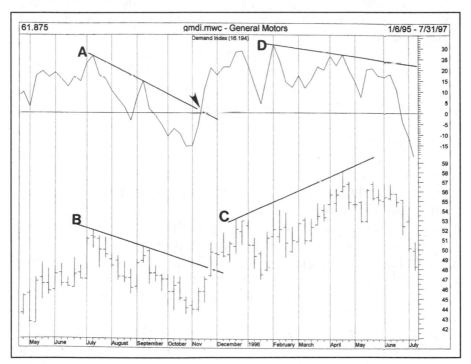

Figure A.2   *The Demand Index (solid line) compared to a weekly chart of GM. Trendline breaks on the DI line often preceded trendline breaks on the price chart. Notice the negative (bearish) divergence in April 1996. (Courtesy MetaStock, Equis International.)*

a week before the corresponding price downtrend (line B). As this chart indicates, buying just one week earlier could have significantly improved the entry price. The DI also warned of a price high in mid-April 1996. While GM was making a new price high (line C), the DI had formed lower highs (line D). This warning signal came well ahead of the serious price decline in June and July.

HERRICK PAYOFF INDEX (HPI)

This indicator was developed by the late John Herrick as a way of analyzing commodity futures through changes in the open interest. As discussed in Chapter 7, changes in the open interest can give traders important clues as to whether a market trend is well supported or not.

The *Herrick Payoff Index* uses price, volume, and open interest to determine money flow into or out of a given commodity. This helps the trader spot divergences between the price action and the open interest. This is often quite important as buying or selling panics can often be identified through analysis of the open interest by the Herrick Payoff Index.

The most basic interpretation of the HPI is whether it is above or below the zero line. A positive value means that the HPI is projecting higher prices and that open interest is rising along with prices. Conversely, negative readings suggest that funds are flowing out of the commodity being analyzed.

One of the more volatile commodity markets is coffee, featured in Figure A.3. During March and April of 1997, the HPI had four crossings of the zero line with the last positive signal in early April (B) lasting until early June. The HPI dropped below zero in June, and even though prices were well below the highs, coffee dropped another 70 cents. Once again the HPI turned positive in late July very close to the lows. Over the next two months there were two short term signals and then another longer term sell signal. This is characteristic of the HPI when used on the daily data as it will cross above and below the zero line several times before a longer lasting buy or sell signal is given.

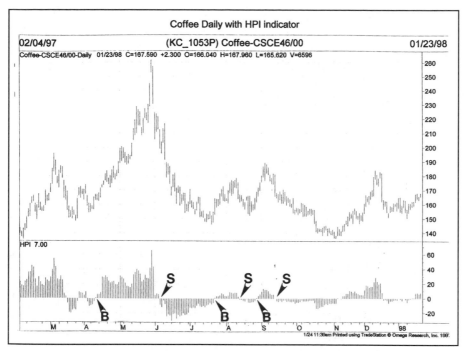

Figure A.3 *The Herrick Payoff Index (HPI) shown as a histogram with coffee prices. HPI uses price, volume, and open interest in its calculation and is used in futures markets. Crossings above zero are buys (B); crossings below are sells (S).*

The HPI, like the Demand Index, is most effective when used on the weekly data, as fewer false signals are evident. Divergence analysis can also be used to warn the trader of a change from positive to negative money flow. There are several good examples on the weekly T-Bond futures charts (Figure A.4) that covers approximately six years of trading. The HPI stayed positive from late 1992 until late 1993. The HPI peaked in early 1993 and, when bonds were almost 10 points higher (line A), the HPI was forming a lower high (line B). This negative divergence warned bond traders of the decline in prices that took place in 1994. The HPI violated the zero line in late October of 1993, but then turned slightly positive in early 1994 before plunging back below the zero line. The HPI reached its lowest

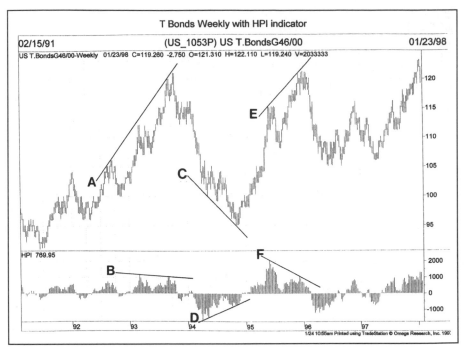

Figure A.4 *A weekly version of Herrick Payoff Index with Treasury Bonds. Notice the bearish divergences in 1993 and 1995, and the bullish divergence in 1994.*

level in the first half of 1994 and bottomed well ahead of prices. As prices were making lower lows (line C), the HPI was forming higher lows and therefore a positive divergence (line D). The HPI moved back into positive territory in December 1994 as bonds were very close to their lows. A negative divergence was formed in late 1995 (line F), after bonds had rallied over 25 points from the late 1994 lows. The zero line was crossed several times in 1996 and early 1997 before the HPI moved firmly into positive territory. These two examples should illustrate why the HPI and its analysis of open interest can be helpful in analyzing a commodity market's direction.

STARC BANDS AND KELTNER CHANNELS

As discussed in Chapter 9, banding techniques have been used for many years. Two types that I prefer are based on the *Average True Range*. Despite this common factor, these two types of bands are used in very different ways. Average True Range is the average of true price ranges over x periods. *True Range* is the greatest distance from today's high to low, yesterday's close to today's high, or yesterday's close to today's low. See Welles Wilder's *New Concepts in Technical Trading Systems*.

Manning Stoller, a well known expert in the commodity business, developed the Stoller Average Range Channels or *starc* bands. In his formula the 15 period *Average True Range* is doubled and added to or subtracted from a 6 period moving average (MA). The upper band is starc+; the lower is starc–. Movement outside of these bands is uncommon and indicates an extreme situation. In this manner they can be used as trading filters. When prices are near or above the starc+ band, it is a high risk time to buy and a low risk time to sell. Conversely, if prices are at or below the starc– band, then it is a high risk selling zone and a more favorable point to buy.

The weekly continuation chart of gold futures (Figure A.5) is plotted with both the starc+ and starc– bands. In Feb. 1997 at point 1, gold prices slightly overshot the starc– band. Though the price action was weak, the starc bands indicated that this was not a good time to sell. By waiting, a better selling opportunity was likely to occur. Just three weeks later gold was $22 higher and at the starc+ band (point 2). Point 2 was a low risk selling opportunity. In July (point 3), gold prices dropped well below the starc-band, but instead of declining further, prices moved sideways for the next 12 weeks. Gold prices then started to move lower from November to December 1997 and touched the starc– band three times (points 4). In all instances prices did stabilize or move higher for 1–2 weeks. These bands work well in all time frames even as short as 5 to 10 minute bar charts. Starc bands can help the trader avoid chasing the market, which almost always results in a poor entry price.

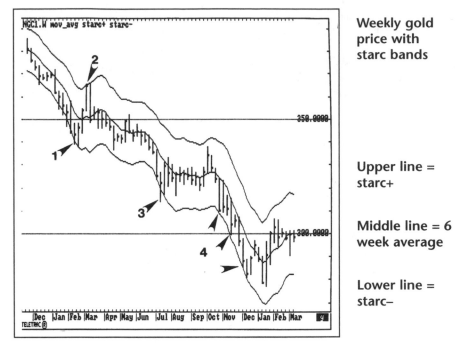

Weekly gold
price with
starc bands

Upper line =
starc+

Middle line = 6
week average

Lower line =
starc–

Figure A.5 *Starc bands plotted around a 6 week moving average of week-ly gold prices. Points 1 and 3 show prices bouncing after dipping below the lower band. Point 2 shows prices falling after rising above the upper band.*

The *Keltner channels* were originally developed by Chester Keltner in his 1960 book *How to Make Money in Commodities*. Linda Raschke, a very successful commodity trader, has reintroduced them to technicians. In her modification, the bands are also based on the *average true range (ATR)*, but the ATR is calculated over 10 periods. This ATR value is then doubled and added to a 20 period exponential moving average for the plus band and subtracted from it for the minus band.

The recommended use of the Keltner channels is much different from the starc bands. When prices close above the plus band, a positive signal is given as it indicates a breakout in upward volatility. Conversely, when prices close below the lower band, it is negative and indicates prices will move lower. In many respects, this is just a graphical representation of a four week channel breakout system discussed in Chapter 9.

Figure A-6 is a daily chart of March 1998 copper futures. Prices closed below the minus band in late October 1997 at point 1. This indicated that prices should begin a new downtrend and copper prices dropped 16 cents in the next two months.

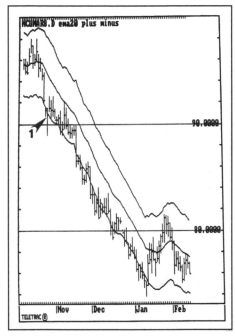

Daily copper prices with Keltner Channels

Upper line = plus channel

Middle line = 20 day exponential average

Lower line = minus channel

Figure A.6 *Keltner Channels plotted around a 20 day exponentially smoothed average of daily copper prices. With this indicator, moves below the lower channel (such as point 1) are interpreted as a sign of weakness.*

There were many other closes below the minus band during this period. Until prices close above the plus band, the negative signal will stay in effect. The second chart is March 1998 coffee prices (Figure A.7) and illustrates a positive signal at point 1. After two consecutive closes above the plus band, prices then declined to the 20 period EMA. In a rising market the 20 period EMA should act as support. Several days after the EMA was touched (point 2), coffee prices began a dramatic 30 cent rise in just a few weeks.

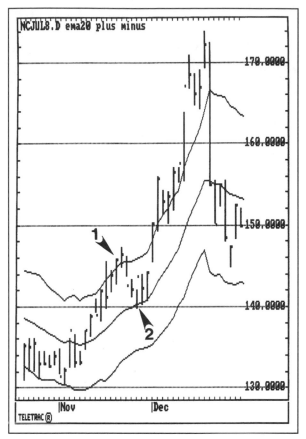

Daily coffee chart with Keltner Bands

Figure A.7   *Keltner Channels with a daily coffee chart. Point 1 shows prices breaking the upper channel which is a sign of strength. Notice that after that buy signal, prices found support at the 20 day exponential moving average (middle line) at point 2.*

Both of these techniques offer an alternative approach to either percentage envelopes or standard deviation bands (like Bollinger Bands). Neither is presented as a stand-alone trading system but should be considered as additional tools of the trade.

FORMULA FOR DEMAND INDEX

The Demand Index (DI) calculates two values, Buying Pressure (BP) and Selling Pressure (SP), and then takes a ratio of the two. DI is BP/SP. There are some slight variations in the formula. Here's one version:

> If prices rise:

> > BP = V or Volume
> > SP = V/P where P is the % change in price

> If prices decline:

> > BP = V/P where P is the % change in price
> > SP = V or Volume

> Because P is a decimal (less than 1), P is modified by multiplying it by the constant K.

> > P = P(K)
> > K = (3 × C)/VA

Where C is the closing price and VA (Volatility Average) is the 10 day average of a two day price range (highest high – lowest low).

> If BP > SP then DI = SP/BP

> The Demand Index is included on the MetaStock charting menu.

Appendix B:
Market Profile*

INTRODUCTION

The purpose of this writing is to illustrate what Market Profile is and to define its underlying principles. Before the early 1980s, the only technical tools available were the bar chart and the point and figure chart. Since then Market Profile®[1] was introduced to expand the arsenal of technical tools. Market Profile is essentially a statistical approach to the analysis of price data.[2] For those without a statistics background, a familiar example may be helpful. Consider a group of students taking an exam. Typically, some score very high (say 90 or higher), some score very low (say

*This appendix was prepared by Dennis C. Hynes.

[1]The Market Profile® is a registered trademark of the Chicago Board of Trade (CBOT), hereafter referred to as Market Profile or the *profile*. The concept was developed by J. Peter Steidlmayer, formerly of the CBOT. For further information on the subject, contact the CBOT or read Mr. Steidlmayer's latest book: *141 WEST JACKSON*—1996.

[2]Originally introduced for commodity futures prices, the format can be used for any price data series where continuous transaction activity is available.

475

60 or lower), but most scores tend to be clustered around the average score (say 75). A *histogram* can be used to depict the *frequency distribution* of these test scores in a "statistical picture" (Figure B.l).

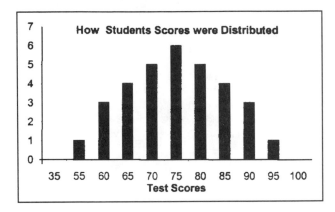

Figure B.1

As can be seen, the most frequent score, or *modal* score, is 75 (6 students) while the *range* of scores is defined by the lowest and highest scores (55 and 95). Note how the scores distribute evenly around the modal score. For a perfectly *symmetric* distribution, the modal score will be equal to the *mean,* or average score. Next observe that the distribution is "bell-shaped," the telltale sign of a *normal* distribution. For a perfect normal distribution, specific *standard deviation* intervals correlate to specific numbers of observations. For example, if the test scores are, in fact, perfectly normally distributed, then 68.3% of these scores will fall within one (1) standard deviation of the mean. While actual data is unlikely to form a perfect normal distribution, it is often close enough that these relationships can be employed.

Prices, like other physical measurements (e.g., school test grades, population heights, etc.), *distribute* around a mean price level as well. What is the Market Profile *graphic*? Visualize it as simply, a frequency distribution of prices displayed as a price histogram turned on its side (see Figures B.2a and B.2b).

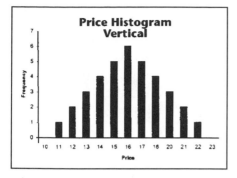

Figure B.2a   *Traditional.*

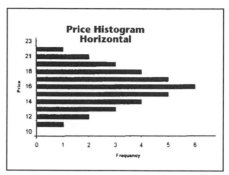

Figure B.2b   *Flipped on its side.*

The centerpiece of the Market Profile graphic is the (bell-shaped) *normal* curve used to display the evolving price distribution. Once the normal curve assumption is acknowledged, a modal or average price can be identified, a price dispersion (standard derivation) can be computed and probability statements can be made regarding the price distribution. For example, virtually all values fall within three (3) standard deviations of the average while about 70% (68.3% to be exact) fall within one (1) standard deviation of the average (see Figure B.3).

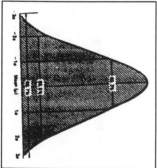

Figure B.3   *The profile graphic reveals that market activity is regularly normally distributed.*

Market Profile provides a picture of what's happening *here and now* in the marketplace. In its pursuit of promoting trade, the market is either in equilibrium or moving toward it. The profile's natural tendency toward symmetry defines, in a simple way, the degree of balance (equilibrium) or imbalance (disequilibrium) that exists between buyers and sellers. As the market is dynamic, the profile *graphic* portrays equilibrium as periods of market balance—when price distributions are symmetric, and represents disequilibrium as periods of market imbalance—when price distributions are not symmetric or are skewed.

Market Profile is not a trading system nor does it provide trade recommendations. The aim of the profile graphic is to allow the user to witness a market's developing value on price *reoccurrence* over time. As such, Market Profile is a *decision support* tool requiring the user to exercise personal judgment in the trading process.

MARKET PROFILE GRAPHIC

The Market Profile format organizes price and time into a visual representation of what happens over the course of a single session. It provides a logical framework for observing market behavior in the *present tense* displaying price distributions over a period of time. The price range evolves both vertically and horizontally throughout the session. How is a profile graphic constructed?

Consider a 4 period bar chart (see Figure B.3a). This traditional bar chart can be converted to a profile graphic as follows: (1) assign a letter for each price within each period's price range, letter A for the 1st period, B for the 2nd, and so on (see Figure B.3b) and then (2) collapse each price range to the leftmost or first column (see Figure B.3c). The completed profile graphic reflects prices on the left and period frequency of price occurrence on the right, represented by the letters A through D.

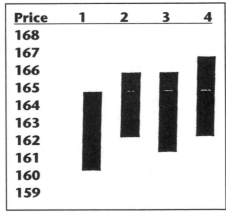

Price	1	2	3	4
168				
167				D
166		B	C	D
165	A	B	C	D
164	A	B	C	D
163	A	B	C	D
162	A			
161	A			
160				
159				

Figure B.3a

Figure B.3b

Each letter represents a *Time Price Opportunity* or TPO to identify a specific price at which the market traded during a specific time period (e.g., in B period prices traded between 163 and 166). These TPOs are the basic units of analysis for the day's activity. In other words, each TPO is an *opportunity* created by the market at a certain *time* and certain *price*. Market Profile distributions are

Price				
168				
167	D			
166	B	C	D	
165	A	B	C	D
164	A	B	C	D
163	A	B	C	D
162	A	C		
161	A			
160				
159				

Figure B.3c

constructed of TPOs. The Chicago Board of Trade (CBOT) assigns a letter to each half-hour trading period on a 24 hour basis; upper-case letters A through X represent the half-hour periods from midnight to noon while lowercase letters from a through x represent the half-hour periods from noon to midnight.[3]

MARKET STRUCTURE

When you visit a commodities trading pit on a busy day, you observe what is best described as "controlled chaos." Beneath the screaming and gesturing *locals* and other traders, there is a describable process. Think of the market as a place where participants with differing price needs and time constraints compete with each other to get business done. Emotions can run high as anxiety levels soar.

The Market Profile concept was introduced by Mr. Steidlmayer in an attempt to help describe this process. As a

[3]Letter assignments can vary between vendors. For example, CQG assigns upper-case letters A through Z from 8:00 am CST while lowercase letters from a through z from 10:00 p.m. CST.

CBOT floor trader (*local*) and student of market behavior, he observed recurring patterns of market activity, which ultimately lay the foundation for his understanding of the market. Since the CBOT trading floor conducts trade in an auction-like manner, he defined Market Profile principles in auction terms. For example, an off-the-floor trader would describe an advancing market as one that is *rallying* or *trading up,* whereas Mr. Steidlmayer would instead say something like, "the market continues to *auction up, advertising* for sellers to appear in order to *shut off* buying."

To explain why a trading pit auction process works the way it does, he invented some new terms unfamiliar to off-the-floor traders. He began with a definition of a market's purpose, which is to *facilitate* trade. Next, he defined some operational procedures, namely that the market operates in a *dual auction* mode as prices *rotate* around a fair or mean price area (i.e., similar to the way school grades were distributed). Lastly, he defined the behavior characteristics of market participants, namely that traders with a short term time frame seek a *fair* price, while traders with a longer term time frame seek an *advantageous* price.

MARKET PROFILE ORGANIZING PRINCIPLES

Auction Setting: The purpose of the marketplace is to *facilitate* or promote trade. All market activity occurs within this auction setting. Initially, as price moves higher, more buying comes in, as price moves lower, more selling comes in. The market moves up to *shut off* buying (i.e., auctioning up until the last buyer buys) and moves down to *shut off* selling (i.e., auctioning down until the last seller sells). The market actually operates through a *dual auction* process. When price moves up and more buying comes in, the up-move *advertises* for an opposite response (i.e., selling) to stop the directional move. The opposite is true when price moves down.

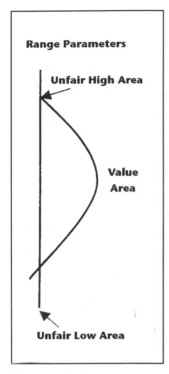

Range Parameters

Unfair High Area

Value Area

Unfair Low Area

Figure B.4

Continuous Negotiation: When a market moves directionally it establishes price parameters, an *unfair high* and an *unfair low,* and then trades between them to establish a *fair value* area. All trade takes place through this *negotiating process* and remains within these parameters until one side or the other side is eventually taken out (i.e., a new high or new low is formed). (see Figure B.4.)

Market Balance and Imbalance: The market is either in equilibrium or working toward equilibrium between buyers and sellers. To facilitate trade, the market moves from a state of balance (equilibrium) to one of *imbalance* (disequilibrium) and back to balance again. This pattern of market behavior occurs in all times frames, from intraday session activity to single session activity to aggregated or consolidated sessions activity which form the longer term auction.

Time Frames and Trader Behavior: The concept of different time frames was introduced to help explain the behavioral patterns of market participants. Market activity is divided into two timeframe categories, short term and longer term. The short term activity is defined as *day time frame* activity where traders are forced to trade today (e.g., locals, day traders and options traders on expiration day fall into this category). With limited time to act, the short term trader is seeking a *fair* price. Short term buyers and sellers *do* trade with each other at the same time and at the same price. Longer term activity is defined by all *other timeframe* activity (e.g., commercials, swing traders, and all other position traders fall into this category). Not forced to trade today and with time as an ally, these traders can seek a more *advantageous price.* In pursuit of their interests, longer term buyers seek lower prices while longer term sellers seek higher prices. As their price objectives differ, longer term buyers and sellers generally *do not* trade with each other at the same price and at the same time. It is the behavioral interaction between these two distinct timeframe types of activity that causes the profile to develop as it does.

The Short Term Trader and Longer Term Trader Play Different Roles: Short term and longer term traders play key, but different, roles in facilitating trade. A market's *initial balance* (i.e., a place where two-sided trade can occur) is usually established in the first hour of trade by short term buyers and sellers (day timeframe activity) in their pursuit of a fair price. Most of the day's activity occurs in the fair price or value area. Prices above and below this developed fair value area offer opportunity and are advantageous to longer term traders. With time on their side, longer term traders can either accept or reject prices away from fair value. By entering the market with large enough volume, longer term buyers and sellers can upset the *initial balance,* thereby extending the price range higher or lower. The longer term trader is responsible for the way the day's range develops and for the duration of the longer term auction. In other words, the role of the longer term trader is to move the market directionally.

Price and Value: The distinction between price and value defines a market-generated opportunity. There are two kinds of prices: 1) those that are accepted—defined as a price area where the market trades over time and 2) those that are rejected—defined as a price area where the market spends very little time. A rejected price is considered excessive in the market—defined as an unfair high or unfair low. Price and value are all but synonymous for short term traders as they ordinarily trade in the fair value area. For longer term traders, however, the concept that price equals value is often inaccurate. Price is *observable* and *objective* while value is *perceived* and *subjective,* depending upon the particular needs of longer term traders. For example, a price at the top of today's range, while excessive or unfair for today, is *cheap* to the longer term trader who believes that prices next week will be much higher (i.e., today's price is *below* next week's anticipated value).

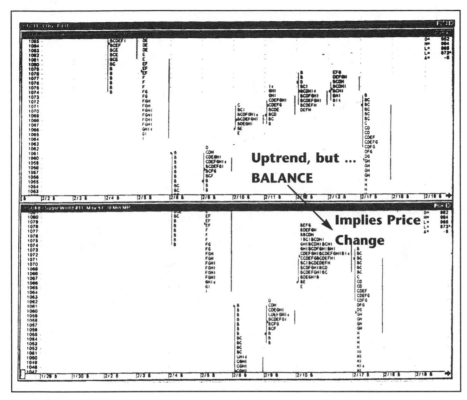

Figure B.5 *By combining daily consecutive profile graphics (upper) into a larger cumulative profile graphic (lower), an evolving picture of long term balance or imbalance emerges. (See explanation on page 489.)*

The longer term trader distinguishes between price and value by accepting or rejecting current prices away from his perception of fair value. Recall that rising prices advertise for sellers while falling prices advertise for buyers. When the longer term trader responds to an advertised price, this behavior is expected and is referred to as *responsive*. On the other hand, if the longer term trader did the opposite (i.e., buy after prices rose or sell after prices declined), then this unexpected activity is referred to as *initiating*. Classifying longer term activity as responsive or initiating relative to yesterday's or today's evolving value area provides anecdotal evidence of longer term trader confidence. The more confident the trader becomes, the more likely he is to take initiating action.

RANGE DEVELOPMENT AND PROFILE PATTERNS

Since market activity is not arbitrary, it's not surprising that over time recognizable price patterns reveal themselves. A skillful trader able to anticipate such pattern development in its early stage may be able to capitalize. Mr. Steidlmayer loosely identifies the following daily *range development* patterns:

1. A ***normal day*** occurs when the longer term trader is relatively inactive. The day's range is established in the *pioneer range* (defined as the first column of prices) during the session's first half-hour period of trade. The short term trader establishes the initial balance, the unfair high and low, and then prices rotate between these *parameters* for balance of the day (see Figure B.6: *Panel #1*—Orange Juice).

2. A ***normal variation day*** occurs when the longer term trader is more active and extends the range beyond the initial balance. In this instance, the short term traders initial balance parameters do not hold and there is some directional movement which extends the range and sets a new high or new low parameter. As a rule, the range extension beyond the initial balance can be anywhere from a couple of ticks to double the initial balance. This profile type is probably the most common (see Figure B.6: *Panel #2*—Dow Jones Industrial Average).

3. A ***trend day*** occurs when the longer term trader extends the range successively further. In this instance, the range is considerably more than double the initial balance with the longer term trader controlling direction as the market continues its search for a fair price. Here the market moves in one direction and closes at or near the directional extreme (see Figure B.6: *Panel #3*—Japanese Yen).

4. A ***neutral day*** occurs when the longer term trader extends the range after the initial balance in one direction, then reverses and extends the range in the opposite direction. Neutral days indicate trader uncertainty and occur when the market probes or tests for price trend continuation or change (see Figure B.6: *Panel #4*—Cattle).

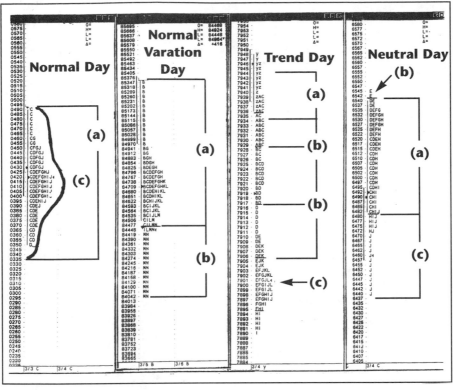

Panel #1
Orange Juice

NORMAL DAY

(a) Initial Balance established by short term traders in the first two periods: C & D

(b) Longer term traders are inactive

(c) Symmetrical or balanced price distribution

Panel #2
Dow Jones Industrials

NORMAL VARIATION DAY

(a) Initial Balance established by short term traders in periods: B & C

(b) Longer term traders extended the range down to almost double the initial balance

Panel #3
Japanese Yen

TREND DAY

(a) Initial Balance established by short term traders in periods: y & z

(b) Longer term traders extend range successively further.

(c) Market closes near the directional low

Panel #4
Cattle

NEUTRAL DAY

(a) Initial Balance established by short term traders in periods: C & D

(b) Longer term traders first extend up in E period, then

(c) Longer term traders extend down in H period

Figure B.6

TRACKING LONGER TERM MARKET ACTIVITY

With the exception of option sellers who profit when prices remain static, the profit strategy of most traders requires directional price movement. The trader wins when he gets the direction right and loses when he is incorrect. Because the longer term trader is responsible for determining the market's directional movement, we monitor this activity to help detect evidence of a price trend. After identifying and evaluating longer term trader activity, an educated conclusion regarding price direction can be reached. We begin the process by identifying the longer term trader's influence in today's session and then considering how that influence extends into the future.

- **Influence in day's range development:** The profile graphic helps identify longer term trader behavior during daily range development. By monitoring longer term activity throughout the range, particularly at the *extremes,* at *range extension*, and after *value area* completion, we can determine whether longer term buyers or sellers are more active and hence control market direction. Activity at the extremes provides the clearest indication of longer term trader influence, followed by range extension and then value area buying and selling.

  1. *Extremes* are formed when the longer term trader competes with the short term trader for opportunities at a particular price level (which later becomes either the session high or low). A minimum of two single prints is required to establish an extreme. The more eager the longer term trader is in this price competition, the more the single prints and the longer the single print extreme. Anything less than two prints suggests that the longer term trader is not very interested in competing at that price. A *local* top or bottom is formed when only one single print defines the top or bottom of the range. This condition implies that the market offered a price opportunity which no one really wanted (i.e., no evidence of competition [see Figure B.7: *Panel #1*—Intel Corporation].

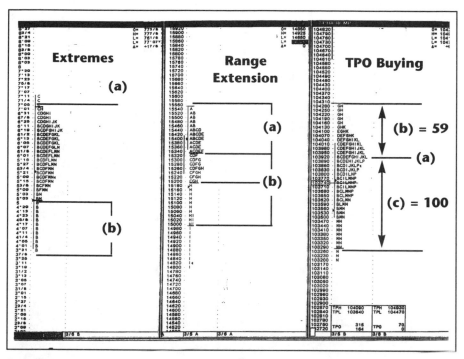

Panel #1	Panel #2	Panel #3
Intel Corporation	Coffee	S&P 500 Index

Extreme: formation requires at least two TPOs

(a) Selling Extreme from 77 11/32 to 77 5/32
(b) Buying Extreme from 73 31/32 to 75 reveals spirited competition between short term and longer term traders.

Range Extension: occurs when longer term traders upset the initial balance

(a) Initial Balance established in periods: A & B.
(b) Range extension down in periods C, H, and I

Value Area/TPO Buying or Selling: assessment of whether longer term buyers or sellers control the current session in the value area

(a) Modal or Fairest Price at 1039.20
(b) TPO selling count equals 59
(c) TPO buying count equals 100
(d) Imbalance to the buy side implies that prices need to go higher for market balance.

Figure B.7

2. ***Range Extension*** occurs when the longer term trader enters the market with enough volume to tip the initial balance and extend the range up or down. Range extension up indicates longer term buying while range extension *down* indicates longer term selling. However, there are occasions when both the longer term buyer and seller are active at a range extreme, but not at the same price and time (recall that longer term buyers and sellers generally do not trade with each other). For example, if an extreme is formed after a range extension up, the market moves up first to shut off buying and then moves down to shut off selling. This is an example of both longer term buyers and sellers trading in the same price area but at different times. Both kinds of activity at the extremes are identified to evaluate the impact of longer term buying and selling (see Figure B.7: *Panel #2—* Coffee).

3. The ***Value Area*** is determined each trading session by price rotations around the modal price (i.e., the price with the highest TPO count or the *fairest* price). The value area is computed by counting 70% of all TPOs surrounding the fairest price. In other words, the value area is an estimate of fair value which is approximated by one standard deviation of the session's trading volume (recall the student example earlier). When a longer term trader makes a trade in the value area, he is buying low or selling high in relation to a longer term view, not in relation to today's value. This behavior creates an imbalance in today's value area. Longer term trader activity is measured by counting TPOs. The following procedure can be used to determine which side contains the longer term imbalance, 1) a line is drawn through the fairest price, and 2) TPOs are counted on either side of the fairest price until a single print is encountered. The imbalance is assigned to the side with the smaller number of TPOs because the longer term trader activity represents the smaller percentage of total trade in the value area. For example, if the TPO count was 22 above and 12

below the fairest price, that would indicate net TPO selling with a mild bias toward lower prices (see Figure B.7:
Panel #3—S&P 500 Index). Note that TPO buying and
selling in the value area *is not applicable on trend days,* as
the market is still in search of a fair value area.

After identifying and evaluating longer term trader activity correctly in today's profile graphic, the user can readily determine whether longer term buyers or sellers were in control of the
current trading session.

- **Influence beyond today:** The profile graphic also helps
  identify longer term trader behavior beyond today's range
  development. A key goal of the trader is to determine
  whether the current market price trend will continue or is
  likely to change. A change in market direction is a *reversal* of
  the current price trend. The standard technical approach to
  trend assessment, without Market Profile, is to draw an
  appropriate trendline and monitor subsequent price action
  against it. Unless the trendline is violated, the current price
  trend is expected to continue. Trendline analysis is the most
  important of basic technical tools, particularly given its universal usage and applicability to different time intervals (i.e.,
  hourly, daily, weekly, monthly, etc.).

  Market Profile, on the other hand, offers an alternative
  approach to traditional trend analysis by evaluating market
  activity over different time periods. In its simplest form, an
  evaluation of the profile graphic on consecutive days can
  help define the start or continuation of the short term price
  trend. For example, if today's value area is higher than yesterday's value area, then the current market price trend is
  up. Moreover, if tomorrow's value area is higher than
  today's, then the current market uptrend has continued. By
  monitoring market activity in this fashion, the trader is
  able to readily identify trend continuation or change.
  Similarly by combining daily consecutive profile graphics
  into a larger cumulative profile graphic, an evolving picture
  of longer term balance or imbalance emerges. The profile
  graphic in Figure B.5 (*Sugar*) on page 483 illustrate this

point. A cursory review of the individual sessions (2/10—2/13) in the upper panel suggest an uptrending market without a hint of reversal. When these four (4) consecutive sessions are combined (lower panel), however, a cumulative balanced picture springs forth. Once balanced, a market moves to a state of imbalance which, more often than not, begins after a final test at the fairest price.

CONCLUSION

The Market Profile method can be used to analyze any price data series for which continuous transaction activity is available. This includes listed and unlisted equities, U.S. government notes and bonds (prices or yields), commodity futures and options, where applicable. The *profile graphic* presents the movement of prices, per unit of time, in two dimensions—vertically (i.e., directionally) and horizontally (i.e., frequency of occurrence). When price action is viewed in this way, a picture of *price discovery* unfolds which is unavailable in the traditional one dimensional (vertical) bar chart.

The profile graphic offers unique advantages over the standard bar chart:

- The *symmetry* attribute of the profile graphic allows the trader to assess the market's state of *balance* (or *imbalance*) in any timeframe. When a market is symmetric, a condition of balance or equilibrium exists between buyers and sellers. A market imbalance implies price trend continuation, as the market works toward a new equilibrium. Market balance, however, is fleeting and implies market *change* or a directional move (either up or down) is likely to occur, a signal for traders to consider employing trend following methodologies.

- Every trend change occurs at a single moment in time, not conveniently at the end of the hour, day, week or month. The profile graphic can be used to more accurately identify that specific time where control changed hands between buyers and sellers. By pinning down such control shifts, the profile graphic allows the trader to identify key support and resistance levels.

In short, the profile graphic provides a substantial amount of price information per unit of time, allowing the trader to identify patterns and dynamics which would not be readily apparent using other methods.

Appendix C: The Essentials of Building a Trading System*

Trading system development is part art, part science, and part common sense. Our goal is not to develop a system that achieves the highest returns using historical data, but to formulate a sound concept that has performed reasonably well in the past and can be expected to continue to perform reasonably well in the future.

Ideally, we would prefer an approach that is 100% mechanical, increasing the odds that past performance can be replicated in the future. Mechanical means objective: if 10 people follow the same rules and achieve the same results, those rules are said to be objective. It does not matter whether a mechanical system is written on paper or entered into a computer.

*This appendix was prepared by Fred G. Schutzman.

Here, however, we'll assume that we are using a computer and will use the terms "mechanical" and "computerized" interchangeably. This does not imply that a computer is mandatory for trading system development, although it certainly helps.

The mechanical approach offers us three main benefits:

- **We can back test ideas before trading them.** A computer allows us to test ideas on historical data rather than on hard earned cash. By helping us see how a system would have performed in the past, it allows us to make better decisions when it really counts—in the present.

- **We can be more objective and less emotional.** Most people have trouble applying their objective analysis to actual trading situations. Analysis (where we have no money at risk) is easy, trading (where we have money at risk) is stressful. Therefore, why not let the computer pull the trigger for us? It is free of human emotion and will do exactly what we had instructed it to do at the time when we developed our system.

- **We can do more work, increasing our opportunities.** A mechanical approach takes less time to apply than a subjective one, which allows us to cover more markets, trade more systems, and analyze more time frames each day. This is especially true for those of us who use a computer, since it can work faster and longer than we can, without losing its concentration.

5 STEP PLAN

1. Start with a concept
2. Turn it into a set of objective rules
3. Visually check it out on the charts
4. Formally test it with a computer
5. Evaluate the results

STEP 1: START WITH A CONCEPT (AN IDEA)

Develop your own concepts of how markets work. You can begin by looking at as many charts as you can, trying to identify moving average crossovers, oscillator configurations, price patterns or other pieces of objective evidence which precede major market moves. Also attempt to recognize clues that provide advance warning on moves that are likely to fail. I studied chart after chart after chart in the hope of finding such answers. This "visual" approach has worked for me, and I highly recommend it.

In addition to studying price charts and reading books such as this one, I suggest you read about trading systems and study what others have done. Although no one is going to reveal the "Holy Grail" to you, there is a great deal of useful information out there. Most importantly, think for yourself. I have found that the most profitable ideas are rarely original, but frequently our own.

Most of the successful trading systems are trend following. Counter trend systems should not be overlooked, however, because they bring a degree of negative correlation to the table. This means that when one system is making money, the other is losing money, resulting in a smoother equity curve for the two systems combined, than for either one alone.

Principles of Good Concept Design

Good concepts usually make good sense. If a concept seems to work, but makes little sense, you may be sliding into the realm of coincidence, and the odds of this concept continuing to work in the future diminishes considerably. Your concepts must fit your personality in order to give you the discipline to follow them even when they are losing money (i.e. during periods of drawdown). Your concepts should be straightforward and objective, and if trend following, should trade with the major trend, let profits run and cut losses short. Most importantly, your concepts must make money in the long run (i.e. they must have a positive expectation).

Designing entries is hard, but designing exits is harder and more important. Entry logic is fairly straightforward, but exits have to take various contingencies into account, such as how fast to cut losses or what to do with accumulated profits. I prefer systems that do not reverse automatically—I like to exit a trade first, before putting on another trade in the opposite direction. Work hard to improve your exits, and your returns will improve relative to your risk.

Another suggestion—try to optimize as little as possible. Optimization using historical data often leads one to expect unrealistic returns that cannot be replicated in real trading. Try to use few parameters and apply the same technique across a number of different markets. This will improve your chances of long run success, by reducing the pitfalls of over optimization.

The three main categories of trading systems are:

- **Trend following.** These systems trade in the direction of the major trend, buying after the bottom and selling after the top. Moving averages and Donchian's weekly rule are popular methodologies among money managers.

- **Counter trend**

  - Support/Resistance. Buy a decline into support; sell a rally into resistance.

  - Retracements. Here we buy pullbacks in a bull market and sell rallies in a bear market. For example, buy a 50% pullback of the last advance, but only if the major trend remains up. The danger of such systems is that you never know how far a retracement will go and it becomes difficult to implement an acceptable exit technique.

  - Oscillators. The idea is to buy when the oscillator is oversold and to sell when it is overbought. If divergence between the price series and the oscillator is also present, a much stronger signal is given. However, it is usually best to wait for some sign of a price reversal before buying or selling.

- **Pattern recognition** (visual and statistical). Examples include the highly reliable head and shoulders formation (visual), and seasonal price patterns (statistical).

STEP 2: TURN YOUR IDEA INTO A SET OF OBJECTIVE RULES

This is the most difficult step in our 5 step plan, much more difficult than many of us would at first expect! To complete this step successfully, we must express our idea in such objective terms that 100 people following our rules will all arrive at exactly the same conclusions.

Determine what our system is supposed to do and how it will do it. It is with this step that we produce the details needed to accomplish the programming task. We need to take the overall problem and break it down into more and more detail until we finalize all the details.

STEP 3: VISUALLY CHECK IT OUT ON THE CHARTS

Following the explicit rules we just determined in Step 2, let us visually check the trading signals that are produced on a price chart. This is an informal process, meant to achieve two results: first, we want to see whether our idea has been stated properly; and second, before writing complicated computer code, we want some proof that the idea is a potentially profitable one.

STEP 4: FORMALLY TEST IT WITH A COMPUTER

Now its time to convert our logic into computer code. For my own work, I use a program called TradeStation®, Omega Research, Inc. in Miami, FL. TradeStation is the most comprehensive technical analysis software package available for formulating and testing trading systems. It brings together everything from the visualization of your idea, to assistance in trading your system in real time.

Writing code in any computer language is no easy task and TradeStation's EasyLanguage™ is no exception. The job with EasyLanguage, however, is greatly simplified because of the program's user friendly editor and the inclusion of many built in functions and plenty of sample code. See Figure C.1.

Once our program has been written, we then move into the testing phase. To begin with, we must choose one or more data series to test. For stock traders this is an easy task. Futures traders, however, are faced with contracts that expire after a relatively short period of time. I like to do my initial testing using a continuous (spread adjusted) price series popularized by Jack Schwager. (*Schwager on Futures: Technical Analysis*, Wiley, 1996.) If those results look promising, I then move on to actual contracts.

Next, we must decide how much data to use when building our system. I use the entire data series, without saving any for out-of-sample testing (building your system on part of the data and then testing it on the remaining "unseen" data). Many experts would disagree with this approach, but I believe it to be the best with my methodology that relies on good solid concepts, virtually no optimization, and a testing procedure that covers a wide range of parameter sets and markets. I start with a methodology that I believe to be sound and then test it to either prove or disprove my theory. I have found that most individuals do the reverse, they test a data series to arrive at a trading system.

I do not account for transaction costs (slippage and commissions) when testing systems, but instead factor them in at the end. I believe that this keeps the evaluation process more pure and allows my results to remain useful should certain assumptions change in the future.

I require my systems to work across:

- **Different sets of parameters.** If I were considering using a 5/20 moving average crossover system, then I would expect 6/18, 6/23, 4/21, and 5/19 to also perform reasonably well. If not, I immediately become skeptical of the 5/20 results.

```
{*********************************************************************************

//fileName: JJMBook.Four%Model
//Written by Fred G. Schutzman, CMT
//Logic by Ned Davis
  //see Zweig book: Martin Zweig's Winning with New IRAs, pages 117–128
//Model was designed to be applied to a weekly chart of the Value Line Composite Index
(VLCI)
//Program uses the weekly (usually Friday) close of the VLCI to initiate trades
  //buy if the weekly close of the VLCI rises 4% or more from its lowest close (since the last
sell signal)
  //sell if the weekly close of the VLCI falls 4% or more from its highest close (since the last
buy signal)
//Date last changed: February 8, 1998

********System Properties********
Properties tab:
Pyramid Settings = Do not allow multiple entries in same direction
Entry Settings = default values
Max number of bars system will reference = 1

*********************************************************************************}

Inputs:              perOffLo(4.00),      { percent off lowest close }
                     perOffHi(4.00);      { percent off highest close }
Variables:           LC(0),               { lowest close}
                     HC(0),               { highest close }
                     trend(0);            { 0 = no trades yet, +1 = up, –1 down }
{ initialize variables }
If currentBar = 1 then begin
  LC = close;
  HC = close;
  trend = 0;
end;

{ update trend variable and place trading orders }
if trend = 0 then begin
  if ((close-LC) / LC) > = (perOffLo / 100) then trend = +1;
  if ((HC-close) / HC) > = (perOffHi / 100) then trend = –1;
end
else if trend = +1 and ((HC-close) / HC) > = (perOffHi / 100) then begin
  sell on close;
  trend = –1;
  LC = close;
end
else if trend = –1 and ((close-LC) / LC) > = (perOffLo / 100) then begin
  buy on close;
  trend = +1;
  HC = close;
end;

{ update LC & HC variables }
If close < LC then LC = close;
If close > HC then HC = close;

{ End of Code }
```

Figure C.1 *(EasyLanguage Code): This EasyLanguage code was written using TradeStation's Power Editor™. It has the look—and power—of a full blown programming language. See Figures C.2 and C.3 for the results on this trend following system described by Martin Zweig.*

- **Different periods of time** (e.g. 1990–95 and 1981–86). A system that tests well in the Japanese Yen over a recent five year period should also test reasonably well over any other five year interval. This is another area where I appear to hold the minority point of view.

- **Many different markets.** A system that has worked well in crude oil should also work well in heating oil and unleaded gasoline over the same period of time. If not, I will look for an explanation and will usually discard the system. I go even further than this, however, and test that same system across my entire database of markets, expecting it to perform well in the majority of them.

Once our testing is complete, let us visually inspect the computer generated trading signals on a price chart to ensure that the system does what we intended it to do. TradeStation facilitates this process by placing buy and sell arrows directly on the chart for us! If the system does not do what it is supposed to do, we need to make the necessary corrections to the code and test it again. Keep in mind that very few ideas will test out profitably, usually less than 5%. And, for one reason or another, most of these "successful" ideas will not even be tradable.

STEP 5: EVALUATE RESULTS

Let us try to understand the concept behind our trading system. Does it make sense or is it just a coincidence? Analyze the equity curve. Can we live through the drawdowns? Evaluate the system on a trade-by-trade basis. What happens if a signal is a bad one? How quickly does the system exit from losers? How long does it stay with the winners? Make sure we are completely comfortable with the test results, otherwise we will not be able to trade this system in real time.

Three key TradeStation statistics to analyze are:

- **Profit factor.** Equals *Gross profit* on winning trades/*Gross loss* on losing trades. This statistic tells us how many dollars our system made for every $1 it lost, and is a measure of risk. Long term traders should aim for profit factors of 2.00 or higher. Short term traders can accept slightly lower numbers.

- **Avg trade (win & loss).** This is our system's mathematical expectation. It should at least be high enough to cover transaction costs (slippage and commissions); otherwise we will be losing money.

- **Max intraday drawdown.** This is the biggest drop, in dollar terms, from an equity peak to an equity trough. I prefer to do this calculation on a percentage basis. I also differentiate between drawdowns from a standing start (where I am losing money from my own pocket) versus drawdowns from an equity peak (where I am giving back profits taken from the markets). I am usually more lenient with the latter.

MONEY MANAGEMENT

Money management, while outside the scope of this appendix, is an extremely important topic. It is the key to profitable trading, every bit as important as a good trading system.

Money management techniques should be well thought out. Accept the fact that losses are part of the game. Control your downside and profits will take care of themselves.

In this area, practice diversification as much as possible. Diversification will enable you to increase your returns while holding your risk constant, or decrease your risk while holding your returns constant. Diversify among markets, systems, parameters, and time frames.

CONCLUSION

We have discussed the basic philosophy of trading systems and why objective is better than subjective. We covered the three main benefits of a computerized approach and designed a 5 step plan for building a trading system. And last, but not least, we touched upon the importance of money management and diversification.

Trading systems can improve your performance and help to make you a successful trader. The reasons for that are clear:

- they force you to do your homework *before* making a trade
- they provide a disciplined framework, making it easier for you to follow the rules
- they enable you to increase your level of diversification

With lots of hard work and dedication, anyone can build a successful trading system. It is not easy, but it certainly is within reach. As with most things in life, what you get out of this effort will be directly related to what you put into it. (See Figures C.2 and C.3.)

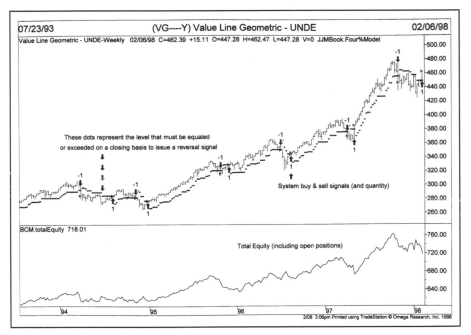

Figure C.2   *(Price Chart): This trading system was designed to be applied to a weekly chart of the Value Line Composite Index (VLCI), but also tested well on a daily chart of the VLCI and on both weekly and daily charts in other markets, votes of confidence in the underlying concept. This is the system described in Figure C.1.*

```
┌──────────────────────────────────────────────────────────────┐
│                                                          ┌┐┌ ┌│
│  [  ][  ][  ][Pr][  ][№][  ][?][  ][  ][  ][  ][  ][  ]  │     │
│ UMBook.Four%Model  Value Line Geometric - UNDE-Weekly  06/30/61 - 02/06/98 │
│                                                                │
│                    Performance Summary:  All Trades            │
│                                                                │
│ Total net profit        $   718.01   Open position P/L    $    0.00 │
│ Gross profit            $  1118.15   Gross loss           $ -400.14 │
│                                                                │
│ Total # of trades           137      Percent profitable        49% │
│ Number winning trades        67      Number losing trades       70 │
│                                                                │
│ Largest winning trade   $    78.06   Largest losing trade  $  -15.95 │
│ Average winning trade   $    16.69   Average losing trade  $   -5.72 │
│ Ratio avg win/avg loss       2.92    Avg trade(win & loss) $    5.24 │
│                                                                │
│ Max consec. winners          7       Max consec. losers         5 │
│ Avg # bars in winners       21       Avg # bars in losers       7 │
│                                                                │
│ Max intraday drawdown   $   -45.01                             │
│ Profit factor               2.79     Max # contracts held       1 │
│ Account size required   $    45.01   Return on account      1595% │
│                                                                │
└──────────────────────────────────────────────────────────────┘
                        Created with TradeStation by Omega Research ® 1996
```

Figure C.3 *(Performance Summary): Here is a 36 year Performance Summary of the system shown in Figures C.1 and C.2. Performance over the last 12 years has been consistent with the overall results. The Profit factor, Avg trade (win and loss) and Max intraday drawdown are all excellent.*

Appendix D: Continuous Futures Contracts*

With a clean database of "raw" commodity data, there are numerous types of contracts that can be gleaned from the raw data, such as: Nearest Contracts, Next Contracts, Gann Contracts, and Continuous Contracts. Following, are ideas for constructing these futures contracts derivatives. The symbols used are for illustration purposes only. These continuous contracts can be created through the Dial Data Service (56 Pine Street, New York, NY 10005, [212] 422-1600.)

*This appendix was prepared by Greg Morris.

NEAREST CONTRACT

A nearest contract is primarily used by traders who just want a large file of continuous data made up of actual trading prices. They are content with the data going to expiration and then rolling over automatically.

It is quite probable that no one trades the nearest contract within 15 to 30 days of expiration. This is because the liquidity dries up very fast in the latter days of a contract. The number of days before expiration that an individual rolls over to the next contract is a function of the commodity that is being traded (the number of months till the next contract), and the individual's trading style. It is quite conceivable that the same individual will rollover at different times for different commodities.

When to rollover to the next contract will more than likely be based upon the current contract's volume. When it begins to erode, that is the time to roll forward.

Therefore, one should have available a choice as to when to rollover his Nearest Contract. Remember, Nearest Contracts are made up of actual data. Here are some examples: Portfolio Manager A is content to rollover at expiration; so all he wants is the "standard" Nearest Contract with symbol TRNE00 (Treasury Bonds). Manager A is probably managing money and needs equity calculations which he can derive from the data. Trader B feels that trading in the month of expiration is not liquid enough for him; so he wants his Nearest Contract to roll over 15 days prior to expiration—the symbol could be TRNE15. Analyst C would like to evaluate different roll-over dates, so he might like to download multiple Nearest Contracts, such as: TRNE00, TRNE05, TRNE12, and TRNE21 (which roll-over 5, 12, and 21 days before expiration).

Keep in mind that all of these contracts are Nearest Contracts and contain actual contract data. The only difference is which actual contract the data comes from.

NEXT CONTRACT

A Next Contract is a unique offspring of the Nearest Contract. It is exactly the same as the Nearest Contract except that it is *always* the contract that follows the Nearest Contract. In other words, if the Nearest Contract is using December data for T-Bonds (TR), then the Next Contract is using data from the March T-Bond contract. When the December contract expires, the Nearest rolls to the March and the Next rolls to the June contract. This is defined as the Next-1 contract.

From this concept, another Next Contract is available, called a Next-2. Here, the data is always coming from the contract that is two contracts away from the Nearest Contract. Keeping with the above example, if the Nearest is using data from the December contract, the Next-2 Contract is using data from the June contract. When the December contract expires, the Nearest begins to use data from the March contract and the Next-2 Contract uses data from the September contract and so on.

Ticker symbols for the Next contracts are: TRNXT1 and TRNXT2. Of course, the actual futures ticker will be used instead of the TR used in this example.

GANN CONTRACT

Gann Contracts refer to the use of a specific contract month and rolling over only to the same contract in the next year. For example, July Wheat would be used until the July contract expires, then the Gann Contract would start using data from the July Wheat contract of the next year.

Examples of ticker symbols for Gann Contracts are: W07GN, GC04GN, JY12GN, etc. (representing July Wheat, April gold, December Japanese yen).

CONTINUOUS CONTRACTS

Continuous Contracts were developed to help analysts overcome the problem of liquidity dry up and premium (or discount) gaps in futures data. This becomes a problem whenever an analyst is testing a trading model or system over many years of data. It allows for a continuous stream of data with compensation being made for rollover jumps in price trends.

CONSTANT FORWARD
CONTINUOUS CONTRACTS

A Constant Forward Continuous Contract looks a constant length
of time into the future. It uses more than one contract to do this.
A common method is to use the nearest two contracts and do a
linear extrapolation of the data. (See Figure D.1.)

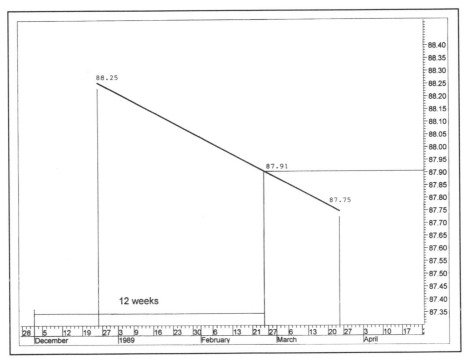

Figure D.1   *A visual representation of a continuous contract.*

One possibility is to give the futures trader (as with the
Nearest Contracts) the ability to construct his own Constant
Forward Continuous Contract. Three things are needed to do this:
The commodity symbol, the number of contracts he wants used
in the calculation, and the number of weeks into the futures he
wants to look. For instance, if he wanted T-Bonds, using 3 of the

nearest contracts, and looking 14 weeks into the future, the symbol could be: TRCF314. TR is the symbol, CF is for Continuous (Forward Looking), 3 is the number of contracts used, and 14 is the number of weeks the price is projected.

The mechanics of this are fairly simple. First, a fixed rollover date would need to be set for each commodity. A good one to start with could be 10 days prior to expiration. What is important is that there is a rollover sometime prior to actual expiration. Second, the number of contracts used will never be less than 2 and probably never greater than 4. The number of weeks used should probably always be greater that 3 and could go up to 40 in some cases.

Example: This is the method used by Commodity Systems, Inc. (See *Perpetual Contract* in Chapter 8.)

T-Bonds will be used again, because they have a uniform expiration cycle of every 3 months. Let's say a trader wants a Continuous Contract of T-Bonds using the 2 nearest months and looking 12 weeks into the future (symbol = TRCF212). Today's date is December 1. A graphical portrayal makes this easier to understand (see Figure D.1). The vertical axis is price and the horizontal axis is time. Today's date is marked on the horizontal axis and the expiration dates of the two nearest contracts (December and March), are also marked. He wants to look 12 weeks into the future so a mark is made 12 weeks from today which is about February 25. The close price of the December contract was 88.25 and the close of the March contract was 87.75 These points are then put above their expiration dates at the corresponding prices. Then a linear extrapolation is made by merely drawing a line between the two points. The slope of this line will vary up and down depending upon the outlook for long term interest rates (in this T-Bond example). In this particular example the outlook is for higher rates because the March futures price is lower than the December price.

To find the value of the TRCF212 close price for today, find the point on the horizontal axis that is 12 weeks from today (Feb 25th) and go up to the line drawn on the chart. Then from the line go to the right and that is the price of the close for this Constant Forward Continuous Contract (about 87.91). You can also visually see from the chart that the March contract is carrying more weight than the December contract because the point of interception is closer to March. This method can be done on the Open, High, Low, and Close in the exact manner. Of course, a computer does it mathematically; this is just a visual explanation of how a Perpetual Contract is constructed.

Glossary

Advance-decline line: One of the most widely used indicators to measure the breadth of a stock market advance or decline. Each day (or week) the number of advancing issues is compared to the number of declining issues. If advances outnumber declines, the net total is added to the previous cumulative total. If declines outnumber advances, the net difference is subtracted from the previous cumulative total. The advance-decline line is usually compared to a popular stock average, such as the Dow Jones Industrial Average. They should trend in the same direction. When the advance-decline line begins to diverge from the stock average, an early indication is given of a possible trend reversal.

Arms index: Developed by Richard Arms, this contrary indicator is a ratio of the average volume of declining stocks divided by the average volume of advancing stocks. A reading below 1.0

indicates more volume in rising stocks. A reading above 1.0 reflects more volume in declining issues. A 10 day average of the Arms index over 1.20 is oversold, while a 10 day average below .70 is overbought.

Ascending triangle: A sideways price pattern between two converging trendlines, in which the lower line is rising while the upper line is flat. This is generally a bullish pattern. (*See* Triangles.)

Bar chart: On a daily bar chart, each bar represents one day's activity. The vertical bar is drawn from the day's highest price to the day's lowest price (the range). A tic to the left of the bar marks the opening price, while a tic to the right of the bar marks the closing price. Bar charts can be constructed for any time period, including monthly, weekly, hourly, and minute periods.

Bollinger bands: Developed by John Bollinger, this indicator plots trading bands two standard deviations above and below a 20 period moving average. Prices will often meet resistance at the upper band and support at the lower band.

Breakaway gap: A price gap that forms on the completion of an important price pattern. A breakaway gap usually signals the beginning of an important price move. (*See* Gaps.)

Channel line: Straight lines drawn parallel to the basic trendline. In an uptrend, the channel line slants up to the right and is drawn above rally peaks; in a downtrend, the channel line is drawn below price troughs and slants down to the right. Prices will often meet resistance at rising channel lines and support at falling channel lines.

Confirmation: Having as many market factors as possible agreeing with one another. For example, if prices and volume are rising together, volume is confirming the price action. The opposite of confirmation is divergence.

Continuation patterns: Price formations that imply a pause or consolidation in the prevailing trend. The most common types are triangles, flags, and pennants.

Descending triangle: A sideways price pattern between two converging trendlines, in which the upper line is declining while the lower line is flat. This is generally a bearish pattern. (*See* Triangles.)

Divergence: A situation where two indicators are not confirming each other. For example, in oscillator analysis, prices trend higher while an oscillator starts to drop. Divergence usually warns of a trend reversal. (*See* Confirmation.)

Double top: This price pattern displays two prominent peaks. The reversal is complete when the middle trough is broken. The double bottom is a mirror image of the top.

Down trendline: A straight line drawn down and to the right above successive rally peaks. A violation of the down trendline usually signals a reversal of the downtrend. (*See* Trendlines.)

Dow Theory: One of the oldest and most highly regarded technical theories. A Dow Theory buy signal is given when the Dow Industrial and Dow Transportation Averages close above a prior rally peak. A sell signal is given when both averages close below a prior reaction low.

Elliott wave analysis: An approach to market analysis that is based on repetitive wave patterns and the Fibonacci number sequence. An ideal Elliott wave pattern shows a five wave advance followed by a 3-wave decline. (*See* Fibonacci numbers).

Envelopes: Lines placed at fixed percentages above and below a moving average line. Envelopes help determine when a market has traveled too far from its moving average and is overextended.

Exhaustion gap: A price gap that occurs at the end of an important trend, and signals that the trend is ending. (*See* Gaps.)

Exponential smoothing: A moving average that uses all data points, but gives greater weight to more recent price data. (*See* Moving average.)

Fibonacci numbers: The Fibonacci number sequence (1, 2, 3, 5, 8, 13, 21, 34, 55, 89, 144…) is constructed by adding the first two numbers to arrive at the third. The ratio of any number to the next larger number is 62 percent, which is a popular Fibonacci retracement number. The inverse of 62 percent, which is 38 percent, is also used as a Fibonacci retracement number. The ratio of any number to the next smaller number is 1.62 percent, which is used to arrive at Fibonacci price targets. (*See* Elliott wave analysis).

Flag: A continuation price pattern, generally lasting less than three weeks, which resembles a parallelogram that slopes against the prevailing trend. The flag represents a minor pause in a dynamic price trend. (*See* Pennant.)

Fundamental analysis: The opposite of technical analysis. Fundamental analysis relies on economic supply and demand information, as opposed to market activity.

Gaps: Gaps are spaces left on the bar chart where no trading has taken place. An up gap is formed when the lowest price on a trading day is higher than the highest high of the previous day. A down gap is formed when the highest price on a day is lower than the lowest price of the prior day. An up gap is usually a sign of market strength, while a down gap is a sign of market weakness. Three types of gaps are breakaway, runaway (also called measuring), and exhaustion gaps.

Head and shoulders: The best known of the reversal patterns. At a market top, three prominent peaks are formed with the middle peak (or head) slightly higher than the two other peaks (shoulders). When the trendline (neckline) connecting the two intervening troughs is broken, the pattern is complete. A bottom pattern is a mirror image of a top and is called an inverse head and shoulders.

Intermarket analysis: An additional aspect of market analysis that takes into consideration the price action of related market sectors. The four sectors are currencies, commodities, bonds, and stocks. International markets are also included. This approach is based on the premise that all markets are interrelated and impact on one another.

Island reversal: A combination of an exhaustion gap in one direction and a breakaway gap in the other direction within a few days. Toward the end of an uptrend, for example, prices gap upward and then downward within a few days. The result is usually two or three trading days standing alone with gaps on either side. The island reversal usually signals a trend reversal. (*See* Gaps.)

Key reversal day: In an uptrend, this one day pattern occurs when prices open in new highs, and then close below the previous day's closing price. In a downtrend, prices open lower and then close higher. The wider the price range on the key reversal day and the heavier the volume, the greater the odds that a reversal is taking place. (*See* Weekly Reversal.)

Line charts: Price charts that connect the closing prices of a given market over a span of time. The result is a curving line on the chart. This type of chart is most useful with overlay or comparison charts that are commonly employed in intermarket analysis. It is also used for visual trend analysis of open end mutual funds.

MACD: Developed by Gerald Appel, the moving average convergence divergence system shows two lines. The first (MACD) line is the difference between two exponential moving averages (usually 12 and 26 periods) of closing prices. The second (signal) line is usually a 9 period EMA of the first (MACD) line. Signals are given when the two lines cross.

MACD histogram: A variation of the MACD system that plots the difference between the signal and MACD lines. Changes in the spread between the two lines can be spotted faster, leading to earlier trading signals.

McClellan oscillator: Developed by Sherman McClellan, this oscillator is the difference between the l9 day (10% trend) and the 39 day (5% trend) exponentially smoothed averages of the daily net advance decline figures. Crossings above the zero line are positive and below zero are negative. Readings above +100 are overbought while readings below –100 are oversold.

McClellan summation index: A cumulative sum of all daily McClellan oscillator readings that provides longer range analysis of market breadth. Used in the same way as an advance–decline line.

Momentum: A technique used to construct an overbought–oversold oscillator. Momentum measures price differences over a selected span of time. To construct a 10 day momentum line, the closing price 10 days earlier is subtracted from the latest price. The resulting positive or negative value is plotted above or below a zero line. (*See* Oscillators.)

Moving average: A trend following indicator that works best in a trending environment. Moving averages smooth out price action but operate with a time lag. A simple 10 day moving average of a stock, for example, adds up the last 10 days' closing prices and divides the total by 10. That procedure is repeated each day. Any number of moving averages can be employed, with different time spans, to generate buy and sell signals. When only one average is employed, a buy signal is given when the price closes above the average. When two averages are employed, a buy signal is given when the shorter average crosses above the longer average. There are three types: simple, weighted, and exponentially smoothed averages.

On balance volume: Developed by Joseph Granville, OBV is a running cumulative total of upside and downside volume. Volume is added on up days and subtracted on down days. The OBV line is plotted with the price line to see if the two lines are confirming each other. (*See* Volume.)

Open interest: The number of options or futures contracts that are still unliquidated at the end of a trading day. A rise or fall in open interest shows that money is flowing into or out of a futures contract or option, respectively. In futures markets, rising open interest is considered good for the current trend. Open interest also measures liquidity.

Oscillators: Indicators that determine when a market is in an overbought or oversold condition. When the oscillator reaches an upper extreme, the market is overbought. When the oscillator line reaches a lower extreme, the market is oversold. (*See* Momentum, Rate of change, Relative strength index, and Stochastics.)

Overbought: A term usually used in reference to an oscillator. When an oscillator reaches an upper extreme, it is believed that a market has risen too far and is vulnerable to a selloff.

Oversold: A term usually used in reference to an oscillator. When an oscillator reaches a lower extreme, it is believed that a market has dropped too far and is due for a bounce.

Pennant: This continuation price pattern is similar to the flag, except that it is more horizontal and resembles a small symmetrical triangle. Like the flag, the pennant usually lasts from one to three weeks and is typically followed by a resumption of the prior trend.

Percent investment advisors bullish: This measure of stock market bullish sentiment is published weekly by Investor's Intelligence of New Rochelle, New York. When only 35% of professionals are bullish, the market is considered oversold. A reading of 55% is considered to be overbought.

Price patterns: Patterns that appear on price charts and that have predictive value. Patterns are divided into reversal and continuation patterns.

Rate of change: A technique used to construct an overbought–oversold oscillator. Rate of change employs a price ratio over a selected span of time. To construct a 10 day rate of change oscillator, the last closing price is divided by the closing price 10 days earlier. The resulting value is plotted above or below a value of 100.

Ratio analysis: The use of a ratio to compare the relative strength between two entities. An individual stock or industry group divided by the S&P 500 index can determine whether that stock or industry group is outperforming or underperforming the stock market as a whole. Ratio analysis can be used to compare any two entities. A rising ratio indicates that the numerator in the ratio is outperforming the denominator. Trend analysis can be applied to the ratio line itself to determine important turning points.

Relative strength index (RSI): A popular oscillator developed by Welles Wilder, Jr. and described in his self published 1978 book, *New Concepts in Technical Trading Systems*. RSI is plotted on a vertical scale from 0 to 100. Values above 70 are considered to be overbought and values below 30, oversold. When prices are over 70 or below 30 and diverge from price action, a warning is given of a possible trend reversal. RSI usually employs 9 or 14 time periods.

Resistance: The opposite of support. Resistance is marked by a previous price peak and provides enough of a barrier above the market to halt a price advance. (*See* Support.)

Retracements: Prices normally retrace the prior trend by a percentage amount before resuming the original trend. The best known example is the 50% retracement. Minimum and maximum retracements are normally one third and two thirds, respectively. Elliott wave analysis uses Fibonacci retracements of 38% and 62%.

Reversal patterns: Price patterns on a price chart that usually indicate that a trend reversal is taking place. The best known of the reversal patterns are the head and shoulders and double and triple tops and bottoms.

Runaway gap: A price gap that usually occurs around the midpoint of an important market trend. For that reason, it is also called a measuring gap. (*See* Gaps.)

Sentiment indicators: Psychological indicators that attempt to measure the degree of bullishness or bearishness in a market. These are contrary indicators and are used in much the same fashion as overbought or oversold oscillators. Their greatest value is when they reach upper or lower extremes.

Simple average: A moving average that gives equal weight to each day's price data. (*See* Exponential smoothing and Weighted average.)

Stochastics: An overbought–oversold oscillator popularized by George Lane. A time period of 14 is usually employed in its construction. Stochastics uses two lines—%K and its 3 period moving average, %D. These two lines fluctuate in a vertical range between 0 and 100. Readings above 80 are overbought, while readings below 20 are oversold. When the faster %K line crosses above the slower %D line and the lines are below 20, a buy signal is given. When the %K crosses below the %D line and the lines are over 80, a sell signal is given.

Support: A price, or price zone, beneath the current market price, where buying power is sufficient to halt a price decline. A previous reaction low usually forms a support level.

Symmetrical triangle: A sideways price pattern between two converging trendlines in which the upper trendline is declining and lower trendline is rising. This pattern represents an even balance between buyers and sellers, although the prior trend is usually resumed. The breakout through either trendline signals the direction of the price trend. (*See* Ascending and Descending triangles.)

Technical analysis: The study of market action, usually with price charts, which includes volume and open interest patterns. Also called chart analysis, market analysis and, more recently, visual analysis.

Trend: Refers to the direction of prices. Rising peaks and troughs constitute an uptrend; falling peaks and troughs constitute a downtrend. A trading range is characterized by horizontal peaks and troughs. Trends are generally classified into major (longer than a year), intermediate (one to six months), or minor (less than a month).

Trendlines: Straight lines drawn on a chart below reaction lows in an uptrend, or above rally peaks in a downtrend, that determine the steepness of the current trend. The breaking of a trendline usually signals a trend reversal.

Triangles: Sideways price patterns in which prices fluctuate within converging trendlines. The three types of triangles are the symmetrical, the ascending, and the descending.

Triple top: A price pattern with three prominent peaks, similar to the head and shoulders top, except that all three peaks occur at about the same level. The triple bottom is a mirror image of the top.

Up trendline: A straight line drawn upward and to the right below reaction lows. The longer the up trendline has been in effect and the more times it has been tested, the more significant it becomes. Violation of the trendline usually signals that the uptrend may be changing direction. (*See* Down trendline.)

Visual analysis: A form of analysis that utilizes charts and market indicators to determine market direction.

Volume: The level of trading activity in a stock, option, or futures contract. Expanding volume in the direction of the current price trend confirms the price trend. (*See* On-balance volume.)

Weekly reversal: An upside weekly reversal is present when prices open lower on Monday and then on Friday close above the previous week's close. A downside weekly reversal opens the week higher but closes down by Friday. (*See* Key reversal day.)

Weighted average: A moving average that uses a selected time span, but gives greater weight to more recent price data. (See Moving average.)

Bibliography

Achelis, Steven B., *Technical Analysis from A to Z*, Probus, 1995.

Allen, R.C., *How to Build a Fortune in Commodities* (Windsor Books, Brightwaters, NY) (Best Books, Chicago) 1972.

Allen, R.C., *How to Use the 4 Day, 9 Day, and 18 Day Moving Averages to Earn Large Profits in Commodities*, Best Books 1974.

Arms, Richard W., *The Arms Index (TRIN)*, Dow Jones-Irwin, 1989.

———*Volume Cycles in the Stock Market: Market Timing Through Equivolume—Charting*, Dow Jones-Irwin, 1983.

Bressert, Walter J., *The Power of Oscillator/Cycle Combinations*, Bressert & Associates, 1991.

Burke, Michael L., *Three-Point Reversal Method of Point & Figure Construction and Formations*, Chartcraft, 1990.

Colby, Robert W. and Thomas A. Meyers, *The Encyclopedia of Technical Market Indicators*, Dow Jones-Irwin, 1988.

deVilliers, Victor, *The Point and Figure Method of Anticipating Stock Price Movements* (1933: available from Traders' Library, P.O. Box 2466, Ellicott City, MD 20141 [1-800-222-2855]).

Dewey, Edward R. with Og Mandino, *Cycles, the Mysterious Forces That Trigger Events,* Manor Books, 1973.

Dorsey, Thomas J., *Point & Figure Charting,* Wiley, 1995.

Edwards, Robert D. and John Magee, *Technical Analysis of Stock Trends,* 5th Edition, John Magee, 1966.

Ehlers, John F., *MESA and Trading Market Cycles,* Wiley, 1992.

Elder, Alexander Dr., *Trading for a Living,* Wiley, 1993.

————*Study Guide* for Trading for a Living.

Freund, John E. and Frank J. Williams, *Modem Business Statistics,* Prentice-Hall.

Frost, Alfred J. and Robert R. Prechter, *Elliott Wave Principle, Key to Stock Market Profits,* New Classics Library, 1978.

Gann, W.D., *How to Make Profits in Commodities,* revised edition, Lambert-Gann Publishing, orig. 1942, reprinted in 1976.

Granville, Joseph, *Granville's New Key to Stock Market Profits,* Prentice Hall, Englewood Cliffs, NJ, 1963.

Hadady, R. Earl, *Contrary Opinion: How to Use It for Profit in Trading Commodity Futures,* Hadady Publications, 1983.

Hamilton, William Peter, *The Stock Market Barometer.* Robert Rhea developed the theory even further in the *Dow Theory* (New York: Barron's), published in 1932.

Hurst, J.M., *The Profit Magic of Stock Transaction Timing,* Prentice-Hall, 1970.

Kaufman, Perry, *Smarter Trading,* McGraw-Hill, 1995.

Kondratieff, Nikolai, translated by Guy Daniels, *The Long Wave Cycle,* New York: Richardson and Snyder, 1984. (Two other books on the subject are *The K Wave* by David Knox Barker and *The Great Cycle* by Dick Stoken.)

LeBeau, Charles and David W. Lucas, *Technical Traders Guide to Computer Analysis of the Futures Market,* Business One Irwin, 1992.

Lukac, Louis, B. Wade Brorsen, and Scott Irwin, *A Comparison of Twelve Technical Trading Systems,* Traders Press, Greenville, SC, 1990.

McMillan, Lawrence G., *McMillan on Options,* Wiley, 1996.

Moore, Geoffrey H., *Leading Indicators for the 1990s,* Dow Jones-Irwin, 1990.

Morris, Gregory L., *Candlestick Charting Explained,* Dow Jones-Irwin, 1995 (Originally published as CandlePower in 1992).

Murphy, John J., *Intermarket Technical Analysis,* Wiley, 1991.

———*The Visual Investor: How to Spot Market Trends,* Wiley, 1996.

Neely, Christopher, J., *Technical Analysis in the Foreign Exchange Market: A Layman's Guide,* Federal Reserve Bank of St. Louis Review, September/October 1997.

Neill, Humphrey B., *The Art of Contrary Thinking,* Caldwell, OH: The Caxton Printers, 1954.

Nelson, S.A., *ABC of Stock Market Speculation,* First published in 1903, Reprinted in 1978 by Frasier Publishing Co.

Nison, Steve, *Japanese Candlestick Charting Techniques,* NY Institute of Finance, 1991.

———*Beyond Candlesticks,* Wiley, 1994.

Prechter, Jr., Robert R., *The Major Works of R. N. Elliott,* Gainesville, GA: New Classics Library, 1980.

Pring, Martin J., *Technical Analysis Explained,* Third Edition, McGraw-Hill, 1991.

———*Pring on Market Momentum,* Intl. Institute for Economic Research, 1993.

Ruggiero, Murray A., *Cybernetic Trading Strategies,* Wiley, 1997.

Schwager, Jack D., *Schwager on Futures Technical Analysis,* Wiley, 1996.

Steidlmayer, Peter J., *141 West Jackson,* Steidlmayer Software, 1996.

————Steidlmayer on Markets, A New Approach to Trading, Wiley, 1989.

Teweles, Richard J., Charles V. Harlow, Herbert L. Stone, *The Commodity Futures Game,* McGraw-Hill.

Wheelan, Alexander, *Study Helps in Point & Figure Technique,* Morgan Rogers & Roberts, 1954, reprinted in 1990 by Traders Press.

Wilder J. Welles, *New Concepts in Technical Trading Systems,* Greensboro, NC: Trend Research, 1978.

Wilkinson, Chris, *Technically Speaking: Tips and Strategies from 16 Top Analysts,* Traders Press, 1997.

Selected Resources

FINANCIAL BOOK DEALERS

Fraser Publishing Company, P.O. Box 494, Burlington, VT 05402, (800) 253-0900

Traders Library, PO Box 2466, Ellicott City MD 21041 (800) 272-2855

Traders Press, PO Box 6206, Greenville, SC 29606 (800) 927-8222

TECHNICAL MAGAZINES

Futures Magazine, 250 S. Wacker Drive, #1150, Chicago, IL 60606 (312) 977-0999

Technical Analysis of Stocks & Commodities, 4757 California Avenue S.W., Seattle, WA 98116 (800) 832-4642

TECHNICAL SOFTWARE

Metastock, Equis International, 3950 S. 700 East, Suite 100, Salt Lake City, UT 84107 (800) 882-3040

North Systems, Inc., CandlePower, S. Salem, OR (503) 364-3829

SuperCharts and TradeStation, Omega Research, 8700 Flager Street, Suite 250, Miami, FL (305) 551-9991

MARKET DATA

Dial Data, Track Data Corp., 56 Pine Street, New York, NY 10005 (800) 275-5544

Telescan, 5959 Corporate Drive, Suite 2000, Houston, TX 77036 (800) 324-8246

CHART SERVICES

Chartcraft, 30 Church Street, New Rochelle, NY 10801 (914) 632-0422

Futures Charts, Commodity Trend Service, PO Box 32309, Palm Beach Gardens, FL 33420 (800) 331-1069

SRC Stock Charts, Securities Research Company, 101 Prescott Street, Wellesley Hills, MA 02181 (781) 235-0900

The Business Picture, Gilman Research Corporation, PO Box, 20567, Oakland, CA 94620 (510) 655-3103

TECHNICAL ORGANIZATIONS

International Federation of Technical Analysts (IFTA), PO Box 1347, New York, NY 10009

Market Technicians Association (MTA), One World Trade Center, Suite 4447, New York, NY 10048 (212) 912-0995

INDEX